CONNECT FEATURES

---

my portfolio 3.1

Company Research

Research three companies that interest you, or that you might like to work for. Use the Internet, library, trade journals, Chamber of Commerce, or other sources to locate this information. Most companies have websites, which are great places to start.

After you have researched your chosen companies, complete the following information:

Company 1

Company or organization name: _____

Briefly describe what the company does: _____

Location(s): _____

Website address: _____

Phone number: _____

Type of position you are interested in within the company: _____

How to apply: _____

Positive aspects of the company: _____

Negative aspects of the company: _____

Three things you learned about the company or organization. These might include size, mission statement, growth projection, etc.: _____

Interactive Form Submission

Connect allows students to record their responses to key exercises from the text and submit them directly to the instructor for grading and review. Many exercises automatically grade based on completion, and students can revisit their projects in the system, including resumes, cover letters, mock interviews, and sample applications.

Interactive Applications

Interactive Applications offer a variety of automatically graded exercises that require students to **apply** key concepts. Whether the assignment includes a *click and drag*, *video case*, or *decision generator*, these applications provide instant feedback and progress tracking for students and detailed results for the instructor.

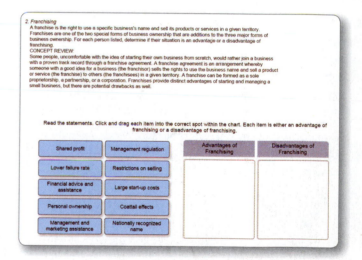

Connect Insight

The first and only analytics tool of its kind, Connect Insight is a series of visual data displays, each of which is framed by an intuitive question and provides at-a-glance information regarding how an instructor's class is performing. Connect Insight is available through Connect titles.

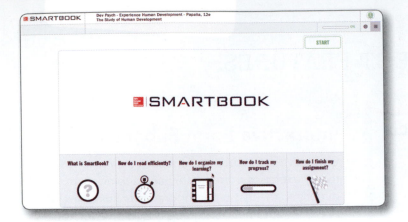

eBook

Connect includes a media-rich eBook that allows you to share your notes with your students. Your students can insert and review their own notes, highlight the text, search for specific information, and interact with media resources. Using an eBook with Connect gives your students a complete digital solution that allows them to access their materials from any computer.

EASY TO USE

Learning Management System Integration

McGraw-Hill Campus is a one-stop teaching and learning experience available to use with any learning management system. McGraw-Hill Campus provides single sign-on to faculty and students for all McGraw-Hill material and technology from within the school website. McGraw-Hill Campus also allows instructors instant access to all supplements and teaching materials for all McGraw-Hill products.

Blackboard users also benefit from McGraw-Hill's industry-leading integration, providing single sign-on to access all Connect assignments and automatic feeding of assignment results to the Blackboard grade book.

The **Best** of **Both Worlds**

POWERFUL REPORTING

Connect generates comprehensive reports and graphs that provide instructors with an instant view of the performance of individual students, a specific section, or multiple sections. Since all content is mapped to learning objectives, Connect reporting is ideal for accreditation or other administrative documentation.

CAREER*achievement*
GROWING YOUR GOALS

Karine B. Blackett, Ed.D.
American Public University System APUS
Kaplan University
National American University
Virginia College Online
Walden University

CAREER ACHIEVEMENT: GROWING YOUR GOALS, SECOND EDITION

Published by McGraw-Hill Education, 2 Penn Plaza, New York, NY 10121. Copyright © 2016 by McGraw-Hill Education. All rights reserved. Printed in the United States of America. Previous editions © 2011. No part of this publication may be reproduced or distributed in any form or by any means, or stored in a database or retrieval system, without the prior written consent of McGraw-Hill Education, including, but not limited to, in any network or other electronic storage or transmission, or broadcast for distance learning.

Some ancillaries, including electronic and print components, may not be available to customers outside the United States.

This book is printed on acid-free paper.

2 3 4 5 6 7 8 9 0 RMN 21 20 19 18 17 16

ISBN   978-0-07-783188-2
MHID   0-07-783188-8

Senior Vice President, Products & Markets: *Kurt L. Strand*
Vice President, General Manager, Products & Markets: *Michael Ryan*
Vice President, Content Design & Delivery: *Kimberly Meriwether David*
Managing Director: *Scott Davidson*
Director, Product Development: *Meghan Campbell*
Product Developer: *Alaina Tucker*
Executive Marketing Manager: *Keari Green*
Digital Product Developer: *Kevin White*
Digital Product Analyst: *Thuan Vinh*
Director, Content Design & Delivery: *Terri Schiesl*
Executive Program Manager: *Mary Conzachi*
Content Project Manager: *Danielle Clement*
Buyer: *Laura Fuller*
Design: *Matthew Backhaus*
Content Licensing Specialists: *Keri Johnson, Ann Marie Jannette*
Cover Images: Front Cover: © *Gandee Vasan/Getty Images*
Back Cover: © *Don Farrall/Getty Images*
Compositor: *Aptara®, Inc.*
Printer: *R. R. Donnelley*

All credits appearing on page or at the end of the book are considered to be an extension of the copyright page.

Library of Congress Cataloging-in-Publication Data

Blackett, Karine.
     Career achievement : growing your goals / Karine B. Blackett. — Second edition.
        pages cm
     ISBN 978-0-07-783188-2 (alk. paper) — ISBN 0-07-783188-8 (alk. paper)
     1. Job hunting. 2. Vocational guidance. I. Title.
HF5382.7.B583 2016
650.14—dc23
                                                              2014046593

The Internet addresses listed in the text were accurate at the time of publication. The inclusion of a website does not indicate an endorsement by the authors or McGraw-Hill Education, and McGraw-Hill Education does not guarantee the accuracy of the information presented at these sites.

dedication

This book is dedicated to the light of my life, my son, Kevin. And to my students—it is an honor and privilege to work with you as you grow your goals.

about the AUTHOR

DR. KARINE B. BLACKETT is a certified life coach whose professional credentials span more than 20 years of student success and career management experience. Dr. Blackett studied at the University of Malta and worked in Kenya, Africa, through her undergraduate degree with the University of Minnesota. She holds an English Language Teaching Certificate from New School University in New York and taught English as a second language in Southern Japan. Dr. Blackett received her master's degree in Student Affairs in Higher Education from Colorado State University. She received her doctorate in Higher Education Administration from the University of South Dakota.

Dr. Blackett has taught for several institutions, including doctoral online courses for Walden University and Aspen University, master's online courses for Kaplan University, and undergraduate online courses for Virginia College Online, National American University, and the American Public University System. In addition to teaching, Dr. Blackett is a course instructional designer and consultant for several institutions. In the past, she has served as the career services manager for National American University. She is a published author and contributor in the college success and career management fields and is an accomplished public speaker.

Dr. Blackett is a Master Facilitator with The Pacific Institute, an advisor to Jim Madrid and Advanced Sports Technology (http://jimmadrid.com/ast), and consults with many colleges and universities worldwide. Dr. Blackett was also a consultant with Coach Pete Carroll's "A Better LA" anti-gang program (http://www.abetterla.org).

NOTE TO STUDENTS

After several years of teaching career development and management courses, I realized that something was missing from the course materials I was using. The basic elements could be found in nearly all of the textbooks available, but many of the critical topics that I taught were absent. In my classes and coaching practice, I stress the importance of using success tools. Over the years, many former students and clients have told me how those principles and tools literally transformed their lives and set their careers on the paths they truly desired.

I determined that in order to ensure that career-seekers everywhere could apply and reap the benefits of those career tools, I needed to compile them into an easy-to-use text, packed with leading success strategies from scholarly resources and industry professionals, proven career planning and search processes, thought-provoking questions, relevant examples, and action-oriented activities. *Career Achievement* is the complete, current, and invaluable result of that need.

Career growth is a lifelong development process, not just a onetime search. Your career continually changes as your life path and your professional goals change. That said, the concepts and lessons covered in this book underscore the fact that having a job, and ultimately a career, is critical to your current well-being. By opening this book and preparing to apply its concepts and support tools to your career planning process, you have taken the first step toward finding a career that fulfills both your personal and financial needs.

Career Achievement will help you discover a wealth of information not only about yourself and your career goals, but also how to grow those goals throughout the job-search process using straightforward, easy-to-follow steps. The conversational style allows for easy reading and makes you feel as though you have a personal career coach by your side, offering support as you work toward and achieve each of your career goals and providing encouragement, tips, and suggestions to guide you through any obstacles. This winning combination is missing from other career planning textbooks; with it, you become unstoppable!

This book is about you. It is about you living your best life and achieving a fulfilling career. It is about defining your own meaning of "success" and really believing that it is possible. A single mother who returns to school to change her life and work in a purposeful career, allowing her to provide for her family, is a success. A retiree who decides to pursue an entirely new career, so that he or she can remain fulfilled through a chosen vocation is a success. A young adult who goes against what most of his or her friends are doing and attends college while working to earn a degree in a field he is passionate about is a success. When you utilize success tools and principles on your journey, success is not only possible, it is probable. Most of us never received these tools and principles growing up. If you did, the ideas in this book will provide reinforcement and show you how to put what you know into action. If you did not, fear not, as this book was designed with you in mind!

Karine B. Blackett

PREFACE

Welcome to *Career Achievement: Growing Your Goals!* This text was specifically designed with your success as our top priority. We understand the immense preparation, energy, time, and dedication that the career planning process requires. This book was developed to simplify the process. It provides necessary information and support to help career-seekers reach their objectives and succeed beyond what they might have thought possible.

Each chapter covers vital topics—supported by dynamic activities and relevant examples—that will help you identify, grow, and ultimately achieve your career goals. In addition to concept discussion, embedded questions, real-world examples, and application-oriented activities, each chapter in *Career Achievement* presents the opportunity for you to create your own portfolio materials. Whether you are searching for your first job, planning a career change, or have unexpectedly found yourself searching for employment, *Career Achievement* provides the valuable information you need to land the perfect job and advance on your desired career path.

This comprehensive text couples the most tried-and-true steps to achieving career goals with new principles and tools that are absent in other career development books. In the ever-changing job market, these new tools will help you stay in front of hiring managers and strides ahead of other applicants in the hiring pool. With the continually growing need to stay at the forefront of technology during the career planning process, it also provides the opportunity not only to apply traditional career planning and search techniques, but also to incorporate the Internet and online resources into the process. *Career Achievement* is a powerful combination of both proven and new career assessment, marketing, communication, and management tools.

Exploring, Growing, and Achieving

The features included in *Career Achievement: Growing Your Goals* are specifically designed to ignite and cultivate your students' interests and career objectives, while allowing you to teach the course easily, effectively and comprehensively.

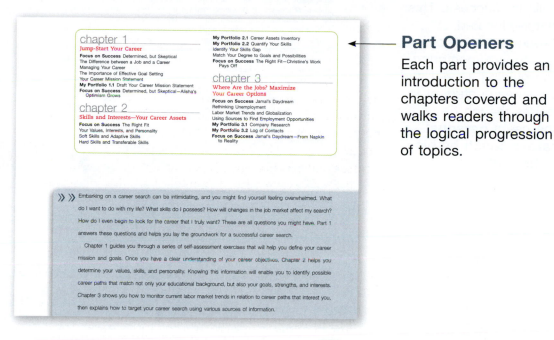

Part Openers

Each part provides an introduction to the chapters covered and walks readers through the logical progression of topics.

Chapter Openers

Chapter-opening quotes inspire students, while the target competencies and learning outcomes plant the seeds for what is to come. Each learning outcome is linked directly to a main heading in the chapter, emphasizing important topics throughout, and providing a **chapter-by-chapter outline for self-study**.

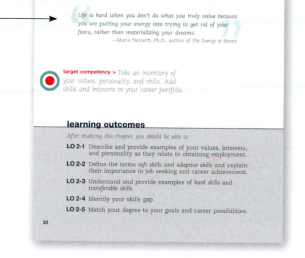

Focus on Success

These are scenarios that focus on real-world career planning and development issues. A dilemma is presented at the beginning of each chapter, allowing students to consider and discuss how they might handle the situation. At the end of the chapter, the problem is resolved, and students can react to the characters' actions and choices. This feature will spark **discussion** among students with questions and references to concepts presented in the chapter.

Career Coaching

Career Coach boxes provide enhanced concepts, reinforcement, tools, principles, and skills for success. This feature, located throughout each chapter, lends a mentoring and guiding aspect and allows each student to feel as though he or she has a **personal career coach by his or her side**.

careercoach 3.1
Seeing the Opportunities

Part of finding available jobs involves being open to opportunities. We can understand the trends, but it is also as important to learn how to see what you were unable to see previously. In Chapter 1 you learned how your mind works in terms of goal setting. If you believe there are no jobs in your field, you will not be able to find them (Rutherford, 1998; Tice & Quick, 2004).

Your brain is well-equipped to blind you from seeing everything, from your misplaced car keys to job opportunities. You will learn more about this in future chapters, but essentially your mind is created to keep you sane. So if you think there are no jobs in your area, your mind will block information to the contrary. It is more important to your brain to be sane than right. You may have found yourself in the past seeing some people as "lucky." We can create our own luck. Being lucky and staying fortunate over the long haul involve knowing and applying the tools and principles found in this book.

Another principle to keep in mind is: *money loves speed* (Killoran, 2009; Proctor, 1997; Vitale, 2008). This universal principle means that when opportunity presents itself, you need to react with enough speed and wisdom to capitalize on it.

My Portfolio

Included in each chapter, these action-oriented activities assist students in **creating their own personal marketing materials** throughout the course, resulting in a complete, ready-to-use portfolio.

my portfolio 1.1

Draft Your Career Mission Statement

You are the expert on you! With this in mind, you will construct a career mission statement that works for you and your life's purpose. Now that you have learned about the career mission statement, and viewed several websites to learn more about developing one, you are ready to draft your own. Remember that you can modify your career mission statement over time. At this point, draft your best guess. Write something on paper as a starting point about what you want to do with your life. This may be similar to an objective on a resume. Do not be afraid to revise it several times until you have determined your best career mission statement. When you are satisfied, either rewrite your career mission statement on a clean sheet of paper and keep it in a binder specifically for your portfolio documents, or type it into an electronic word processing document and save it to your computer or a portable storage device, such as a USB drive.

Exercises

Hands-on practice exercises directly related to key concepts allow students to **immediately apply what they have learned**.

e x e r c i s e 2.2
Five People You Admire

This exercise will help you identify the qualities that you value in yourself and others.

Directions: List five people (living or dead, fictional or real) you admire. Next to each name, list characteristics you admire or value in that person or character. For example, you might admire someone for being brave, funny, and creative. Next, list your admirable characteristics. The resulting two lists represent all of the characteristics that you value in yourself and in others. If you feel you don't possess a particular quality that someone else on your list has, keep this in mind—that quality must already exist in you to some extent, or you would not identify with it. It might be a quality you wish to enhance or improve.

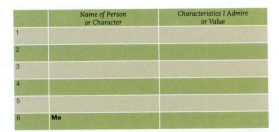

	Name of Person or Character	Characteristics I Admire or Value
1		
2		
3		
4		
5		
6	Me	

Cyber Trips

Web-based activities encourage students to utilize the Internet during the career planning and development process. These are also fully assignable and gradable in **Connect**.

Cyber Trip 3.1

Unemployment Rates   Visit the Department of Labor website (http://www.bls.gov/eag/) to see the national unemployment rate and the unemployment rate in your state. Note that men and women have roughly the same unemployment rate, yet the unemployment rate varies substantially among female racial groups: The unemployment rate of white women was 6.2 percent; black or African-American women, 12.1 percent; Asian women, 4.8 percent; and women of Hispanic or Latino ethnicity, 10.9 percent (DOL Women's Bureau, 2014. Data from the Bureau of Labor Statistics, Labor Force Statistics from the Current Population Survey http://bls.gov/cps/cpsaat03.htm, http://bls.gov/cps/cpsaat04.htm, http://bls.gov/cps/cpsaat07.htm (2013 annual averages). (DOL Women's Bureau). After visiting the Department of Labor website, answer the questions below:

1. What is the current national unemployment rate?

   _____

2. Research a particular state. What is the current unemployment rate for that state?

   _____

✓ **SELF-CHECK**

4. Name three qualities that employers look for in a worker.

5. Consider the three qualities you chose above. What type of skill is each quality?

6. What are some ways you can use your skills-gap identification information?

Self-Check Questions

Questions positioned at key learning points throughout each chapter reinforce learning outcomes and **promote concept retention**.

[chapter summary]

As you seek your ideal job, it is as important to know what you are seeking as it is to know what is going on in the economy. You want a great match. This chapter examined the top 10 employment trends, and how these trends can be used to generate opportunities for your personal career growth. As noted, employment trends come and go. Therefore, you want to gather accurate information to ensure your long-term career success. In this chapter, you also learned how to research industries, target jobs, research specific companies, and log your contacts in an organized manner.

[skill/term check]

1. What is frictional unemployment? (LO 3-1)
2. How can frictional unemployment benefit one's job search? (LO 3-1)
3. How does globalization impact the labor market? (LO 3-2)
4. What three employment trends do you feel are most significant? Why? (LO 3-2)
5. What do you feel are the pros and cons of working for small firms, medium firms, and large firms? (LO 3-2)
6. How does your educational attainment impact your job and career prospects? (LO 3-2)
7. Which industries are projected to see the greatest job growth between now and 2022? (LO 3-3)
8. List three sources of information you can use to research companies and positions during your job search. (LO 3-3)

[KEY TERMS]

Baby boomer: Someone born between 1946 and 1964. (LO 3-2) [p. 55]

Contact log: A way to record current and potential contacts during the job search and interview process. (LO 3-3) [p. 68]

E-commerce company: Business that is conducted electronically on the Internet. (LO 3-2) [p. 60]

Frictional unemployment: Unemployment that results because people move between jobs, careers, and locations. (LO 3-1) [p. 53]

Globalization: The growing economic interdependence of countries worldwide. (LO 3-2) [p. 54]

Informational interview: An interview that allows you to gather information about a particular occupation or company. (LO 3-3) [p. 66]

McDonaldization: Term coined by George Ritzer to explain how society takes on the characteristics of a fast-food restaurant. (LO 3-2) [p. 60]

McJob: A low-paying job requiring few skills and offering little chance of advancement. (LO 3-2) [p. 60]

Outsourcing: Hiring and paying an outside firm or third party to handle internal company functions. (LO 3-2) [p. 54]

Service workers: Those who perform services for the public. (LO 3-2) [p. 57]

Small to medium employer (SME): Generally defined in the United States as a firm

End-of-Chapter Materials

Chapter Summaries review learning outcomes and important concepts. Skill/Term Checks **promote recall and reinforcement** of vital chapter concepts; each question is linked to the appropriate learning outcome. Key Terms are listed for reference, and also linked to page numbers and learning outcomes.

Instructor Supplements

What's New to This Second Edition

Macro Updates

- Updated research throughout.
- New art added throughout.
- Additional focus on social networks and Internet job hunting.

Chapters 1–3

- Updated technology references.
- New discussions of social networking and sites such as LinkedIn.

Chapters 4–6

- Updated discussions of top jobs and earnings.
- Refreshed coverage of networking and the use of cold contacts.

Chapters 7–9

- Additional examples of business cards.
- Updated resumes.

McGraw-Hill Connect

Connect is an all-digital teaching and learning environment designed from the ground up to work with the way instructors and students think, teach, and learn. As a digital teaching, assignment, and assessment platform, *Connect* strengthens the link among faculty, students, and coursework, helping everyone accomplish more in less time.

LearnSmart

The smartest way to get from B to A   LearnSmart is the most widely used and intelligent adaptive learning resource. It is proven to strengthen memory recall, improve course retention, and boost grades by distinguishing between what students know and what they don't know and honing in on the concepts that they are most likely to forget. LearnSmart continuously adapts to each student's needs by building an individual learning path. As a result, students study smarter and retain more knowledge.

SmartBook

A Revolution in Reading   Fueled by LearnSmart, SmartBook is the first and only adaptive reading experience available today. SmartBook personalizes content for each student in a continuously adapting reading experience. Reading is no longer a passive and linear experience, but an engaging and dynamic one where students are more likely to master and retain important concepts, coming to class better prepared.

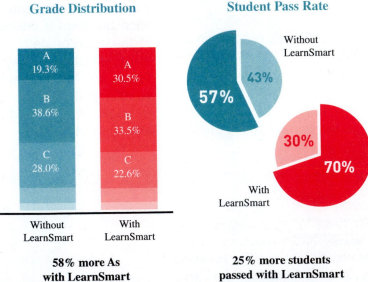

Grade Distribution

Without LearnSmart: A 19.3%, B 38.6%, C 28.0%
With LearnSmart: A 30.5%, B 33.5%, C 22.6%

58% more As with LearnSmart

Student Pass Rate

Without LearnSmart 43%
57%

With LearnSmart 70%
30%

25% more students passed with LearnSmart

Efficient Administrative Capabilities

Connect offers you, the instructor, auto-gradable material in an effort to facilitate teaching and learning.

Reviewing Homework

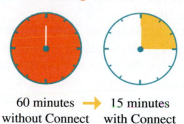

60 minutes → 15 minutes
without Connect   with Connect

Giving Tests or Quizzes

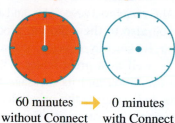

60 minutes → 0 minutes
without Connect   with Connect

Grading

60 minutes → 12 minutes
without Connect   with Connect

Student Progress Tracking

Connect keeps instructors informed about how each student, section, and class is performing, allowing for more productive use of lecture and office hours. The progress tracking function enables instructors to:

- View scored work immediately and track individual or group performance with assignment and grade reports.
- Access an instant view of student or class performance relative to learning objectives.
- Collect data and generate reports required by many accreditation organizations, such as AACSB.

Actionable Data

Connect Insight is a powerful data analytics tool that allows instructors to leverage aggregated information about their courses and students to provide a more personalized teaching and learning experience.

Connect Instructor Library

Connect's instructor library serves as a one-stop, secure site for essential course materials, allowing you to save prep time before class. The instructor resources found in the library include:

- PowerPoint Slides: These slide presentations are created specifically for each chapter to reinforce key concepts and provide a visual for students. They are excellent for in-class lectures, as well as for supplemental learning.
- Test Bank: A comprehensive test bank and answer key is available for use in classroom assessment. The test bank includes a variety of question types, with each question linked directly to Learning Outcome, Bloom's Taxonomy, difficulty level, and page number in the chapter.
- Instructor's Manual: The Instructor's Manual includes lectures, additional activities, and help for instructors while planning and teaching the course.

Acknowledgments

This book is the result of the synergy brought about by my *posse,* my team of supportive people. I extend my sincere gratitude to the following people: Paul Hubbeling, for your editing and writing contributions, and for believing in this work and my abilities from its inception. Melanie Venhuizen and Krista

Osburn, for your assistance. Dave Kulish, Frank Cawley, and Ken Palmer, for your professional opinions on the subject matter. Paul Sedlacek, for your friendship, formatting expertise, and professional support. While there are too many to name, I also want to thank those who were gracious in allowing me to use their quotations and material to enhance the message of this textbook and bring the coaching principles and tools to life.

Thank you also to the editorial, production, and design teams at McGraw-Hill. Alaina Tucker, my developmental editor, is professional, insightful, and authentic, as well as a great editor. Thank you for the spirit and energy you brought to this book and its message to students. Scott Davidson, managing director, for believing in the principles and ideas of this book. Keari Green, marketing manager, for your efforts on behalf of this book's message and helping it reach the student population. Danielle Clement, for your expert schedule coordination and close attention to production details. Matthew Backhaus, for creating the beautiful cover and interior design. Keri Johnson and Ann Marie Jannette, for your help with permissions and citations, respectively. I would also like to extend a big thank you to Doug Hughes, for seeing the potential of this book, and helping it take shape.

Many thanks to all of the authors and industry professionals who were instrumental in shaping my career and the ideas in this book. Thank you so much for allowing me to cite your work and pass your ideas on to my students, as well as those to come who will learn from you through this book. To my students—all of you—for allowing me to work with you, learn from you, share my ideas, and watch you accomplish your goals.

McGraw-Hill Education and Dr. Blackett would like to acknowledge the instructors and academic professionals who offered their time and expertise in reviewing this book. The invaluable suggestions and insight they provided contributed directly to its development and success.

Jon Arriola,
Tyler Junior College

Isabelle Bajeux-Besnainou,
George Washington University

Ardyn Barton,
Morgan State University

Pamela Bilton Beard,
Houston Community College—Southwest

Laura Jean Bhadra,
Northern Virginia Community College, Manassas

Anastasia Bollinger,
Georgia Military College

Christi Boren,
San Jacinto College

Vickie Brown,
Daytona State College

Cindy Burgess,
Dickinson State University

Todd Butler,
Jackson College

Gail Carr,
Plymouth State University

Miriam Chirico,
Eastern Connecticut State University

Dawnette Cigrand,
Winona State University

Amy Colon,
SUNY Sullivan

Michelle Conklin,
El Paso Community College

Bernadette Connors,
Dominican College of Blauvelt

Michelle Detering,
Lansing Community College

Kathryn DiCorcia,
Marist College

Mark A. Dowell,
Randolph Community College

Kristina Ehnert,
Central Lakes College, Brainerd, Minnesota

Terri Fields,
Lake Land College

Kerry Fitts,
Delgado Community College

Stephanie Foote,
Kennesaw State University

Linda Gannon,
College of Southern Nevada

Linda Girouard,
Brescia University

M. Sheileen Godwin,
Kings College, Wilkes-Barre, Pennsylvania

Paige Gordier,
Lake Superior State University

Joseph Goss,
Valparaiso University

Catherine Griffith,
Argosy University

Deana Guido,
Nash Community College

Bethany Gwin,
Lawson State Community College

Faye Hamrac,
Reid State Technical College

HelenMarie Harmon,
Indiana University Northwest

Jessica Hasson,
California State University Channel Islands

Richard Heiens,
University of South Carolina, Aiken

Dixie Elise Hickman,
American InterContinental University, Atlanta

Walter Huber,
Muskingum University

Julie Jack,
Tennessee Wesleyan College

Irene Jackson,
Palm Beach State College

Kim Jameson,
Oklahoma City Community College

Misty Joiner,
Bainbridge State College

Bonnie Kaczmarek,
Mid-State Technical College

Lisa Kahookele,
Des Moines Area Community College

Russell Kellogg,
University of Colorado Denver

Elizabeth Kennedy,
Florida Atlantic University

Deborah Kindy,
Sonoma State University

Betty J. Klein,
Ivy Tech Community College

Keith Klein,
Ivy Tech Community College, Bloomington, Indiana

Michael Kuryla,
SUNY Broome Community College

Christopher Lau,
Hutchinson Community College

Gary R. Lewis,
Southern Technical College, Fort Myers

Vinzanna Leysath,
Allen University

Kim Long,
Valencia College

Sandy Lory-Snyder,
Farmingdale State College

Susan Loughran,
St. Edwardís University

Maleeka T. Love,
Western Michigan University

Eva Menefee,
Lansing Community College

Megan L. Meyer,
Holy Family University

Nicki Michalski,
Lamar University

Valamere Mikler,
University of Phoenix

Carra Miskovich,
Randolph Community College

DJ Mitten,
Richard Bland College

Amanda Mosley,
York Technical College

Pamela Moss,
Midwestern State University

brief TABLE OF CONTENTS

table of
CONTENTS

Chapter 6 **Professional Cover Letters and Applications** 163

PART

3

Moving Forward: Interview, Follow-Up, and Managing Change 194

Chapter 7 **Successful Interviews** 195

CAREER*achievement*

You and Your Career:
Finding and Cultivating A Great Match!

Embarking on a career search can be intimidating, and you might find yourself feeling overwhelmed. What do I want to do with my life? What skills do I possess? How will changes in the job market affect my search? How do I even begin to look for the career that I truly want? These are all questions you might have. Part 1 answers these questions and helps you lay the groundwork for a successful career search.

Chapter 1 guides you through a series of self-assessment exercises that will help you define your career mission and goals. Once you have a clear understanding of your career objectives, Chapter 2 helps you determine your values, skills, and personality. Knowing this information will enable you to identify possible career paths that match not only your educational background, but also your goals, strengths, and interests. Chapter 3 shows you how to monitor current labor market trends in relation to career paths that interest you, then explains how to target your career search using various sources of information.

Part 1 helps you to establish clear goals, helps you identify the specific skills you possess, gives you techniques for researching career information, and details how to gain confidence in your abilities and in your career choices. Combined, these tools ensure that you have a solid advantage over other candidates in the job market.

chapter 1

Jump-Start Your Career

> *Make no little plans; they have no magic to stir men's blood . . .*
> *Make big plans; aim high in hope and work.*
>
> —Daniel H. Burnham,
> architect and urban planner

 **target competency >** *Develop a career mission statement based on your career goals.*

learning outcomes

After studying this chapter, you should be able to:

LO 1-1 Differentiate between a job and a career.

LO 1-2 Determine how to manage your career.

LO 1-3 Recognize the role of effective goal setting in relation to career success.

LO 1-4 Understand the importance of having a career mission before you create a career plan.

Determined . . . but Skeptical

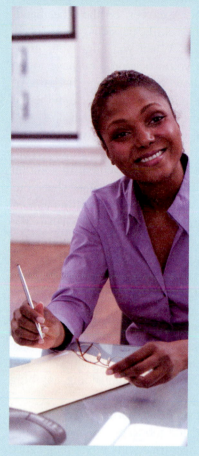

Alisha waited after class to speak with her career development instructor. She needed clarification on how to do the homework Dr. Harris had assigned. She waited patiently, but she wondered how long it would take for the student before her to finish talking to Dr. Harris. Alisha's daughter was at after-school care, and Alisha knew she couldn't be late picking her up.

Alisha had worked hard to graduate from high school, and had spent the last five years working as a home care aide for the elderly. She enjoyed her work, and the pay she earned as an aide covered her daughter's needs, but recently she had become increasingly aware that her opportunities for advancement were limited. After determining it was time to make a change, she researched her options online, and decided she wanted to be a dental assistant. Coupled with working, Alisha knew that taking college classes would limit her time with her daughter, but she hoped that earning an associate's degree would allow her to earn more money and provide a better life for her family. Making more money was a goal she had kept in the back of her mind for several years.

The career development course was required for the dental assisting program, but Alisha didn't really think it was necessary. She already knew she wanted to do dental assisting, and she had been hired for good jobs in the past without the help of a class. Now Dr. Harris' homework assignment required each person in the class to write down at least five specific career goals. With just one goal of making more money, Alisha didn't know how she was going to come up with four more.

As the other student gathered his books and left the classroom, Dr. Harris turned to Alisha.

"Alisha, right?" she asked.

Alisha nodded. "Yes, and I think I need some help," she said.

"Of course!" said Dr. Harris. "That's what I'm here for. What can I do for you?"

"Well, I really don't know how I'm going to do the homework assignment," Alisha replied. "You asked us to write down five specific career goals, and I only have one. My goal is to make more money, and I don't really see the point in writing that down."

"I can understand why writing your goals down might not seem to hold much value right now, but I promise it will make sense by our next class," said Dr. Harris. "If you don't mind my asking," she continued, "exactly how much more money would you like to make?"

Alisha thought for a moment. She had never really had a target income in mind.

"I'm not sure," she told Dr. Harris. "I'm just not satisfied with what I make now, and my raises are never enough."

Dr. Harris smiled. "Don't worry," she said. "You are not alone in that feeling! I think I can help you get started on the assignment. Let's begin at the most logical place—tell me about you."

Discussion Questions

1. Alisha is at a point where she feels like she needs a change. Have you ever felt the same way? Did you do anything about it? Why or why not?

2. How might specifying her desired income help Alisha reach her goal of "making more money"?

3. How do you think writing down her goals will help Alisha achieve them?

» LO 1-1   The Difference Between a Job and a Career

What is the difference between a job and a career? Some say that J.O.B. stands for Just Over Broke. That makes a lot of sense when you think about it. A **job** is a work situation you take to earn money. You might like it and you might not. A **career,** on the other hand, is a profession built on one's skills, passions, experiences, education, and preferences. When you align your gifts, talents, and desires with your vocation, you have found your career. This will allow you to endure the parts of your work that you don't totally enjoy, because in the big picture you have a purpose and like what you do.

Some people like to paint, volunteer, or exercise in their free time. What hobbies, or avocations, do you enjoy?

The terms job *and* career *are used interchangeably, but they are quite different.*

Job A work situation in which you earn money.

Career A profession built on one's skills, passions, experiences, education, and preferences.

Avocation An activity or hobby that is done for enjoyment in addition to one's regular work.

You may find that you want to turn an **avocation** you have now into a full-time career. An avocation is an activity or hobby that is done for enjoyment in addition to one's regular work. If you are not sure what your purpose is, or what you should do for a fulfilling career, that is fine. This chapter will help you reaffirm the choices you have made, or it will get you moving in the right direction if you are not yet clear.

Ask yourself the question "Live to work, or work to live?" This question is the essence of the line between a job and a career. Keep this question in mind as you do the assessments in this chapter and when you formulate your career mission. A full-time job will take up more than 2,000 hours of your time each year. You will spend more time on the job than doing anything else, except sleeping if you are lucky.

The terms *job* and *career* are used interchangeably, but they are quite different. A job is a means to an end. You work at a job to get by and pay bills. A career is a life path. You build your career over time with a long-range goal. You strategize for your career. Once you have a firm idea of what you want to do for your career, you will find a way to carry out your plan. You will map out and follow a career path. Jobs, on the other hand, are often unrelated and do not typically reflect what you really want to do with your life.

Should you take a job? Absolutely. There is a definite time and place for working at a job. For example, jobs are helpful while you are in school, looking for a better position for your career, or if you were laid off and take a temporary job to make ends meet while you search. Employers prefer to hire people who are working, so having a job is an important part of landing your career.

careercoach1.1

Do What You Love and the Money Will Follow

The saying "Do what you love and the money will follow" (Canfield & Hansen, 1996; Rann & Arrott, 2005; Roman & Packer, 2007; Sher & Gottlieb, 2003; Shinn, 2008) is based on a success principle. In the 1960s, a man by the name of Scrully Blotnick conducted a study of 1,500 people who set out to become millionaires. He divided them into two groups. The first group, 1,245 individuals, said they would pursue money first and then later do what they truly wanted to do with their lives. The second group was made up of only 255 people who said they would follow their interests first and trust the money would follow. These 1,500 individuals were tracked 20 years later. Guess what? There were 101 millionaires from the whole group. Only one millionaire came from the first group. The other 100 millionaires came from the 255 people in the second group—those who said they would follow their interests and dreams first.

This chapter is designed to bring about a personal awareness to the natural gifts, talents, inclinations, skills, and abilities you possess. This will help you align your career search with your career goals. You cannot fail when your own interests and natural talents are involved.

Doing what you love so the money and success follow does not mean you can sit on the couch watching television all day and expect to get rich. It means that if you go after the money first, you may find yourself burned out in a field that does not fit you. When you go after your career, it is important to do something you like, or even love. Think of it as a lifestyle decision.

Some of the happiest people are those who say "*My job is not really like work*" or "*I lose track of time when I am working because it is easy to focus.*" For your career it makes logical sense to do something you love. As Barbara Sher, author of *Live the Life You Love* and *Wishcraft*, explained, "Nothing will make you really happy but doing what you love." With all of the possible employment positions in the world, there may be hundreds of careers you would truly enjoy. The key is figuring out what would be a great career match for you. Finding a fulfilling career should not be guesswork. You could be retired by the time you figure out what you really want to do if you go about it by trial and error.

> *Do what you love and success and satisfaction will follow.*
>
> —Money Principle

Driven by a passion for coffee, Doug Zell and Emily Mange founded Intelligentsia Coffee & Tea Inc. in 1995. The company has consistently produced millions in revenue over the past several years. If you could turn any dream into a successful career path, what would you do?

» LO 1-2   Managing Your Career

Career management does not happen in a class. Career management, or career development, is a lifelong process you unfold and build upon. Think of this metaphor: A job is like a sprint, whereas your career is like a marathon. You will train, plan, and gradually make your career happen with many unexpected diversions, peaks, and a few valleys. Career management is exciting. It is your life's vocation. The best part is that you get to decide! It is totally up to you what you will do with the next 20, 30, or even 50 years of your life's work.

To get started in building your career, you need to do some inside work. This involves reflecting on your values, passions, gifts, and talents.

Many do not take the time to look inside themselves to discover the clues for finding their ideal career. They take on hand-me-down goals from others such as their parents, teachers, mentors, and coaches. These people may have good intentions, but if the passion or drive for the goal or dream is not in you, you will find it hard to get motivated, not only to achieve the goal, but also to sustain it. Luckily, you have been leaving yourself clues all along regarding your interests and talents. Now you just need to find them.

Success leaves clues.

—Anthony Robbins

exercise 1.1

Clues in Your Life

Take a few minutes to jot down your answers to the following:

1. List some of your childhood wishes.

_____

_____

2. List compliments you most frequently receive (now and in the past).

_____

_____

3. Whom do you admire?

_____

_____

4. If you could be paid to do what you most enjoy, what would you be doing?

_____

_____

5. What are some things you are naturally good at without really trying?

_____

_____

6. Name two or three of your unique qualities, such as creativity or helpfulness.

_____

_____

Cyber Trip 1.1

H.O.T.S. Survey: If You Are Doing What You Love, Who Are You? To complete this activity, visit http://oneminutemillionaire.com/hots-survey/. This quick survey will help you understand more about your work preferences and will reveal some of your innate strengths. You can use this information for insight as you search for your ideal job.

When you are finished taking the survey, write down some of the descriptions from your survey results.

1. Your role:

_____

_____

2. Your approach:

_____

_____

3. A few key words or phrases that describe you:

_____

_____

4. What you contribute to the team:

_____

_____

5. Some of your weaknesses:

_____

_____

6. What you do by instinct:

_____

_____

The survey answers will help you begin framing your career preferences.

✔ SELF-CHECK

1. What does J.O.B. stand for?

2. What is the difference between a job and a career?

3. Explain the statement *"Do what you love and the money will follow."*

» LO1-3 The Importance of Effective Goal Setting

Learning how to create and achieve goals is crucial, not only for landing your dream job, but also for soaring in your career. All too often, long-range goals are neglected. The need to pay bills forces us to seek employment—a job. Consequently, many jobs turn into careers by default. The result is often job dissatisfaction. You are not alone if you sometimes feel there are "no good jobs out there." Consider Deb Smart's story that follows. Deb is studying health care administration at National American University. Before deciding to go back to school, though, she felt lost.

I know I am guilty of wanting to "stay stuck." I have done this more than once in my life. I worked in one job for 21 years. I knew that the last three years I worked there it was the wrong job for me. I was jaded, uninspired, burned out, and every other term you can come up with for needing to make a job change. Yet, I had friends at work and I was comfortable so I stayed.

One day, I got up to go to work and began to tear up at the thought of having to spend another day there. I had to do some soul searching. Did I want to stay at the job because I had friends there and was comfortable, or did I want to take a chance on something new? I was afraid of quitting without something to fall back on. Getting my degree while working seemed like a positive step, but I wasn't sure what field to go into or what I really wanted to do. I also didn't know how to figure out what would make me happy, or even what I was good at doing. I was stuck, and the feeling of despair was taking all of my energy. I needed to find a spark; something that I wanted to do on a daily basis, but how was I supposed to do that?

After some soul searching and goal setting, I decided to do something new, and it was a great decision. I took the time to think about what I loved to do. I examined several career choices within the framework of my life goals and personal skills and abilities. After some deliberation, I decided the best career path for me involved returning to school to get my bachelor's degree. In the beginning, I was afraid I would not do well because I had been out of school for so long. I did enroll though and today I am doing well at school. I have had other jobs. Since that tearful day when I dreaded going to work I have had other jobs that I have really enjoyed, and I have learned so much at each one of them. If I had not made the choice to get "unstuck," I'm sure I'd still be tearing up at the thought of going to work."

Used with permission
from Deb Smart.

Deb Smart, B.A. in health care administration, National American University, class of 2012.

Through introspection, Deb determined her true interests and desires. She was able to connect those interests and desires to a fulfilling career path only after establishing clear goals.

Whether you are a stay-at-home parent or training to be on the next space mission, you need goals. Goals are so important that without them people can find themselves stuck. They focus on the past, and worry and complain about the way things are today. If you do not give yourself goals, you will either take on other's goals, re-create your goals from last year, or life will give you something to do. "Nature abhors a vacuum" is an important axiom to consider and remember. In short, if you don't decide what you want in your life and go after it, your life will go on with or without your input.

High-performance people know how to make and achieve their goals. Those who achieve their goals do so by adopting a winner's mentality, and, as we will learn later, having structure and support. You will learn to have each of these, regardless of your current mind-set and support system.

A very important success principle is to *begin with the end result in mind* (Bristol, 1991; Dooley, 2007; Klauser, 2001; Tice & Quick, 2004; Canfield, 2004; Canfield & Hansen, 1996; Shinn, 2008; Covey, 2014). Essentially, you move toward what you think about the most and with the most emotion. This is also why worrying is actually negative goal setting. Your job is to create your career goals based on your desires, gifts, and talents. In order to get from "here" to "there" you need to know where "there" is in your career. For some of you that is easy. You are either working in your chosen field or getting ready to launch your career. For others, you are still considering many options and have a vague idea of what you want to do, but have not fully defined your career goals. In any case, systematic goal setting will launch you in the direction you wish to go.

> *Life can be pulled by goals just as surely as it can be pushed by drives.*
> —Viktor E. Frankl, neurologist and psychiatrist

Creating short-term and long-term career goals is essential to making them happen. Robert A. Heinlein is a highly influential science fiction writer who is well known for his maxim "Reach low orbit and you're halfway to anywhere in the solar system." In other words with each baby step we take, we get that much closer to reaching our career goals. Keep this maxim in mind when setting goals, because if you can generate the energy to reach your short-term goals, you can achieve your long-range dreams. As you create your career strategy, you will begin to work toward the short-term goals that will ultimately lead you to your career landmarks.

To reach your career goals and dreams, it is essential to learn the specifics of goal setting that get results. Establishing concrete goals within the context of your interests, values, and talents is the fuel that will ensure you achieve them.

Goals are different from tasks. Tasks are things on your "to do" list. They, too, are important, but a goal excites you. It fills you with energy. One way you can assess if the goal is right for you is to write it out and think about it. Ask yourself if achieving the goal excites you. See if there is any energy around this goal. A quick tool to use if you are ever stuck or needing guidance is to *follow the energy*. This is the same energy that gets us out of bed in the morning and invigorates us to create the day.

Humans Need Goals

It is easy to discount the importance of goal setting. One might think, "I have goals, but I don't need to write them down— I just know what they are." The following research is provided to drive home the point of *why* it is important to set and write out career goals. Research has demonstrated that without goals you can literally die. In other words: No goals equals no life. Dr. Gary Latham, the Secretary of State Professor of Organizational Effectiveness at the University of Toronto, has done extensive research on this topic. With Dr. Latham's permission, the research findings are condensed here for you. In his book, *Work Motivation* (2012), Latham explained that during the Korean War, terminal mind control experiments were conducted by the North Koreans on young prisoners of war (POWs) to find out what would happen if men and women were deprived of meaningful work-related goals. In one experiment, they sent a group of young POWs into a mental downward spiral by giving them only negative news from home such as "Your wife left you." The POWs were given a job of shoveling and moving dirt. Day in and day out they were instructed to put dirt into a wheelbarrow and move it to another location, where they were to empty the dirt and then fill the same dirt back into a wheelbarrow and move it back to its original place. They would continue this activity without being told when this duty would end. The result was damaging. Although the POWs were adequately fed and allowed sleep, these young men died within 48 hours for no apparent medical reason.

A second part of the experiment involved a different group of POWs who were told to complete the same task, but this time with a goal in mind. The activity of moving dirt was turned into a competition. These men survived despite the conditions. The only difference between the two groups was the addition of the goal. The second group of men had a reason to move the dirt around—a purpose.

The tragedy of these Korean War POWs is also examined in the book, *How Full Is Your Bucket?* (Rath & Clifton, 2009). U.S. Army chief psychiatrist Dr. William Mayer (Schein, 1963; Wilson, 2006) studied 1,000 American soldiers in a North Korean POW camp, and found that although their basic needs were met, and they were not physically tortured, more than 38 percent of the POWs died. According to Mayer's report, the POWs simply lacked motivation to live under the negative conditions and gave up hope. This condition, labeled *mirasmus*, means lacking the will to live. The young men would literally go to a corner alone, sit down, put a blanket over their head, and pass away within two days.

Similarly, the Germans conducted experiments to see what would happen when prisoners were forced to do meaningless work during World War II (Latham, 2012). The Germans required the prisoners to shovel debris into carts and move it from one end of a compound to another. Within weeks, dozens of prisoners went mad and ran from their work. They were either shot by the guards or electrocuted by the fence.

Remember how essential it is to set and achieve goals.

These stories are dire and might even seem outlandish, but they do exemplify the power of purpose and the necessity of goal setting. The point of this research is to remember how essential it is to set and achieve goals. As Benjamin Mays, mentor to Martin Luther King Jr., explained it, "The tragedy of life doesn't lie in *not* reaching your goal. The tragedy lies in having no goal to reach." Whatever your circumstance is, it is essential to set goals.

You don't have to push wheelbarrows to survive or to be successful, but you do need goals that will drive you to advance and grow in your career. While there are various ways to go about this, it is imperative to acquire goal-setting tools and enhance the skills to make them work for you.

Writing Down Your Goals

Thoughts accumulate to form beliefs, beliefs accumulate to form habits, and habits run your life (Gage, 2006; Fengler & Varnum, 1994; Ray, 1999; Roman & Packer, 2007; Tice & Quick, 2004; Vitale, 2006; Hyatt, 2014; Matthews, 2014). This sentence is a common success formula, meaning that in order to change your life, you must change your thoughts. Writing down your goals is one way to get started on changing your life, providing you with a career launching pad. Dr. Gail Matthews, a psychology professor at Dominican University in California, conducted a study on the effects of written goals on short-term goal achievement. She found study participants who wrote down their goals were 50 percent more likely to achieve their goals than those who did not. She also found that sharing these written goals with others increased accountability and further increased the likelihood that those goals would be achieved. (Matthews, www.dominican.edu) About five-sixths of your thoughts are subconscious, where you create your belief systems. If you do not like what is happening in your life, then changing your mind is the first step. Make a conscious decision to plant different thought patterns, and in return you will get different results. Writing down your goals will only reinforce your thoughts. It has been said that the thoughts you had six months ago provided the groundwork for what is showing up in your life today. What were your thought patterns six months ago? Do you think the thoughts you had then are related to what is currently happening in your life? Once you have created and written down your career goals using the techniques in this chapter, compare your goals to what is happening in your life six months from now.

careercoach1.2

Write It Down!

Writing down your goals tells your brain to wake up and take notice—*this is important!* The sheer act of writing down your career goals sends a signal to your brain that these goals are important and worthy of your attention, much like the flashing light of a well-lit billboard along a highway. It fires up your brain to begin the task of reaching your goals. In fact, there is even an entire book on this subject entitled, *Write it Down, Make it Happen* by Henriette Anne Klauser (2001). Nearly every success expert will tell you to write down your goals to make them happen (Canfield & Hansen, 1996; Gage, 2006; Hansen & Allen, 2002; Klauser, 2001; Rutherford, 1998; McColl, 2007; Proctor, 1997; Vitale, 2008; Hyatt, 2014; Matthews, 2014).

Obviously, it will take more than merely writing down your goals to turn them into reality, but don't get discouraged, as new behaviors will eventually become habit with practice.

exercise 1.2

Who Are You in Five Years?

Imagine that you are attending your family or class reunion five years from now. Picture being at this event, having the career you desire, and living your best life. Consider this exercise your chance to make up a "true" story for yourself. At the top of a blank page write "In five years I see myself. . . ." Let go of the "how" and write down your highest career vision. What would you do if you had no excuses? This is a clue to your career vision. Prepare your ideal day below.

1. What do you do on a daily basis?

_____

_____

2. Where is your job located?

_____

_____

3. What is your office or work setting like?

_____

_____

4. What kind of people would you work with?

_____

_____

5. What is your title?

_____

_____

6. What type of clothing do you wear to work?

_____

_____

7. How do you get to work? Do you drive, walk, bike, take public transportation, or do you work from home?

_____

_____

8. Where do you take your lunches and what do you eat?

_____

_____

9. What hours do you work?

_____

_____

10. What do you enjoy about your work?

_____

_____

11. How are your skills and gifts being used?

_____

_____

12. What is your salary? Do you earn bonuses?

_____

_____

13. How are you advancing in your career?

_____

_____

14. Do you travel for work? If so, how often and where do you go?

_____

_____

15. What professional development groups do you belong to?

_____

_____

16. In what major ways does your life in five years compare with your life today?

_____

_____

17. What are three obstacles that might keep you from reaching this vision?

_____

_____

18. What skills or training might you need to develop to reach this vision?

_____

_____

There is a saying _you get what you are willing to settle for in life._ You can get more of what you desire by clearly defining what you truly want. Do not settle too cheaply when it comes to your career goals and life goals.

Attitude and Self-Talk

Your attitude will be the determining factor of your career success. Whether you work for yourself or someone else, you will decide your fate largely based on the attitude you bring to work each day.

Your attitude is often driven by the conversations you have with yourself. **Self-talk** (Kasl, 2005; Forleo, 2009; Osteen, 2007; Rann & Arrott, 2005; Rutherford, 1998; Sylver, 1997; Tice & Quick, 2004; Heer, 2011; Hesselbein & Goldsmith, 2009; Goldsmith & Reiter, 2007) is the mental chatter that you say to yourself on a constant basis. It is the running dialogue you have with yourself. It is believed that up to 90 percent of the mind's constant chatter is irrelevant to what is actually going on. This is another reason why worrying is a habit to break. Remember that worrying is negative goal setting. If you tell yourself that there are no good jobs out there, chances are you won't find any.

Most of the thoughts you have are random conversations in your head. You are constantly thinking, replaying events, strategizing, judging, and so on. Start paying attention to the chatter you have with yourself. Those conversations have power; they can lead you in the direction you want to go in your career—or away from it. Think of your thoughts like a bus; make sure it is taking you in the direction you want to go before you jump on board.

There is a difference between "happy" thoughts and constructive thoughts. To achieve your goals, you need constructive thoughts. These may or may

> _I can tell you ... with the utmost confidence: the secret of success is attitude._
> —Lou Tice, author and founder of The Pacific Institute

> _You can't stop your thoughts, but you don't have to listen to them, either._
> —Joe Vitale, author of _Life's Missing Instruction Manual_

Self-talk The mental chatter that you say to yourself on a constant basis.

Think of your thoughts like a bus; make sure it is taking you in the direction you want to go before you jump on board.

not be considered happy thoughts. You want your mind to generate the energy to move toward your goals; to inspire you to act on your goals. Some realistic people are quite good at achieving their goals. They see problems and fix them, keeping their thoughts focused on the outcome and taking action. Remember, you want to increase your awareness to make sure you are having thoughts that take you in the direction you wish to go.

Controlling your thoughts will lead to self-mastery. Change the conversation you have with yourself so it is positive and constructive. The subconscious does not differentiate between what is true and what is not. The subconscious takes you at your word—literally. If you tell yourself that you cannot interview well, you will likely struggle with interviewing as a result. You have built beliefs from your thoughts, and you regulate what happens to you at your belief level.

exercise 1.3

The Smart-Band™ Negative Self-Talk Buster

Wear a rubber band, or Smart-Band, on your wrist as you work on changing your mental talk. If you fall back into negative thinking, send a mental signal to your brain by gently snapping the band on your wrist. This is a very simple, yet effective, success tool recommended by many success experts including Will Bowen, author of *A Complaint Free World,* that can work to improve many habits. For example, you can practice this exercise when you decide to change your eating pattern, alter your physical activity, or vary your workload.

Change your mental chatter to include words such as *want to, desire,* or *enjoy.* Think about it: even if you think you *have to* pay taxes, you really don't. There are people in jail who chose not to pay their taxes. Instead, tell yourself you are proud to pay your taxes as a responsible citizen, or grateful that you are able to do so. Furthermore, there are those that may say, "I *have to* care for my children." Think again. Social services will find loving families to care for your children if you don't want to. Change your mind, and the words you feed your brain, and watch your life change dramatically. The same goes for going to work and moving ahead in your career. Positive self-talk is one of the most powerful tools you have in your tool kit as you work toward your successful career. Remember, it is more than just having a positive mental attitude; this tool will change your life.

Your subconscious keeps you in a constant state of balance. When something happens, or when you try to do something outside the box, the subconscious will do everything it can to get back to a state of balance and comfort. If you tell yourself you "have to," "must," or "need to" do an activity, your subconscious pushes back with "I don't *have to*." It will find ways and reasons for you to avoid doing what

Successful people never drink from a glass that's half empty.

—Marshall Goldsmith, author of *What Got You Here Won't Get You There* you say you must do. This is one of the reasons that procrastinators are always late. They constantly "have to, must, and need to" get things done or be on time. The more they force themselves, the more their subconscious fights back. Knowing this in advance can be used to your advantage. You can learn to change the way you think about an activity prior to experiencing that activity. After all, you can set all the goals you want, but if you are fighting them due to your adverse self-talk, then you are going to go one step forward followed by two steps back. *That which you resist, persists* (Grant, 2007; Katz, 2009; Killoran, 2009; Proctor, 1997; Rutherford, 1998; Vitale, 2008).

exercise 1.4

Eliminate "Should/Have to" Self-Talk

Eliminate *force* talk. Stop saying *have to* phrases for one week. Instead of *have to, must, should,* or *need to,* use *choose to, want to,* and *am going to.* Use the Smart-Band exercise along with this exercise for maximum benefit.

exercise 1.5

"What If"

Many times people hold back due to worrying about all of the reasons they cannot do what they want to do. This worrying becomes negative goal setting. Often the words "what if" are used to perpetuate the negative thinking and worrying. What if I fail? What if I make a fool out of myself? What if I lose money? What if I have to move home?

For this exercise stick with the "what if" questions, but this time use them for winning. List five "what if" statements from a positive point of view. What if you do not fail and can have your dream career?

Example: What if I am hired by the company I want to work for?

1. What if _____

_____

2. What if _____

_____

3. What if _____

_____

4. What if _____

_____

5. What if _____

_____

Affirmations

One way to change your self-talk is to use affirmations (Canfield & Hansen, 1996; Gage, 2006; Gregory, 2004; Kasl, 2005; Klauser, 2001; Ray, 1999; Roman & Packer, 2007; Rutherford, 1998; Shinn, 2008; Tice & Quick, 2004; Matthews, 2014). An **affirmation** is a conscious, positive statement you say to yourself even if it is not true at the moment. Whatever you say after the words "I am . . ." you become. Even in your self-talk, when you say to yourself "I am . . ." you have just given yourself an affirmation. Affirmations are tools. They are very powerful when used, but it is up to you to use them. To use affirmations to your advantage, make constructive statements and say (and feel) them frequently. For example, "I always say and do the right thing" or "I am always in the right place at the right time." Feed your brain constructive statements in order to offset the defeating messages you have fed yourself in the past. Affirmations are most powerful when using positive, first person, present tense language. You will find affirmations corresponding to each chapter in Appendix B at the end of this book.

> **Affirmation** A conscious, positive statement you say to yourself even if it is not true at the moment.

✓ SELF-CHECK

4. How does writing down your goals affect your ability to achieve them?

5. Explain how constructive self-talk can help you reach your goals.

6. Define affirmations, and explain their purpose.

SMART Goals and Stretch Goals

To help turn your goals into reality, you can use a powerful goal setting technique called **SMART goals**. SMART is an acronym that stands for:

> **SMART goals** An acronym technique that produces specific, measurable, attainable, realistic, and tangible goals.

S pecific

M easurable

A ttainable

R ealistic

T angible

The following are a few variations of SMART that also work. Use the definition that is most meaningful to you.

S — significant, stretching, specific

M — measurable, motivational, meaningful

A — attainable, achievable, acceptable, action-oriented

R — realistic, relevant, reasonable, results-oriented

T — time-frame based, timely, tangible, able to be tracked

How SMART Goals Work

When writing a goal, it is important to be very specific. For example, compare "I want to be a manager" to "I want to be a financial manager in the health care industry." See the difference? The work you do now to create specific career goals will help when you learn to write your resume and career summary (or objective) in later chapters.

Next, you want to make certain you can measure your goal. Measuring implies numbers, so you must quantify your goal. This is also what you will learn to do when you write a winning cover letter and resume. The brain likes numbers. It will work toward a specific goal if it can be measured. For example, if you state that you want to earn "more money," your brain does not know exactly what you are seeking. Your subconscious will find you "more money," but that may be a dollar on the street. Unfortunately, your subconscious may be satisfied with that amount of extra money. You now have "more" money and the outcome has been met. Since that was not your intention, you want to be specific and write measurable goals. "I want to earn $35,000 over the next year" is a precise and measurable goal.

How do you plan to quantify your goals?

Set attainable, realistic goals.

Set attainable, realistic goals. For example, to set a goal that you are going to win the lottery is not using the SMART formula, and it can be seen as a lack of faith in your ability to get what you truly want. It is fine to say you are going to earn more than $1 million next year, if you are already earning half of that amount now. If you are not sure what certain careers pay, you will want to do some research. Make your goals large enough so you generate enough energy and momentum to motivate you into action. On the other hand, if you set them too high, fear and doubt may limit your ability to take action, resulting in career paralysis or apathetic thinking. To find out what different positions are worth, research career worth by visiting websites that have salary calculators.

Cyber Trip 1.2

How to Find Salaries for Specific Careers   Many excellent websites are available that allow you to find out what a job or career is paying for entry-level, mid-level and executive-level positions. These sites are often broken down by region. Conduct salary research not only before you set your goals, but also before you interview and negotiate. Here are a few sites where you can find online salary calculators, as well as information on additional salary resources: Salary.com, www.salary.com; Bureau of Labor Statistics Occupational Outlook Handbook: http://stats.bls.gov/ and http://www.bls.gov/ooh/; The Salary Wizard from Monster.com, http://promotions.monster.com/salary/?WT_srch=1; Job Search Intelligence, http://www.jobsearchintelligence.com/.

You can also search for the key words "salary calculator" to find information online.

exercise 1.6

Smart Goals

Look at the following goals written by university students, and decide if they fit the SMART format for goal writing. If not, rewrite them so they do.

The question these students answered was "What are your goals after graduation?"

1. *Student 1*: One of my goals after graduation is to find a job that has better pay.

   _____

   _____

2. *Student 2*: I would like to find a job that I can be happy with and get paid well.

   _____

   _____

3. *Student 3*: One of the goals I have set is to move up in the management career ladder after graduation, and get out of front line supervision in the banking industry. I also intend to continue my education by completing my MBA degree within 18 months.

   _____

   _____

4. *Student 4*: My minor is Internet Business Systems. After graduation, with the use of my education, I am going to have my own e-commerce business that will generate at least 60K a year.

   _____

   _____

5. *Student 5*: My goals after graduation are to pay off my loans as quickly as possible, and have a job where I'm financially comfortable.

   _____

   _____

How Stretch Goals Work

Stretch goal A goal that is large enough to create the energy and motivation needed to achieve it, but not so lofty that it is unattainable.

If you know exactly how you will achieve your career goals, the rule of thumb is you have set your goals too low. A **stretch goal** is one that is large enough to create the energy and motivation needed to achieve it, but not so lofty that it is unattainable.

Once you get close to reaching your career goals, you need to set new goals. Your subconscious will help drive you to your goals, but once you achieve them, your subconscious shuts down. This is why some students who simply want to attain a career or job after college tend to flounder in the workplace once they get that job. They forget to set goals to move them ahead within the new job.

Several studies have concluded that many people pass away within 16 to 18 months after retiring. The thinking behind this is that their work was their life (Tice & Quick, 2004; Lin, 2002). Without a new career goal or other life goals, they literally shut down. Few realize the need for career goals after the "job" is done. Just as determining one's major in college is considered the step leading to a career, retirement should be considered an extension of that process. The point of all of this is to make your career goal setting a priority, and to make lifelong goals.

It is important to stay active and goal-oriented even after retiring. It may seem far in the future, but what kinds of goals do you think will benefit you during retirement?

✓ SELF-CHECK

7. What does the acronym SMART stand for?

8. What is a stretch goal?

9. Why is it important to set new goals once you get close to achieving your current goals?

What if you don't always have a positive attitude, or visualizing (a tool explained more in later chapters) is not your thing? Fortunately, if you do enough of the right things correctly, you can still achieve success. In other words, if you plant corn seeds in fertile soil, and water them, corn will grow. You don't need to visualize corn, or have positive thoughts about corn; you get what you plant. That said, it is good to remember that working the success tools, along with having great marketing tools, will give you the edge over the hundreds or thousands of other applicants for that one sought-after position.

Achieving Your Goals

The following steps will help you clear out what you don't want and get to what you do want.

Step 1: Write down what you don't want.

Step 2: Write down the opposite of what you don't want so that you are writing down what you *do* want.

Step 3: Write your statement SMART.

Step 4: Use tools: visualization, constructive self-talk, and affirmations.

Step 5: Focus, get clear, and take action.

Many people talk about what they don't want in a job (i.e., "I don't want a job that is boring"). If that is all you know right now, then you can start there. Once you get what you don't want down on paper, the next step is for you to reverse the negative. Knowing what you don't want is the springboard to attaining what you do want.

For example, the negative statement "I don't want a dead-end job" can be turned around by stating "I want a job that I can grow with, and move up the career ladder." Refocusing on what you do want starts moving your energy in the direction you actually want to go.

exercise 1.7

Five Steps to Achieving Your Goals

Use Figure 1.1 to complete steps 1 through 3.

Step 1: Write Down What You Don't Want

Make a list of the items you know you don't want in your career on the left side of a piece of paper, or use the chart in Figure 1.1.

Step 2: Write Down What You Do Want

Next, reverse the negative statement. "I don't want a boring job" becomes "I want a job that changes from day to day." The result is a list of goals.

Step 3: Write Your Goal Statement SMART

Make your final list specific using the SMART technique. You may want to define what you are saying prior to writing out a SMART list. Use a separate sheet of paper to define any term that is vague. In this case, what careers actually offer day to day change and challenges? This is where goal setting becomes subjective and personal. What one person calls *change*, another person might call *mundane*.

List as many descriptive, or defining, terms as you can during this step to make your terminology meaningful for you. You can then rewrite the goal

	Step 1: What I Don't Want in My Career	Step 2: Reverse the Negative—What I Do Want	Step 3: Write It SMART
Example:	I don't want a boring job.	I want a job that changes day to day.	I want a fast-paced career working in emergency medicine.
1.			
2.			
3.			
4.			
5.			
6.			
7.			
8.			

Figure 1.1   **Five Steps to Achieving Your Goals: Steps 1–3**

with more specificity. "I want a job that changes from day to day" becomes "I want a fast-paced career working in emergency medicine." Remember that vague goals get very little attention from your subconscious, and consequently not much happens.

Step 4: Use Tools

Use your tools! This includes constructive self-talk, affirmations, and other tools you will learn in the chapters ahead.

Step 5: Focus, Get Clear, Take Action, and Get Support

You will learn more about these success tools and how to apply them throughout this book.

If goal-setting is so wonderful, why don't some people set any? The answer lies in the fear of failure. Once you declare something as a goal, you risk not getting it. You work on your goals, make excuses for not working on them, or give them up entirely. When you learn to use the principle, *success is always failure turned inside out,* you will begin to recognize obstacles as signs you are moving toward your goals, rather than signs to quit. Think of highly successful people and the amount of obstacles, and even failures, they endured to reach their goals. For example, Thomas Edison learned more than 5,000 ways how *not* to make a lightbulb before he was finally successful.

> *Success is failure turned inside out.*
>
> —Unknown

careercoach1.3

The Power of Focus

What you focus on expands.

(Canfield & Hansen, 1996; Choquette, 1997; Dooley, 2007; Grant, 2007; Rann & Arrott, 2005; Tice & Quick, 2004; Vitale, 2008; Killoran, 2009; Matthews, 2014; Roman & Packer, 2007; Proctor, 1997)

This is an often overlooked, yet powerful, coaching principle you will want to remember. It means that the object of your mental attention is what you will produce more of in your life. If you have a negative thought, it won't amount to much as long as the majority of your thoughts are constructive. If you can get into the habit of thinking positive thoughts 51 percent of the time, you are on your way to great success.

> *Whatever you focus on will happen to you if you focus on it long enough and with feelings, whether it is good or bad.*
>
> —Bob Grant, licensed psychologist and relationship coach[1]

There are people who know how to focus their intention and goals, and while they seem to not work very hard, they do get a great deal accomplished. Focus is their success tool. For instance, Warren Buffett, a well-known and highly successful U.S. business investor, has many quotes on using *focused intention.*

---

[1] **www.relationshipheadquarters.com**

Focused intention is a synergistic combination of focus, desire, and belief. Having a clear career mission statement will condense all of your career goals into one concise statement you can focus on intently. Once you write your statement, you can look at things you are doing daily and ask yourself, "Is this thing I am doing, or about to do, taking me closer to my career mission statement and goals, or away from them?" If it is not moving you in the direction you wish to go, you can decide if you still want to do that particular thing. This is a great time-management tool for use in any area of your life.

e x e r c i s e 1.8

Jump-Start Your Career Goals

The goal of this activity is to write down as many goals as you can think of. You can do this on 3 × 5-inch index cards, with each goal on its own card, or you could use the notepad feature on your phone to create digital note cards. Whichever you prefer, make it easy to keep your goals with you. Each goal can be something you wish to do, be, or have, and should include the date you set it. Whenever you think of a new goal, write it down and date it. When you achieve the goal, pull out the card or note, and write a word of your choice on the card that represents victory, achievement, or gratitude, and put it in a separate pile of "completed goals." Having a visual representation of the goals you wish to achieve, and watching the "completed goals" pile grow larger, is a great way to remind yourself that your hard work is paying off.

» LO 1-4 Your Career Mission Statement

We spent time on goals and goal setting because it leads to uncovering our career purpose. By having a career destination in mind, you will be able to formulate a **career plan.** A career plan is a series of steps taken over a period of time to achieve a desired career. A career plan allows you to acquire the skills you need, and to make strategic choices, so that you are on course toward your career destination.

Can you imagine a person getting on an airplane without any regard to where the plane was headed? Perhaps he or she just wanted to go *somewhere.* However, when the plane arrived at its destination, the person became frustrated because the particular destination was not really where he or she wanted to be at all. The destination might be too hot, too cold, too crowded, or too lonely. Without having a destination in mind for your career, you will end up working *somewhere,* but most likely not where you want to be.

A **career mission statement** is a brief description of your overall career purpose: what you are doing or what you plan to do. It is a broad statement of

Career plan A series of steps taken over a period of time to achieve a desired career.

Career mission statement A brief description of your overall career purpose.

intent that allows you to encompass all of your goals, and helps you achieve them. When you look at any one career goal it should be able to fit within your career mission statement. In other words, think of your career mission statement as an umbrella for your career goals (see Figure 1.2). Companies and organizations have mission statements so that all activity is aligned to the common end as stated in the mission statement. When you make choices in your career, you can ask yourself, "Is this choice going to take me closer to my career destination?" As you move closer to your career destination, you will know more about yourself and your profession, and your career mission will change based on your new insights.

Focus on the next five years of your career to create your mission statement. Do not worry about getting this wrong. Start somewhere. Remember, if you are vague, life will happen with or without your input, so be as specific as possible. Your job then, as the expert on you, is to look inside yourself and become conscious of your thoughts. For some, this means tuning into the vision or picture of what you see yourself doing. For others, this may mean listening to your words and thought processes. Are you working at a construction site or tending to sick patients? Begin to focus on your career mission. This is an important step when beginning with the end in mind. You want your mission statement broad enough so you can do many things with your skills and experiences, yet specific enough to keep out that which is not what you seek to do. Revisit your goals, as you will find many clues leading to your mission statement.

Your mission statement is not designed to be measured. However, your goals and purposes within your mission statement should be measurable if you wrote them SMART. To stay on purpose, ask yourself, *"Am I doing what I say I want to do with my career life?"*

The following are examples of career mission statements:

My Career Mission is to work as a Correctional Officer, make a difference in the community by keeping order within my institution, and help inmates move forward with their lives by avoiding recidivism.

Maintain a 3.5 GPA while working towards my associate's degree.

Earn a position as a correctional officer within three months of earning my associate's degree.

Continue my education by working toward a bachelor's degree in Criminal Justice.

Graduate with my associate's degree in Criminal Justice.

Gain experience consulting with the courts as part of my job.

Gain employment as federal correctional officer within one year of earning my bachelor's degree.

Figure 1.2

The Career Mission Statement acts as the umbrella under which your career goals should fall.

- My career mission is to become a leader in my community as a trainer and coach, consulting with businesses and other organizations.
- My career mission is to help others lead healthy, high-quality lives through my work as a nurse.
- My career mission is to raise the self-esteem and knowledge of children with special needs.
- My career mission is to earn my CPA and work in the accounting field, building a reputation of integrity and loyalty.
- My career mission is to faithfully and ethically serve clients and lawyers as an outstanding professional paralegal.
- My career mission is to affect, change, and raise awareness of the environment through my teaching, speaking, and writing.

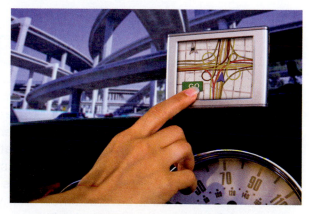

It would be unwise to begin a road trip without first consulting a map. In terms of beginning your career search, how are creating a career mission statement and creating goals similar?

Cyber Trip 1.3

Career Mission Statement Before you construct your own mission statement, it will help to read some outside information, as well as view samples. You should also visit several company websites and look at professional business mission statements to get a feel for how to write them. Here are two sites where you can learn more: CollegeGrad, http://www.collegegrad.com/jobsearch/Job-Search-Prep/Develop-a-Personal-Career-Mission-Statement/, and Quintessential Careers, http://www.quintcareers.com/mission_statements.html. Both sites contain additional valuable information about your Mission Statement. You can also search online using the key words "Career Mission Statement" or "Company Mission Statement" to find additional examples.

Creating a Portfolio

Portfolio A grouping of hard copy or electronic documents that represent one's work and can be used during the job search.

You will be compiling documents to create your own portfolio as you work through this book. A **portfolio** is a grouping of documents that represent your work and can be used during the job search.

Many employers now expect to be able to access these important career documents electronically. Consider posting your portfolio documents on a personal website, on a career site like LinkedIn, or if you work in a creative field such as graphic design, web design, or photography, on a platform such as Behance. If you prefer to limit access to your portfolio documents, you could keep them in a digital folder on Google Drive, Dropbox, or Box, and share the link to that folder with prospective employers.

Keeping your portfolio documents in digital format lets you easily update them when you gain new experiences, and it also makes it easy to print your portfolio to bring to an interview or job fair. The first item you will add to your portfolio is your career mission statement.

my portfolio 1.1

Draft Your Career Mission Statement

You are the expert on you! With this in mind, you will construct a career mission statement that works for you and your life's purpose. Now that you have learned about the career mission statement, and viewed several websites to learn more about developing one, you are ready to draft your own. Remember that you can modify your career mission statement over time. At this point, draft your best guess. Write something on paper as a starting point about what you want to do with your life. This may be similar to an objective on a resume. Do not be afraid to revise it several times until you have determined your best career mission statement. When you are satisfied, either rewrite your career mission statement on a clean sheet of paper and keep it in a binder specifically for your portfolio documents, or type it into an electronic word processing document and save it to your computer or a portable storage device, such as a USB drive.

10. Why is it important to determine your career mission statement before creating your career plan?

11. What is a portfolio and when is it used?

12. After reading this chapter, how can you examine your goals to make a better career choice?

focus on success

Determined . . . but Skeptical— Alisha's Optimism Grows

Alisha wasn't sure how to describe herself to Dr. Harris.

"Well," she began, "I am 28 years old, and I have a seven-year-old daughter who is the light of my life. I graduated high school 10 years ago, and I've been a home care aide ever since. Now I'm enrolled in the dental assisting program here. That's about it!"

"In the past minute, you've just told me three of your goals," replied Dr. Harris with a smile.

"Really?" asked Alisha, somewhat confused.

"Sure," said Dr. Harris. "You just need to put some work into making them specific. For instance—a moment ago, you said you wanted to make more money. Many people share that desire. The problem is most do not have a clear idea of what they consider 'enough,' and they never write down their target amount, so the raises that they *do* earn never reach a specific goal."

Alisha looked unconvinced. "So, if I write down that I want to make $100,000, it will just happen?"

"Not exactly," said Dr. Harris, "but you are on the right track. Your goals should be specific, but they still need to be realistic. Once you have specific and realistic goals written down, you will have accomplishments to work toward, and the actions you take will have purpose."

"I guess that makes sense," Alisha agreed. She thought about how much extra money she wanted to make per month. She also wanted to be able to put money into a savings account each month for her daughter's college fund. She pulled a small calculator out of her purse and multiplied the extra amount she wanted by 12 months, and added it to what she currently made in one year. Lastly, she added an appropriate annual amount for taxes and other items taken out of her earnings. She ended up with $28,000, but the amount seemed too low to enjoy the life she wanted with her daughter.

"So my target income one year after graduating is $28,000, but that seems a little low for working so hard for this degree," she said.

"Ok," said Dr. Harris, "that is why I demonstrated how to find online salary calculators in class today. Let's look up the average salary for dental assisting."

It only took Dr. Harris and Alisha two minutes to find the national's average salary for dental assisting. Figure 1.3 shows what they found on Salary.com.

"Now how do you feel about your career goal and salary?" asked Dr. Harris. "Perhaps this is the salary range you should be writing down and working toward. Alisha smiled broadly and nodded in agreement.

"OK then," said Dr. Harris. "Write it down!" While Alisha wrote her income goal in her notebook, Dr. Harris continued. "You are currently in the two-year dental assisting program, right?"

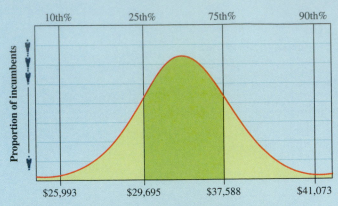

Figure 1.3 Dental Assistant Salary Ranges: U.S. National Average

© Source: HR reported data as of August 2014, http://www1.salary.com/Dental-Assistant-Salary.html.

Alisha looked up from her notebook and nodded. "So there is your second goal," said Dr. Harris. "Graduate from the dental assisting program in two years."

Alisha's eyes lit up. "Of course," she said, writing it down. "That one is so clear—I can't believe I didn't think of it first! You said I had three goals already, though. What's the third?"

"You said you have a daughter. Think about what type of family life you want. How much time do you want to spend with her?" asked Dr. Harris.

Alisha responded immediately. "I definitely want a more flexible schedule," she said. "I want to spend as much time with her as I can, especially in the mornings between six and eight, and in the afternoons when she is home from school. My current job requires me to be at work each morning by six."

"There's your third goal!" said Dr. Harris. "An ideal work schedule for you would involve working more normal hours during the day—perhaps eight in the morning until four in the afternoon."

"Wow, I never thought of an ideal work schedule as a career goal before," said Alisha, "but it makes complete sense."

"Write it down!" Dr. Harris said, with a smile.

Alisha thanked Dr. Harris, and as she walked out of the building, she thought about how many goals she really had. By the time she reached her daughter's school, not only had she pinpointed two more specific career goals to complete her homework assignment, she was also feeling more positive and confident than ever about her future and providing for her daughter.

Discussion Questions

1. From what you've learned in this chapter, describe in your own words why it was important for Alisha to write down her goals.

2. Alisha had never considered an ideal work schedule to be a goal. Through the exercises in this chapter, what goals did you come up with that you wouldn't have thought of before?

3. Describe yourself in 10 seconds—either out loud, or in your mind. How many career goals can you draw just from your description?

[chapter summary]

Understanding the difference between a job and a career is the first step toward determining what you want to do with your life. It is largely true that if you do what you love, money and satisfaction will follow. While you may like certain jobs you have held, a true career path that encompasses your passions is likely to fulfill you more than a job that pays the bills. The goal is to figure out what is driving you, and to find out what careers are available that match those passions. The results from the work you did in this chapter—defining specific goals and creating your career mission statement—have laid the foundation for your career achievement. The next chapter will help you recognize your skills and values and identify which skills you still want to obtain. You will also expand your career possibilities by learning what you can do with your major.

[skill/term check]

1. What is the difference between a job and a career? **(LO 1-1)**

2. Can career management be learned in a classroom? Why or why not? **(LO 1-2)**

3. Why is it important to have career goals? **(LO 1-3)**

4. How can changing your self-talk assist you in attaining your career goals? **(LO 1-3)**

5. What is the purpose of a career mission statement? **(LO 1-4)**

6. How can having a portfolio help your career development? **(LO 1-4)**

[KEY TERMS]

Affirmation: A conscious, positive statement you say to yourself even if it is not true at the moment. **(LO 1-3)** *[p. 18]*

Avocation: An activity or hobby that is done for enjoyment in addition to one's regular work. **(LO 1-1)** *[p. 6]*

Career: A profession built on one's skills, passions, experiences, education, and preferences. **(LO 1-1)** *[p. 6]*

Career mission statement: A brief description of your overall career purpose. **(LO 1-4)** *[p. 24]*

Career plan: A series of steps taken over a period of time to achieve a desired career. **(LO 1-4)** *[p. 24]*

Job: A work situation in which you earn money. **(LO 1-1)** *[p. 6]*

Portfolio: A grouping of hard copy or electronic documents that represent your work and can be used during the job search. **(LO 1-4)** *[p. 26]*

Self-talk: The mental chatter that you say to yourself on a constant basis. **(LO 1-3)** *[p. 15]*

SMART goals: An acronym technique that produces specific, measurable, attainable, realistic, and tangible goals. **(LO 1-3)** *[p. 18]*

Stretch goal: A goal that is large enough to create the energy and the motivation needed to achieve it, but not so lofty that the goal is unattainable. **(LO 1-3)** *[p. 20]*

chapter 2

Skills and Interests—Your Career Assets

" *Life is hard when you don't do what you truly value because you are putting your energy into trying to get rid of your fears, rather than materializing your dreams.* "

—Maria Nemeth, Ph.D., author of *The Energy of Money*

target competency > Take an inventory of your values, personality, and skills. Add skills and interests to your career portfolio.

learning outcomes

After studying this chapter, you should be able to:

LO 2-1 Describe and provide examples of your values, interests, and personality as they relate to obtaining employment.

LO 2-2 Define the terms *soft skills* and *adaptive skills* and explain their importance in job seeking and career achievement.

LO 2-3 Understand and provide examples of *hard skills* and *transferable skills*.

LO 2-4 Identify your skills gap.

LO 2-5 Match your degree to your goals and career possibilities.

The Right Fit

Christine worked as the front office assistant for Dr. Gary Nelson, a busy general practitioner. Christine had been employed there for just two weeks, but she already knew she wanted to become a medical assistant because it paid more than her current position, and because the medical assistants moved about and interacted with the patients. In her position, Christine remained at the front desk to answer the phone, pull files, and make copies of insurance cards. She was unable to leave the front desk area unless she was going to the restroom or to lunch. Christine was very personable and outgoing, and liked working with people. She realized, however, that she had to acquire the technical skills needed to be a medical assistant, so she enrolled in the medical assisting program at a college close to the office, so she could attend classes after work.

On her first day of class, the instructor, Mrs. Cook, reviewed the requirements of the program and then asked, "Are there any questions?"

Christine raised her hand. "Is it possible to be a medical assistant without drawing blood or giving shots? Needles make me pretty queasy."

Mrs. Cook smiled and replied, "Not if you're going to be a good medical assistant!" Both Mrs. Cook and Christine realized that perhaps medical assisting wasn't the right career for Christine. In her heart, Christine realized she did not have the stomach to perform the necessary procedures required for those working as medical assistants.

After class was over, Christine asked Mrs. Cook if she could talk with her for a moment because she was considering dropping out of the program. When Mrs. Cook asked Christine why she wanted to become a medical assistant, Christine told her about her current job. She explained how she wanted to make more money, move about the office during the day, and interact more with the public.

"Mrs. Cook," Christine said, "honestly, I'm a little discouraged. I like interacting with people and I like the medical field, but I just don't think I can perform all the duties that you said medical assistants have to do, specifically the blood work."

"Don't be discouraged," said Mrs. Cook. "I think I might know of a better career fit for you, and the program for it is also offered here. You would still be able to work in a fast-paced, medical setting. If you apply yourself, your earning potential will be greater than it is now. You can use your people skills, and you will be able to move about the office. The best part is you won't have to handle any needles!" They both laughed.

Christine was interested in the career Mrs. Cook had in mind for her. "That sounds great—can you tell me more?" she asked.

Discussion Questions

1. Did Christine have the right motives for wanting to become a medical assistant? Why or why not?

2. What should Christine have researched before enrolling in the medical assisting program?

3. How can you find out what careers might be a good fit for you?

» LO 2-1 Your Values, Interests, and Personality

Your career mission statement and career goals provide you with the foundation for your career achievement. Another integral aspect of your career plan is ensuring your values and skills are aligned with your career goals and mission.

It would be tragic to "climb" the career ladder only to find it is leaning against the wrong wall. Take the time now to become more aware of your values, strengths, skills, personality, and passions. This can save you time and energy in the long run toward achieving your career goals and mission.

Most people apply for many jobs at a time, accept the job they can get, and hope the position turns out to be a good fit. Assessing your values, and making sure they align with your career desires, is one way to determine if the position is right for you. Values are what you feel strongly about. Values stir your emotions.

What Do You Value?

Workplace values Values that are upheld and honored in the workplace.

Workplace values are values that are upheld and honored in the workplace. Along with your skills and preferences, for you to have a good career fit, your values need to be aligned with your career choice and work environment. For example, if you are a vegetarian or vegan, you would find it difficult to work in a meat packing plant. If you value living in an urban center, pursuing a career in livestock management would not be aligned with your desire to live in the city; however, pursuing a marketing or advertising career path might be a great match.

When you truly are on purpose, the people, resources, and opportunities you need naturally gravitate toward you.
—Jack Canfield, success author[1]

Your career should be aligned with the type of environment you value.

Your inner state of being attracts and creates your outer results.
—Joe Vitale, author of *The Attractor Factor: 5 Easy Steps for Creating Wealth (or Anything Else) from the Inside Out*[2]

Your values determine your choices, attitude, and actions. There is nothing wrong with placing status and income high on your value list. Just ask a not-for-profit agency about the importance of money. Ask a well-known philanthropist the same question. Money can bring happiness for many people. For example, many enjoy supporting scholarships. Happiness can certainly be found in supporting the right cause. It is what a person does with wealth that is the defining question. When wealth is attained without clear values, those people tend to overspend and often go broke. Because your values are so personal, do not judge yourself incorrectly. Instead, become very clear about your values so your career and possible subsequent wealth support your values and lifestyle.

---

[1] www.jackcanfield.com/
[2] www.mrfire.com

The coaching principle, *Like Attracts Like* (Holmes, 2009; Gage, 2006; Gregory, 2004; Matthews, 2014; Rann & Arrott, 2005; Rutherford, 1998), is about finding a great career fit. Once you are clear about what you truly value, you can be more conscious about making sure you find or "attract" a workplace and career that support your values. Being in a mismatched workplace in terms of your values can crush your spirit.

How we perceive things is a large part of what is real for us. People who are chronic complainers see situations in negative light, and consequently experience more negative situations in their life to complain about. For example, a complainer who needs to return something at a store will be thinking about how difficult the return will be before he even arrives. He will focus on how long the wait will be, and how unfriendly the worker will be to him. He does not realize that his frown and defensive tone create an unpleasant situation for the worker right away, causing the worker to respond in an unfriendly manner. This is the essence of *like attracts like*.

There are experiences that are out of our hands. However, 80 to 90 percent of what happens to us is under our control, and because of this, the axiom *like attracts like* suggests that you are accountable for what happens in your life. Adversity comes to all of us—it is how we respond to it that makes the difference between success and failure.

> *I am convinced that life is 10 percent what happens to me and 90 percent how I react to it. And so it is with you. We are in charge of our attitudes!*
>
> —Chuck Swindoll

Like attracts like is not about magical thinking. It is about accountability, and taking responsibility for the results in your life so you are more likely to find yourself in a career that is congruent with your goals, interests, values, and personality. By consistently practicing the coaching tools in this book, it may seem like magic is taking place. Remember, *"learn what the magician knows and it's not magic anymore."* —Richard Bach.

We each value different things. Exercise 2.1 will make you aware of what you value most in terms of your career and work. With this information, you can make sure your mission statement—and ultimately your career—is aligned with your values. This alignment can help you find a good career fit. When you are offered a job, revisit your values. Being aware of your values is one of your guides to good career decision making.

exercise 2.1

Values Clarification

Next to each value in the table below, enter the score that describes you the best (3 = Value a Great Deal, 2 = Value Somewhat, 1 = Value Very Little).

	Score		Score
Ability to telecommute		Integrity	
Accomplishment		Intellectually challenging	
Admired		Location	
Advancement		Making decisions	
Adventure		Order/structure	
Aesthetics		Outdoors	
Autonomy/independence		Pleasure	
Caring and supportive		Power	
Challenging		Public contact	
Creating things/building		Quiet	
Creativity		Recognition	
Deadlines		Social activism	
Detail oriented		Stability/security	
Education		Status/prestige	
Excitement		Stress free	
Fast paced		Supervising	
Financial gain/high income		Support family obligations	
Flexible hours		Travel	
Freedom		Variety	
Helping others		Warm relationships	
Humor		Working on the computer	
Independence		Working with people face-to-face	
		Other	

To determine your top five values, look at all those you scored as "3," and choose your top five. List those five in the space below:

1. _____
   _____

2. _____
   _____

3. _____
   _____

4. _____
   _____

5. _____
   _____

exercise 2.2

Five People You Admire

This exercise will help you identify the qualities that you value in yourself and others.

Directions: List five people (living or dead, fictional or real) you admire. Next to each name, list characteristics you admire or value in that person or character. For example, you might admire someone for being brave, funny, and creative. Next, list your admirable characteristics. The resulting two lists represent all of the characteristics that you value in yourself and in others. If you feel you don't possess a particular quality that someone else on your list has, keep this in mind—that quality must already exist in you to some extent, or you would not identify with it. It might be a quality you wish to enhance or improve.

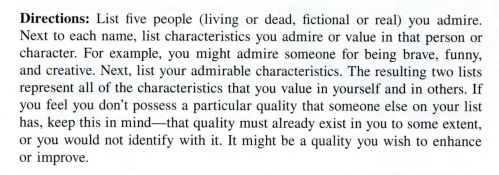

	Name of Person or Character	Characteristics I Admire or Value
1		
2		
3		
4		
5		
6	**Me**	

As you take different assessments and inventories, remember that regardless of the results, you are always the expert on you. Assessments are merely snapshots of parts of you at any given moment, valuable when used in the context of guiding you to a good career fit, or in reinforcing choices you have made. They might also suggest new career possibilities that you had not previously considered. If any assessment gives you results you instinctually know are not correct, go with your gut because the purpose is to become more self-aware and reflective as you move toward your ideal career.

[*Only you know what is true for you.*
—Dr. Dain Heer

The coaching principle discussed in Career Coach 2.1 allows you to become more conscious of what you value. Taking assessments and identifying your values and skills are ways for you to learn more about what makes you tick. You are being coached to success by deliberate intention and creation versus default. The work you do in these early chapters will pay off, and that is why it is so important to understand the value of self-assessments and identify your

skills, values, and personality. Businesses regularly take inventories so they know where they stand. If they did not, they could end up with disastrous results. They need to know what inventory they have, what they need to add, and what they need to unload. You will be doing the same thing on a personal level. Lasting change starts on the inside and works its way out (Heer, 2012; Tice & Quick, 2004; Vitale, 2008).

How is completing a self-assessment exercise similar to taking a snapshot of yourself?

Your Unique Personality

Along with your values, your distinct personality needs to fit with your career and workplace. If you are an outgoing, loud, funny person, with a great laugh, you might not fit well in a stuffy professional office. You need the career and workplace that will value what you have to contribute, including your great laugh. Becoming sharply aware of the characteristics that make up your personality will allow you to be conscious of whether or not you will fit into a workplace culture. You want to ensure that all parts of you are aligned with your career (Dooley, 2007; Hansen & Allen, 2002; Shinn, 2008). There are many qualities that make up your personality. Cyber Trip 2.1 will help you identify the aspects unique to you through a **personality assessment** that categorizes your personality traits to determine if your personal attributes are a good fit in a particular work environment.

Personality assessment Categorizes your personality traits to determine if your personal attributes are a good fit in a particular work environment.

Cyber Trip 2.1

Personality Inventory   There are many personality inventories available to you on the internet. One of the best is the Keirsey™ Temperament Sorter (Keirsey, 1998), a tool designed to help you better understand your unique set of characteristics and personality type. Conduct an online search for a free personality inventory, or use the assessment you find at http://www.humanmetrics.com/cgi-win/JTypes2.asp. When you take the assessment, you will receive a four-letter sequence. Read the descriptions regarding each of the types and see if this information fits you.

Below are the 16 personality types:

ESFP	ISFP	ENFJ	INFJ
ESTP	ISTP	ENFP	INFP
ESFJ	ISFJ	ENTJ	INTJ
ESTJ	ISTJ	ENTP	INTP

Remember, the results are on a scale from 0 to 100, and you can fall anywhere along the scale. You might be an introvert in some or most situations, but not all. You will use this information as you develop your personal profile and consider possible career fits.

Personality Type and Careers   To find additional information and activities related to your personality type and career fit, explore the following websites:

The Holland Occupational Themes (Holland Codes) inventory helps you match your interests with compatible jobs. Visit http://personality-testing.info/tests/RIASEC.php.

Kingdomality© is an assessment that links your personality preferences to medieval vocations, then links those to vocations in the modern corporate world. Searching for a fulfilling career can seem frustrating, but thinking about the perfect job for you in the time of kings and dragons can help lighten your spirit and provide some insight. Visit http://www.careermanagement.com/kingintro.php. You can also use a key word search with your specific personality type, if you know it. For example, if your personality type is ENFP, you could search "ENFP careers." Explore some of the links you find to learn more about careers that fit your personality profile.

✔ SELF-CHECK

1. How can being more aware of your personality and values help you in your career or when job hunting?

2. What are three things you learned about yourself from the assessments on personality or on values?

3. Finish the following statement in your own words: *If you want to make money, you should find work that you. . . .*

» LO 2-2   Soft Skills and Adaptive Skills

> *Everyone has his own specific vocation or mission in life; everyone must carry out a concrete assignment that demands fulfillment . . . everyone's task is unique as his specific opportunity.*
>
> —Viktor E. Frankl

Now that you have assessed your values, personality, and preferences, you should be seeing some patterns and inclinations to help you clarify what careers might be natural fits for you. You also have many skills, and it is helpful to identify them so you have a career language to use in your resume, cover letter, and interviews. Creating your **skills vocabulary** means identifying your skills in order to market and sell yourself to potential employers, or to your current employer if you want to be considered for advancement. In the job search and career promotion process, you are selling yourself as a product. The buyer (employer) wants to know what you can do for them. Your job is to be very clear about your skills so you can market yourself effectively and sell yourself to employers.

Soft skills are all of the skills, excluding technical expertise, that you need to do a job. **Adaptive skills** are also soft skills, related to your work

Skills vocabulary Identifying your skills in order to market and sell yourself to potential employers or to your current employer if you want to be considered for advancement.

Soft skills Skills, excluding technical expertise, that you need to do a job.

Adaptive skills Soft skills related to your work style that help you function as a good employee on a day-to-day basis.

Listening is a soft skill. What soft, or adaptive, skills do you have?

style, and help you function as a good employee on a day-to-day basis. Adaptive skills include time management, honesty, dexterity, active listening, and having a great memory.

You may find it surprising to learn that employers are eager to find employees with strong soft skills and adaptive skills, and often prefer these types of skills over technical expertise. Among other attributes, employers are looking for good interpersonal skills, honesty, a positive attitude, and competence. According to the National Association of Colleges and Employers' *Job Outlook 2014* (http://www.naceweb.org), the top 10 attributes employers look for on a candidate's resume are:

1. Communication skills (written).
2. Leadership.
3. Analytical/quantitative skills.
4. Strong work ethic.
5. Ability to work in a team.
6. Problem-solving skills.
7. Communication skills (verbal).
8. Initiative.
9. Detail-oriented.
10. Computer skills.

exercise 2.3

Your Soft Skills

To become aware of your soft skills (adaptive skills), in the following list place a check mark by the skills that you feel you have.

✓ Adaptable to working alone and in a team	✓ Easy to work with, cooperative spirit
✓ Agreeable	✓ Effective
✓ Appreciates diversity	✓ Efficient
___ Attention to detail	___ Energy management
✓ Client skills (customer service)	___ Enthusiastic
✓ Communicates effectively	✓ Friendly
✓ Completes work on time	✓ Follow directions/instructions
✓ Confident	✓ Good humor
___ Conscientious	✓ Great attendance record
___ Copes well with frequent deadlines	___ Great memory
___ Creative	✓ Hardworking
✓ Dependable	✓ High standards
✓ Detail oriented	✓ Imaginative
___ Diplomatic	✓ Industrious
	___ Intuitive

✓ Logical	✓ Respects supervisors/authority/
✓ Loyal	others
___ Manages time well	✓ Sees the big picture
___ Mature	✓ Self-confident
___ Mentor	✓ Self-motivated
✓ Multitasks	✓ Sincere
___ Organized	✓ Social niceties
✓ Patient	(please, thank you)
✓ Performs well under stress	✓ Solves problems
✓ Positive attitude	___ Strong leader
✓ Practical	✓ Trustworthy
✓ Professionally express	✓ Winner's attitude
opinions	___ _____ (add your own)
___ Punctual	___ _____ (add your own)
___ Quick learner	___ _____ (add your own)
✓ Reliable	
___ Resourceful	

» LO2-3 Hard Skills and Transferable Skills

Your skills can be a catalyst for change and success in your career. By developing your skills vocabulary, you will have the power words needed for writing a winning resume and cover letter and for having a positive interview experience. By knowing the skills you *do* possess, you will also be able to identify skills you need to acquire to obtain your ideal job. Identifying skills gives you another plan of action as you move toward your career goals.

hard skills The technical expertise you need to do a job well.

transferable skills The skills you gain from your experiences.

You have more skills than you probably realize. We have already discussed soft and adaptive skills. In contrast to soft skills, **hard skills** are the technical expertise you need to do a job well. These skills can be gained from education and experience. **Transferable skills** are the skills you learn from your experiences. They include such skills as decision making, communication, and team building, and can be used in a variety of work settings. For example, you may have obtained great research skills while pursuing your degree. If you are interested in becoming a paralegal, a position requiring extensive research skills, you can transfer your research expertise to your new job.

Working in a restaurant requires excellent communication and teamwork skills. What transferable skills have you gained from your past jobs, activities, or experiences?

exercise 2.4

Your Transferable Skills

The following is a partial list of transferable skills. Place a check mark under the headings Proficient or Expert, depending on your estimate of your skill level.

Transferable Skill	Proficient	Expert
Motivate others/team building	✓	
Public speaking	✓	
Listening		✓
Writing/editing	✓	
Keyboarding/typing	✓	
Building rapport	✓	
Identifying problems		✓
Solving problems/creating alternatives	✓	
Setting and achieving goals	✓	
Analyzing	✓	
Forecasting/predicting	✓	
Teaching/training/coaching	✓	
Decision making	✓	
Arbitration/conflict management	✓	
Selling/persuading	✓	
Time management/organization	✓	
Delegating	✓	
Research	✓	
Speaking foreign language(s)	✓	
Building/designing/constructing	✓	
Managing	✓	
Record keeping/data collection/handling quantitative data	✓	
Coordinating/fundraising	✓	
Supervising	✓	
Internet skills/web design	✓	

Job-Specific Skills

Job skills are what people usually think of when they think of *career skills*. These are the skills specific to the job. **Job-specific skills** require special training, experience, education, or certification. Job-specific skills are typically hard skills obtained from many sources, including jobs or volunteer work, courses you have taken, your hobbies, avocations, and other experiences. Examples of job-specific skills include computer skills, keyboarding skills, and accounting skills. To determine if you already have the required skills for a certain position, or need to acquire them, you can look at any job description and find listed many of the required job skills. Job postings are another great source of the specific terms you will want to identify and use in your resume, cover letter, and interview. We will revisit how to identify your skills from a job posting in later chapters.

Job-specific skills Skills that require special training, experience, education, or certification.

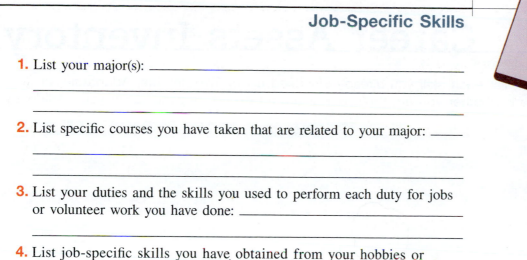

e x e r c i s e 2.5

Job-Specific Skills

1. List your major(s): _____

_____

_____

2. List specific courses you have taken that are related to your major: _____

_____

_____

3. List your duties and the skills you used to perform each duty for jobs or volunteer work you have done: _____

_____

4. List job-specific skills you have obtained from your hobbies or avocations: _____

_____

_____

5. Double-check the skills you have listed to ensure they do not include items such as time management, honesty, and so on. Those skills fall under the categories already discussed, such as transferable and adaptive skills. Job-specific skills include knowing how to take blood pressure or give CPR.

Congratulations! You have completed some critical groundwork toward securing your ideal job. You systematically identified your transferable, adaptive, and job-specific skills. You are ahead of the majority of people in the job search market who cannot identify or speak of their skills. Now you need to organize your skills, so that you will be better prepared when you begin work on your resume, cover letter, and prepare for interviews.

> **Achievement** An accomplishment or success that you attain.

Achievements, Accomplishments, Honors, and Awards

You want to list and describe your accomplishments and achievements. An **achievement** is an accomplishment or success you attain in life. Achievements are important to list in your resume and they fit well with transferable skills. You will be able to refine your skills and achievements when you create your cover letter, resume, and portfolio. In other words, you will make your skills and achievements specific and quantifiable in your marketing documents. For now we will focus on identifying them. Some examples might include the following: paid off credit card debt or student loans, stuck to fitness program and lost 30 pounds, made successful career transition, worked and went to school full-time while raising a family, bought first home, and so on.

Achieving something can give you a wonderful feeling. What types of accomplishments, big or small, have you attained in life so far?

my portfolio 2.1

Career Assets Inventory

In the chart below, list each skill you already identified under Transferable, Adaptable, or Job-Specific. Then mark whether you are proficient or are an expert, depending on your skill level.

Career Assets Inventory			
Type of Skill	List Skill	Proficient	Expert
Transferable Skills			
Adaptive Skills			
Job-Specific Skills			

Quantify Your Skills

This portfolio exercise sets the foundation for resume building, cover letter writing, and interviewing. First, identify several skills you wish to include in your marketing documents. Next, consider how you might be able to quantify each skill. This means that you will need to add numbers to the skill so it is measurable. Figure 2.2 shows examples of how to quantify your skills.

Skill	Quantified Skill
Typing/keyboarding	Type or keyboard 50 wpm (words per minute).
Selling	Top salesperson for two quarters last year, with over $150,000 in total sales per quarter.
Supervising	Supervised 12 employees on a daily basis.

Figure 2.2 **How to Quantify Your Skills**

Now you try it:

List Skill	Quantify the Skill

You will expand on the process of quantifying skills in upcoming chapters to help you create superior marketing documents.

e x e r c i s e 2.6

Achievements and Accomplishments

List five of your achievements, accomplishments, honors, or awards:

1. _____

_____

2. _____

_____

3. _____

_____

4. _____

_____

5. _____

_____

TV and radio advertising is an important medium to get information out to mass audiences. The advertising strategy is to make you remember a business, product, or service. When you hear it over and over again, it begins to stick in your head, and even though you may not recall it immediately, when you have a need, the companies will count on you remembering those advertisements. Networking strategies are identical. You are marketing yourself for someone to recruit and hire you, and when the time comes to do so, you want that person to undoubtedly think of you; just like in business advertising.

—Kevin Brewster, National American University, career management student

You are your product.

Brand identity Your personal marketing image that highlights your worth and value to employers.

Your Brand Identity

Have you ever heard the saying "You don't sell the steak, you sell the sizzle?" You are your product. Start thinking about your **brand identity.** This is your personal marketing image that highlights your worth and value to employers.

If you are in any way active in social media, you are already cultivating your brand identity, whether you realize it or not. Whenever you post something online—a picture on Facebook, a link on Twitter, your thoughts on a personal blog, or new work experience on LinkedIn—you are shaping how people see you.

Think about how your friends present themselves online. Do you have a friend who always posts cat videos? A friend who regularly shares articles about politics and argues in the comments? If somebody immediately came to mind, you understand the idea of having a brand identity online. Now, think about the identity you are developing for yourself online.

While some of your social network activity is private, some can be seen by anyone, including potential employers. Are you showing them the brand identity of a person they would want to hire? We'll examine this more closely in Chapter 4, but now is the time to think about the brand identity you want to present for yourself online.

In this chapter you are identifying the qualities, skills, and values that make you stand out from your competitors. You are identifying those skills and qualities you possess that bring value or benefit to the employer. Perhaps you are skilled at crisis management. This would be part of your brand identity. How might you present this online?

Identifying your marketable skills is crucial in the job search. You possess hundreds of skills, yet most job candidates can only list a few of their marketable skills, and very few can specifically link their skills to the position they are interviewing for. You will learn how to market your skills and relate them to the positions you seek in a way that is attractive to potential employers.

In Chapter 1, you formulated your career goals. However, goals without the framework of your internal interest, inclinations, gifts, and skills can be futile. When you combine your dreams, values, skills, and talents with effective goal setting, you have a winning combination. You cannot fail with this combination. Look at your goals again and ask yourself if these goals reflect your interests and values.

exercise 2.7

Brand Yourself:

First, read through the following brands, and try and come up with the slogan they are identified with:

- Nike, Inc.
- Skittles
- Subway
- Energizer
- Ford
- Verizon Wireless
- Michael Jordan

Next, create a short marketing slogan based on you. To do this, revisit your goals and career mission statement in Chapter 1 and, from this chapter, keep your values, personality, and skills in mind. Create a slogan for yourself in 20 words or less, as if you hired a marketing company to do it for you. Focus on what you can do that adds value to organizations. This slogan might turn into a personal affirmation. After you write this down, share it with your peers, instructor, family, and friends to get their feedback. How might you incorporate it into your online identity? Below is a sample slogan from the student quoted earlier:

When you need a leader in your organization.

—Kevin Brewster

You can refine your slogan, but keep it with you and read it often. Write your slogan here:

_____

_____

_____

» LO 2-4 Identify Your Skills Gap

You know a great deal about your skills at this point. Now it is time to determine what skills you need to acquire for your ideal job. This is also known as your **skills gap.** Your skills gap compares the skills you need in your chosen profession to those you currently possess. Most employers will provide additional training, and even if they do not, you will acquire and learn new skills while working on the job. A proactive approach is to examine the positions you seek and see what requirements you still need to obtain.

Skills gap The skills you must acquire to obtain your ideal job.

exercise 2.8

Skills Gap Identification

Complete the following chart to identify three to five skills you need to acquire for your chosen career. If you are not sure what skills you need, locate job postings for the job you are seeking, and look at the requirements and qualifications. You can find many postings on job search websites, such as Monster .com or CareerBuilder.com.

	Qualification or Skill Required for Your Profession	How You Plan to Acquire This Skill	Date by Which You Plan to Acquire This Skill
1.			
2.			
3.			
4.			
5.			

careercoach 2.2

Awareness as a Success Tool

Now that you are aware of your current skills and the skills you still need, you are empowered. Your skills vocabulary comes from the ability to articulate your skills in your marketing tools and in the interview process. In addition, the process of identifying the skills you still need gives you new goals you can set and achieve. Being aware is a simple, yet powerful tool. It has been said that awareness alone is 50 to 90 percent of the solution to any problem. By spending the time and energy to identify and write down your skills, you will be at least 50 percent closer to mastering the art of finding your ideal job (Chopra, 2005; Heer, 2012; Kasl, 2005; Forleo, 2009; McColl, 2007; Price, 1998; Rutherford, 1998; Proctor, 1997; Shinn, 2008).

Cyber Trip 2.3

MindTool's Essential Skills for Your Excellent Career Not only is it important to pinpoint the skills you currently have, but it is also important to continuously hone those skills. Visit the MindTools website, http://www.mindtools.com, where you can learn more about skills identification and improvement (MindTools, 2014).

4. Name three qualities that employers look for in a worker.

5. Consider the three qualities you chose above. What type of skill is each quality?

6. What are some ways you can use your skills-gap identification information?

» LO2-5 Match Your Degree to Goals and Possibilities

Many people end up working in a field unrelated to their majors. This is not necessarily a bad thing. Having a degree demonstrates that you have many transferable skills that are valued by employers. Your completed degree will demonstrate you have the ability to achieve a long-term goal. The employer will also know you have skills such as time management, organization, and are teachable. In fact, your degree will make you valuable for careers you have not even considered, and as quickly as the workplace changes, there are certain to be careers 10 years from now that don't even exist today.

For example, a decade ago, few people would have imagined making a living as a social media manager. But today, thousands of jobs like that are available. People who hold those jobs probably didn't major in social media, since colleges only recently started offering social media degrees. Instead, social media managers may have majored in subjects such as communications, English, creative writing, journalism, public relations, marketing, or advertising. Those degrees may not have provided them with the specific skills they use as a social media manager today, but they helped them develop transferable skills that they are able to apply to their jobs in this exciting new field. A degree can lend itself to any number of careers.

Cyber Trip 2.4

Matching Your Major to Your Career Mission   Please visit the following school websites to learn more about matching your major to your career mission: http://www.uncw.edu/career/WhatCanIDoWithaMajorIn.html or http://www.iup.edu/page.aspx?id=9913. This is an excellent way to expand your thinking about what your major will allow you to do career-wise.

Next, list three career possibilities suited to your major that you are interested in pursuing.

1. _____

2. _____

3. _____

The Right Fit–Christine's Work Pays Off

After discussing her options with Mrs. Cook, Christine decided to switch her program of study from Medical Assisting to Medical Coding and Billing. Coding and Billing was Mrs. Cook's recommendation, and Christine realized that it was the perfect career for her. Christine's career mission was to work with people in a medical environment. By doing Medical Coding and Billing, she could fulfill her mission and achieve the earning targets she had set for herself. Christine knew her soft skills would transfer well to Medical Coding and Billing, but she also knew she would have to learn the hard skills needed to close her skills gap.

Christine did very well in her classes. She had near-perfect attendance, and earned a 3.6 GPA. Her high school GPA had been a 2.5, so she was quite proud of what she had accomplished in the college program. Just before graduation, Christine spoke to Dr. Nelson about her future plans. Christine was an excellent employee, and Dr. Nelson was more than happy to meet with her. Christine explained how she had been taking classes to prepare for a Medical Coding and Billing career, and that she would graduate soon. She said she was sad to leave his office since she had made close friendships with the other employees, but at the same time she was excited about her future. After telling Dr. Nelson her plans to look for a new career, she handed her written two weeks' notice to him.

Dr. Nelson was impressed with Christine's professionalism. He had experienced a few occasions over the past years where employees had quit without notice, or just stopped showing up without explanation. He was also impressed with Christine's capacity to learn quickly, and her ability to succeed in school even while working.

"Thank you for being so upfront and professional," began Dr. Nelson. "You have been a great employee, and I fully understand why you are making the career change. I can tell you have put time into your decision, and that you have worked hard in school to learn the skills you will need for your new career path."

Christine was elated at Dr. Nelson's praise. She had been nervous about the meeting and afraid he was going to be annoyed or even angry at her decision to leave.

Dr. Nelson surprised Christine even further. "As a matter of fact," he said, "Since my practice has been expanding, I have decided to open up another office. I will need to hire additional Coding and Billing specialists to help with the workload. Would you be interested in staying with my practice?"

Christine could hardly contain her smile, but she tried to stay calm. Her hard work had paid off and she had accomplished her goal of creating a new career path for herself. She hadn't even considered asking about a Coding and Billing position with Dr. Nelson's office. She had just assumed all of the needed positions were filled. Christine accepted Dr. Nelson's offer and happily began transitioning to her new Coding and Billing role within the month.

Discussion Questions

1. What types of soft skills do you think Christine had that transition well from a receptionist position to a Coding and Billing position?

2. Think about two skills that Christine might have acquired from going to college that could transition to her new role in Dr. Nelson's office.

3. What lessons do you think Christine may have learned from her experience in terms of communicating with her instructors and/or employers?

[chapter summary]

The work you did in this chapter will set the foundation for much of the work you will do when creating your resume, cover letter, and portfolio. You have made your task for creating those documents much easier by organizing and outlining your skills, values, and accomplishments. You also have a heightened awareness of what careers you might consider or qualify for based on your interests, values, and skills. This awareness is the foundation that will expand your career possibilities as you learn new skills, and grow and change. Chapter 3 will help you identify which careers, industries, and companies are a good fit for you and are booming. It is important to have a career in a field where there is a demand for product, thus creating a growing job market in that field. That said, the product in demand may be you.

[skill/term check]

1. Describe how being more aware of your personality, values, and interests assists you in finding a great career fit. **(LO 2-1)**

2. Explain the difference between hard skills and soft skills and provide two examples of each term. **(LO 2-2), (LO 2-3)**

3. Explain transferable skills and provide two examples. **(LO 2-3)**

4. Define skills gap. Explain how you might close this gap. **(LO 2-4)**

5. Name two different careers (job titles/positions) you could consider with your degree. **(LO 2-5)**

[KEY TERMS]

Achievement: An accomplishment or success that you attain. **(LO 2-3)** [p. 41]

Adaptive skills: Soft skills related to your work style that help you function as a good employee on a day-to-day basis. **(LO 2-2)** [p. 37]

Brand identity: Your personal marketing image that highlights your worth and value to employers. **(LO 2-3)** [p. 44]

Hard skills: The technical expertise you need to do a job well. **(LO 2-3)** [p. 39]

Job-specific skills: Skills that require special training, experience, education, or certification. **(LO 2-3)** [p. 40]

Personality assessment: Categorizes your personality traits to determine if your personal attributes are a good fit in a particular work environment. **(LO 2-1)** [p. 36]

Skills gap: The skills you must acquire to obtain your ideal job. **(LO 2-4)** [p. 45]

Skills vocabulary: Identifying your skills in order to market and sell yourself to potential employers or to your current employer if you want to be considered for advancement. **(LO 2-2)** [p. 37]

Soft skills: The skills aside from technical expertise that you need to do a job. **(LO 2-2)** [p. 37]

Transferable skills: The skills you gain from your experiences. **(LO 2-3)** [p. 39]

Workplace values: Values that are upheld and honored in the workplace. **(LO 2-1)** [p. 32]

chapter 3

Where Are the Jobs? Maximize Your Career Options

> *Market trends should always dictate labor opportunities, the question is . . . How long will those trends be viable for long term employment?**

—David Kulish, general manager
M.G. Oil Company, Inc.

 target competency > *Learn how to monitor employment and economic trends as they relate to your career choice.*

learning outcomes

After studying this chapter, you should be able to:

LO 3-1 Define frictional unemployment and understand how to use it to your advantage in the job search.

LO 3-2 Understand labor market trends and globalization as they relate to the job market.

LO 3-3 Use various sources of information to find employment opportunities.

---

* Used courtesy of Dave Kulish. Copyright © 2015.

Jamal's Daydream

"I hate my job," said Brandon.

Brandon had been making the same complaint to Jamal at the lunch table almost every day for the past couple of months. "I hear that there are layoffs coming soon, too," Brandon continued.

Jamal nodded in agreement. He had heard the same rumors, and recent newspaper articles pointed toward corporate downsizing. While working at the call center was not his dream job, it did pay the bills and supported his wife and son. He hoped that the job at the call center would keep him afloat until he found a better one. Brandon continued to chatter on about positions moving overseas and how no one appreciated the job they did.

Jamal stifled a yawn as a familiar daydream popped into his head. He saw himself sitting at a desk in front of a computer answering e-mails. Checking his watch, he gathered several papers together and walked down the hall. He knocked on a large office door and, once inside, discussed the balance sheet in his hand. The CEO looked it over and congratulated him for finding an error that saved the company $100,000.

"Why are you smiling?" Brandon inquired, interrupting Jamal's daydream.

Jamal shook his head, startled back to reality. "Oh, I was just thinking about what I'm going to do this weekend," he said.

While Brandon went off to the soda machine, Jamal wrote the word "accountant" on a napkin, folded it up, and put it in his pocket. Jamal knew he would need to go to college to make this daydream come true. He would be the first in his family to go, but definitely not the last. When his son was born, Jamal had made a silent vow that he would be financially secure enough to send his son to college. Maybe this was the time to start thinking seriously about the accounting field and the opportunities that it offered. Jamal had always loved working with numbers. He helped several people in his neighborhood with their taxes each year, and he always enjoyed the challenge of solving number problems. While his current employer could send the call center overseas, there were no plans to move the accounting department.

In the same business section of the newspaper where he had learned about the possible layoffs, he had also spotted an article about the upcoming expansion of nearby Jackson Hospital. Not only were they building a new wing, they were also purchasing some smaller clinics in the area with plans of adding staff and services—including patient billing and other financial services necessary to manage the expansion. Jamal drove home that evening with many questions running through his mind, but no answers. Tomorrow, he decided, he would find a way to avoid sitting with Brandon at lunch. He needed a positive, peaceful environment to begin his first steps.

Discussion Questions

1. What questions does Jamal need answered in order to make his decision about his next step?
2. What are some resources he could use to find out if the accounting field offered him job security?
3. How did you make the decision to continue, or return to, school? Was it similar to Jamal's story? What was your "job daydream" like?

» LO 3-1 Rethinking Unemployment

When we hear the word *unemployment,* we often think the worst. Images of soup lines and poverty may come to mind. There is, however, a type of unemployment that is normal and healthy in the job market. This type of unemployment is called frictional unemployment. **Frictional unemployment** results from people moving between jobs, careers, and locations. It is important to have a good understanding of frictional unemployment, and to know how to use it to your advantage.

Frictional unemployment
Unemployment that results from people moving between jobs, careers, and locations.

As the definition explains, when someone resigns, is fired, moves, or is promoted, a gap is created in the workforce. This gap is frictional unemployment, and it occurs in both a strong and weak job market. When someone tells you there are no good jobs out there, you need to remember frictional unemployment and avoid locking onto incorrect perceptions. Instead, be aware of frictional unemployment and be there when the gap is created. Remember, most people land jobs through personal contacts and networking. So do not wait until the job is posted. Timing is critical in the job market. If you interviewed with a company in the past and were unable to secure a position, keep following up on your leads, as there may be a perfect opening available today. Companies do not like to interview, as it requires time and money, so following up with them saves them the work, and shows them you are motivated.

Cyber Trip 3.1

Unemployment Rates Visit the Department of Labor website (http://www.bls.gov/eag/) to see the national unemployment rate and the unemployment rate in your state. Note that men and women have roughly the same unemployment rate, yet the unemployment rate varies substantially among female racial groups: The unemployment rate of white women was 6.2 percent; black or African-American women, 12.1 percent; Asian women, 4.8 percent; and women of Hispanic or Latino ethnicity, 10.9 percent (DOL Women's Bureau, 2014. Data from the Bureau of Labor Statistics, Labor Force Statistics from the Current Population Survey http://bls.gov/cps/cpsaat03.htm, http://bls.gov/cps/cpsaat04.htm, http://bls.gov/cps/cpsaat07.htm (2013 annual averages). (DOL Women's Bureau). After visiting the Department of Labor website, answer the questions below:

1. What is the current national unemployment rate?

   _____

2. Research a particular state. What is the current unemployment rate for that state?

   _____

» LO 3-2 Labor Market Trends and Globalization

As we move toward becoming a service-workforce nation, the concept of *meaningful work* is one to consider. Remember the discussion in Chapter 1 regarding goal setting and prisoners of war? The German commandant of the war camp was asked why he required the prisoners to move huge piles of

> *If one wants to utterly crush a human being, just give the person completely senseless, irrational work.*
>
> —Fyodor Dostoevsky (1911), Russian novelist

How can staying up-to-date on labor market trends help your job search?

rubble back and forth from one end of the prison camp to the other. The commandant explained it was an experiment to see what happens when people are given what they perceive to be meaningless work (Latham, 2012). What do *you* perceive to be meaningful work? That is the key. There are seemingly endless jobs and careers in the world. Now that you know what is meaningful to you in terms of your career, you must become aware of the labor market and job trends.

Millennial Employment Trends

Being aware of market trends will allow you to plan, respond quickly, and adapt to these trends and changes. This awareness helps you discover where the jobs are and gives you the knowledge to make informed decisions about your career path. Gaining this awareness is what we will explore in this chapter. See Figure 3.1 for a list of the top 10 labor market trends. These trends are discussed in more detail below.

Trend 1: Globalization and Outsourcing

There is nothing worse than getting a degree in widget design, only to find out that widget production has been outsourced to India. Take a look at your wristwatch. Very likely the watch parts were made in China, Mexico, or the Philippines, and then shipped to the United States, assembled, and marketed as "made in the USA." This is known as globalization. **Globalization** is the growing economic interdependence of countries worldwide. Outsourcing goes hand-in-hand with globalization. **Outsourcing** involves hiring and paying an outside firm or third party to handle internal company functions. American companies often outsource call centers, technology support, manufacturing, and other functions to countries overseas, where the cost of performing these functions is lower. Outsourcing has become a major issue in the global market. Companies are able to save money by using more cost-efficient labor in other countries. On the other hand, this diminishes work domestically. Ethical considerations have been argued both ways. Some feel it is wrong to employ workers abroad and pay them very low wages in what is often referred to as "sweatshop conditions." Others feel we have an obligation to share the wealth with other countries, and we should expand outsourcing.

Globalization The growing economic interdependence of countries worldwide.

Outsourcing Hiring and paying an outside firm or third party to handle internal company functions.

Trend 1:	Globalization and Outsourcing
Trend 2:	People Changing Jobs More Often
Trend 3:	Baby Boomers in the Workplace
Trend 4:	Diversity in the Labor Market
Trend 5:	Small to Medium Employers (SMEs)
Trend 6:	Health Care Is Fastest Growing Field
Trend 7:	Accounting, Paralegal, Finance, Service, Management, Health Care, IT, and Insurance Are Booming
Trend 8:	Education Is Essential for Highest Paying Jobs
Trend 9:	More Working Poor
Trend 10:	Technology and Automation

Figure 3.1   **Top 10 Labor Market Trends**

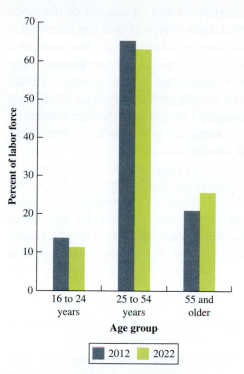

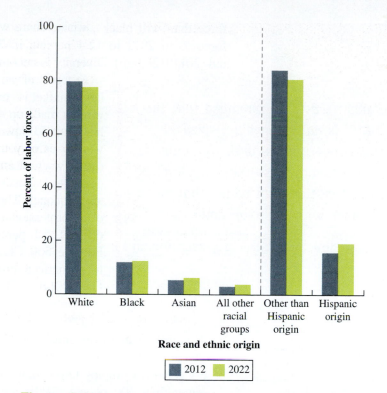

Figure 3.2 Percent of Labor Force by Age Group, 2012 and Projected 2022

Source: U.S. Department of Labor, Bureau of Labor Statistics. (2014b). Retrieved July 13, 2014, from http://www.bls.gov/opub/ted/2014/ted_20140124.htm.

Figure 3.3 Percent of Labor Force by Race and Ethnic Origin, 2012 and Projected 2022.

Source: U.S. Department of Labor, Bureau of Labor Statistics. (2014b). Retrieved July 6, 2014, from http://www.bls.gov/news.release/ecopro.t01.htm.

Trend 2: People Changing Jobs More Often

Employees are less loyal toward their employers. In times past, people often would take a job and stay through retirement. Now, workers look for opportunities and change companies when better offers are presented. According to a study conducted by the U.S. Bureau of Labor Statistics (http://www.bls.gov/news.release/nlsoy.htm), workers surveyed held on average more than 11 jobs between ages 18 and 46. Along with this trend, many people are changing entire career fields during their lifetime, often more than once. Life stages may account for some of these changes.

Trend 3: Baby Boomers in the Workplace

The **baby boomer** generation is defined as those born between 1946 and 1964. Between 2012 and 2022 the number of workers 55 and older is projected to increase from 15.9 percent of the labor force to 17.3 percent of the labor force, due to the aging of the baby-boomer generation. (See Figure 3.2.)

Baby boomer Someone born between 1946 and 1964.

Trend 4: Diversity in the Labor Market

As shown in Figure 3.3, the U.S. workforce will be more diverse by 2022. White, non-Hispanic persons will continue to make up a decreasing share of the workforce, falling from 65.7 percent in 2012 to 60.8 percent in 2022 (http://www.bls.gov/opub/ted/2014/ted_20140124.htm), but will remain the overwhelming majority of the labor force. Hispanics are projected to be the fastest growing of the four labor force groups, growing by 27.8 percent. By 2022, Hispanics will continue to constitute a larger proportion of the labor force than will blacks, whose share will grow from 11.9 percent of the labor force to in 2012 to 12.4 percent in 2022 (http://www.bls.gov/opub/ted/2014/ted_20140124.htm). Diversity is becoming one of America's greatest strengths.

In terms of gender, while the number of women in the labor market is comparable to the number of men (in 2012, women made up 46.9 percent of the workforce, while men made up 53.1 percent), yet on average, full-time working women earn just 77 cents for every dollar a man earns (http://www.whitehouse.gov/equal-pay/career). When it comes to leadership in major corporations, the numbers are also unequal. Though women hold more than 50 percent of all professional-level jobs, only 14.6 percent of executive officers, 8.1 percent of top earners, and 4.6 percent of Fortune 500 CEOs are women, according to the Center for American Progress' report, The Women's Leadership Gap (2014).

> *"Graduates need to be reminded that the term 'SME' [small to medium-sized enterprise] covers firms with . . . millions of people in turnover, so they shouldn't be seen as one or two-man bands that share a photocopier with the shop downstairs."*
>
> —Jonathan Evans,
> director of Discovery Recruitment

Trend 5: Small to Medium Employers (SMEs)

Small to medium employer (SME) Generally defined in the United States as a firm employing between 1 and 500 full-time employees.

A **small to medium employer (SME)** is generally defined in the United States as a firm employing between 1 and 500 full-time staff. Small employers generally employ fewer than 100 people, while medium employers have fewer than 500 people. SMEs are important engines of job growth. The Bureau of Labor Statistics reports that in 2013, 53.8 percent of private-sector employees were employed by companies with fewer than 500 employees, and that 74.2 percent of job gains came from those companies (http://www.bls.gov/bdm/bdmfirmsize.htm).

Trend 6: Health Care Is Fastest Growing Field

The United States Department of Labor predicted the 10 occupations with the highest projected job growth through 2022 (http://www.bls.gov/ooh/most-new-jobs.htm). They are:

1. Personal care aides.
2. Registered nurses.
3. Retail salespeople.
4. Home health aides.
5. Combined food preparation and serving workers, including fast food.
6. Nursing assistants.
7. Secretaries and administrative assistants (except legal, medical, and executive).
8. Customer service representatives.
9. Janitors and cleaners (except maids and housekeeping cleaners).
10. Construction laborers.

How many small to medium-sized businesses can you think of in your community? Why do you think these types of businesses are on the rise?

As you can see from the preceding list, the job sectors in the United States that project to see the most job growth are health care and retail sales. In fact, health care occupations are expected to make up 11 of the 20 fastest growing occupations (based on percentage growth) (DOL BLS, 2014b). Figure 3.4 shows the percent change in the occupations projected to grow the fastest between 2012 and 2022. Aging baby boomers require more health care and account for much of the rapid growth in health-related occupations. They are a wealthier population that can afford better health care, and advances in medical technology permit more health problems to be treated more aggressively (DOL Women's Bureau, 2011a).

Trend 7: Accounting, Paralegal, Finance, Service, Health Care, IT, and Insurance Are Booming

The shift from goods-producing to service-providing employment is expected to continue. Service-providing industries are expected to account for approximately 18.7 million of the 18.9 million new wage and salary jobs generated through 2014. According to National Association of Colleges and Employers (NACE) (NACEWeb, 2009b), even in volatile financial markets, employers surveyed expect to hire about 1.3 percent more graduates from the class of 2009 (see Figure 3.5). For example, the government sector significantly increased hiring in 2009 by 19.8 percent.

Service workers are those who perform services for the public. Employment in service occupations is projected to increase by 5.6 million, or 1.3 percent, between 2012 and 2022. Unfortunately, many jobs in the service sector have median annual earnings lower than the average for all occupations (http://www.bls.gov/emp/ep_table_101.htm).

Management occupations are projected to grow 7.2 percent and add 636,000 new jobs between 2012 and 2022, while business and financial operations occupations are projected to grow 12.5 percent and add 898,000 jobs in that same period. Among managers, the number of medical and health services managers and social and community service managers will grow the fastest, by 23.2 percent and 20.8 percent, respectively. General and operations managers will add the most new jobs—265,000—between 2012 and 2022. Among business and financial occupations, accountants, auditors, and management analysts will add the most jobs—300,000 combined.

Trend 8: Education Is Essential for Highest Paying Jobs

Among the 20 fastest growing occupations, a bachelor's or associate degree is the most significant source of postsecondary education or training for seven of the careers, while advanced degrees such as a master's or doctorate are expected

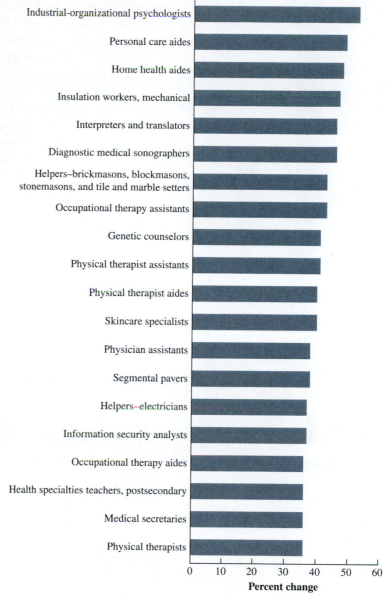

Figure 3.4 Percent Change in Employment in Occupations Projected to Grow Fastest, 2012–2022

Source: U.S. Department of Labor, Bureau of Labor Statistics. http://www.bls.gov/ooh/fastest-growing.htm.

Service workers Those who perform services for the public.

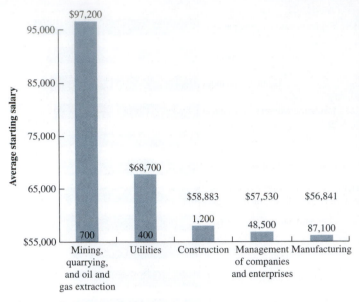

Figure 3.5 Top Industries for the Class of 2014

Source: https://www.naceweb.org/uploadedFiles/Content/static-assets/downloads/executive-summary/2014-april-salary-survey-executive-summary.pdf.

for five occupations in that grouping. On the whole, the outlook for college graduates is improving. Figure 3.6 lists the fastest growing occupations, by level of postsecondary education or training, as well as those projected to have the largest numerical increases in employment between 2012 and 2022.

The individual and societal benefits of completing a college degree are well documented. Higher education is necessary for advancing in the 21st century. Workers with a bachelor's degree earn an average of $24,000 a year more than those with a high school diploma, and workers with advanced degrees earn on average up to $55,000 more a year than workers with only a high school diploma (DOL, BLS, 2014). The average annual earnings for those with a bachelor's degree are $57,616, while those with an associate's degree average $40,404, and those with only a high school diploma average $33,852.

Figure 3.6 Fastest Growing Occupations from 2012 through 2022

Source: Occupational Outlook Handbook, http://data.bls.gov/projections/occupationProj.

	Fastest Growing Occupations	Occupations Having the Largest Numerical Job Growth
Doctoral or Professional Degree		
	Audiologists	Postsecondary teachers
	Postsecondary teachers	Physical therapists
	Physical therapists	Lawyers
	Anesthesiologists	Physicians and surgeons
	Optometrists	Clinical, Counseling, and School Psychologists
Master's Degree		
	Genetic Counselors	Education Administrators
	Organizational Psychologists	Librarians
	Orthotists and Prosthetists	Postsecondary teachers
	Marriage and Family Therapists	Educational, Guidance, School, and Vocational Counselors
	Nurse Practitioners	Speech-Language Pathologists
Bachelor's Degree		
	Information Security Analysts	Secondary School Teachers, Except Special Education
	Meeting, Convention, and Event Planners	Accountants and auditors
	Interpreters and translators	Computer and Information Systems Managers
	Market Research Analysts and Marketing Specialists	General and Operations Managers
	Geographers	Management Analysts

(Continued)

	Fastest Growing Occupations	*Occupations Having the Largest Numerical Job Growth*
Associate Degree		
	Cardiovascular technologists and technicians	Preschool teachers, except special education
	Diagnostic Medical Sonographers	Registered Nurses
	Medical and Clinical Laboratory Technicians	Dental hygienists
	Occupational and Physical Therapy Assistants	Computer Network Support Specialists
	Veterinary Technologists and Technicians	Paralegal and Legal Assistants
Postsecondary Vocational Award		
	Skincare Specialists	Dental Assistants
	Surgical Technologists	Emergency Medical Technicians and Paramedics
	Dental Assistants	Medical Assistants
	Emergency Medical Technicians and Paramedics	Nursing Assistants
	Medical Assistants	Heating, Air Conditioning, and Refrigeration Mechanics and Installers
High School with On the Job Training		
	Medical Secretaries	Medical Secretaries
	Substance Abuse Counselors	Pharmacy Technicians
	Pharmacy Technicians	Bill and Account Collectors
	Paving, Surfacing, and Tamping Equipment Operators	Bookkeeping, Accounting, and Auditing Clerks
	Pest Control Workers	Operating Engineers and Other Construction Equipment Operators

According to a recent study, the median family income for a high school graduate decreased by 13.1 percent, while an individual with four years of college saw an increase of 9.9 percent, and the gap continues to grow (Newman et al., 2004).

Here is another way to look at the disparity: the unemployment rate for those age 25 and over, without a high school diploma, is 11 percent; however, this rate falls to 4 percent with a bachelor's degree (DOL BLS, 2014). Figure 3.7 is another look at earnings by degree.

Working poor Individuals whose income falls below the official poverty threshold.

Trend 9: More Working Poor

According to the U.S. Bureau of Labor Statistics, 7.1 percent of all individuals in the U.S. labor force are classified as **working poor** (http://www.bls.gov/cps/cpswp2012.pdf). The working poor are individuals who are active in the labor force (either working or looking for work), but whose income falls below the official poverty threshold. Economic turmoil is creating even more challenges

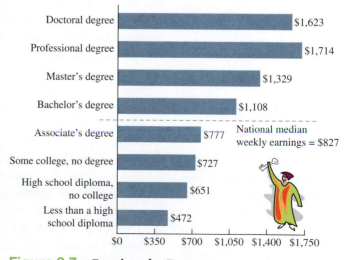

Figure 3.7 **Earnings by Degree**
Source: http://www.bls.gov/emp/ep_chart_001.htm.

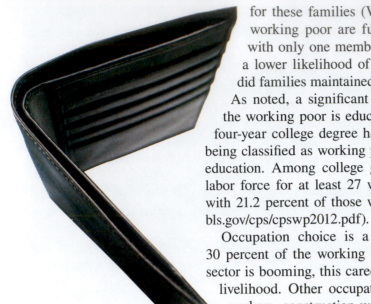

What does "working poor" mean? What contributes to this trend?

for these families (Workingpoorfamilies.org, n.d.). Nearly half of the working poor are full-time employees. Furthermore, among families with only one member in the labor force, married-couple families had a lower likelihood of living below the poverty level (9.6 percent) than did families maintained by women (26.8 percent) or by men (16.8 percent).

As noted, a significant factor that reduces the risk of becoming part of the working poor is education. In fact, those with an associate degree or a four-year college degree have the lowest rates of poverty. The likelihood of being classified as working poor diminishes as workers attain higher levels of education. Among college graduates, 2.1 percent of those who were in the labor force for at least 27 weeks were classified as working poor, compared with 21.2 percent of those with less than a high school diploma (http://www.bls.gov/cps/cpswp2012.pdf).

Occupation choice is a key factor affecting the working poor. About 30 percent of the working poor are in the service sector. While the service sector is booming, this career field does not substantially support the worker's livelihood. Other occupations with high levels of working poor are farm workers, construction workers, and maintenance workers.

Another factor affecting the working poor is what is referred to as **McDonaldization,** a term coined by George Ritzer in his book, *McDonaldization: The Reader,* in which he used the global giant McDonald's as a business model. Ritzer used McDonald's to explain how society takes on the characteristics of a fast-food restaurant. Relatedly, Ritzer also coined the term **McJob.** A McJob is a low-paying job requiring few skills and offering little chance of advancement. It is a representation of the many de-skilled service jobs that are on the rise. Many of these underskilled positions are also part-time, often leaving the working-poor employees without health care coverage or retirement benefits.

Trend 10: Technology and Automation

Trend 10 is also linked to the increase in the number of the working poor. In essence, with the expansion of technology and automation, there has been a reduction in the number of jobs that were once high paying, hands-on, and unionized.

Factory automation accounts for the majority of the 20 occupations with the largest projected numerical decreases. These include office and administrative support, and production occupations. The implementation of technology reduces the needs for these workers. For example, employment of word processors and typists is expected to decline due to proliferation of personal computers. Other workers are able to perform duties formerly assigned to word processors and typists, eliminating the need for these positions.

Other Employment Trends

The global economy has created the need for multilingual workers and those who are flexible, skilled in technology, and culturally adaptive. **Virtual companies** are online companies that may or may not have physical locations. Virtual companies, also known as **e-commerce companies**, involve business that is conducted electronically on the Internet. These types of businesses are expanding from education to business. Many employees of virtual companies interview online, are trained online, and work online. They communicate with their supervisors, co-workers, and clients on a daily basis, but may never see them in person. In terms of online education, the product (knowledge) is invisible—there are no physical classrooms because students and teachers are connected virtually. The need to communicate well

McDonaldization Term coined by George Ritzer to explain how society takes on the characteristics of a fast-food restaurant.

McJob A low-paying job requiring few skills and little chance of advancement.

Virtual companies Online companies that may or may not have physical locations.

E-commerce company Business that is conducted electronically on the Internet.

in writing and via the phone is critical when face-to-face communication is missing.

Temporary agencies are staffing companies that find jobs for people searching for employment, and find qualified people for companies that are seeking to fill specific positions. Temporary agencies are also known as *headhunters* or *professional recruiters*. These types of companies and workers are on the rise. In the past, temporary agencies staffed mostly clerical workers; however, health care workers, accountants, paralegals, as well as those in other fields are now in demand. Other employment trends include:

- Hiring process is online.
- Increase of drug screening and other prescreening.
- Networking and changes due to social media.
- Rising costs of medical care.
- Downsizing and restructuring.
- Job sharing and part-time jobs on the rise.

> The need to communicate well in writing and via the phone is critical when face-to-face communication is missing.

Temporary agencies Staffing companies that find jobs for people searching for employment, and find qualified people for companies that are seeking to fill specific positions.

✓ SELF-CHECK

1. What are three of the fastest growing career fields?

2. How is education linked to income?

3. How is globalization affecting domestic employment?

careercoach3.1

Seeing the Opportunities

Part of finding available jobs involves being open to opportunities. We can understand the trends, but it is also as important to learn how to see what you were unable to see previously. In Chapter 1 you learned how your mind works in terms of goal setting. If you believe there are no jobs in your field, you will not be able to find them (Rutherford, 1998; Tice & Quick, 2004).

Your brain is well-equipped to blind you from seeing everything, from your misplaced car keys to job opportunities. You will learn more about this in future chapters, but essentially your mind is created to keep you sane. So if you think there are no jobs in your area, your mind will block information to the contrary. It is more important to your brain to be sane than right. You may have found yourself in the past seeing some people as "lucky." We can create our own luck. Being lucky and staying fortunate over the long haul involve knowing and applying the tools and principles found in this book.

Another principle to keep in mind is: *money loves speed* (Killoran, 2009; Proctor, 1997; Vitale, 2008). This universal principle means that when opportunity presents itself, you need to react with enough speed and wisdom to capitalize on it.

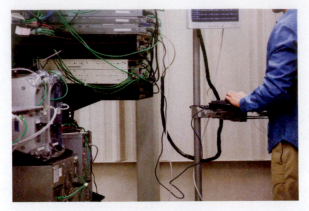

Occupations that involve computers are expected to continue growing over the next several years. What is the growth outlook for the career you are most interested in pursuing?

» LO3-3 Using Sources to Find Employment Opportunities

You need accurate, current information in order to make wise career decisions and moves. One place to find such data is the Occupational Outlook Handbook, that can be found online at http://www.bls.gov/ooh/ (DOL BLS, 2014).

As mentioned previously, health care occupations are expected to grow the fastest over the projection period. Health care occupations make up four of the top six fastest growing occupations shown in Figure 3.8 those four health care occupations are projected to. Combined, add more than 1.8 million new jobs to the economy between 2012 and 2022 (DOL BLS, 2014b).

Figure 3.8 Occupations with the Largest Numerical Increases in Employment, Projected 2012–2022

Source: U.S. Department of Labor, Bureau of Labor Statistics. (2014). Most New Jobs. Retrieved August 3, 2014, from http://www.bls.gov/ooh/most-new-jobs.htm.

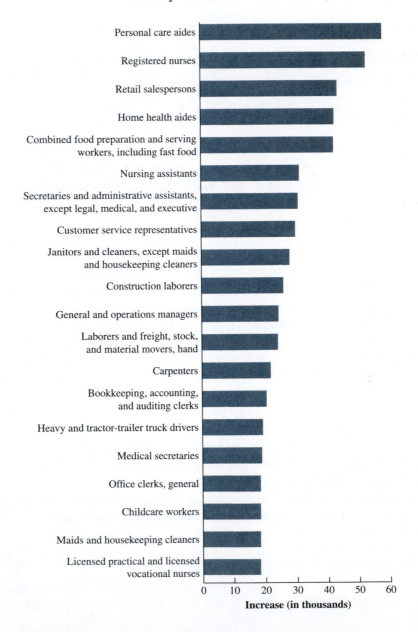

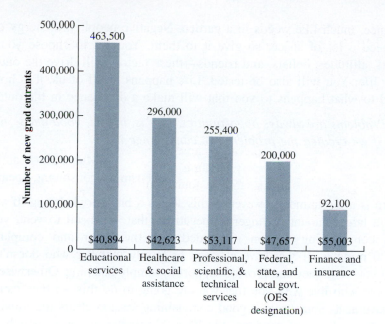

Figure 3.9 Top Hiring Industries/Average Starting Salaries

careercoach3.2

Accountability

Another principle to remember for locating your ideal job is accountability. Accountability means to take responsibility for one's life. If you leave your career up to the career center, your instructors, or other forces outside of yourself, you are giving up accountability. Blaming external forces, such as the economy, is a way to stay stuck. When you become fiercely accountable for your life and your results, you will begin to reap your rewards. To say you cannot find an ideal job because the economy is bad is simply an excuse. It allows you to give up and literally not see, hear, or find opportunities. When you say *"That's just the way it is . . . ,"* you give up accountability (Chopra, 2005; Gage, 2006; Katz, 2004; Hayden, 1992; Matthews, 1990; Niven, 2006; Tice & Quick, 2004; Vitale & Len, 2007).

This is a difficult concept for many to wrap their minds around, especially if they have had a hard life thus far. Many don't want to take responsibility for their lives. Any time success or failure shows up in your life, you are accountable for it. For many it is difficult to imagine taking personal responsibility for failure. It is much easier to pat ourselves on the back when things go right. For instance, it is easier to blame the weather for a lost championship than it is to focus on the elements of the plays that were not executed correctly. When opportunity shows up at your door, you must take personal accountability for its presence. If that opportunity happens to be further training or more education, seize the moment.

Remember the principle: *like attracts like?* That fits here as well. On some level, you attracted the results in your life up to this moment, and you can now use your power to attract new results if you so choose. The beauty of this principle is that if you were somehow responsible in causing the situation, you also have the power to change it!

Becoming entirely responsible for the quality of your life also means you forfeit the right to complain and blame. Negative attitudes and people are in abundance, much like weeds in a garden. Negative people are energy drains. They need a lot of space, so give it to them. You get to choose your own thoughts, attitudes, beliefs, and friends—these factors will drive the outcomes in your life. You will also be tested. Life happens to all of us; it is how you respond to what happens to you that will make a difference in the outcome.

> *. . . Problems are always opportunities. This is, in fact, good news, given that if we created the problem, we can change it.*
>
> —Mabel Katz, author, business consultant, speaker[1]

There is a disclaimer, however, if this seems a bit overwhelming. If you are feeling a large amount of lingering negativity that you need to vent, you can take a complaining session if needed. Set the timer and complain for 10 to 20 minutes. If you have a friend or family member who doesn't mind hearing you vent, they can provide support by simply listening. Otherwise, warn the people who live with you that you are going to do this, so they can leave. Then have at it. Sometimes a good complaining session clears the mind like a thunderstorm clears the air. Once the 10 or 20 minutes are over, though, get on with your life. Move forward and leave the complaints behind. Move toward the solutions and get clear. We will learn more about getting clear in later chapters.

Cyber Trip 3.2

Industry and Occupation Search   Research three interesting industries or occupations that fit you and your career goals. You may use periodicals, websites, industry professionals, or any other appropriate sources. Here is a list of helpful online sources: The Occupational Outlook Handbook: http://www.bls.gov/ooh/ O*Net: http://www.onetonline.org/find/ Riley Guide, Employment and Industry Trends: http://www.rileyguide .com/trends.html Vault Industry Search: http://www.vault.com/industries-professions.aspx Quintessential Careers: http://www.quintcareers.com/career_centers/ After you have done your research, fill in the following chart regarding the jobs you selected:

	Industry/Career Title	Industry/Career Outlook or Trends	Industry/Career Projected Earnings
1			
2			
3			

Targeted Job Search

Researching the companies you want to work for is part of a targeted job search. A **targeted job search** is one in which you take the lead to research and select industries, companies, and even positions or people you want to work for. Once you gather information, you can focus your time and net-working efforts toward these companies.

You will search not only for specific openings in the companies, but also for potential opportunities. Just because the position you seek is not

Targeted job search When you take the lead to research and select industries, companies, and even positions or people you want to work for.

---
[1] www.mabelkatz.com, www.businessbyyou.com, www.hooponoponowithmabelkatz.com

available now, does not mean it won't be in the future. Many job seekers think they are only looking for positions currently advertised or open. That is faulty thinking. As you will learn in the upcoming chapter on networking, most jobs are found through contacts—this includes positions not yet advertised. Landing your ideal job is largely about contacts and timing. Targeting companies and positions, while leveraging your efforts through networking, significantly improves your outcome.

Research—The First Step in Targeting Companies

There are many reasons to research a company, including finding out the future outlook for the company, the reputation, the company climate, financial conditions, and compensation, to name a few. You also want to find a good fit between yourself and the company. Researching companies will give you an inside edge as you custom-create your resume and cover letters for the positions within the company. Furthermore, you will learn valuable information for your interview. To make an informed employment decision, you want to arm yourself with accurate information on companies you are generally interested in, and those you are applying to.

It is important to know how to research a company. The first key to conducting effective research is to know what you are looking for. Think about what is important to you in a job.

Perhaps a company's financial importance is important because you want to work for a company that is financially healthy, growing, and not likely to lay off workers soon. You may want to know the company's policy and track record regarding mentoring, training, promotion, or diverse hiring practices. Perhaps you'd like to learn about the company's history, culture, values, or philosophy. Or maybe you want to get a sense of a company's personality, or get to know some of the people who work there.

How do you think an informational interview can help you during your job search?

All of these factors can impact your interest in a company, as well as your experience as an employee if you go to work there. Learning about these things can also help you ask informed questions if the company offers you an interview.

Where can you find this kind of information? A good starting point is the company's website. There you can find things such as press releases, company history, values and philosophy, and public financial records. You can also find social media links, where you can click to see what the company posts to Twitter, Facebook, Instagram, and Google+, as well as the company blog, if one exists.

However, while you can find a lot of valuable information online, do not limit your search to the Internet. Visit the library, and explore trade journals, directories, and business files. You can ask a library employee to assist you in your search.

Another source of information on companies is your college resource center. Most colleges and universities, including online universities, have this service for students. The Internet can be your friend and foe for researching companies. You can find accurate information on the Internet *if* you know where to look. My Portfolio 3.1 and 3.2 will help you hone your Internet research skills.

A great way to elicit information is to conduct an informational interview with someone at the company where you are interested in working. An **informational interview** is an interview that allows you to gather information about a particular occupation or company. Its purpose is not for you to necessarily land the job, but rather to assist you in your job search by providing you with information and networking contacts. It may lead to a job, but that should not be the primary intent. You will learn the specifics on how to conduct an informational interview in later chapters. You can also use any contact you have at the company to gain opinions. This will have some value, especially for networking.

my portfolio 3.1

Company Research

Research three companies that interest you, or that you might like to work for. Use the Internet, library, trade journals, Chamber of Commerce, or other sources to locate this information. Most companies have websites, which are great places to start.

After you have researched your chosen companies, complete the following information:

Company 1

Company or organization name: _____

Briefly describe what the company does: _____

Location(s): _____

Website address: _____

Phone number: _____

Type of position you are interested in within the company: _____

How to apply: _____

Positive aspects of the company: _____

Negative aspects of the company: _____

Three things you learned about the company or organization. These might include size, mission statement, growth projection, etc.: _____

_____

_____

Company 2

Company or organization name: _____

Briefly describe what the company does: _____

Location(s): _____

Website address: _____

Phone number: _____

Type of position you are interested in within the company: _____

(Continued)

How to apply: _____

Positive aspects of the company: _____

Negative aspects of the company: _____

Three things you learned about the company or organization. These might include size, mission statement, growth projection, etc.: _____

_____

_____

Company 3

Company or organization name: _____

Briefly describe what the company does: _____

Location(s): _____

Website address: _____

Phone number: _____

Type of position you are interested in within the company: _____

How to apply: _____

Positive aspects of the company: _____

Negative aspects of the company: _____

Three things you learned about the company or organization. These might include size, mission statement, growth projection, etc.: _____

_____

_____

Most communities have a Chamber of Commerce. The chamber is where local businesspeople network. Look online or in the phone book for the Chamber of Commerce and find out when there are meetings or mixers. Ask to be added to their mailing list.

exercise 3.1

Cost of Living and Salaries

The more information you are armed with, the better equipped you will be to find your ideal career. You want to know what a job is worth, as well as the cost of living in that geographical location. Having salary and cost of living information will help you in the job negotiation process. It will also add to your knowledge of different types of possible jobs and titles.

Use the first table below to make a realistic guess about the salary of two positions that you are interested in.

	Title of Position	Estimated Salary (Your Guess)
1.		
2.		

Then use resources such as the library, periodicals, people in the industry, and websites such as http://www.salary.com/ or http://www.bls.gov/bls/blswage.htm, to find the actual estimated salary for the two positions you chose. You also can find this information by conducting a keyword search of the job title plus "salary calculator" using your favorite Internet search engine.

Enter your findings in the second table below. In addition, visit http://www.bestplaces.net/cost-of-living/ or another site that calculates cost of living, and make a comment in the chart below regarding the cost of living for that area.

	Title of Position	Average Salary (Actual)	Geographical Location	Cost of Living Comment
1.				
2.				

Now that you know how to research industries, trends, and specific companies, you need an efficient and effective method to keep track of job search information. My Portfolio 3.2 is a start to this process. You may be applying to hundreds of companies and you don't want to waste time repeating your efforts, or trying to remember the contact person's name and number for follow up. A **contact log** is a way to record current and potential contacts during the job search and interview process. By utilizing a contact log, you can easily update contact information for networking and interviewing, and ensure that you follow up effectively.

Contact log A way to record current and potential contacts during the job search and interview process.

my portfolio 3.2

Log of Contacts

Transfer the information from one of the companies you researched to the contact log below. This is how you can keep track of the companies you target, their contact information, and what action you took or plan to take. Consider also creating a digital version of this log of contacts that you can keep on your computer or phone.

Log of Contacts	
Company name:	
Address:	
City:	
State:	
Zip code:	
Website address:	
Contact person name and title:	
Phone number:	
Fax number:	
E-mail:	
Date applied:	
Follow-up date:	
Additional comments:	

Jamal's Daydream—From Napkin to Reality

It had been three weeks since Jamal sat with Brandon at lunch. He didn't think Brandon missed him much. A decent-sized lunch crowd continued to listen to Brandon's rants about his terrible job. In his quiet corner, Jamal pulled out the crumpled napkin with the word "accountant" on it. He smiled and opened the notebook he had been using to keep track of his research.

The past few weeks had been busy. He went to the local library the same day he had written his dream down on the napkin. There, he found a helpful woman named Marilyn who showed him Internet resources pertaining to the accounting field. He spent a few hours exploring the Occupational Outlook Handbook for information about salaries, career paths, educational requirements, and labor trends. He learned that accounting is one of the fastest growing occupations due to the trend toward service industry jobs, and the fact that workers with good financial experience often direct business activities in business, government, and other organizations.

He was surprised at how much more money he could make by completing an associate's degree, or even continuing toward a bachelor's degree, master's degree, or his CPA certification. Jamal was especially interested in the online courses offered by each of the schools, since they would enable him to continue working while in school. Marilyn showed him a list of colleges in the area that offered accounting programs and how to contact them. On his own, Jamal wrote down all of his questions about starting college, including those about time commitment, financial aid, placement tests, and career services. He contacted each school and asked a lot of questions. He then wrote out the pros and cons of each school, and ultimately made the decision to attend a nearby college that offered evening, weekend, and online courses. This meant he could continue to provide for his family while working toward his degree.

He paged through his notebook and found the worksheets he had created to organize his research information. One of his neighbors whom he regularly helped with taxes offered to take Jamal on a tour of the accounting department at the company where he worked. Jamal jumped at the chance, and it proved to be a great opportunity to ask the staff questions about day-to-day duties, job security, average pay, advancement, and a number of other topics. Hearing answers and explanations from those who currently worked in the field provided valuable insight beyond what Jamal had read online and in other sources.

While all of this had taken time and energy, Jamal was enthusiastic about taking control of his career. He did not want to just sit around complaining and waiting for a possible layoff notice. He was now in charge of his own destiny and was determined to see his daydream through to reality. School would take time away from his family, but his wife supported his decision and had encouraged him to go for it.

He looked at the crumpled napkin and debated throwing it away. Instead, he folded it neatly and put it into his backpack, which also contained his new textbook, *Introduction to Accounting*. After work, he would drive to campus and attend his first college class, confident that his decision would lead to a fulfilled daydream and a better life.

Discussion Questions

1. Why was it important for Jamal to stop having lunch with Brandon?
2. In what ways did Jamal take responsibility for his career and life?
3. Are there other resources, besides the ones that Jamal used, that can help you make informed choices about your career?

chapter summary

As you seek your ideal job, it is as important to know what you are seeking as it is to know what is going on in the economy. You want a great match. This chapter examined the top 10 employment trends, and how these trends can be used to generate opportunities for your personal career growth. As noted, employment trends come and go. Therefore, you want to gather accurate information to ensure your long-term career success. In this chapter, you also learned how to research industries, target jobs, research specific companies, and log your contacts in an organized manner.

skill/term check

1. What is frictional unemployment? **(LO 3-1)**
2. How can frictional unemployment benefit one's job search? **(LO 3-1)**
3. How does globalization impact the labor market? **(LO 3-2)**
4. What three employment trends do you feel are most significant? Why? **(LO 3-2)**
5. What do you feel are the pros and cons of working for small firms, medium firms, and large firms? **(LO 3-2)**
6. How does your educational attainment impact your job and career prospects? **(LO 3-2)**
7. Which industries are projected to see the greatest job growth between now and 2022? **(LO 3-3)**
8. List three sources of information you can use to research companies and positions during your job search. **(LO 3-3)**

KEY TERMS

Baby boomer: Someone born between 1946 and 1964. **(LO 3-2)** [p. 55]

Contact log: A way to record current and potential contacts during the job search and interview process. **(LO 3-3)** [p. 68]

E-commerce company: Business that is conducted electronically on the Internet. **(LO 3-2)** [p. 60]

Frictional unemployment: Unemployment that results because people move between jobs, careers, and locations. **(LO 3-1)** [p. 53]

Globalization: The growing economic interdependence of countries worldwide. **(LO 3-2)** [p. 54]

Informational interview: An interview that allows you to gather information about a particular occupation or company. **(LO 3-3)** [p. 66]

McDonaldization: Term coined by George Ritzer to explain how society takes on the characteristics of a fast-food restaurant. **(LO 3-2)** [p. 60]

McJob: A low-paying job requiring few skills and offering little chance of advancement. **(LO 3-2)** [p. 60]

Outsourcing: Hiring and paying an outside firm or third party to handle internal company functions. **(LO 3-2)** [p. 54]

Service workers: Those who perform services for the public. **(LO 3-2)** [p. 57]

Small to medium employer (SME): Generally defined in the United States as a firm employing between 1 and 500 full-time employees. **(LO 3-2)** *[p. 56]*

Targeted job search: When you take the lead to research and select industries, companies, and even positions or people you want to work for. **(LO 3-3)** *[p. 64]*

Temporary agencies: Staffing companies that find jobs for people searching for employment, and find qualified people for companies that are seeking to fill specific positions. **(LO 3-2)** *[p. 61]*

Virtual company: Online companies that may or may not have physical locations. **(LO 3-2)** *[p. 60]*

Working poor: Individuals whose income falls below the official poverty threshold. **(LO 3-2)** *[p. 59]*

Marketing Tools:
Promoting Your Skills

In Part 1 you explored and determined your goals, career mission, values, and skills. You learned the importance of monitoring labor market trends, and how to use several sources of information to search for a career. You also learned how to brand yourself. Part 2 builds upon the principles and tools presented in Part 1. It is always important to try new tools while allowing the supporting principles to work in the background. The tools in Part 2 are some of the most critical that you will use during your career search.

Chapter 4 shows you the importance of networking. Networking is a proven way to make career contacts, land interviews, and ultimately find a job. It is imperative that you are comfortable meeting potential networking contacts and presenting yourself, both in person and through social media. Part of networking includes creating your own networking business card, as well as knowing how to approach warm and cold contacts, give a proper handshake, and work a room. Chapter 5 then guides you through creating a professional and attention-grabbing resume using a simple formula. Relatedly, Chapter 6 shows you how to create effective cover letters and error-free applications. A polished resume, cover letter, and application provide the confidence you need to approach key potential employers.

Creating and using the marketing tools in Part 2 give you the ability and self-assurance to promote yourself with ease. Each tool supports the idea that you are your own product and allows you to successfully communicate your skills to potential employers and networking contacts—on paper, online, and in person.

chapter 4

Networking—It's Always Who You Know

> *Good things come to those who wait, but better things come to those who go out and get them.*
>
> —Anonymous

target competency > *Use networking skills and tools successfully.*

learning outcomes

After studying this chapter, you should be able to:

LO 4-1 Explain the importance of networking in reaching your career goals.

LO 4-2 Identify networking opportunities and potential contacts.

LO 4-3 Employ social media in your job search

LO 4-4 Demonstrate how to use warm and cold contacts.

LO 4-5 Use specific tools to enhance networking results.

Making Connections

Is this seminar ever going to end? Richard felt time crawling by, and he was starting to lose interest in the speaker. His father had made him come to the workforce development seminar about networking. After high school, Richard had drifted from one low-wage job to another, never really finding the challenge and opportunity to prove his worth. After three years, he was starting to doubt that he had a bright future, and his father had made him attend the seminar series, in hopes that it would provide Richard with new job-seeking skills. The other 50 people in the room had begun to shift in their metal folding chairs, and Richard was relieved when a break was finally called.

While pouring a cup of coffee, a woman next to him in line smiled. *Please don't talk to me,* Richard thought to himself. He had never been completely comfortable speaking to strangers, and he just wasn't in the mood. The woman didn't seem to notice Richard's attempt to avoid her, though. She sat down next to him and introduced herself as Amanda. Amanda had been in the workforce for 15 years and had just recently been laid off from her administrative assistant position. She now wanted to work in human resources, especially in the benefits area. Richard listened politely and began to sympathize with Amanda's plight. He shared some of the workplace frustrations that she had, and his desire to work with computers matched her desire to work in human resources. Richard had not shared his IT career dream with too many people, thinking they would either laugh at him, or assume he was trying to be better than them. Richard slowly began to feel more comfortable conversing with Amanda, though, and just as he was ready to exchange contact information with her, the seminar began again.

The presenter had spoken earlier about the benefits of networking and was now talking about imaginary networks—which sounded a little "out there" in Richard's opinion. Nonetheless, he was really trying to concentrate now. He started to make a mental list of people he would put into his imaginary network and what qualities they possessed. As he reflected, he thought about this newest connection he had made with Amanda. She already seemed supportive, intelligent, and trustworthy, which were three of the qualities he listed in his imaginary network. As she was searching for a human resource position, she might meet people in the IT field that she could introduce him to, and he may be able to repay the favor by introducing her to any HR professionals he came across. In fact, his sister Laurie was attending community college as a business student, and he knew she had friends who were going into the HR field. All of these ideas were running through his head when the seminar ended.

As he was getting up to leave, Amanda walked over and handed him her networking business card. Richard had never seen a networking business card before—he had always assumed that people who had jobs were the only ones with business cards. Her contact information was listed on the card, as well as a brief description of her qualifications. She told him that she was sure that they could create a mutually beneficial connection, and if he felt the same, to give her a call. Richard smiled and shook her hand, pleased to have added the first person to his network.

Discussion Questions

1. What are Richard's next steps in creating a network?
2. How could Richard use the workforce development workshop series to help him grow his network?
3. What actions did Amanda take at the workshop that showed she was using good networking skills?

» LO4-1 The Importance of Networking

How many opportunities do you get each day to network yourself? If you're like most people, you have more chances to connect with people who can help you in your job search than you realize.

Are you aware of the number of chances each day you are given to network yourself? By becoming conscious of these often overlooked opportunities, you can better leverage the time and energy spent job searching. You can do this by harnessing the energy of others. Using the power of synergy is nothing new in the career development process. **Synergy** is known as the enhanced results when two or more people combine efforts or energy.

Cyber Trip 4.1

Test Your Networking IQ Visit http://www.execunet.com/e_download_quiz.cfm to take a fun quiz that tests your networking IQ. Be prepared to discuss your results in class.

Synergy The enhanced results when two or more people combine efforts or energy.

Networking Using contacts for purposes beyond the reason for the initial contact, especially in business and career searches.

Hidden job market A network that consists of real people you will associate with in your career search, and while climbing the career ladder; also known as a hidden network.

The Hidden Job Market

This chapter will explain how most jobs are obtained—not through job boards or online ads, but through networking. **Networking** is using contacts for purposes beyond the reason for the initial contact, especially in business and career searches. Networking can help you find your hidden job market. The **hidden job market** is a network that consists of real people you will associate with in your career search and while climbing the career ladder. It can also be referred to as a hidden network. Most positions and job openings are never advertised to the public; they are made available only to people within a specific network. In fact, only about 20 percent of jobs are ever advertised; the remaining are filled through referrals.

It is difficult to determine exact statistics about the number of jobs obtained through this "hidden," or unpublicized, job market. Some estimates suggest as many as 80 percent of job openings are unadvertised (see Figure 4.1). But a review of the U.S. Bureau of Labor Statistics Job Openings and Labor Turnover Survey (http://www.bls.gov/jlt/) shows that month after month, there are more hires than posted job openings—meaning that millions of employees are hired without a posted job opening. How are those workers finding those jobs? Through personal contacts and networking.

In my experience, most jobs originate internally, and many are staffed from recommendations provided through employed personnel. The organization saves agency fees and receives a personal profile on the potential hire directly from its employees.

—Irene Teutonico, student, National American University

Percentage of Jobs Attained	Source Used
74.5	Networking
9.9	Advertising
8.9	Employment agencies
6.7	Other sources

Figure 4.1 **Percentage of Jobs Attained in Relation to Source Used**

Source: M. Granovetter, Getting a Job: A Study of Contacts and Careers (Chicago: University of Chicago Press, 1995).

In this chapter, you will learn how to tap into the hidden job market successfully and how to find and use your allies "posse" and mentors. In the process, you will also create your networking business card (NBC). Your NBC will put you a step ahead of the game as you leverage your career network, now and in the future.

Headhunter Jorg Stegemann (2013) lists the following as the six best ways to find your next job:

1. Tap your network.

2. Connect with alumni.

3. Attend events.

4. Use LinkedIn and other social media sites to maximum effect.

5. Check job boards.

6. Contact headhunters.

Where Companies Look for Employees

It is important to understand how companies find employees. Many job seekers look to online job boards when they begin their search. But do employers begin their search for new employees there?

Actually, those online job boards are often the last place they look. Most employers first look within their organization. If no good candidate emerges there, they'll reach out to people within their network. If they have no luck there, then they'll turn to hiring agencies, and public job postings.

One reason they turn to these places last is the cost of posting jobs. Even more than wanting to avoid the expense, though, employers want to avoid the unknown. Hiring from within their company or professional network helps them identify candidates who are known commodities, with trusted references who can speak on their behalf.

This is not to suggest there is no value in looking at online job boards. If a company posts a job there, it is usually looking to fill a position and probably hasn't found an inside candidate who is a good fit. Just understand that what you see on those job boards does not represent the entire universe of available jobs—far from it.

More important, understanding how and where companies look for employees should help encourage you to develop your professional network, so you can tap into this hidden job market.

careercoach4.1

Water Rises to Its Own Level

Water rises to its own level is a principle that works for water as much as it works for you. We will expand on what we learned about this principle in earlier chapters to maximize using it in networking. First, if you do not like the people you are attracting, you need to change your "internal water level." Essentially, you attract what is in you. John C. Maxwell, the author of *The 21 Irrefutable Laws of Leadership,* said it best: "If you think the people you attract could be better, then it's time for you to improve yourself. Who you are is who you attract." If you find that you are always attracting employers who do not see your true abilities, or people who do not fully appreciate you, then you need to make some changes from the inside out.

Next, it is important to realize that you possess properties that are somewhat magnetic (Gage, 2006; Matthews, 1990; McColl, 2007; Proctor, 1997; Rann & Arrott, 2005). You align with people and things subconsciously. The people you hang around influence you. Some people are very negative and this can rub off on you if you are not diligent about repelling that energy.

The ideas in Career Coach 4.1 might sound a bit far-fetched, but many experts in coaching and science support the basic concept (Braden, 2009; Canfield, 2009; Gage, 2006; Demartini, 2005; Hill, 1997; Holmes, 2009; Gregory, 2004; Matthews, 1990; Rann & Arrott, 2005; Rutherford, 1998; Vitale, 2008). The mind is very powerful. If you treat your thoughts as being part of a legitimate energy system, you will see the results or consequences of your thinking. Thoughts of fear and uncertainty do not produce prosperity. Meanwhile, thoughts of gratitude and abundance attract like thoughts, minds, and circumstances.

We sow our thoughts, and reap our actions; we sow our actions, and reap our habits; we sow our habits, and reap our character; we sow our character, and reap our destiny.

—Desiderius Gerhard Erasmus

Your income and prosperity will be the average of your five closest friends.

—Randy Gage, success coach (2009)

Think of a tuning fork. Tuning forks are used to calibrate pianos through sound vibrations. Law enforcement uses them to check the calibration of radar units. In layman's terms, tuning forks are used to make sure the radar units function properly. Tuning forks do not transport matter, they transport energy. Your thoughts have energy as well.

This analogy is actually more real than you might think. Think of your thoughts as radio waves, in much the same way your favorite radio station transmits to its audience. Some people tune in and some do not. By the same token, you will pick up on frequencies of some people and not others. Incidentally, negative people have powerful frequencies, and it is important to give them a lot of space. Do not tune into their thought patterns.

Your thoughts are made up of the frequencies of the five individuals you spend the most time with (Gage, 2006; Vitale, 2006). If you are serious about changing the results that you get in your career search and in life, then you must get serious about who surrounds you.

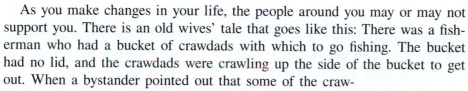

exercise 4.1

Awareness of Your Influencers

Make a list of the five people you spend the most time with:

1. _____
2. _____
3. _____
4. _____
5. _____

Next, decide if you like the results that they are getting in their lives. If the results they are getting are not representative of what you want in your own life, start thinking about how you might need to change the people you spend time with.

As you make changes in your life, the people around you may or may not support you. There is an old wives' tale that goes like this: There was a fisherman who had a bucket of crawdads with which to go fishing. The bucket had no lid, and the crawdads were crawling up the side of the bucket to get out. When a bystander pointed out that some of the crawdads were about to escape, the fisherman responded, "No need to worry. When one of them is about to get out, the others pull it back down."

The point of this adage is that it is very important that you surround yourself with those who will not try to sabotage your efforts. At the very least, become conscious of how others might be holding you back so you can do the internal work to overcome the blocks. It is an inside job. Blaming others for glass ceilings or other career obstacles makes you a victim of circumstances. In essence, blaming others allows you to give up accountability. When you find this happening, return to the fundamentals of career management found in earlier chapters. This way, you can succeed regardless of what others may have in mind for you.

As the crawdad tale exemplifies, some events and people in your life may not always support your goals. How can you overcome these obstacles, and ensure you escape "the bucket"?

careercoach4.2

Find Your Posse

If you think about people who have "made it" in your opinion, you will notice that they had a support network. Even if they did not have the ideal family to support them, they found people to aid them on their quest to fulfill their goals. In the same way, identify your coaches, family, teachers, sponsors, and friends who are available to give you energy and support in your job search. In essence, you want to find your posse.

Your posse is made up of the people you can use in many different ways in your career life. They can pick you up when you don't land the job interview. They can proof your resume, cover letter, and networking business cards. They can send you positive energy whenever you need it. They can be the starting point for tapping into the hidden job market. They will also be the ones to help you identify skills and gifts that you possess that you do not see within yourself.

You will find that some of your supporters won't be able to help you as much as you were hoping. Do not despair, as you will soon be attracting new members to your cheering team. Remember, as we change our thought waves, we will attract some people and repel others. Be aware of these changes and be open to receiving a new audience. Soon, you will appreciate the fact that an aligned group will always achieve more than the individual. Harness the synergy.

Now that you know that most jobs are not found through online job boards, your goal is to tap into the hidden job market. With the Internet, all sorts of new and exciting ways to network are available to you.

e x e r c i s e 4.2

Who Is in Your Posse?

Think of former teachers, coaches, bosses, co-workers, family, and friends. Do not feel obligated to put people on your list if you do not feel they support you unconditionally. Often our supporters are simply people who make us smile. Sometimes they are those individuals who believe in us and do not attempt to hold us back. They may be the ones who encourage your dreams. Supporters, like negative influencers, are sometimes not easily identified. You need to identify them!

For this exercise, list the names of your supporters in the following chart. See how many names you can list.

Names of Supporters	Names of Supporters
1.	11.
2.	12.
3.	13.
4.	14.
5.	15.
6.	16.
7.	17.
8.	18.
9.	19.
10.	20.

Mentors

In *My American Journey,* Colin Powell recounts how he used role models and former co-workers as resources within his personal career management strategy. Having good mentors is as important in life as it is in defining our own career management strategies. A **mentor** is an experienced person who helps and guides another. Finding and using your mentor is one of the best forms of leverage you will have in networking. Find a mentor who has the character you desire. Find a mentor who is willing to share intimate details (Canfield, 2004; Gage, 2006; Proctor, 1997). John Maxwell describes his *Law of Connection* by saying "People don't care how much you know until they know how much you care."

> **Mentor** An experienced person who helps and guides another.

Find a mentor who will push you to share your details. Your mentor should know the ropes. They should also believe in you and your dreams. If you choose wisely, your mentor should have done the "impossible." They should be able to affirm with you that you can succeed at anything. John Morley stated, "No man can climb out beyond the limitations of his own character." Mentors are essential in reaching your career goals and dreams, but choose wisely. Make sure they have a personal character that you would be proud to have as your own.

> *All successful people we have ever encountered have had a great and inspiring mentor with whom they were attuned.*
> —Mark Victor Hanson and Robert Allen, authors of *The One Minute Millionaire*

> *The quality of the help you receive along the way can make all the difference.*
> —Lou Tice

exercise 4.3

Identify a Mentor

Write down the names of people who you trust and who you cannot manipulate. You are looking for someone who will remind you of your goals and commitments to your job search. This person's role is to help hold you accountable. It is highly likely that these names appear on some of your other networking lists.

1. Make a list of five possible people who might fit the above description:

a. _____

b. _____

c. _____

d. _____

e. _____

2. Write down the things you are doing in your job search, including making your resumes, cover letters, searching for jobs, expanding your network, scheduling informational interviews with people at the places you want to work, sending follow-up correspondence, and so on.

3. Choose someone from your list whose help you would like in your job search.

4. Call this person within the next few days and ask her or him if she or he would help keep you accountable in your job search. Be very clear that you will need to let her or him know what you are doing on a weekly basis, and ask that she or he help you keep your commitment to your progress.

5. Decide what action you are willing to take in your job search this week and give a deadline to yourself and the other person. If you want to raise the bar for yourself, make your action a stretch goal.

6. Determine a time when you will check in with your mentor each week. If your mentor does not have time for a call each week, you could send your mentor an e-mail with your weekly update. Using e-mail for these check-ins also lets you easily document your progress.

If you do not keep the commitments you make, that is OK, just get back on track and move forward. Use your self-talk, such as "Next time I will do what I set out to do."

Keep Your Commitments

Although this may seem simple, you will find that making and keeping commitments in your job search will actually help propel you to your career faster and with less work. Like a workout buddy or personal trainer, a mentor can help push you to meet your goals. Your mentor can also proofread your letters and resume, brainstorm new ideas with you, and lift your spirit when you are not feeling your best or seeing results.

The Power of the Invisible Network

As noted earlier, the hidden job market—or hidden network—can be found through networking with real people. You are now going to learn another tool called the invisible network. The invisible network is an imaginary network that can be as powerful as your hidden network. Although an imaginary network might seem impractical, it is an idea worth testing for at least 30 days. The invisible network allows you to gain confidence by thinking of being supported by your personal heroes.

Most success gurus suggest using an imaginary network for business results when a real network is lacking. Mark Victor Hanson (author of the *Chicken Soup* books) and Robert G. Allen co-authored a book called *The One Minute Millionaire* (2002). In the book, they stress the importance of using what they call the Infinite network. This is the same as the invisible network: a realm where there is coincidence, serendipity, chance, and twists of fate that link us all (2009). They explain that the invisible network or imaginary network can be as powerful as a real network. Other success leaders suggest that this imaginary network works through coincidences, or what Henriette Anne Klauser refers to as "Go-Incidences," in her book, *Write It Down, Make It Happen* (2001).

Tapping into the imaginary, invisible network will put you a step ahead of the rest as you take charge of your career. As mentioned earlier, your mind is a magnet of sorts. You attract what you think about the most and with the most emotion. If you are worried all the time, then in effect you are attracting that which worries you most. In his book, *The Magic of Believing* (1991), Claude Bristol wrote, "What may appear as coincidences are not coincidences at all but simply the working out of the patterns which you started with your own weaving." Success guru Robert Scheinfeld wrote an entire book on the power of the invisible network, *The 11th Element* (2003). Scheinfeld outlines how to tap into the power of the invisible network and how to use your "Inner CEO" to find the people, ideas, resources, techniques, and strategies to reach your goals.

Another success author and career counselor, Barbara Sher, explains that your imaginary, invisible network is just as powerful and necessary as your real network. Whether the power comes from your higher power or imagination is not the point. The point is that you harness the energy of those who unconditionally and unmistakably support you when you need it. Most people fail in their dreams not because they are weak or unmotivated, but because they do not have adequate structure and support. Unless you are among the lucky few to be born into a family who propels you to succeed, you need to create this structure and support for yourself (Sher, 1997; Sher & Gottlieb, 2003).

As we discussed in both Career Coach 4.2 and Exercise 4.2, you need to have a support network. Your team of supporters will not always be available at the moment you need them, but your invisible network will still be there. The invisible network is a part of your posse. If you can suspend your judgment, you can experiment with your invisible network and see what kind of results you get.

So how do you form an imaginary, invisible network? Simply choose a group of allies that makes you feel stronger when you imagine they are there to support you. You can change this as you go. For example, you might want Albert Einstein or even an animal to be on your team. I have a mongoose in my invisible network. Do you know the story of *Rikki-Tikki-Tavi,* by Rudyard Kipling? In this story, a mongoose takes on king cobra snakes to save a child and his family. When I am up against similar odds, I like believing that such a force is on my side. Call upon your invisible network during your job or career search when you need support, or you feel weak, alone, or afraid.

e x e r c i s e 4.4
Your Invisible Network

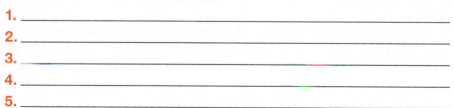

Create a list of allies that you would like to be on your side. Since they are imaginary, you can add names of authors, saints, characters, animals, or any other type of helper for your list. Some examples include: Rocky (Sylvester Stallone), Helen Keller, LeBron James, Lance Armstrong, Maya Angelou, or even a superhero. Add the type of support you receive from each chosen ally. These should be people or characters that symbolize success, comfort, and positive energy to you. Have fun with this!

1. _____
2. _____
3. _____
4. _____
5. _____

☑ SELF-CHECK

1. Explain the hidden job market and how that relates to where companies most often look for employees.

2. Have you ever used your hidden job market, networking, or other unique ways to land a job or internship? Explain.

3. What is a mentor, and how can having a mentor assist you in your job search?

» LO 4-2 Networking Opportunities

Awareness alone is said to be 50 to 90 percent of the solution to a problem. Without awareness, you are unable to see the people or opportunities that are available in your life. The goal is to wake up to the network that is all around you in your everyday life. The following activities will help you develop your networking awareness.

Without awareness, you are unable to see the people or opportunities that are available in your life.

As you begin to network, start examining your contacts in new ways. The chart in Exercise 4.5 will help you identify individuals in your immediate network. You will also begin to look for the "hinges" in your life—those individuals who are connected to the greatest number of opportunities. For example, if you knew Oprah or her personal secretary, you would be fortunate enough to have a very strong connector. Have you seen the film, *Six Degrees of Separation?* The movie is based on a universal principle that we are all connected in social networks by only six degrees of separation. The key is to identify, and then expand, your network. The person with the greatest network has access to the greatest amount of leverage. You are the center of your network.

exercise 4.5

Your Networking Wheel

Complete the wheel in Figure 4.2 by using the list to see how the power of networking works. If you need more space, redraw the wheel on a blank sheet of paper. First, draw as many spokes in the wheel as you need in order to make wedges that represent different areas in your life such as: school, work, church, civic groups, family, friends, services you use, and so on.

Next, list the people you know from each category or "wedge." You most likely have a much bigger network than you realize. The following categories are listed to give you an idea of the number of potential categories you can use. If you end up with a large number of categories and people, don't worry; in the end we will narrow your list of connectors.

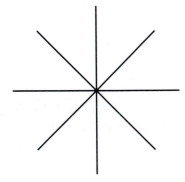

Figure 4.2 Networking Wheel

- Family, friends, and neighbors
- Acquaintances
- People you have worked with, both past and present
- People whose services you use: hair stylists, coffee shop workers, automotive workers, insurance agents, stockbrokers, travel agents, and people whom you see often at the places where you shop

- Church, synagogue, temple, mosque, or other place of worship
- Parents of your children's friends
- Trade groups: meetings you attend, conventions, or directories
- If you are military: your connections
- Professional organizations on campus

- Alumni organizations you belong to
- Social clubs
- Health clubs
- PTA members
- Your classmates: past or present
- Teachers: your teachers, professors, your children's teachers
- Anybody to whom you wrote a check in the last year
- Lawyer, accountant, real estate agent
- Doctor, dentist, optician, and other health care providers
- Dry cleaner
- Politicians
- Community and civic workers
- Places you volunteer
- Your parents' friends

You do not know who will assist you at this point, so do not rule anyone out. Add the names of possible connectors that follow:

Family and Friends	Social Contacts/ Neighbors	Professional Contacts	Education Contacts	Service Providers	Others

Next, choose a contact and obtain two names and numbers from them for your job search. Write the first contact's name on the far left line in Figure 4.3. Then write the names of the two additional contacts on the second two lines. The figure exemplifies how your network can grow quickly. Remember, always ask those in your network for possible contact names! You are sure to obtain several reliable networking contacts from this exercise.

Think for a moment of the top people you would like to have in your network. Once you get an idea of the top three or four, brainstorm how you might enlist their help.

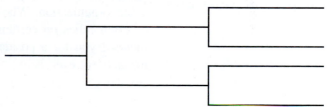

Figure 4.3 **Growth of Networking Contacts**

Your job is to get the word out about your job search. Some students have even made a list of 100 people they want to network with, work for, surpass, or simply meet for the first time. Remember that thoughts are energy. The positive energy you are putting forth as you make a list like this begins to create the circumstances that will produce opportunities for networking, and ultimately employment. This does not mean that if you write down a person's name, you are guaranteed to meet them, but you will

If less than 100 people know you are looking for a job, you are not in the ballpark.
—Frank Cawley, recruiter

Why is it important to network with people who hold both position power and personal power?

begin to work toward the overall goal. The people on your list will begin to show up in your thoughts, conversations, and experiences. As noted in a later section, these coincidences can be seen as evidence that your efforts are working. Your team of supporters knows people. Use them.

Leverage Your Career through Networking

Remember the concept from Chapter 3 that money loves speed? There is also the universal principle *leverage equals speed*. The more leverage you have, the faster you can achieve your goals. In a nutshell, **leverage** is the power to *do more with less*. In networking, it is always "who you know." Like it or not, this world works through associations. We have all heard stories—or know of first-hand situations—where the person with the least experience goes straight to the top, regardless of credentials.

Favoritism prevails in environments that allow managers to tap into that energy. Who you know matters. While it might not seem fair, the practice of hiring and promoting friends, acquaintances, and relatives can work for you in your job search. Some people want to succeed on merit alone, not through connections. While it is important to be qualified, it is often the person who has the qualifications *and* the connections who gets the job or promotion.

Find the power. Within any organization, there are many forms of leadership and many forms of power. Leaders are not always in positions of power and managers are not always leaders, nor are they always in power. Some positions exert power regardless of the person in the position. Similarly, you will find people without any position (like a business owner's spouse, son, or daughter) who hold immense power. It is important to know about each type, and how to network with each type. This is true in the searching process and even after you land the job.

Position power is the power that a title brings to an individual. A president of a company yields power due to this title. Personal power is the power an individual holds regardless of the title. Find out who moves and shakes within an organization. Who holds both types of power? For example, a president often relies on certain people as advisors. If one of these advisors recommended you for a position, that could make the difference between landing a job and not even being "in the ballpark." Find these people.

Leverage Your Efforts

Learning how to make and nurture contacts is a skill that can be learned. Leverage allows you to do a lot with a little. There are many ways to leverage in business. In job hunting and promoting your career, leveraging time, people, and the invisible network all pay off. Leverage equals speed. Some examples of leverage include investing, where your money begins to work for you. Another example is royalties. This is where your screenplay, book, or idea is bought, produced, and sold to the masses, creating income and subsequently leverage. In networking, the efforts of connecting pay off by securing and/or advancing your career. It's always who you know.

You can also move your offline contacts online, to leverage your social and professional network. There are many ways to do this. One is by setting up a profile on an online networking site, such as LinkedIn. You can also join professional groups on social networks, such as Facebook and Twitter.

Leverage The power to do more with less.

Position power The power that a title brings to an individual.

Use Professional Organizations for Leverage

Professional organizations are one of the best ways to network in your field. If you're not sure how to find the professional organizations in your field, ask your advisor or one of your professors, or simply search online for the name of your field and "professional organization." Most professional organizations have student memberships at a discounted rate, and many have special programs and events for students. Once you find a professional organization that's a good fit for your career goals, join and become active! Volunteer for committees and get involved. If there is a student version of the professional organization at your school, join that as well—it's another opportunity to network. Although it may seem like you do not have time to do these types of activities, the time spent will leverage your networking for your career. In the long run, your time will be well spent. Not only will you grow professionally and provide service to your field, you will also gain long-lasting networking connections. Adding service to your field is great for your resume as well.

Cyber Trip 4.2

Mine the Internet for Professional Networks   You have access to enormous networking opportunities via the Internet. Work all of the networking angles, but pay special attention to leveraging your time and energy. Using the professional networks, along with targeting the companies you want to work for, will allow you to get the most out of your networking efforts.

Questions for you:

1. What are some professional organizations related to the type of work you seek?

2. What activities and organizations are you (or have you been) involved in?

3. What companies hire positions that you are looking for?

Let's look at the first question. If you are looking for a job in human resources, you could immediately go to the website of the national organization that regulates the human resources industry. If you don't know the address, search for "human resources code of ethics" online. One of the first results returned from that search should be www.shrm.org. The SHRM (Society for Human Resource Management) has a wealth of networking information at its site, including a link to the names of individuals within various communities who belong to SHRM, and even a job board for you to post your resume for human resource positions.

Another example is the Association of Information Technology Professionals, found at http://www.aitp.org. This organization helps IT professionals stay current with trends and offers networking opportunities. There are ways for you to network yourself, find jobs, and find the key people who are the "connectors" in whatever field interests *you*.

Here are a few more examples of professional organizations to explore:

American Dental Assistants Association (http://www.dentalassistant.org).

National Association for the Education of Young Children (http://www.naeyc.org).

National Criminal Justice Association (http://www.ncja.org).

The Professional Association of Healthcare Coding Specialists (http://www.pahcs.org).

The second question posed above is another way for you to mine connections via the Internet. For example, if you are a member of the Honor Society of Phi Kappa Phi, you could go to the website for the group by searching "Phi Kappa Phi" using your preferred online search engine. There, you will find a wealth of networking information, names of members, and a job board for Phi Kappa Phi members.

exercise 4.6

Your Internet Connections

Under each of the questions that follow, list several groups or keywords you could search on the Internet to expand your network.

1. **What are some professional organizations related to the type of work you seek?**

   You might search online or at the library for trade journals in your field. A trade journal is a publication targeted at a specific industry. This is one more way to network, as the journals will be filled with valuable networking information.

   _____

   _____

2. **What activities and organizations are you (or have you been) involved in?**

   _____

   _____

3. **What companies or industries hire positions that you are looking for?**

   There are some great websites you can use to begin your company search. For example: www.rileyguide.com and http://online.onetcenter.org are helpful resources.

   _____

   _____

As you find websites that look to be valuable resources in building your network or searching for a job, keep track of them. You could bookmark each of them and create a "Job Search" or "Networking" bookmark folder to keep them all in one place in your browser, you could add all the links to a note on your phone, or you could create a document that you keep on your computer desktop where you can paste new links as you find them. Whatever your preference, make sure you know where to find—and to put—these valuable links, so you don't have to waste time finding them again.

Professional Recruiters

Another way to network is to use a **professional recruiter,** or headhunter, in your job search. These are professional agencies and individuals who work on your behalf to help you land a job. It is their job to find you employment and provide leads that you would not otherwise have access to. While many recruiters charge their clients a fee, the most reputable employment agencies charge the companies the placement fee. Recruiters are just one more tool for you to utilize in your search. To find a professional recruiter in your area, search online for "professional recruiter" or "headhunter" plus your city or region.

Professional recruiter Professional agency or individual, also known as a headhunter, who works on your behalf to help you land a job.

Reaching your career goals might not happen easily. Once you set a goal, the universe will provide challenges for you to overcome. It is as if the universe is saying "Are you sure you really want this?" Many people view obstacles or rejections in the interview process as signs that they are not going to get what they want. Instead, you should view blocks or rejection as temporary setbacks and one more step toward achieving your ideal job. Remember how Edison tried thousands of times to create the lightbulb? According to Edison, none of those attempts were failures; they were just one more way *not* to make a lightbulb. This is the attitude you need for your job search. We will discuss this further in chapters to come.

careercoach4.3

The 100th Monkey

You need the momentum and the energy that comes from synergy. Remember when you wrote down your goals? You are telling your brain *I am ready for this!* regardless of what "this" is. Now you need to circulate the energy. Ken Keyes performed an experiment in the late 1950s in which monkeys were taught to wash the sand off of sweet potatoes on the Pacific island of Koshima. In brief, the scientists found that monkeys liked the sweet potatoes given to them, but they did not like sand on them. One monkey solved the problem by washing the sand off of the sweet potatoes. She then taught other monkeys to wash the sand off of the potatoes, until many monkeys were doing the same.

The result was that a critical mass (thus the 100th monkey), or virtual awareness, had been achieved. Not only did all of the monkeys on Koshima begin to wash the sweet potatoes without being taught individually, but entire colonies of monkeys on *other* islands began doing the same! The theory behind this experiment—and many more of its kind—is that when a critical number or mass achieves awareness, this awareness is somehow a part of a universal mind or knowledge.

Of course, there have been those who have questioned the Keyes experiment. Keyes presented his work as a phenomenon, but the concepts behind his work are the pieces that you can be mindful of as you keep working your contacts and network. Eventually, you will reach whatever critical mass is needed for the word to get out about your job search, and it will ideally help you land your best job.

4. How can you utilize professional networks? Provide an example of one of the professional networks in your field.

5. What is a recruiter, or headhunter, and why might someone use this service?

6. Why is it helpful to write down your contacts?

» LO 4-3 Social Media in Your Job Search

If you approach a cold contact in the correct way, your professionalism and effort will likely result in a valuable addition to your network.

Much as it has transformed so many things in our world, the Internet has completely changed the job search process. Even before the emergence of **social media,** things such as online job boards, the ability of companies to post job listings on their own websites, and classified ad sites like Craigslist had dramatically changed the way people looked for jobs. Social media has taken this shift further, changing professional networking as well as the job search process.

If you have ever used Facebook (and as of July 2014, 1.4 billion people had), you are familiar with social media. But while many people join Facebook just to share pictures and connect with friends, social media has grown up as it has evolved. Many people have referred to LinkedIn as "Facebook for work," and it has become a hub for professional networking.

With more than 300 million registered users in over 200 countries and territories, LinkedIn has become the world's largest online professional network. And LinkedIn reports that more than 39 million students and recent college graduates are members.

LinkedIn allows you to create a profile that works like an online resume, where you can list your education, experience, and skills. By connecting with friends, fellow students, and current and former co-workers on LinkedIn, you can easily grow your professional network. Reviewing profiles of your connections, you can learn about different types of careers, the skills and experience needed for different positions, and the career paths that led people to their current jobs.

You've got to ask. Asking is, in my opinion, the world's most powerful and neglected secret to success and happiness.

—Percy Ross

You can also write recommendations for others, and others can write recommendations for you. Recommendations you write, and those others write for you, will appear on your profile, making it more in-depth than a standard resume. You can also endorse your LinkedIn connections for skills and expertise, and your connections can do the same for you. If you've had a positive experience with a supervisor, co-worker, professor, or advisor, consider asking them to write a recommendation for your LinkedIn profile—and offering to return the favor!

Social media Digital technology, websites, and other online means of communication that are used by large groups of people to share information and to develop social and professional contacts.

Like many job sites, LinkedIn also offers job postings. As a member of the network, you have the ability to see which of your connections works for the company posting the job, or if you don't have any connections there, to see how you might be connected to someone who does work there. If you find that you have a connection at a company that has posted a job that interests you, you can reach out to that person to get some insight into the nature of the position, what the company is looking for in a candidate, the culture of the company, and more. If you learn that you don't have a direct connection in the company, but you are connected to someone who does have a direct connection, you can ask your contact to make an introduction.

Recruiters also use LinkedIn. In addition to posting jobs there, when they receive an application, they will often look to LinkedIn, not only to review your job experience, but also to see how connected you are to others in the industry and to read recommendations about you and that you have written. The more you have developed your professional network on LinkedIn, the more valuable LinkedIn will be for you in your job search, and the better your experience will be using the site.

Your Social Media Presence

In today's professional world, LinkedIn is an important social network. But it's not the only one to pay attention to.

Many people use multiple social networks today: LinkedIn, Facebook, Twitter, Instagram, Tumblr, and more. These are all great ways to share your thoughts and connect with friends, family, and like-minded individuals. However, many people share private information on these networks, which are mostly public—and sometimes job seekers pay a price for their sharing.

In addition to reviewing your resume, recruiters and hiring managers today will research your online presence. They will certainly check LinkedIn, because that's where you put on your best professional face. But they will also look to see if you have profiles on other social media sites, and if so, what you have posted there. It may not seem fair, but if a recruiter or hiring manager finds something you have posted that appears unprofessional or inappropriate, it may cost you a chance at getting hired.

With that in mind, think about your online presence as an extension of your resume. Assume that recruiters, hiring managers, and others in your professional network can and will find you there, and post accordingly. This doesn't only mean you should avoid posting questionable photographs or comments to stay safe. It also means that you can enhance your standing online by posting things that show that you are up-to-date in your field. You could post interesting articles you have read, or if you have opinions about what's happening in your field, you could share them in short form on a site such as Twitter or in longer form in a blog.

Many people today establish themselves as strong job candidates because of the reputation and network they have built for themselves on social media, and many others have found career opportunities because of connections they have made through social media.

The widespread use of social media does come with challenges, but if you think about how it can help you in your career, it is also a source of great opportunity.

Case Study: Utilizing Social Media

Nathan felt well equipped to land his dream job as he prepared to graduate with his degree in information technology, but he did not think about how social networking might play into the equation. Nathan did not want to relocate his family from his home town in the Midwest, so he spent a great deal of time scouring online job boards for positions in his area. While Nathan had a Facebook account, he did not have an account on LinkedIn or any other social media site. He also felt Facebook was not really for him and spent very little time using it. One day, his wife, Jolene, took it upon herself to update her status announcing and congratulating her husband's accomplishment and what he hoped to do.

Here is what Jolene posted:

Congrats to my hubby, Nathan, for graduating with his IT degree!!!! Now he needs a great paying job lol. FB me if you know of anyone hiring in the area-we don't want to move.

While several people "liked" her post, no one contacted Nathan regarding a position.

Case Study Assignment

Answer the following questions:

1. Do you feel Jolene's post was appropriate? Why or why not?
2. What could Jolene have said that would be more likely to generate a response of interest?
3. What other sites besides Facebook might be better for Nathan to use in finding positions?
4. Have you ever used social media sites to locate a position or to help someone find a job? If so, explain.
5. With employers able to view potential candidate's sites, what caution would you use? Why?
6. Here is a quote from one hiring manager:

   "If your Facebook posts are public, it makes me NOT want to hire you."

   What are your thoughts on her opinion?

» LO 4-4 Warm and Cold Contacts

The key to success in the hidden job market—to finding jobs and advancing in your career—is networking. Of course, to succeed at networking, you need contacts with whom to network. There are two types of contacts: warm and cold. A **warm contact** is someone you know and are comfortable contacting. This person is usually a friend, a former co-worker, an acquaintance, or maybe even a relative.

A **cold contact** is someone you don't know personally, but who you have identified as someone you would like to connect with regardless.

There are successful ways to approach each type of contact while you are searching for a job. Of course, warm contacts are the easiest to approach. Because you already have a relationship with them, they are likely to take your call or reply to your e-mail.

Warm contact Someone you are comfortable contacting.

Cold contact A person with whom you have no connection, but you are going to call or connect with regardless.

To start your conversation with warm contacts, reach out and let them know you're looking for a job and would like to talk with them to get their insight and perspective. It's best if you can set up an in-person meeting or a phone call, to allow for a more in-depth conversation.

Once you set up a conversation, let your warm contacts know the kind of job you are looking for, why you would like that kind of job, and the skills and experience you could bring to such a position. Then, ask them for any advice or suggestions they might have for you. If they already work in the field that interests you, they are likely to have a lot of insight, but even if they work in an unrelated field, they may know people in their professional network who work in careers similar to the one that interests you.

Many times in these conversations, your contacts will think of somebody in their network they think you should talk to about finding a job or about the field generally. If your warm contact suggests a person you should meet, be sure to get that person's contact information: name, employer, e-mail address, and phone number. If your warm contacts do not volunteer any specific names, as you get toward the end of the conversation, ask if they can suggest anybody else you should talk to who might help you in your job search. Usually, they will be able to think of at least one person. If your warm contacts do suggest someone, be sure to ask if it is OK to use their name when contacting the referral.

Any name recommended to you in this way is a cold contact (unless it's someone that you already know). The best way to open the door with cold contacts is by explaining how you got their name and why they were recommended to you.

E-mail is a good place to start when reaching out to cold contacts because e-mail doesn't interrupt someone's day and lets people respond at their convenience. E-mail also lets you use the name of your mutual connection to help open the door. For example, in the subject line of your e-mail, you could write, "Referral from Bob Jones." Cold contacts are more likely to open the e-mail and respond because you have gotten their attention with the name of your mutual friend.

In your e-mail, explain why your friend recommended you contact this person and what you hope to get out of the connection. For example, you might write:

Dear Ms. Smith,

Bob Jones recommended I contact you. Bob and I were speaking recently, and I shared with him my interest in the field of information technology. He mentioned that you were very knowledgeable in the field, and would be a great person to talk with, and that you might have some suggestions to help me in my job search.

I would very much appreciate the opportunity to talk with you about your experiences in the IT field. Would it be possible to schedule a phone call or an in-person meeting? I am happy to find a time that works with your schedule.

Thank you for considering my request. I look forward to the opportunity to speak with you.

Sincerely,
Anna Suarez

Note that this e-mail does not come right out and ask about a job opening. Starting off your e-mail by asking about an opening can come off as desperate and puts the person you're contacting in a bad situation. Most people are willing to meet with you to talk about their company or industry, particularly if you share a mutual connection. But asking someone you don't know yet about a job is usually asking too much—at least right way. Once you have had a productive conversation with the person, you are in a better position to ask about job openings.

When you get the chance to meet or talk with people, approach it as an informational interview and be curious. Ask them about their job and their company. Ask them for their thoughts on the state of the field today and where the field is going. Ask what they really like about their position and what they find challenging or difficult about it. Ask what skills they think are essential to succeed in their field and what advice they would offer to someone looking to break into the field. Ask about their career path and how they got to the position they are in today.

That may sound like a lot of things to ask. But if you are interested in a career in this field, isn't that all information you want to know? If the people talking with you feel that you are truly interested in a career in the field, and not just looking for a job right now, they are much more likely to be generous with their time, expertise, and connections. If you jump right to asking if they know about a job for you, you may leave the meeting and never hear from them again. But if the conversation goes well, and you prove yourself to be a thoughtful, mature candidate, you could possibly find yourself with a new mentor, with someone who wants to introduce you to other people in the field, or even someone willing to recommend you to the hiring manager for an open position.

No matter how the conversation with cold contacts goes, there are a few things to remember to do at the end. First, thank them for their time, ask them if you can follow up with them again if you have more questions, and ask if they can think of anybody else in the field you should talk to. (If they recommend someone, ask for that person's contact information and if it's OK to mention their name when contacting the referral.) Second, if you have met in person, ask for their business card, and give them your networking business card. Finally, send a thank-you note (a written card is best, but e-mail is better than nothing) to the contact, as well as to your warm contact who offered you the referral. Include your NBC in notes that you send. These small gestures help show your gratitude and appreciation, which help to strengthen your professional network.

careercoach4.4

Ask!

Not many people like making cold contacts or calls. In the job search game, those who make connections and use them win. Asking is a skill. It is also a success principle. Ask and you shall receive is even biblical. People do not like making cold contacts for many reasons. Some are afraid of rejection while others are afraid that they will look foolish. Most of the time, people are simply not hungry enough. They want desperately to break out of their familiar ruts, but often not desperately enough. They lack the tools and belief in themselves to break out. Life is a whole lot more fun when you let yourself play the game. By using these tools, you will not only get in the game, but you will also eventually claim your personal career victories. Asking is one of the powerful tools you can use in your career journey to success (Canfield, 2004; Proctor, 1997; Vitale, 2006).

Cold contacts (or cold calls) in the job search is not the same as cold-calling people to sell them something. Your goal in these cold calls is to make a connection, get a lead, and see if you can meet the hiring authority for an informational interview or find out any piece of information that would help you in your job search. While many companies will not allow anyone from the outside to submit a resume, many small to medium-sized firms (remember where the jobs are) will. I know of individuals who dressed like they were going to an interview, walked into the companies they wanted to work for, presented their resume, and not only did they get an interview, but they also landed a job. Presentation and persistence matter. Consider the following student's perseverance and professionalism:

Sometimes I would hand-deliver my resume to different doctors' offices. That is how I found my current job. I wore my scrubs because I was a medical assistant, and delivered my resume to each office. When I arrived at my current workplace to give them my resume, I did not know that I was giving it to the office manager! She said what she liked most about me was that I had a smile on my face when I walked into the office, and that I used correct grammar and spoke well when she asked me questions.

—Marcia Biggers, student, Virginia College Online

Staking a claim on the career you seek requires stepping outside your comfort zone. It might also require wandering in a state of confusion, at least for a short time. Take things one step at a time and use your support system.

Break Out of Your Comfort Zone

To be successful you need to take some risks. In the job search, this means introducing yourself to strangers, such as cold contacts. It means applying for jobs you want and risking rejection. It means putting yourself out there. You will want to stretch out of your comfort zone. Your **comfort zone** consists of the environment, situations, or people that make you feel the most safe and normal. Everyone's comfort zone is different. If you grew up in a privileged family, you will do what you can to make sure you keep the lifestyle you are accustomed to. Likewise, if you grew up with very little, it may take an internal adjustment or growth before you move outside your comfort zone. Otherwise, like the lotto winners who blow their winnings and return to the financial status they had before their winnings, you will not have the personal foundation to stay at that status level for long. Using your self-talk, affirmations, visualization, goal setting, and other tools, you will begin to change your internal comfort zone. Once this happens, you will go to work matching your outside world with your inside beliefs.

> To be successful you need to take some risks.

Comfort zone The environment, situations, or people that make you feel the most safe and normal.

More tips for cold contacts:

- Be sincerely interested in the other person.
- Assume he or she is helpful and friendly.

- Be clear and specific about your intent. Be able to verbalize the type of job you are seeking and the type of help you need (a referral).
- Be grateful for whatever anyone can do. Send a thank-you note to follow up. Gratitude, as you will later learn, is one of the most potent success principles.
- Be truthful.

careercoach4.5

Persistence

If you make new connections that fail to produce interviews, don't sweat it. This is expected. You might be wondering why you need to meet and contact so many people. Why can't you find the perfect job without much effort? After all, you are a great candidate! There are many layers to the answer. For one, you need to remember that you are working with visible marketing schemes and *invisible* energy systems. Second, you need to understand that this is not a linear process. Most of us neither need, nor want, the laws of gravity spelled out in order to appreciate their validity. Integrate these tools into your job search method. "Stir the energy pot." Hammer away at the rock. More than likely, you will never know for sure which blow caused the rock to shatter, but it *will* shatter. Keep at it. *"Not hiring"* can mean *"Not hiring at this moment."* Winners win, not because they hammer longer, but because they hammer smarter. They created their own good luck, and so can you!

exercise 4.7

Identify Your Fears or Limiting Beliefs

Asking and receiving help from others is sometimes scary. To overcome fears, you first must identify them. Identifying your fears is half the battle. The following are some fears and limiting beliefs that you might have about asking for help. Add your own to this list in the space provided.

Examples:

1. It is weak to ask for help.
2. I don't want anyone to know how badly I need a job.
3. People have always let me down. Why would I want to involve anyone else?
4. They are too busy. I do not want to bother them.
5. I should be able to figure this out for myself.

My fears:

1. _____
2. _____
3. _____
4. _____
5. _____

SELF-CHECK

7. What is a comfort zone?

8. Define the term *warm contact*, and describe how to network effectively with one.

9. Define the term *cold contact*, and describe how to network effectively with one.

» **LO4-5** Specific Tools to Enhance Networking Results

Now that you are finding many people to network with, you need networking tools that will give you an edge over the competition. The following tools—networking business card, professional handshake, working a room, informational interviews, and organizing your contacts—are all valuable ways you can step above other job seekers in your chosen field.

Networking Business Card (NBC)

Think about how many times you have gone to an event or convention and met new people, and wished you could have handed them a mini resume of yourself as a way to let them know your skills. Handing out your business card is nice, but if you are looking to land a different job, you need a **networking business card (NBC).** A networking business card is a personal business card that includes your name, contact information, desired field of employment, and a brief description of your skills or qualifications. A business card usually means "I have a job. Give me a call if I can be of service." Your NBC introduces you by saying, "I am capable and professional. You want me on your team." Furthermore, if you are changing fields or not working, your NBC can demonstrate your current ability and desire to be gainfully employed. In order to leverage your networking effort, it will help you immensely to know how to make a NBC.

Beyond your resume and cover letter, the NBC is a tool that you can immediately use to leverage your abilities and help you land your ideal job. When put on the spot, inner insecurity

> **Networking business card (NBC)**
> A personal business card that includes your name, contact information, desired field of employment, and a brief description of your skills or qualifications.

> *I had never heard of networking business cards before this class, but they definitely sound like a useful tool to use when looking for a job and spreading the word about services that you can provide. I think it's neat how something so small has the hidden potential of something huge!*
>
> —Maria Johns, student, Virginia College Online

can show up for those who do not have a business card. A logical step to thwart this feeling is to prepare for the inevitable by creating a business card now. Believe it or not, there comes a time when your purpose in life will be clear. It will be so clear that the world will come to you without the need to market yourself. Until you reach that point, use these tools to your advantage. The winning combination is to use the universal principles and marketing techniques previously discussed.

Imagine having an opportunity to meet one of the people from one of your networking lists. Now imagine meeting that person but not being able to speak. This might be what it feels like when an opportunity arises, but you are not in a position to market yourself. Instead, prepare yourself for opportunity. Many students think they cannot have personal business cards because they do not have professional jobs. That is incorrect thinking. You are not only permitted, but it is essential if you intend to market yourself as a professional. How will you use your NBC? The ways are endless. Here are a few of the ways students use their NBCs:

- Give to a new professional contact.
- Hand out at conferences and job fairs.
- Attach to resumes and cover letters.
- Enclose one with thank-you notes.

Cyber Trip 4.4

NBCs Visit these websites to find further information regarding NBCs: http://www.collegegrad.com/jobsearch/Network-Intelligence-Gathering/The-Networking-Business-Card-Technique/ and http://www.quintcareers.com/networking_business_cards.html.

Networking Business Card Samples

The NBC samples shown in Figures 4.4 through 4.14 may give you some ideas to get started on your own card. Several are from students who took the initiative to create their own marketing tools.

Figure 4.4 **NBC Example 1**

Used with permission of Christian Sean Caspers

Figure 4.5   NBC Example 2

Used with permission of Geneva E. Wolfe

Figure 4.6   NBC Example 3

Used with permission of Matthew Mark Banken

Figure 4.7   NBC Example 4

Used with permission of Jamie Tschida

Sheila Helm

Degree: B.S. Healthcare Management
Phone: 555-555-1234
Email: xrayadama@email.com

Position Desired: Clinic Manager

Skills: Strong communication skills & efficient work ethic in a fast-paced
environment. Excellent computer skills & x-rays skills. Internship completed
at Chiropractic Clinic.

Figure 4.8 NBC Example 5

Used with permission of Sheila Helm

Front of Card:

Back of Card:

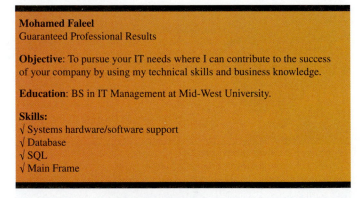

Figure 4.9 NBC Example 6

Used with permission of Mohamed Faleel

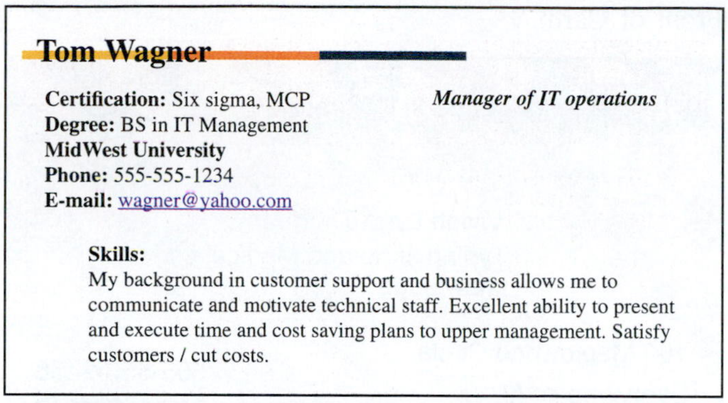

Tom Wagner
Certification: Six sigma, MCP
Degree: BS in IT Management
MidWest University
Phone: 555-555-1234
E-mail: wagner@yahoo.com
Manager of IT operations
Skills:
My background in customer support and business allows me to communicate and motivate technical staff. Excellent ability to present and execute time and cost saving plans to upper management. Satisfy customers / cut costs.

Figure 4.10 NBC Example 7

Used with permission of Tom Wagner

Sheldon Beilke
Professional Security Officer
Currently attending DU for B.A. in
Business Management, maintaining 4.0 GPA
Skills:
• Certified First Responder
• Heart Saver First Aid Certified
• 65 WPM
• Payroll Management
• Training Manager
• Computer Graphics and Data Base Configurations
I strive to excel in everything I do. Dreams are reachable, and goals attainable. With over 4 years of security experience, I am confident that I have secured my future as a successful business associate in fast-paced and ever-changing environments. I will be an upbeat and unbeatable addition to your team, and will help your company reach a whole new level.
E-mail: Sheldon.Beilke@gustr.com
Cell: 612-555-5555

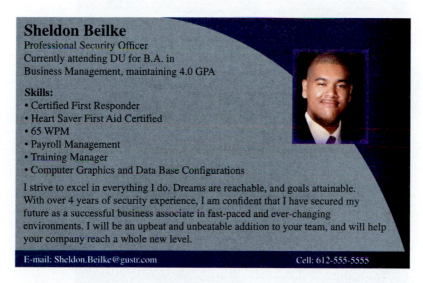

Figure 4.11 NBC Example 8

Used with permission of Sheldon Beilke

Jamie Braunesreither
Degree: Early Childhood Education
Position Desired: Childcare Center Director
Skills: Over five years of childcare experience as a lead teacher, good communication and organization skills.
E-mail: jbraunesreither@dayrep.com
Phone: 605-555-0032

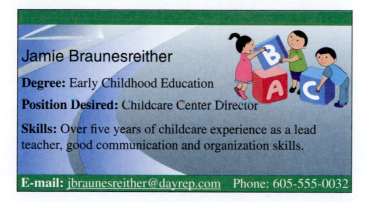

Figure 4.12 NBC Example 9

Used with permission of Jamie Braunesreither

Front of Card:

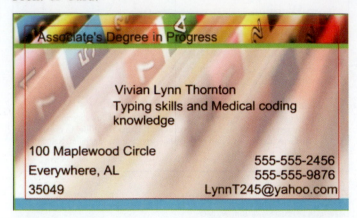

Back of Card:

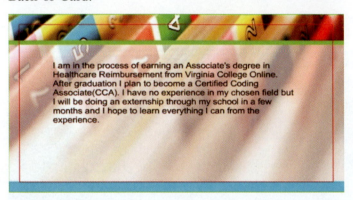

Figure 4.13 NBC Example 10

Used with permission of Vivian Lynn Thornton

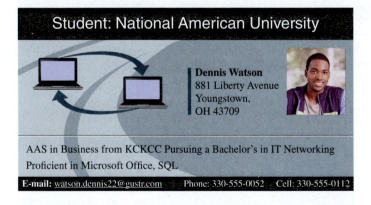

Figure 4.14 NBC Example 11

✓ SELF-CHECK

10. What is the purpose of a networking business card?

11. How might you use an NBC?

12. What type of information should you include on your NBC?

Create Your NBC

Again, your networking business card is your mini resume. It should contain the following information: your skills, contact information, and perhaps an image or icon associated with your career intent. You may find that you continue to use your NBC even after you land a job. The NBC is one of the most powerful, yet underused, tools in leveraging your networking efforts.

To start, see Cyber Trip 4.4 for links to several websites that allow you to experiment with designing your NBC. The suggested sites also provide additional samples for you to view.

Keep in mind there are various approaches to the construction of your NBC outside of the referred links, including Word/clip art, Power Point, and so on. Use the format that works best for you.

It costs nothing to create a design at many of the online business card stores. Explore the different logos. If you are going into an IT field, consider adding a computer icon on your card. These services are very inexpensive, and purchasing the minimum number of cards should last you a sufficient amount of time, depending on how often you hand out your card. It will only cost a few cappuccinos to make and deliver the cards to your home address. As an alternative, you can use heavy paper, also known as card stock, with your own computer software to make your cards. Many students add a photo of themselves to their NBC. Consider adding a picture of yourself as well!

Check to make sure your NBC is professional and easy to read and that it includes the following:

- Your name.
- Your degree (use the words "in progress" if you are still working on your degree).
- Your skills—a few that are essential to your field.
- Professional e-mail address and phone number.
- A visual related to your field.
- Professional and easy to read layout and type.

Lastly, turn in your actual NBC or the information you would include on one, depending on your instructor's requirements.

The Power of a Professional Handshake

Although the handshake seems so simple to do, you would be surprised how many people either forget to shake hands when they network or use a very weak handshake that gives the wrong impression. Women are notorious for giving weak handshakes. Perhaps it is not considered ladylike, or they were never taught to give strong handshakes. The only times a firm handshake is not warranted in networking is if there are cultural or other similar factors in the meeting. For example, some religions do not allow shaking of hands between the sexes.

The rule of thumb is to shake hands in Western cultures, unless you know of specific reasons a handshake would not be valued.

When you shake someone's hand, don't let go until you can determine the color of their eyes.
—Mark Victor Hansen and Robert Allen, authors, *The One Minute Millionaire*

exercise 4.8

Your 30-Second Marketing Commercial

Advertisers understand the importance of capturing the attention of their audience in a mere 30 seconds or less. You can also nail down a short script to market yourself in networking. This way, you will not be at a loss for words when the opportunity to market yourself appears. First impressions matter.

Write down a 30-second commercial that you could use in future networking opportunities. Once you have your commercial written, practice saying the script until you can fluently and convincingly repeat it out loud. Thirty seconds is not much time, so you will only need to write 75 to 100 words. Each word should be meaningful and descriptive. Although it is a script, you want it to sound authentic. You might start by thinking of how you could answer the question "What do you do?"

- I have a bachelor's degree in project management, work in my field for XYZ Corporation, and recently my team was first in the region for . . .
- My background is in _____, and . . .
- I have been working in the _____ field quite successfully for over three years. Now I am looking to move into the _____ _____ field to better utilize my _____ degree and skills. My skills include _____.

How to Work a Room

While it might seem obvious to you, you would be surprised how many people are clueless when it comes to successfully working a room. While working a room, you use your professional handshake, 30-second commercial, and give your NBC to new contacts. Remember to ask for business cards as well. It may be a wise move to send follow-up cards after the event or meeting to the new contacts you meet. This is covered in more detail in future chapters. Keep in mind the success tool: *progress not perfection.* You are seeking progress in networking. If you focus on perfection, it can get in the way. Any success in moving out of your comfort zone is a step in the right direction.

exercise 4.9

Working a Room Successfully

Practice this activity in class for 10 to 15 minutes. Make sure you use name tags, a firm handshake, your NBC, and your 30-second commercial.

After you practice in class, decide on a networking opportunity in the near future, such as a Chamber of Commerce mixer, job fair, or other professional meeting. Any meeting will do, as long as you use it to make new contacts. Again, the goal will be to use your handshake, NBC, and 30-second commercial in one setting while you practice working a room. Set a goal of making three new contacts at this meeting. "Meet and greet" people, leave them with your NBC, and collect business cards and contact names. You want to be authentic, so focus on listening and learning as well.

- Name tags are worn on the right side.
- Print your first and last name, as well as place of employment, if applicable.
- Write your name large enough that it can be easily read.
- Use your effective handshake.
- Use each person's name at least once while you talk to him or her.
- Introduce yourself by saying *"Hi or Hello, my name is _____. It's nice to meet you."* Or *"It's a pleasure to meet you."* As you are doing this, hold your right hand out as a gesture to shake hands.
- Use a shortened version of your marketing commercial for your introduction. Say who you are and what you do in 15 seconds or less.
- Make polite small talk. Stay away from topics such as money, religion, politics, personal problems, or depressing news.
- Listen as much, or more, than you talk. Use active listening skills. You will be surprised how smart others will think you are when you engage in active listening.
- Be present, and stay in the moment (Kane & Kane, 2008; Forleo, 2009).
- Do not stay in one group or location too long. You are there to network with as many people as possible.
- Offer your networking business card to each person you speak with, and ask politely for their card in return.

Informational Interview

One of the best approaches for networking is to set up a meeting to gather information. Your goal is to get an idea of what someone in a specific position does from day-to-day, or to learn more about the company they work for. As noted in Chapter 3, this is also known as an informational interview. Most people enjoy talking about themselves and helping others. Use this to your advantage.

exercise 4.10

The Informational Interview

For this exercise, you will interview a professional who has a job of interest to you. The person you select should have a minimum of three years in his or her field. Use the following techniques and questions during your informational interview:

- How did this individual land his or her job?
- What education does this person have?

- How long has he or she held this job?
- What steps did he or she follow in his or her profession leading up to this position?
- Ask for his or her advice for people like yourself, who are seeking a similar career.
- What advice does he or she have regarding working in this field?
- Collect the contact information of the person you interviewed. One of the best ways is to ask for his or her business card.

Make sure you leave your NBC with this person, and that you send him or her a formal thank-you note after the interview. Then ask yourself the following questions:

- What insights or ideas did you gain from interviewing this person?
- Does his or her career seem like a good fit for you?
- Does this job fit with your career direction, values, and goals?

Cyber Trip 4.5

Informational Tutorial   Visit http://www.quintcareers.com/informational_interviewing.html to find a helpful tutorial that offers tips on the informational interviewing process.

Organizing Your Contacts

In Chapter 3, you learned how to organize contacts at specific companies. Now you will expand this to include general networking contacts. There are a couple of tried-and-true methods to organizing contacts. The first, and perhaps the best, is to save them electronically in a Word document or spreadsheet. Also, a number of software applications and websites, such as Evernote, can help you save and organize your contacts. Organizing your contacts electronically allows you to update the information quickly, easily, and neatly. Keep information such as names, titles, company names, addresses, phone numbers, fax numbers, e-mail addresses, dates of contact, and notes regarding follow-up.

You can also purchase a businesses card organizer at any office supply store. With a business card organizer, you can save and categorize all of the business cards you collect, and write comments about the contact next to or on the business card. Some people use both methods to keep track of their networking contacts. This will serve you even when you land your ideal job. Networking is an ongoing process and will always be an integral part of your career success.

Cyber Trip 4.6

Tracking My Contacts   Visit http://www.jibberjobber.com/networking.php to see an example of one online service available for organizing and tracking your job search contacts. Many services like this one are free.

Making Connections—Richard Builds His Network

The workforce development workshops had proved to be a valuable asset to Richard. He started coming out of his shell since meeting Amanda and had been working with her in pursuing both of their goals. Amanda had recently been hired by the HR department of a health care organization. While she wasn't working exclusively with benefits, there were definitely opportunities for growth. Richard knew that his future was also bright, and he was ready to move forward.

At every workshop, he forced himself to talk to at least two new people, and he met many others who were searching for their dream jobs. He began to spend much of his job search time in networking activities. He also began slowly getting the word out to his friends that he was interested in working in the IT field. While some of his friends gave him a hard time, the majority of them surprised Richard by being supportive of his plan. A couple of his friends even introduced him to people they knew in the IT field.

In addition to telling his friends, he sat down with Laurie to seriously discuss her college experience and to ask her advice about starting school. She encouraged his decision to pursue his dream, and generously provided him with the name and contact information of someone she knew in IT who was willing to do an informational interview with Richard. The informational interview went extremely well, thanks to Richard's preparation, and the interviewer referred him to an acquaintance who was looking for an entry-level computer hardware technician assistant. Richard had been extremely nervous for his first "real" job interview, but found that he was speaking easily and feeling comfortable with the questions that were asked. The informational interview prepared him well! While the interview did not result in a job offer, Richard remained positive and knew that the interview practice would only help him in the long run. He also knew that he might have to go on quite a few interviews before finding the right position.

He followed all of the instructions given in the seminar, and vigorously pursued his connections via phone and e-mail. Not all of his connections had been successful, but his network continued to grow. He created a networking business card through an online program, printed 150 cards, and already needed to reorder! On a few professional websites, he also created profiles and made connections with a wide variety of people, including some international IT professionals. He was continuously learning the industry jargon and was amazed by the number of different career paths he could take.

Richard felt proud of his network—not only how he benefitted from it, but also how he was able to share his own thoughts and ideas, and give support to others. Instead of feeling alone and frustrated as he had once been, he was now feeling proud of his accomplishments and knew that the work he was putting in would give him the results he hoped for. In two months, he would begin going to school part-time. There, he could add even more connections to his network. Who knew how far he could be in two years?

Discussion Questions

1. What were the key elements to the success of Richard's network?
2. Richard had to get out of his comfort zone to attend the seminar. What are some things that you can do to network that might be outside your comfort zone at the moment?
3. What does Richard need to do to continue the health and growth of his network?

[chapter summary]

Networking is the way most great jobs are obtained. The positions that are advertised are the leftovers after all of the networked jobs are filled. In order to be in the right place at the right time—to get the jobs before they are advertised—you need to make connections and network. Professional networking is an art and a skill that can be learned. Making and keeping connections is important not only to landing your dream job, but also in ascending the career ladder.

[skill/term check]

1. Why is networking referred to as the *hidden job market?* **(LO 4-1)**

2. How can a mentor help you in your job search? **(LO 4-1)**

3. How can the tools of synergy and leverage assist you in networking your job search? In your career? **(LO 4-1, LO 4-2)**

4. What are some advantages and disadvantages in using professional recruiters for networking jobs? **(LO 4-2)**

5. How can you use social media in your job search? **(LO 4-3)**

6. What is the best way to approach a cold contact? **(LO 4-4)**

7. What are three ways you could use your networking business card? **(LO 4-5)**

8. What is an informational interview? What are some questions you might ask during one? **(LO 4-5)**

9. Describe a professional handshake. Why is a good handshake important? **(LO 4-5)**

[KEY TERMS]

Cold contact: A person with whom you have no connection but you are going to call or connect with regardless. **(LO 4-4)** [p. 92]

Comfort zone: The environment, situations, or people that make you feel the most safe and normal. **(LO 4-4)** [p. 95]

Hidden job market: A network that consists of people you will associate with in your career search and while climbing the career ladder; also known as a hidden network. **(LO 4-1)** [p. 76]

Leverage: The power to do more with less. **(LO 4-2)** [p. 86]

Mentor: An experienced person who helps and guides another. **(LO 4-1)** [p. 81]

Networking: Using contacts for purposes beyond the reason for the initial contact, especially in business and career searches. **(LO 4-1)** [p. 76]

Networking business card (NBC): A personal business card that includes your name, contact information, desired field of employment, and a brief description of your skills or qualifications. **(LO 4-5)** [p. 97]

Position power: The power that a title brings to an individual. **(LO 4-2)** [p. 86]

Professional recruiter: Professional agency or individual, also known as a headhunter, who works on your behalf to help you land a job. **(LO 4-2)** [p. 88]

Social media: Digital technology, websites, and other online means of communication that are used by large groups of people to share information and to develop social and professional contacts. **(LO 4-3)** [p. 90]

Synergy: The enhanced results when two or more people combine efforts or energy. **(LO 4-1)** [p. 76]

Warm contact: Someone you are comfortable contacting. **(LO 4-4)** [p. 92]

chapter 5

Professional Resumes the Easy Way

Even your marketing pieces carry your energy.

—Dr. Joe Vitale

target competency > *Develop a professional resume for your portfolio.*

learning outcomes

After studying this chapter, you should be able to:

LO 5-1 Understand the importance of a professional resume.

LO 5-2 Differentiate between a chronological resume, functional resume, combination resume, and plain text resume.

LO 5-3 Use keywords and power words to strengthen your resume.

LO 5-4 Understand how to write skills using the Skills Formula™.

LO 5-5 Create a professional resume and measure its success.

Resume Roadblock

"Maria!" exclaimed Marcy from across the parking lot. Maria paused on the way to her car and smiled. Marcy jogged over with their friend Victor.

"Hey, guys!" said Maria. "I haven't seen either of you in a few weeks. How have you been?"

Marcy was grinning. "You're not going to believe it," she said. "I just got called back for a second interview at Lang & Lang!"

" . . . And I have an interview on Friday at the attorney general's office!" Victor chimed in. "We just wanted to see how your job search has been going, too."

Maria was happy for her friends, but hearing their progress made her heart sink a bit. "So far I'm coming up empty," she said. "I haven't gotten a single interview yet! I feel like everyone else is getting interviews. Jessica from class even got a job offer yesterday. I just wonder what I'm doing wrong."

Marcy thought for a moment. "Do you think maybe it's your resume?" she asked. "Victor was initially having problems because of his resume."

"My resume?" replied Maria. "What do you mean?"

"Marcy is right," Victor said. "I wasn't getting any interviews either, but I went to the resume development seminar at the Career Services Center two weeks ago, and one of the advisors spent a lot of time with me. It really helped . . . and now I have my first interview lined up."

Later that evening, Maria sighed as she checked her voice mail and realized she had no new messages from any interested employers. At 38 years old, she had taken a big step when she had decided to return to college to earn her paralegal degree. Now she was beginning to doubt whether her decision had been the right one.

"What if I never get a job as a paralegal?" Maria asked herself. *"How am I ever going to afford to repay my student loans?"*

She wondered what Marcy, Victor, Jessica, and the other students in the program were doing that was landing them interviews. Maria had a solid 3.0 GPA and had done well at her four-week internship at the district attorney's office. She remembered seeing the notice for the resume development seminar, but her son had been ill that day and she hadn't been able to go. She had not really given it a second thought, though. *"A resume is just a list of jobs and schools,"* Maria reflected. *"There's not much more I can do to make my resume better."*

Still, classes were ending soon and Maria was hoping to find a paralegal position as soon as possible. She pulled her resume out of her bag and studied it closely. Maybe her resume really was preventing her from getting interviews after all. *"Hmmm,"* she thought, *"perhaps I should go to Career Services tomorrow, just in case . . . "*

Maria's current resume is shown in Figure 5.1.

Maria Rodriguez

I want to work in a large law office in an entry level paralegal job, which would be exciting. I want to help people.

Work Experience

July/2006 – Dec/2013	Software, Inc. Florida

Senior Receptionist/Switchboard Operator
- I Prepared documents, reports, emails, and general filing
- I Scheaduled corporate condos and conference rooms
- I assisted with travel arrangements
- I greeted clients
- I Assisted HR with applicants and document preparation
- Insure ID tags where worn for security purposes
- I can Type 35 WPM
- Knowledge of MS Office (Word, Power Point, Excel, Outlook), Internet skills

Oct/2000 – July/2006	Vista Resort, Fl

Reservations, Coordinator, Server
- Knowledge of customer service in call center environment
- Reserved hotel rooms throughout the U.S.A.
- Scheduled tee-times for travelers

May/1998 – Aug/2000	**Friendly's Ice Cream, FL**

  - *I worked shifts after school and weekends serving ice cream during the summer*

Education

1996–2000	**City High School, FL**

Diploma
- **Graduated with a 2.7 average, took some honor classes, extra classes were color guard, and after school tutoring.*

2013–2015	**Any College, Florida**

Associate degree-paralegal
  - I have a 3.0 GPA
  - I belong to the paralegal club
  - I did an internship

Interests
  - *I have two children and I volunteer at their school*

Figure 5.1 Maria's Resume

Discussion Questions

1. Do you agree with Maria's view of a resume in that it is simply a list of jobs and schools? Why or why not?
2. What do you notice first about Maria's resume?
3. What are three things Maria could do to improve her resume?

» LO5-1 The Importance of a Professional Resume

As Dr. Vitale said in the chapter opening quote, *your marketing pieces contain your energy.* Your job is to put the energy into your resume and other job marketing tools to reflect your best. You might be the best person for the job, but if your resume and other marketing tools do not represent that, you risk coming across like a Ferrari with flat tires. How can you send clear messages to employers through your marketing tools? How can you make sure your marketing tools are aligned with your career mission, your goals, skills, and who you really are? This chapter will help you do this.

Many students are daunted by the thought of making or even revising their resume. Fear not, this chapter will take the guesswork out of creating a winning resume. Considering the hundreds of ways to create a winning resume, your job is to find a style that appeals to you and merely learn how to use some key elements to make your skills shine.

I have fast eyes.
—Robert Overby,
designer/painter

Did you know most employers will only look at your resume for 30 seconds or less? That is why it is essential to follow some basic *dos* and *don'ts.*

Resume Don'ts

- Don't use sentences.
- Don't hand-write your resume—ever!
- Don't add unnecessary words.
- Don't put your high school information on your resume if you have college experience.
- Don't go back more than 10 years for your job information unless that is your only source for job information.
- Don't cram as much information as you can into one page.
- Don't use font size under 10 or larger than 13.
- Don't use cute or fancy fonts or change fonts in the resume—be consistent (you can use a different font and font size for your name and heading).
- Don't use cute or unusual bullets such as smiley faces ☺
- Don't overuse *italic* or **bold** functions.
- Don't lie! This is cause for termination.
- Don't exaggerate or embellish. This could also be cause for termination—don't risk it.
- Don't list hobbies (unless you are certain they are relevant to the job you are applying for).
- Don't provide personal information including marital status, age, race, religion, health, height, weight, family, and so on.
- Don't provide Social Security number *except* for certain professions that expect or ask for this information needed for background searches such as in law enforcement.
- Don't go over two pages unless you are an executive or you know your profession calls for this. In that case, consider making a curriculum vita (CV). Curriculum vitae are used primarily in academic fields to outline credentials. Each field has its own standard.

- Don't add information about why you are applying for the job.
- Don't right justify (align margins)—only left justify. Block print looks strange in a resume.
- Don't break up words in a resume with a hyphen.
- Don't use first person: no *I, me, my,* and so on.
- Don't leave out details such as company names, locations, or dates of employment.
- Don't assume it is an error-free resume without having someone qualified proof it for you.
- Don't go overboard on extracurricular activities—they are not jobs.
- Don't use your work e-mail address or send it electronically (or apply for jobs) from your work e-mail address.
- Don't use a goofy personal e-mail address such as: funnygirl@spotmail.com, bubba123@bestmail.com, mythreesons@email.com, gonefishing@email.com, or inlove@email.com, for example.
- Don't list using e-mail or the Internet as a skill.
- Don't list a bunch of classes.
- Don't list short-term irrelevant jobs such as a fast-food place you worked at in the summer.
- Don't list references unless asked. Have them ready to send.
- Don't hold back! Humility does not pay off in the job search.
- Don't list salary information, names of supervisors, or reasons for leaving your jobs.

The *Don't* list might seem long, but they are all important points to remember. Now let's focus on what to do right.

- Do use power words/verbs to highlight your skills.
- Do use keywords to encode your resume.
- Do quantify your skills. In other words, use numbers. For example: Billed over $150K in direct hire revenue in the first three months.
- Do use bullets. Your power word goes right after the bullet, followed by your quantified skill.
- Do list military experience. Military candidates are seen as reliable, responsible, and having excellent work ethics—all are desirable traits. You may be asked to provide a DD-214 if you are seeking veteran's preference in the application.
- Do add collegiate sports. This shows drive, ability to work in teams, and competitiveness.
- Do list jobs in order of importance to the reader. Usually reverse chronological order (most recent to last).
- Do emphasize transferable skills.
- Do keep your resume looking sharp and focused.

- Do give accurate personal contact information so the employer can reach you.
- Do use quality paper.
- Do tailor your resume to the job opportunity.
- Do include special recognitions and awards that are professional.
- Do include honor societies within your major and your GPA if it is 3.0 or higher.
- Do include leadership roles and volunteer work.
- Do have a traditional resume even if you choose to have an electronic resume.
- Do use correct tenses. If you are currently doing the activity listed, use present tense. If it was in the past, use past tense.
- Do use *italic* and **bold** font functions sparingly to highlight information.
- Do make all bullets, italics, and bold items uniform and consistent. This also goes for periods and capital letters.

careercoach5.1

Target the Position

Entities should not be multiplied unnecessarily.

—William of Occam (1284–1347), English philosopher

This maxim by William Occam, also known as *Occam's Razor,* essentially means to *keep it simple.* Focus on the position you are seeking and target your resume to this position. Do not complicate your resume. Stick to the basics and what works. Use more than one resume, so each is targeted to the company and the position.

While your resume is selling you, it is really about the employer's needs. You are targeting your resume to a specific company, position, and even a specific hiring person or committee. The more you know about the position, company, and person who will make the decision, the better. What skills and qualities are they looking for in the perfect candidate? There are several ways to find out what they are looking for in the ideal candidate. You could call and ask, or ask people working in the field. Finally, do not overlook the job listings. The job description is a great source for keywords and gives you an idea of what employers are looking for.

The First Cut

Having a professional resume says volumes about you, even if the employer only glances at it. They will know in just a few seconds whether they should take any time at all to scan your resume and pursue you further. The details matter! One minor typo will land your resume in the circular file (trash).

First cut When employers sort through a pool of applicants and accept or reject them based on their applications or resumes.

Chronological resume A resume that lists specific skills under each position held.

Employers can get hundreds, even thousands, of resumes for a single position. Think of employers who are staring at a large pile of resumes, knowing they need to whittle them down into one small pile. This act of sorting through a pool of applicants, and accepting or rejecting them based on their applications or resumes, is known as the **first cut.** Usually, the candidates whose resumes make it through the first cut are called for an interview. There are specific things you need to do to make the first cut.

Your resume needs to be brief, easy to scan for key information, and well written. Based on your skills, professional goals, experience, and education, you can choose which type of resume will work best for you. Once you learn about the different types of resumes, the choice will be easy to make.

Your resume needs to be brief, easy to scan for key information, and well written.

—Frank Cawley, professional recruiter

The purpose of the resume . . . is to get face to face; not to get the job.

Your resume should have the details to get you the interview, but not your life story. Too much information will cause the employer to lose interest. You want to pique their interest so they call you in for the interview. Essentially, the main purpose of a resume is to get the interview. Once you have the interview, you will learn in future chapters how to get the job offer, and then negotiate your position. It is a process. First, let's review the specifics of how to create a resume the winning way.

» LO 5-2   Types of Resumes

There are four basic types of resumes:

1. Chronological
2. Functional or skills
3. Combination, hybrid, or custom
4. Scannable, plain text, or online

Sample resumes and references are located in the Winning Resume section following this chapter.

Chronological Resume

The most common type of resume used is the chronological resume. A **chronological resume** lists specific skills under each position held. Some people will list education first, while others will list work experience first, followed by education. The way to decide which should go first is based on a couple of things. First, if you are new to the field it is best to list educational degrees first. If you have a great deal of work experience related to the position, then you might want to list your professional experience first. If you were going to apply for a teaching position, you would certainly put your education first. Some IT positions look at experience first. Look at the job description to determine whether an employer seeks experience over education or vice versa. See if you can get a sense of what they are looking for, so you can format your resume accordingly.

Why is it important to do your research and look at the job description closely when choosing which type of resume to use?

All things being equal, consider placing education first if you have a college degree or are working toward one. List the most current degree first and the rest in reverse chronological order. If you are still in college, list your current educational pursuit and denote it with an asterisk followed by "in progress." You can also use verbiage such as "target graduation date June 20XX" or "anticipated graduation date June 20XX." Leave high school information off your resume if you have college experience unless you have recently graduated from high school, and even then you might want to leave it off.

If you do not have any degrees or a college education, then consider placing work experience first. List all educational experiences, including professional study, certificates, or training.

The chronological format works best when the candidate has recent education and/or work experience directly relating to the position. One of the benefits of this type of format is that it is a traditional style and most employers are comfortable and familiar with it. On the other hand, the chronological format places the focus on the positions you have held and degrees you have earned rather than on the skills you have developed. If you have had many job changes, you might avoid this format to downplay what is often perceived as a negative. Also, if you have never held a position comparable to the one you are applying for, you might want to choose one of the other formats and focus on your transferable skills.

Presentation Overview

No matter which type of resume you decide to use, it's important to understand what information to include. This section looks at the parts of the resume.

Resume Header or Identification

This part of the resume contains expected information including your name, address, phone number(s), and e-mail address. Some employers appreciate the phonetic spelling of names difficult to pronounce in parentheses next to your name.

Do not use your work phone number unless you are allowed to take personal calls at work. Keep in mind employers have the right to monitor all workplace communication. If you do not have a personal e-mail account, you can create a free one at hotmail.com, yahoo.com, gmail.com, and so on. Use your name, or a variation of your name to create a professional e-mail address, rather than a cute, confusing, or inappropriate e-mail address. First initial and last name @ the domain name works well, such as jsmith@domainname.com or first name _ (underscore) last name @ domain name such as joann_smith@ domainname.com. If you have a common name (such as Joann Smith), you may have to try a few options to get an e-mail address that isn't taken. Consider using your middle name or middle initial (joann.amanda.smith@ or joann.a.smith@), changing the order of your name (smith_joann.a@) or including a number (joann.a.smith1988@). It's important to find an available professional e-mail address. Using a nickname or funny address is fine for corresponding with friends, but if you put an e-mail address like that on a resume, employers may think you are unprofessional or don't understand how to present yourself professionally. Also, if you are sending your resume electronically, an e-mail with a professional address is more likely to be opened by the person at the receiving end. Anonymous or spam-looking e-mails will often be deleted or overlooked by recipients. Consider how many e-mails you delete on a daily basis from accounts like Fasteddie@spookydomain.com.

Objective

There are mixed feelings about including an objective in your resume. Some experts say *yes* while others say *never*. If you choose to have an objective, one suggestion is to tailor it to the specific position and the specific company. Yes, that means you need to change this part of your resume for each position. You can also make it relatively specific for a broader job search. Vague objectives, such as "To get a well-paying job in my chosen field, with opportunities for advancement," are pointless. You want to target your objective to the position you seek. Do not use a sentence for the objective. In other words, do not say "I want to . . . " or "I am seeking . . . "

For example:

Objective: To use my HR degree and skills to work as a human resource generalist assisting employees with payroll, benefits, and training.

Summary of Skills

This section, like the objective, is also optional. The Summary of Skills can also be referred to as the Summary of Qualifications, Profile, Summary, or other skill references. Here you may bullet up to five relevant skills, or expand each one into a short phrase describing your professional skills and goals.

Education

For most college undergraduates, your degree will separate you from many candidates without one. Therefore, unless you have a great deal of experience in the field you are seeking, you will want to list your education right after the objective or header. You list your degrees from the most recent to the least recent (reverse chronological order) and list the name, city, and state of the institution. If you are currently in college, denote this somehow, but list it first. State your university major and minors as well as specific course work related to the position (this is optional). Your honors and awards may be listed here or in a section for Awards and Honors. You can also list your GPA if it is strong (3.0 and above is considered a strong GPA). Listing other colleges you did not receive degrees from is optional as well. Figure 5.2 shows an example.

Education	
B.S. Human Services, Minor: Earth Science	05/10/20XX
The University of East Coast	City, NY
Dean's list 4 years	4.0 GPA

Figure 5.2 **Education Section**

Work Experience or List of Positions

The format of this section will vary depending on whether you use the chronological resume or the functional resume. If you are using a chronological resume, list your jobs in reverse chronological order, from the most recent to the latest. Give the title of the job, the name of the company, and the city and state the company is located in, as well as the years you worked there. You can omit extra part-time jobs if you have a solid work history. You can include unpaid work if applicable, or you can create a separate section for internships and volunteer work. List skills relevant to the position you are seeking including transferable skills (skills you can transfer from one position to another).

Other Optional Sections

- **Honors or Awards:** You may list honors under your education if applicable.
- **Activities or Community/Civic Involvement:** This could include volunteer work, memberships in clubs and organizations, or sports. Religious and political activities are risky, unless related to the position you are seeking.
- **Professional Affiliations:** List affiliations relevant to the job only. You can combine this section with the community/civic involvement section.
- **Publications:** If you have been published, list your publications in this section.

References

Typically, references should not be included on the resume. You can state *"References, transcripts, additional work history, and any further information available upon request."* Or state *"References available upon request."* However, you should have a reference page ready for when someone asks for it. Your reference page should have headings, font styles, and font sizes that are the same, or similar, to your resume (see Figure 5.3 for an example). The reference page should list three to five references. Make sure most of them are professional references, not personal. A **professional reference** is someone who knows your work, such as an employer or co-worker. A **personal reference** is someone other

Professional reference Someone who knows your work, such as an employer or co-worker.

Personal reference Someone other than an employer who can make statements about your ethics, trustworthiness, and personality.

BETH TICE

7890 Cherry Valley Dr. • Rapid Rock, Texas 01234 • (555) 567-4567
elizabethtice@gustr.com

PROFESSIONAL REFERENCES

Mark Helmann, Fire Marshal
Department of Insurance
State of Texas
(555) 555-1234
mhelmann@dayrep.com

Justin Roe
Assistant to City Manager
City, TX
(555) 555-4321

Kelly Richards, Executive Assistant
City Manager's Office
City, TX
(555) 555-4567

Figure 5.3 Reference List

than an employer who can make statements about your ethics, trustworthiness, and personality. Try not to use family members as references unless you worked for them. The format for references is:

- Name of person
- Title (if appropriate)
- Name of company
- Address
- Phone number (include area code if needed)
- E-mail address (optional)

Functional or Skills Resume

Functional resume A resume that organizes skills and accomplishments into groupings that support the position objective; also known as a skills resume.

Combination resume A resume that combines both the chronological and functional resume types; also known as a custom or hybrid resume.

A **functional resume,** or skills resume, organizes skills and accomplishments into groupings that support the position objective. This resume format works well for candidates changing career fields or who are seeking jobs not related to their majors. Your transferable skills are highlighted, demonstrating your competency for the position. Functional resumes have three to four (no more) skill headings. Functional resumes downplay frequent job changes and also focus on skills, not job titles. However, some employers do not like this type of resume because they cannot link your skills to specific employers or positions you held. For example, you might list a skill for a position you were in for only a couple of months.

If you lack work experience directly related to the job you seek, consider using a skills resume. Your goal is to make sure the skills headings are aligned to the job description for the position you are seeking.

Functional Resumes Organization

- Header
- Summary or objective (optional)
- Targeted skills headings with bulleted skills
- Chronological work experience with company names, dates of employment, and title (don't include skills in this section)
- Education (you can place this earlier in the resume if it is relevant to the position you seek)
- Other optional sections

Imagine you are a hiring manager evaluating 200 resumes, and you open an applicant's electronic resume to discover that the margin alignments are jumbled, and the document is hard to follow. Would you take the time to decipher it or quickly move on to the next resume? How does this show the importance of having a plain text resume?

Combination, Hybrid, or Custom Resume

A **combination resume** combines both the chronological and functional resume types (see Figure 5.4). It is also sometimes known as a custom or hybrid resume. You might choose to use a combination resume if you have had several positions that were similar in nature and a few unique positions. You can then list skills in groupings under the positions that were similar in nature rather than repeating yourself for each job. Then list the unique position(s) on their own with specific bullets under each position.

Scannable, Plain Text, E-Resume, or Online Resume

In certain situations, you cannot control the formatting of your resume because an employer or job-search system requires you to have a scannable or plain-text resume. These are resumes with all of the formatting removed, which

Professional Experience		
Correctional Officer	Orleans Parish Prison	01/20XX – 05/20XX
Chief Deputy Sheriff	LA Department of Labor	09/20XX – 04/20XX
Special Agent	State Commission	06/20XX – 07/20XX
Patrolman	Knoll Police Department	09/20XX – 06/20XX

Summary of Skills

Day-to-Day	**Management**	**Professional Training**
• Responded to calls for service	• Supervised deputies	• D.A.R.E officer trained
• Investigations	• Coordinated day-to-day operations	• Certified Law Enforcement Officer
• Resolved crisis	• Managed budgets	• Basic Narcotics Investigations
• Enforced county ordinances and state/federal laws	• Trained and supervised client managers	• Interview and Interrogations (IPTM)

Military

United States Marine Corps (E-5 Retired)   5/199X – 8/20XX

- Held Military Top Secret Clearance.
- Managed/Coordinated 50 accounts for the Express Travel Management Division.
- Developed, implemented, and directed government travel for musical groups throughout the United States.
- Maintained loss prevention program and supporting plans to protect $2 million in assets of unit materials and facilities.
- Created 150 presentations for military and civilian organizations for all musical commitments and government public relations performances.
- Graduated Non-Commissioned Officers School.

Figure 5.4 Combination Resume Organization

could change when sending electronically. Many employers use computerized scanning systems to review resumes for the first cut. Often a resume does not scan well and this can have a negative impact on making the cut. That's why you want to have a resume that is ready in a scannable format so it retains its professional qualities.

Guidelines for Electronic Resumes

1. Use one of the sans serif fonts or Times New Roman.
2. Keep font size 10–14 for scannable resumes (12–14 for name and headings; 10–12 for the rest of the information depending on font style).
3. Avoid italic, underlining, or shading.
4. Bold sparingly.
5. Send your hard copies if you can as a back up.

Formatting a Scannable, Online, or Plain Text Resume

Many companies will request that you cut and paste your resume into a box, or ask you to submit a **plain text resume**. A plain text resume is one with simplified formatting, in order to prevent errors when sending it electronically. It can also be referred to as a scannable, electronic, or online resume. It is a good idea to have a plain text resume ready to send if an employer

Plain text resume A resume with simplified formatting, in order to prevent errors when sending it electronically.

asks for it. Follow the directions below to change your regular resume into a plain text resume:

- Open your resume in Word.
- Go to resave your resume with a different name. You might save it as "online resume" or "scannable resume."
- Before you click "Save" go to the "Save as type:" at the bottom of the save box. Select either "Plain Text" or "Text Only." You will see it added ".txt" to your file name.
- Now, save the file with the ".txt".
- Stay in Word and reopen your plain text document to edit a few things.
- Your resume will look different.
- Change any bold words to all capital letters.
- Notice your tabs are gone, so use the space key for indents.
- Change any bullets to other symbols such as +, *, or −.
- Fix any indent problems or line problems.
- Save and close out of Word.

careercoach5.2

Use Caution when Applying to Job Boards

Use caution when sending your resume from online job boards or recruiting sites. If you see multiple postings for positions that use the same verbiage, but they don't list the company, chances are likely that the posts are from the same company. This could present a problem if you apply for this position from more than one job board. When your resume shows up at a hiring company from multiple recruiters, it can end up in the trash, regardless of your stellar qualifications. The reason is that the company could open itself up to liability when determining exactly who presented your resume to the hiring company. To avoid this, limit your job search to a couple of recruiting sites or use the company website to apply.

Fonts for All Resumes

The best fonts that can be used safely with any type of resume, including scannable resumes, are fonts with less detail. In general you will want to stick with sans serif fonts or a nondecorative serif like Times New Roman. Stick to using font size 10–12 depending on the font style you choose. You can use up to two fonts in a resume if you want to use one for your name and/or headings and another for the bulk of the information. Experiment with the size and style of fonts. You might consider printing your resume several times with different fonts and font sizes and asking trusted others for feedback. The following (all shown in 11 point font size) are good choices for resumes:

Arial (contemporary look; if you choose Arial use a smaller size font such as 10 or 11, or the resume can look less professional)

Bookman Old Style (traditional look)

Bodoni MT (traditional look)

`Courier New` (traditional look)

Franklin Gothic Book (contemporary look)

Garamond (traditional look)

Helvetica (contemporary look)

Palatino Linotype (traditional look)

Times New Roman (traditional look)

Tahoma (contemporary look)

Verdana (contemporary look)

✓ SELF-CHECK

1. What are some of the differences between a chronological resume, functional or skills resume, and a combination resume?

2. Which type of resume is best if you have several gaps in your work history? Why?

3. What is the difference between a professional reference and a personal reference?

» LO 5-3 What to Include in Your Resume

Keywords are terms related to specific skills or qualifications that employers search for in electronic resumes. Employers use keywords to narrow the candidate resume pool and to find the candidates they want to interview. This is done by digitally scanning online or electronic resumes. Furthermore, many employers source databases of third-party resume-posting boards. Since 75 to 80 percent of resumes are scanned for position-specific keywords, it is critical that your resume contains them.

Keywords Terms related to specific skills or qualifications that employers search for in electronic resumes.

That said, you may be asking, *"How do I know what keywords the employer is looking for?"* While you cannot be certain what keywords employers are looking for, you can increase your odds of having the right keywords in your resume. Keywords are nouns. They are typically nouns describing what you did in the position. You want to match your skills with keywords employers are sourcing when they scan resumes for the first cut. You will find many keywords in the posted job description for the skills they seek. If you do not have a job description, find a similar one in an online database of jobs or even in the newspaper want-ad section. Many positions use similar keywords. Buzzwords and keywords change over time, so keep up-to-date on keywords by looking at job announcements for positions for which you want to apply. The following are some examples of keywords:

- Accountant
- Cost reduction
- CPA
- Financial analyst
- Healthcare
- JAVA

- MBA
- Medical
- Paralegal
- Project management
- Recruiter

Power words are verbs in your resume that best describe and emphasize what actions you did in the position. After each bullet, lead each of your skills with a power word.

Look at the following list of skills you might find on a resume. The power words (verbs) are bolded, while the keywords (nouns) are underlined.

- **Solicited and developed** new clientele for both the <u>staffing and human resources</u> product lines
- **Billed** over $50K in <u>direct hire revenue</u> in the first three months
- **Established** <u>processes and procedures</u> for the administration of <u>sales, recruitment, payroll, benefits, and training</u>
- **Managed** all <u>human resource</u> related issues for 250+ employees
- **Guided** office from start-up to over $500K in <u>sales</u> (projected in one calendar year) with highlights of more than 1,100 <u>contract hours</u> assigned in one week and over $20K in <u>direct hire revenue</u> generated in one month
- **Sourced and interviewed** <u>candidates</u> daily from C-Level executives to entry-level positions
- **Provided** <u>security</u> services for over 200 concerts

exercise 5.1

Power Words for Your Resume

First, circle or highlight the following power words that stand out to you as descriptors of what you have done in your positions. Later, you will narrow this list and select the best power words to use in your resume with the skills they highlight.

abolished	acted	answered	attained
absorbed	actively	applied	audited
accelerated	(participated)	appointed	awarded
accommodated	administered	appropriated	
accomplished	advised	approved	balanced
accrued	aided	arbitrated	billed
achieved	allocated	articulated	brought
acquired	allotted	assisted	bridged

briefed
budgeted
built

calculated
cared for
certified
chaired
charged
checked
cleared
closed
cold-called
collaborated
collected
combined
commissioned
communicated
compiled
computed
conceptualized
conducted
configured
confirmed
consolidated
constructed
consulted
continued
contracted
contributed
controlled
converted
copied
corrected
corresponded
counseled
critiqued
cultivated
cut

dealt
defined
decreased
dedicated
defined
delegated
delivered
demonstrated
deployed
designated
designed
detailed

detected
determined
developed
devised
diagnosed
differentiated
directed
discovered
discussed
dispatched
dispensed
displayed
disposed
disseminated
dissolved
distributed
diversified
divided
documented
doubled
drew up
drove

earned
edited
eliminated
empowered
enforced
engaged
engineered
enhanced
enlarged
enlisted
enriched
enrolled
entered
equipped
estimated
evaluated
examined
exceeded
executed
expanded
expedited
explained
evaluated

facilitated
fielded
filed
filled
financed

fine tuned
focused
forecasted
formulated
fostered
found
founded
funded

gained
gathered
generated
governed
graded
granted
greeted
grew
guarded
guided

halted
halved
handled
helped
hired
honed

identified
impacted
implemented
improved
incorporated
increased
indexed
initiated
influenced
innovated
inspected
inspired
installed
instituted
instructed
instrumental
insured
interacted
interviewed
introduced
invented
invested
investigated
isolated
issued
itemized

joined
judged
justified

launched
lectured
led
licensed
listed
lobbied
logged

made
magnified
maintained
managed
mandated
manipulated
manufactured
mapped
marketed
matched
maximized
mediated
merged
met
minimized
mobilized
modified
monitored
motivated
moved
multiplied

named
navigated
negotiated
nominated
nurtured

observed
obtained
offered
officiated
offset
opened
operated
opted
optimized
orchestrated
ordered
organized
oriented

originated   realized   shipped   taught
outlined   rebuilt   shortened   teamed
outperformed   received   showed   terminated
overcame   recommended   signed   tested
overhauled   reconciled   simplified   testified
oversaw   recorded   simulated   topped
owned   recruited   slashed   totaled
     redesigned   solicited   toured
packaged   reduced   sold   tracked
paid   reengineered   solidified   traded
participated   refocused   solved   trained
partnered   regulated   sorted   transferred
perceived   remodeled   sourced   transcribed
perfected   removed   sparked   transformed
performed   reorganized   spearheaded   translated
persuaded   repaired   specialized   transported
piloted   replaced   specified   traveled
planned   replied   speculated   treated
posted   reported   spent   trimmed
prepared   represented   spoke   tripled
presented   requested   sponsored   troubleshot
presided   rescued   spurred   turned around
prioritized   researched   staffed   tutored
processed   resolved   standardized   typed
procured   responded   started
proficient   restored   steered   uncovered
programmed   revamped   streamlined   underlined
prohibited   revolutionized   strengthened   underscored
projected   reviewed   stretched   undertook
promoted   revised   structured   underwrote
proofread   rotated   studied   unified
proposed   submitted   united
protected   succeeded   updated
provided   salvaged   suggested   upgraded
published   scanned   summarized   upheld
purchased   scheduled   supervised   urged
     screened   supplied   used
quadrupled   searched   supported   utilized
qualified   secured   surpassed
quantified   seized   surveyed   validated
queried   selected   swayed   verbalized
questioned   sent   symbolized   verified
quoted   separated   synthesized   visited
     sequenced   systemized   volunteered
raised   served
ranked   set up   tabulated   waged
rated   settled   tackled   weighed
reached   shaped   tallied   worked
realigned   sharpened   targeted   wrote

Next, put these words in a list so you can use them when you write your resume. Remember, the power words you circled or highlighted are written in past tense, so make sure when you use them in your resume the tense matches the time period. In other words, if you are using the power word for a skill you are currently doing in your present job you will use present tense, but if you select a power word to use in a skill for a former employer, use past tense.

Example:

- **Bill** over $50K in <u>direct hire revenue</u> in the first three months

  Bill would be a current skill for a current employer.

- **Billed** over $50K in <u>direct hire revenue</u> in the first three months

  Billed is past tense for a skill utilized for a former employer.

Cyber Trip 5.1

Mining Power Words and Keywords on the Internet   Search the Internet using the words *"power words/keywords for resumes."* You can also conduct separate searches on the Internet using the words *"power words for resumes"* or *"keywords for resumes."*

List five keywords you might use in your resume that you found in your search.

1. _____
2. _____
3. _____
4. _____
5. _____

List five power words you might use in your resume that you found in your search.

1. _____
2. _____
3. _____
4. _____
5. _____

✓ SELF-CHECK

4. What is the main purpose of a resume?

5. What is a keyword? How might you know which keywords an employer is looking for?

6. What are power words?

» LO 5-4   The Skills Formula™

There is a professional, yet easy-to-use formula for writing your skills in your marketing tools. The **Skills Formula** uses bullets, power words, and keyword skills to create quantified outcomes for your professional resume.

> **Skills Formula**™ Uses bullets, power words, and keyword skills to create quantified outcomes for your professional resume.

Quantifying Skills

Quantified skills: Skills that include specific, measurable amount(s) in numerical form.

Quantifying skills is essential because the reader's eye is naturally drawn to numbers.

Quantified skills are those that include specific, measurable amount(s) in numerical form. Rather than writing out numbers or amounts, a quantified skill emphasizes the impact of number symbols. Quantifying skills is essential whenever possible because the reader's eye is naturally drawn to numbers. For example, "20" is more noticeable than "twenty." When the person reading your cover letter and resume is skimming and scanning, he or she will focus on the numbers that are numerical, not written out. For this reason, you might want to use even small numbers, such as five, written as "5." Read the two bullets below, and decide which one stands out more.

- Maintained loss prevention program and supporting plans to protect two million dollars in assets of unit materials and facilities.
- Maintained loss prevention program and supporting plans to protect $2 million in assets of unit materials and facilities.

The examples below show how to use the Skills Formula effectively. If there is not a way to easily quantify the skills, omit that part of the formula.

The Skills Formula

Bullet + Power Word (verb) + Keyword Skill (noun) = Outcome (quantified results)

Skills Formula Example 1:

- Upgraded company retirement plan from 403-B to 401K, increasing enrollment by 14% and decreasing costs by 10%.

Keywords: Company retirement plan 403-B 401K

Power word: Upgraded

Quantified outcome: Increasing enrollment by 14%; decreasing costs by 10%.

Skills Formula Example 2:

- Instituted changes in drug and alcohol screenings, reducing company costs by 38%.

Keywords: Drug and alcohol screenings

Power word: Instituted

Quantified outcome: Reducing company costs by 38%.

Below are more examples of how to write skills using the Skills Formula:

- Facilitated 10 workshops weekly with 5–40 attendees per session.
- Initiated and implemented customer contact benchmark study recommendations, resulting in a 9% increase in customer satisfaction and service delivery.
- Established key performance indicators for all core leasing operational areas to manage and improve processes, resulting in 7% year over year improvement of KPIs.

Scientists and mathematicians use formulas to simplify complex problems. How is the Skills Formula similar?

- Supervised, trained, and mentored 15 sales associates to work as members of a cohesive, competitive team.
- Monitored and approved expenditures for $80k departmental budget.
- Prepared, updated, and maintained: 250 patient records, reports, departmental budget, and in-house training manual.
- Established, monitored, and maintained strict confidentiality standards for 300+ client accounts.
- Increased regional sales by $1.5 million in first year.
- Expertly organized staff holiday party for 250 employees.
- 100% employment attendance for past 3 years.
- Organized 50 community members, raising over $175,000 for anti-drug education fund.
- Consistently achieved $55,000+ annual income from commission sales.
- Managed and led Girl Scout Troop #43, comprised of 27 girls who completed 20 service projects.

exercise 5.2

Utilizing the Skills Formula

Use three of the skills you identified in Chapter 2, and write them using the Skills Formula. Choose keywords and power words from this chapter to highlight your skill and see if you can add numbers to quantify the skill. You can then use these in your resume, cover letter, or other marketing tools.

Example:

Skill	Power Word	Keywords	Skill Written Using the Skills Formula
management	expertly	managed budget staff	Expertly managed $4M annual budget and staff of 65.

The management skill becomes:

 Expertly managed $4M annual budget and staff of 65.

Practice using the Skills Formula with three of your skills in the following chart.

Skill	Power Word	Keywords	Skill Written Using the Skills Formula

» LO5-5 Formatting, Saving, and Sending Your Resume

Before you create your resume, let's review what we have discussed so far. It is important that you have a clear understanding of the type of resume you will create, the quantified skills you will include, and the various parts, characteristics, and details that make up the resume.

Target the Job

Remember, the purpose of your resume is to get a face-to-face interview with the hiring person. That hiring person usually has specific skills and experience in mind, so you want to customize your resume to highlight the skills and experience you think are the best fit for the job. It's OK to include some experience that isn't directly related to the position you seek, but remember, this is a resume, not a biography. You should not include every detail. Focus on what is important. Keep your resume to one or two pages, depending on your relevant work experience. Don't try to be a Jack of all trades. Create more than one resume so you can target your job search.

Remember, the purpose of your resume is to get face-to-face with the hiring person.

Visual Impact

You have just a few seconds to attract an employer's attention, and entice him or her to read further. Use marketing techniques:

- Bullets
- Power words
- Keywords
- Quantified skills
- White space—margins of at least 1 inch
- Indent
- Fonts—Choose a typeface (font) that is easily readable rather than decorative. Times New Roman, Arial, Courier New, Palatino Linotype, Garamond, or Bookman Old Style are readable.
  - Font sizes 10, 11, or 12 point are recommended, depending on the font you choose.
  - Use bold, italics, or text boxes to set off sections. Do this sparingly.
  - Quality paper
  - Use a laser printer.

Maintain Integrity

Even if you are hired, a lack of integrity on your resume or in person can result in termination. Always be truthful on your resume. It should hold up under scrutiny. You wouldn't want to be hired based on your embellished resume, only to be fired later when your employer finds out you were not honest. Integrity counts. You want to market yourself with finesse, but not deceive the employer. There is a big difference.

Integrity is important both before and after you are hired. What are the possible consequences of embellishing your resume?

Resume Formats

Below is a short review of the different resume format options you can choose from. The advantages and disadvantages of each type are included.

Chronological Resume: This type states work experience in reverse order, and lists skills under positions. It focuses on career growth and development.

Advantages: A traditional format that is familiar to employers, easy to write, and emphasizes steady work history.

Disadvantages: It emphasizes gaps in employment, job-hopping, or career changing.

Functional or Skills Resume: This type focuses on strengths, experience, and skills. It should be used when first entering the job market, changing careers, or for freelance work.

Advantages: Focuses on skills and not your work history; disguises gaps in work history.

Disadvantages: It may lack depth and is not as familiar to employers. You may need education to back up your skills.

Combination Resume: This type combines both the chronological and functional resume types. It offers a complete picture of skills and work history.

Advantages: It presents relevant skills, abilities, and employment record.

Disadvantages: It may become repetitious and long.

Cyber Trip 5.2

Resume Examples on the Internet   Here are a few suggested links to websites that provide resume examples: CareerOneStop: www.careeronestop.com; Purdue Online Writing Lab: https://owl.english.purdue.edu/owl/resource/927/1/; ResumeWriters: http://www.resumewriters.com/sample-resumes/; RileyGuide: http://www.rileyguide.com/letters.html. You can also type "resume samples" into your favorite search engine to find more examples.

Resume Challenges

You may face several challenges when creating your resume. It is helpful to know what these challenges are before you begin, so you know what to expect.

Gaps in Work History

There are a couple of ways to manage gaps in your work history. First, if you were in school or volunteering during this time, make note of this. If the gaps were close together, use seasons for dates of employment. For example: Fall 2012–Spring 2014; Spring 2014–Present. If you were a stay-at-home parent, for example, leave the gap and address this in the interview only if you are asked.

Held Many Positions in One Company

This can be solved by using the chronological format. First list the company and then list the position titles with the corresponding dates you held those positions. Then bullet your skills for the different jobs held.

Fired, Downsized, or Quit

Do not mention reasons for leaving a company on your resume. Only list the required information such as company name, title, and dates of employment with skills. If you have had many short-term jobs, consider using the functional or skills resume. You want face-to-face time with the employer. Be prepared to clarify these items in the interview.

Short-Term, Summer, or Temporary Positions

If you have a solid work history related to the position you are seeking, you can leave these off. If you do not have a solid work history, you can use the functional or skills resume and list these positions last with minimum information. If you worked for a temporary agency and took a variety of jobs, list the positions and note the temporary company or service.

Overqualified

If you are receiving consistent feedback that you are overqualified, or are concerned you will be perceived as such, you need to go back and target your resume to the position you are seeking. Downplay either your education level or seniority of experience if this is a position you truly would like to have. An example of this is a true case where a doctorate-level candidate left that fact off her resume in order to obtain a mid-level management position. Before she decided to take her doctorate off her resume, she was finding it hard to obtain the type of position she wanted. She decided to downplay her doctorate, and she was hired, but after her employer found out she had her doctorate degree, she was promoted rather quickly. She felt that downplaying her education level was necessary in order to get her foot in the door.

If you truly want a position for which you are overqualified, you might have to consider understating your education or extensive experience. For example, if you are over 40, you might consider leaving graduation dates off your resume. Changing the type of resume you have (chronological, functional, or combination) may also help frame your education or experience in a better way for the position you want.

Breaking into a New Field

You will want to use the appropriate type of resume to highlight the education or skills you have for the field you seek to enter. For example, if you have a great deal of retail experience, but just graduated with your paralegal degree, you would list your education first and any skills that transfer to working as a paralegal. A combination or skills resume would work best for this situation.

Below is an example of a similar dilemma.

> ### Student Question
>
> *I hope that I will be able to get the job I want in human resources. My problem is that my experience in HR has been as a secretary/receptionist. I get to interact with potential candidates and assist them with completing their application. What are your suggestions to break into this market?*
>
> —*Ava*

Cyber Trip 5.3

Resumes for Federal Positions   Government positions have specific resume requirements. Visit the websites listed here to learn more about resume writing for federal positions: USAJOBS: http://www.usajobs.opm.gov/; Federal Jobs Network: http://www.federaljobs.net/applyfor.htm.

Portfolios: Putting It All Together

The purpose of a portfolio is to enhance your marketability. It works particularly well for teachers, graphic artists, artists, and journalists, but anyone can create a portfolio, regardless of their profession or program of study. Even if you do not submit all elements of your portfolio, have them ready and available at a moment's notice. For example, if you are a teacher and prospective employers request that you submit your personal teaching philosophy along with your cover letter and resume, you would simply pull this from your portfolio and send it. The following further exemplifies the importance of having a portfolio:

> *I recently interviewed for a position that was offered to me, but I was unable to accept due to my clinical schedule. Before going to the interview, I remember thinking to myself, there are probably five to seven other individuals interviewing this very same day. I asked myself, "How can I stand out?" Other than making sure I looked professional, I also brought along a portfolio illustrating my education, experience in greater detail, and what I felt I could do for the company. This was after already sending my resume. My portfolio worked, and the job offer was made at the end of my interview. I also sent a thank you letter to the hiring manager. I feel that in order to be competitive in today's job market, you must always ask, "What makes me stand out? What makes me outshine the rest?"*
>
> —Carrie Johnson, Virginia College Online student,
> Respiratory Therapy major

You already have completed many of the components for your portfolio. You did this work in each chapter for your My Portfolio assignments. So far you have created your career goals and mission, identified your skills, achievements, and accomplishments, learned how to research companies, and developed your networking business card (NBC) and now your resume. Traditional portfolios include the following:

- Cover Page
- Table of Contents with Clear Divisions
- Career Components
  - Networking business card
  - Cover letter
  - Resume
  - Reference list
  - Letters of recommendation

Carrie Johnson

- Evidence of Skills (job related, transferable, and adaptive)

    Achievements and awards

    Projects

    Presentations

    Transcripts, certificates, and licenses

    Assignments/samples of your best work

    Volunteer/community service

    Conferences and workshops: a list of those you attended and/or presented at Videos/DVDs

Your resume sends a message about you to the world.

—Karine Blackett, author of *College Success Guide*

Take your portfolio with you to interviews even if interviewers do not request any of the information. It will be available, and you can use it as a tool to market yourself and separate yourself from the pack.

careercoach5.3

Dress Your Resume for Success

Details matter! Paper is weighted, and you will want to use a heavyweight white, off-white, or ivory paper. A good resume paper is weighted 20 lbs. to 25 lbs., is at least 25 percent cotton, and has a watermark. Make certain the watermark is facing the right way when you print. Use a laser printer, or consider taking it to a professional printer. For a fee, many printers and copy stores will store, edit, print, and even ship your resume. This might come in handy when time is of the essence.

Consider buying portfolio folders from an office store for sending your resumes. A good one to look for has a vertical left pocket and a horizontal right pocket, with a business card holder. Choose a subtle portfolio color such as olive green or beige. Put your resume in the left pocket and your cover letter in the right. Now that you have a networking business card (NBC), you can put this in the business card slot as well. Send this in a manila envelope of the proper size. Neatly print the address or use a label.

Keep in mind that you want the look and feel of your resume to align with the position you seek. Arial might be considered an informal font, whereas Times New Roman is considered a formal font. You are the expert on you, and you get to decide. If you are not having luck with your resume, and it is not generating many interviews, then consider changing the style and font. Also, remember to have your resume reviewed by your career services department at your college or university, or by a trusted professional.

Delivering Your Resume

There are many ways for your resume to make it into the hiring pool. You can mail it to the company, respond to an ad, apply online, have a networked inside contact pass it on, or present it yourself. The method you choose to deliver the resume matters. Getting your resume into the hiring agent's hands personally is

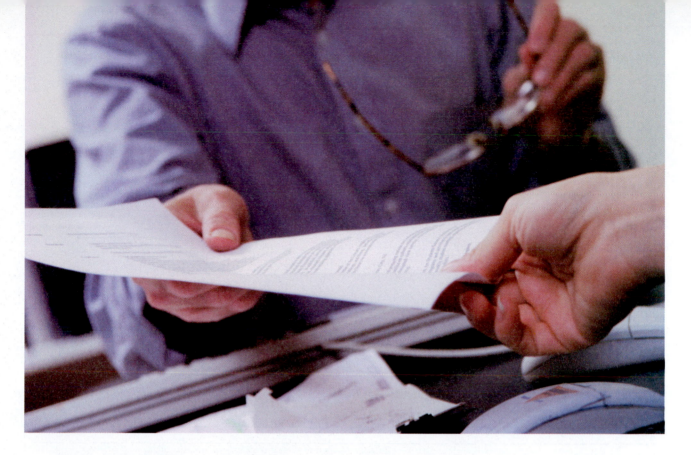

the strongest way to present your resume. This is one of the downfalls of applying online and sending resumes electronically. Any time you can present the resume to the person who does the hiring, do it. The personal presentation is powerful! Remember to dress appropriately for this face-to-face meeting as well.

Cyber Trip 5.4

How Not to Write a Resume   Resumania is a website full of examples of how *not* to write a resume. Please visit the Resumania website at http://www.resumania.com/.

my portfolio 5.1

Create a Resume

Directions: First choose the format—chronological, functional, or combination—that best fits your experience and desired position. Practice with these formats using both the exercises in this book and online using various tools. You can find appropriate worksheets using your favorite Internet search engine, by entering the keywords "resume worksheet," "chronological resume worksheet," or "functional or skills resume worksheet." Revisit My Portfolio 2.1, and use your *Career Assets Inventory.* You already listed many of your skills in that exercise. Now you can organize, bullet, and quantify them for your portfolio. Keep in mind you do not need to use all of the skills you listed in your *Career Assets Inventory* for your resume. You are targeting a job, so use the skills that best support your qualifications for the position you seek. These should agree with your objective if you decide to use one.

(Continued)

Resume Header or Identification

_____
_____
_____

Objective (optional):

To _____

Summary of Skills (optional)

■ _____   ■ _____

■ _____   ■ _____

■ _____   ■ _____

Education
College name, address (city/state):
Degree:
Graduation date (month/year):
Majors/ minors:
GPA if above 3.0:
College name, address (city/state):
Degree:
Graduation date (month/year):
Majors/ minors:
GPA if above 3.0:

Work Experience or List of Positions (most recent first)
Company names, cities, states:

1._____
2._____
3._____
4._____
5._____

Dates of employment at each company:

1._____
2._____
3._____
4._____
5._____

Title held at each company:

1._____
2._____
3._____
4._____
5._____

List skills gained from each company—follow the *Skills Formula*. Once you have a list, put them into bulleted format:

1._____
2._____
3._____
4._____
5._____

Honors and Awards (optional)

_____

Activities or Community/Civic Involvement/Professional Affiliations (optional)

_____

Publications (optional)

_____

Figure 5.5 Chronological Resume Worksheet

(Continued)

Resume Header or Identification

_____

_____

_____

Objective (optional):

To _____

LIST SKILLS IN BULLETED FORM (follow the *Skills Formula*; skills and experience in functional groups such as management, computer skills, training, etc.)

Skill Heading I _____

Example _____

Example _____

Example _____

Skill Heading II _____

Example _____

Example _____

Example _____

Skill Heading III _____

Example _____

Example _____

Example _____

WORK EXPERIENCE OR LIST OF POSITIONS (most recent first)

Company name _____

City, state (abbreviate) _____

Dates of employment _____

Title _____

Company name _____

City, state (abbreviate) _____

Dates of employment _____

Title _____

Company name _____

City, state (abbreviate) _____

Dates of employment _____

Title _____

EDUCATION

Name of college or university _____

College address (city/state) _____

Degree: _____

Majors/minors: _____

Graduation date (month/year) _____

GPA if above 3.0: _____

Honors and Awards (optional):

_____

_____

Activities or Community/Civic Involvement/Professional Affiliations (optional):

_____

_____

Publications (optional):

Figure 5.6 Functional/Skills Resume Worksheet

(Continued)

Resume Checklist	Not Included	Needs Improvement	Well Done
Categories arranged in order of importance			
Organization logical, clear, and consistent			
Information is targeted to position: keywords			
One or two pages only			
No sentences; concise statements			
Information accurate and positive			
Uses *Skills Formula*			
Power words used			
Verbs in correct tense (past or present)			
No slang			
Abbreviations avoided			
Correct spelling, grammar, and punctuation			
Unnecessary repetition avoided			
No use of *I, me, my,* etc.			
Appropriate headings			
White space, indentation, underlining, italic, capitals, and spacing effectively used			
Skills are bulleted			
Space between categories			
Layout: headings, spacing, type face, print size, etc., consistent			
Correct information in the heading			
Overall appearance pleasing, appealing, and easy on the eye			
High-quality paper used (if applicable)			

Reference Checklist			
Separate from resume			
Appropriate format			
Lists 3–5 references			
Heading matches resume heading			
Information is complete			
Phone numbers with area codes			
Addresses include zip codes			
Paper matches resume (if applicable)			

Figure 5.7   Resume Checklist

Resume Checklist and Grading Rubric

Use the Resume Checklist and Grading Rubric to either peer review another student's resume or double check your own. These tools will help ensure all of the elements are included in your winning resume.

(Continued)

Student Name:

Resume Grading Rubric (100 points)	Circle Points		
	Not Included	*Needs Improvement*	*Well Done*
1 Categories are arranged in order of importance	0	1–2–3	4–5
2 Organization is logical, clear, and consistent	0	1–2–3	4–5
3 Information is targeted to position: keywords	0	1–2–3	4–5
4 One or two pages only	0	1–2–3	4–5
5 No sentences; only concise statements	0	1–2–3	4–5
6 Information is accurate and positive	0	1–2–3	4–5
7 Uses *Skills Formula*	0	1–2–3	4–5
8 Uses power words	0	1–2–3	4–5
9 Verbs are in correct tense (past or present)	0	1–2–3	4–5
10 No slang	0	1–2–3	4–5
11 Abbreviations are avoided	0	1–2–3	4–5
12 Correct spelling, grammar, and punctuation	0	1–2–3	4–5
13 Unnecessary repetition is avoided	0	1–2–3	4–5
14 Appealing and easy on the eye; high-quality paper if applicable	0	1–2–3	4–5
15 No use of *I, me, my,* etc.	0	1–2–3	4–5
16 Use of white space, indentation, underlining, italic, capitals, and spacing is effective	0	1–2–3	4–5
17 Skills are bulleted	0	1–2–3	4–5
18 Space between categories	0	1–2–3	4–5
19 Formatting and layout: headings, spacing, type face, print size, etc., are consistent and accurate.	0	1–2–3	4–5
20 Heading information is accurate	0	1–2–3	4–5
Additional comments:			
Total Points for Resume (100 points possible)			
REFERENCES GRADING RUBRIC (25 points)			
1 Reference page is separate from resume; if hard copy, the paper matches the resume	0	1–2–3	4–5
2 Appropriate format	0	1–2–3	4–5
3 Lists 3–5 references	0	1–2–3	4–5
4 References heading matches resume heading	0	1–2–3	4–5
5 Information is complete: phone numbers have area codes; addresses include zip codes	0	1–2–3	4–5
Total Points for References (25 points possible)			
Total Points for References and Resume (125 points possible)			

Figure 5.8 Resume Grading Rubric

exercise 5.3

Resume Peer Review

Exchange resumes with another student. Use the checklist and grading rubric in Figures 5.7 and 5.8 to analyze, review, and provide feedback on your peer's resume.

First, complete the resume grading rubric or checklist to analyze the different elements in the resume. After completing the form and adding comments, answer the following questions:

1. What are three suggestions you have for your classmate to improve his or her resume?

_____

_____

_____

_____

2. What is one idea you received from critiquing your peer's resume that you will adopt or possibly use in your own resume?

_____

_____

_____

_____

exercise 5.4

Measurement of Successful Resumes

Prepare two to three different resumes and measure the response rate of each one. Send each resume to different companies and organizations you targeted in your search. Prior to sending out the resumes, in the chart in Figure 5.9 note which companies received each type of resume. Specifically, which type, style, and method of delivery returned the most interest and invitation to interview? The resume with the largest response rate will become your preferred resume for generating results.

Chart the response rate for your resume over several weeks.

Then look at the results in terms of which types of resumes generated higher and lower response rates. Next, compare your results with other students. Try to compare results with students whose majors are similar to yours. You can add other measurement items to this chart and make additional copies if needed.

	Company Name	Type of Resume: 1. Chronological 2. Functional 3. Combination	Lead: 1. Objective 2. Skills/ Summary 3. Neither	Font: Type/Size	How Presented to the Company: 1. Unsolicited mailed to company 2. Mailed in response to ad 3. Networked 4. Hand delivered 5. Online	Results: 1. # of callbacks 2. Interviews
1						
2						
3						
4						
5						
6						
7						
8						
9						
10						

Your Name:

Figure 5.9   Resume Success Measurement Tool

careercoach5.4

Cleaning and Getting Clear

In order to land the interview, you must *get clear*. Getting clear happens on several levels:

- Clear your deck or space—get organized.
- Get clear about the job you seek—target the job.
- Create a clear and concise resume.
- Clear your mind and regain energy.

You have done an incredible amount of work in earlier chapters by setting goals, identifying your skills, gaining an awareness of market trends, and learning how to network effectively. Now you are ready to launch your marketing tools. You are on the verge of making your career goals unfold. This is the time when your energy could start to leak and pull you away from your goals, not toward them. This happens in a variety of ways. From legal trouble to family problems, there could be hundreds of ways you might be diverted. Many times, students feel this is personal and that bad things happen to them more than to other people. Not true! We all face obstacles and challenges, and when we set goals, the likelihood of encountering challenges increases. You

How can the simple act of cleaning and organizing your work space help you *get clear*?

will be tested. It is your job to manage the stress and changes so you persist in your career goals.

Emotions such as anger, resentment, jealousy, and rage can drain the energy you need to complete tasks and move toward your goals. It has been said that depression is anger without enthusiasm. Who knows if that is true or not, but depression and despair can cause people to go into a downward spiral where it is hard to get motivated to do much of anything, let alone work toward one's goals. If you have lost a job, you know how easy it is to get down on yourself, your finances, and the world in general. Being angry at your current or past place of employment affects your job search and marketing tools. Use the energy to propel you toward something better. This way your anger is constructive.

Being depressed or down can be a dangerous place to be. It is important to get the support you need to move out of this frame of mind. More tools for rebounding from setbacks will be discussed in detail in chapters to come. For now, know that clearing negative emotions and energy is important to reaching your career goals and sending the right message out to the world of who you are and what you want to do.

One of the most powerful, yet simple, ways to clear negative emotions and energy is to use the tool of gratitude. Next to love, gratitude literally transforms people and situations. It is perfect for clearing work. If you feel you have little to be grateful for, then I suggest strongly that you volunteer for a day at a nursing home or a homeless shelter. When we feel grateful, we begin to change our energy level and attract more good things toward us. This is similar to the tuning fork in Chapter 4.

The following are some simple ways to use the power tool of gratitude:

- Make a gratitude journal. Even Oprah uses this tool! (To learn more, use your favorite Internet search engine to search for "Oprah" and "gratitude journal.")
- List 20 reasons this world is better because you are in it.
- Tell two people a day how you appreciate something they did for you.

You also need to get very clear about the position you are seeking. If you have several positions you are seeking and are qualified for, then make several resumes. You target your resume to the job. Once you are clear, you will use keywords targeting this position in your resume. You can do Internet searches to locate positions you would like to have, add the terminology you find to your marketing tools, and then target similar jobs. In this automated world we live in, your resume may not be seen by a live person until it is sourced electronically for keywords. You want to make sure you have those keywords in your resume. Keywords are words that provide a sort of encoding in your resume that will be picked up through automation or searches for these words. Of course, you do not make up skills, but you learn how to market and target the skills you possess to the position you seek. You also want to have power words, or words that highlight and describe the skills you possess. (Success coaches who recommend getting clear: Len, 2009; Vitale, 2009; Proctor, 1997, 2009; Katz, 2009; Katz & Len, 2009; Dooley, 2009; Ferguson, 2004; Truman, 2001; Scheinfeld, 2003; Chopra, 2004, 2009; Rann & Arrott, 2005; Nemeth, 2000, 2009; Remen, 2006; Osteen, 2007; Kane & Kane, 2009; Peale, 2003; Heer, 2012; Zimmerman; 2011.

Resume Roadblock—Maria Clears Her Path

The next day, Maria stopped in at the Career Services Center. She had called ahead to schedule an appointment, and one of the counselors—Janice—greeted her when she arrived.

"I'm glad that you made an appointment to see me," said Janice, shaking Maria's hand. "On the phone you mentioned you were having difficulty getting interviews. Why don't we take a look at your resume?"

Maria followed Janice into her office and took out a few copies of her resume. She handed a copy to Janice, who looked it over thoughtfully (see Figure 5.10).

After a few moments, Janice said, "Maria, you are a good student and you've been a responsible employee since you were in high school, but your resume isn't telling your story in a compelling way."

"What do you mean by compelling?" asked Maria.

"First, you need to start thinking in terms of power words. You are also going into a competitive field, so you need to capitalize on your strengths to make up for the lack of experience you have in the legal field. I recommend focusing on the experiences that will make you stand apart from other candidates."

"What kinds of things do you think I should concentrate on?"

"Your internship is a great example!" said Janice. "Tell me more about what you did at the district attorney's office, and we can start reorganizing and cleaning up your resume. Once you have created a final version of it, you will also want to make sure you have it thoroughly proofread by several qualified people—perhaps a few English teachers here at school. You can even bring it back here to Career Services, and we will proofread it. One grammatical mistake can cost you the interview!"

Maria was surprised at what Janice said. "Thank you so much," she replied. "I had no idea that a resume was such an important tool."

Three weeks later, Maria saw Marcy and Victor on the last day of class. "Guess what!" she said. "I have an interview on Thursday at Hart & Lawrence—one of the most prestigious firms in the area!"

"That's great, Maria!" said Victor. "Marcy and I knew it was just a matter of time."

"Well, not exactly," Maria explained. "I took your advice and went to Career Services last week. One of the counselors really helped me rebuild my resume into a professional marketing tool. I may not get the job with Hart & Lawrence, but I have so much more confidence now knowing that my resume is professional and polished. I definitely think more opportunities will come my way now with a winning resume!"

Discussion Questions

1. Based on Maria's level of experience and education, what type of resume would you recommend that she use—chronological, functional, or combination?

2. How would you rewrite Maria's objective?

3. How would using power words improve Maria's work experience section? How would you rewrite that section?

(Continued)

Maria Rodriguez

555 Any COURT, Somewhere, FL 11111
PHONE 555–555-5555 E-MAIL MariaMRodriguez@dayrep.com

Education

2013-2015 Any College, Florida
Associate degree, Paralegal Studies
3.0 GPA
Member, Paralegal Club

Experience

Jan/2015 – May/2015   District Attorney's Office, Somewhere, FL
Intern
– Shadowed paralegals in District Attorney's office
– Helped paralegals draft briefs and depositions for trial preparation
– Researched cases to identify statues and recent decisions
– Filed legal paperwork

July/2006 – Dec/2013   Software, Inc. Florida
Senior Receptionist/Switchboard Operator
– Prepared documents, reports, e-mails; performed general filing
– Scheduled corporate condominiums and conference rooms
– Assisted guests with travel arrangements
– Greeted clients
– Helped human resources department with applicants and document preparation
– Insured ID tags were worn for security purposes

Skills:
– Knowledge of MS Office (Word, PowerPoint, Excel, Outlook)
– Can type 35 WPM

Oct/2000 – July/2006   Vista Resort, Florida
Reservations, Coordinator, Server
– Delivered customer service in demanding call center environment
– Reserved hotel rooms throughout the U.S.A.
– Scheduled tee times for travelers

Figure 5.10   Maria's Resume

[chapter summary]

There are many ways to create a winning resume; the key is to incorporate the elements necessary to produce the resume that lands the interview. In this chapter, you learned how to choose the resume that will best showcase your skills: chronological, functional, or combination. You learned how to use the Skills Formula tool for writing your skills, including using:

- Keywords to target the position.
- Power words to promote your skills.
- Numbers to quantify your skills.

Minimizing the challenges in resume writing such as gaps in employment history, being a victim of downsizing, or lack of experience is critical to producing a stellar resume.

Winning resumes are the centerpiece of an outstanding portfolio, and in the next chapter you will learn how to write a cover letter to not only complement your resume, but also push it to the forefront of the employers' list of applicants.

[skill/term check]

1. Which type of resume best suits your skills (chronological, functional, combination)? Why? **(LO 5-2, LO 5-5)**

2. When do you use a plain text resume? **(LO 5-2)**

3. What is the difference between a keyword and a power word? Provide an example of each. **(LO 5-3)**

4. Choose one of the skills you might add to your resume and write it using the Skills Formula. **(LO 5-4)**

[KEY TERMS]

Chronological resume: A resume that lists specific skills under each position held. **(LO 5-2)** [p. 114]

Combination resume: A resume that combines both the chronological and functional resume types; also known as a custom resume or hybrid resume. **(LO 5-2)** [p. 118]

First cut: When employers sort through a pool of applicants and accept or reject them based on their applications or resume materials. **(LO 5-2)** [p. 114]

Functional resume: A resume that organizes skills and accomplishments into groupings that support the position objective; also known as a skills resume. **(LO 5-2)** [p. 118]

Keywords: Terms related to specific skills or qualifications that employers search for in electronic resumes. **(LO 5-3)** [p. 121]

Personal reference: Someone other than an employer who can make statements about your

ethics, trustworthiness, and personality. **(LO 5-2)** [p. 117]

Plain text resume: A resume with simplified formatting, in order to prevent errors when sending it electronically. **(LO 5-2)** [p. 119]

Power words: Verbs in your resume that best describe and emphasize what actions you did in the position. **(LO 5-3)** [p. 122]

Professional reference: Someone who knows your work, such as an employer or co-worker. **(LO 5-2)** [p. 117]

Quantified skills: Skills that include specific, measurable amount(s) in numerical form. **(LO 5-4)** [p. 126]

Skills Formula™: Uses bullets, power words, and keyword skills to create quantified outcomes for your professional resume. **(LO 5-4)** [p. 125]

Winning Resumes: Real Student Examples for Resumes and References

Charles Adam Jones

5678 Evens Place   *   Somewhere, IN 12345   *   (555) 001–0001
charlesjones@dayrep.com

OBJECTIVE: Diligent Professional Manager seeking a career in Plant Management where my experiences and education will greatly benefit the organization through conscientious and methodical skill sets.

Education

*Bachelor's Degree in Business Management	*In progress (Graduation August 2016)
Florida Atlantic University	Boca Raton, FL.
Associate's Degree in Supervision	2002
Purdue University	Hammond, IN

Professional Experience

2002–Present   American Candy Company   LaPorte, IN

Production Manager
10/2013–Present

- Develop master scheduling plan for all production
- Manage all daily manufacturing
- Maintain facility and equipment resources
- In charge of hiring and training 23 first line supervisors
- Supervise/manage 5 salary associates and 80 hourly associates
- Transitioning production facility into World Class Manufacturing/Lean

Logistics Manager
07/2009–10/2013

- Established procedures to ensure quality of incoming/outgoing shipments
- Maintained monthly inventory accuracy
- Negotiated $400,000 savings in freight cost
- Responsible for handling, storage, and rotation of all raw materials and finished goods
- 99.5% on time with customer shipments
- Conducted performance appraisals and any necessary discipline

Production Supervisor
06/2007–07/2009

- Managed and led 175 hourly associates
- Designed front line production capacities
- Developed production reporting tools
- Maintained safe work environment
- Accomplished first time quality production

02/2003–06/2007   Bay Ridge Country Club   Schererville, IN

Sous Chef

- Responsible for complete production of entire kitchen
- Supervised 20 hourly employees; managed 15 hourly employees
- Managed inventory and rotation of all food products; placed orders online
- Supervised loading/unloading of all produce trucks
- Established par levels for desired inventory levels
- Managed 15 hourly employees
- Reduced monthly cost by 22% through efficient buying and routing of trucks

Charles Adam Jones

Seminars/Continuing Education

- Supply Chain Redesign and Measurement for Breakthrough Performance. University of Wisconsin-Madison, June 2013.
- Production Planning, Master Scheduling and MRP; University of Wisconsin-Madison, February 2009.
- Kaizen Blitz, University of Wisconsin-Madison, January 2010.

Honors

- Academic Honors—Florida Atlantic University

Awards

- Florida Atlantic University President's List (8 times)
- Certified in Sanitation

References available upon request

Chronological Resume Example 2

BETH TICE

7890 Cherry Valley Dr. • Rapid Rock, Texas 01234 • (555) 001–0001
elizabethtice@gustr.com

OBJECTIVE

To work in a challenging company as a successful human resources manager.

SUMMARY OF QUALIFICATIONS

- Highly motivated, enthusiastic team player
- Detailed oriented, organized, multi-tasker
- Dependable, responsible, reliable
- Dedicated to providing quality customer service
- Skilled at research and in preparing professional presentations

EDUCATION

*Bachelor of Science in Management	*In Progress
Online University	
Associate's Degree of Applied Science in Business	
Phillips College GPA 3.08	Borger, TX

EXPERIENCE

2012–Present	City of Rapid Rock Fire Department	Rapid Rock, TX

Administrative Supervisor

Serve as Fire Chief's Executive Assistant and handle the following duties for the department:

- CAFs *(Citizen Request received byway of City Manager's Office)*
- CIUR *(Mayor & Council Item Requests)*
- Public Information Request
- Manage and oversee Fire Chief's calendar and mail
- Manage and oversee Chief of Staff/Assistant Chief email inbox
- Handle incoming/outgoing mail in Fire Chief's office
- Supervise 2 full-time support personnel at fire headquarters
- Serve as backup on the council agenda management system
- Supervise customer service survey card services program
- Plan and coordinate quarterly meetings, as well as take meeting minutes
- Plan and manage annual City of Rapid Rock Combined Charities Campaign (COACCC) for fire department
- Plan, coordinate, and facilitate Quarterly Promotion & Civilian Employee Recognition Awards Ceremony

BETH TICE

7890 Cherry Valley Dr. • Rapid Rock, Texas 01234 • (555) 001–0001
elizabethtice@gustr.com

EXPERIENCE (continued)

2008–2012   City of Rapid Rock Assistant City Manager's (ACM) Office   Rapid Rock, TX

ACM Executive Secretary

- Managed and coordinated ACM's calendar
- Served as HR liaison for ACM office: Banner Timekeeping, open enrollment, as well as attend quarterly meetings
- Performed office manager-related duties: purchased office supplies and equipment, served as petty cash custodian, maintained records and files, oversaw community work area
- Handled agenda responsibilities; assigned and monitored responses on behalf of ACM and Council request for information; handled day-to-day issues
- Served as Single Point of Contact (SPOC) for ACM Office: Greater Austin Combined Charity Campaign (GACCC)
- Assisted citizens and Council Offices with concerns and complaints Researched and responded to request

2005–2008   Surplus Lines Stamping Office of TX   Rapid Rock, TX

Executive Secretary

- Coordinated off-site Board of Directors meetings
- Assisted General Manager/CEO with requests; attended meetings and took notes
- Created company brochure, employee newsletter, and annual seminar materials
- Created and designed database system to streamline seminar registration process
- Handled day-to-day administrative duties for General Manager/CEO
- Managed and maintained open records request

1998–2005   American Assurance Company   Rapid Rock, TX

Executive Assistant to Regional Vice President

Sr. Field Secretary to Texas State Manager

Sr. Secretary

PROFESSIONAL ACTIVITIES

2012–Current—Steering Committee Member for City of Rapid Rock Combined Charities Campaign
2012–2013—City-wide Coordinator–COACCC
2009–2010—Graduate of City of Rapid Rock LEAPS (Leadership Austin Pubic Service) Program

MEMBERSHIPS

2009–Current—Rapid Rock Rescue Toastmasters

ACCOMPLISHMENTS

2015   Online University President's List
2014   Online University Dean's List
2013
2012   Graduate of City of Rapid Rock (COA) Supervisor Academy

References Available

Michael Kreski

300 Juniper Drive, Ridgewood, New Jersey 07065
Telephone: 555-001-0001
Email: mikekreski@einrot.com

Objective: TO ESTABLISH A CAREER AS A MANAGER IN INFORMATION TECHNOLOGY.

Experience:

HELPDESK ANALYST: 2010–Present

UNITED HOSPITAL—UNION, NJ

- Decreased cost of generating patient registration forms from $0.46 to $0.04 per page
- Trained over 400 employees to use job-specific computer applications
- Provide Active Directory support to Windows-based operating systems to 20 servers, 320 workstations, and over 900 users
- Installed and administer tape library-based backup solution improving backup and recovery times for 13 servers using 2 tape library devices
- Implemented call tracking system, improving call tracking and reporting
- Implemented and support wireless networking to provide more efficient patient care

DEPARTMENT SECRETARY: 2005–2010

UNITED HOSPITAL—UNION, NJ

- Assisted with maintenance of staff scheduling, for 9 staff members
- Automated billing process
- Computerized report generation process
- Managed payroll
- Assisted staff with patient treatment—provided customer service to patients
- Contributed to clinical case studies

Education:

COLLEGE DEGREES:

Bachelor of Science in Information Technology
Midwestern University: Davenport, IA CGPA: 3.9 *January 2015*
Technology Infrastructure, Project Management, Network Design, Network Security, Network Operating Systems, Database Design, Structured Query Language, Advanced Web Languages for Web Design

Associate of Applied Sciences in Computer Information Systems
Midwestern University: Davenport, IA CGPA: 3.96 *September 2012*
LAN Concepts, Introduction to Programming, Computer Systems, Database Management, Technical Writing, Introduction to Web Design, Introduction to Management

TECHNICAL CERTIFICATIONS:

Specific details of the following certifications can be viewed at the official Microsoft Certified Professional transcript site by visiting https://mcp.microsoft.com/authenticate/validatemcp.aspx and entering the following case-sensitive information:

Transcript ID: 714354

Access Code: MCSE2001

Microsoft Certified Systems Administrator (MCS)
November 2013
Stellar Training Center
Certified as Systems Administrator in Microsoft Windows Server 2012 software environment

Microsoft Certified Systems Engineer (MCSE)
September 2011
Stellar Training Center
Certified as Systems Engineer in Microsoft Windows 2007 software environment

Microsoft Certified Database Administrator (MCDBA)
September 2012
Stellacon Training Center
Certified as a Database Administrator in SQL Server 2012 environment

Microsoft Certified Professional (MCP)
January 2009
New Horizons Computer Learning Center
Certified as a Professional for Windows Vista for Business environment

Awards and Memberships:

Patient Satisfaction Service Standards	*October 2014*
National Network of Libraries of Medicine—IT Subcommittee http://nnlm.gov/projects/hosplibit/	*January 2013*
Alpha Beta Kappa National Honor Society	*August 2012*

References: Professional and personal references are available.

Carol Newell

900 Class Court * Paso Robles, CA 93446 * 555-001-0001 *
carolnewell@dayrep.com

Objective

To obtain an interview with San Luis Obispo District Attorney's Office for the position of Paralegal, Investigative Administrative Clerk

Education

Bachelor of Science in Paralegal Studies   2015
  Eastern University

Paralegal Certificate   2012

  California Polytechnic State University,
  San Luis Obispo, CA

Associates of Art Degree   2006

  Ventura Community College,
  Ventura, CA

Professional Experience

05/13 – present   Tobias Law Office, Inc.   San Luis Obispo, CA

Paralegal – Estate Specialist

➢ Assistant to attorney
➢ Prepare probate pleadings, estate planning documents, estate administration documents, corporations, limited liability companies, and foundations
➢ Interview clients for pertinent information regarding estate administration matters
➢ Prepare estate tax returns (Form 706) and gift tax returns (Form 709)
➢ Manage 2 assistants and 30–35 case load
➢ Regulate and originate the monthly billing, including back up and finalization processes

08/12 – 05/13   Law Office of Wane and Wane, LLP   San Luis Obispo, CA

Paralegal – Office Manager

➢ Managed and operated a complex work environment
➢ Answered line phone system
➢ Assisted clients with all concerns and questions
➢ Managed calendaring system including important deadlines & appointments
➢ Compiled and regulated the client's billing system

09/10 – 08/12   Law Office of Stewart D. Jones   San Luis Obispo, CA

Paralegal – Office Manager

➢ Guided and directed by one family law attorney
➢ Answered line phone system
➢ Provided support for clients and attorney
➢ Generated pleadings for 250 family law cases
➢ Assembled and produced trial exhibits
➢ Managed and enabled calendaring system for deadlines and appointments
➢ Utilize time slip program to account for all billable time per client

Carol Newell

| 06/08 – 09/10 | County of San Luis Obispo | San Luis Obispo, CA |

Legal Processor II
➤ Represented San Luis Obispo Superior Court
➤ Assisted Superior and Municipal Court merging
➤ Approved and administered all judgments for dissolution of marriage
➤ Trained and supervised 12 staff with identifying and filing procedures
➤ Executed in-house memorandum communicating recommendations to Superior Court Judges

| 06/07 – 06/08 | Cellphones of San Luis Obispo | San Luis Obispo, CA |

Customer Care Representative
➤ Answered 6-line customer based telephone lines
➤ Assisted customers with their cellular phone needs
➤ Engineered special projects
➤ Persuaded customers with consultative selling skills to change plans and buy products
➤ Developed and demonstrated integrated plan to follow if the cellular system failed
➤ Used programming techniques to troubleshoot problems customers would have with their cellular phones

| 05/03 – 06/07 | Superior and Municipal Ventura Courts | Ventura, CA |

Court Services Assistant II
➤ Processed documents relating to domestic violence, divorce, probate, adoption, and foreign support matters
➤ Helped establish volunteer proper clinic to assist the public with their legal needs
➤ Managed and directed all incoming jury summons
➤ Monitored criminal and civil jury panels for judges
➤ Conducted weekly public speaking orientation to 150 jurors
➤ Initiated and balanced weekly jury payroll
➤ Computed statistical jury data created for State Judiciary

References available

Calvin Matson

2445 Nextover Drive, Crossings, Iowa 55722
555-001-0001 (C.)
555-001-0002 (H.)
calvinmatson@rhyta.com

Summary

A Strong Leader with 28 years of Diverse Experience in DSD Distribution with a Seasoned History of Building and Developing Sales Leadership Capabilities. Major strengths include Leadership, Selling Skills, Analytical Skills, Communication and Presentation Skills

Education

South University, Baton Rouge, La.

- A.A., Business Management and Marketing*   In Progress
- Graduate Fall of 2016
- 3.45 GPA

Experience

2010 – present	Professional Bakery Group	Moline, Ill.

District Manager – Eastern Iowa, Western Illinois

- Lead 2 Routes Specialists, 14 Route Sales Representatives
- 2015 Sales Projected to Deliver $7 Million in Top Line Sales
- Delivering on Plan Performance at 109.0% to Prior Year
- Analyze Sales Data to Create Plan 0 Grams
- Lead Mets Baking Integration into WholeGrains Company in Eastern Iowa

2004 – 2010	WholeGrains Baking Company	Cedar Rapids, Ia.

Sales Manager

- Led 4 Supervisors, 30 Route Sales Representatives, and 5 Relief Sales Representatives in Central Iowa and Northern Missouri
- Conducted Training and Mentoring of New Supervisors
- Responsible for Total Area P&L Performance

1998 – 2003	Checking Baking Company	Des Moines, Ia.

Supervisor

- Responsible for 5 Route Sales Representatives in Southwest Iowa
- Grew Sales Average from $5500 to $7500 per route

1990 – 1998	Checking Baking Company	Hannibal, Mo.

Supervisor

- Responsible for 5 Route Sales Representatives in Northern Mo.
- Grew business to become Market Share Leader

1988 – 1990	Colonial Baking Company	Hannibal, Mo.

Route Sales Representative

Computer Skills

- Proficient in Microsoft Excel, Microsoft Word, Microsoft PowerPoint and Microsoft Outlook

Janet Student

123 Main Street • Atlanta, GA 30342 • phone: 555-001-0001 • email: janetstudent@teleworm.us

PROFESSIONAL OBJECTIVE:

A legal position utilizing administrative, research, and analytical skills

SUMMARY OF SKILLS:

ADMINISTRATIVE
- Created business review presentations for region VP/GM detailing departmental updates
- Organized executive meetings and conferences
- Oversaw team invoices, expenses, and payment processing
- Performed as liaison between parent company and affiliate group

RESEARCH
- Prepared and reviewed medical forms for HIPAA compliance
- Conducted investigation of facts to determine legal cause of action for litigation preparation
- Discovered applicable statutes and codes in completion of legal documents
- Studied patient data for structure and compliance with Department of Health regulations

ANALYTICAL
- Audited medical charts for renewal of federal funding
- Reviewed contracts for accuracy and completion
- Identified transportation errors and implemented new scheduling procedures
- Evaluated company policies for team demonstration and training

EDUCATION:

Best University	Paralegal Studies	July 2016

Best Paralegal Club
GPA 3.51 – Dean's List – July 2015, October 2015, December 2015, March 2016

EXPERIENCE:

Sr. Administrative Assistant   Cellphone Wireless
Atlanta GA
February 2015 – Present

Administrative Assistant   Cellphone Wireless
Albany NY
October 2013 – February 2015

Medical Records Coordinator   Rainbow Senior Care
Schenectady NY
April 2012 – September 2013
- 2012 Quarterly Employee Award Recipient

Secretary/Receptionist   Rainbow Senior Care
Schenectady, NY
June 2011 – April 2012

SKILLS:

MS Word, Excel, PowerPoint, Outlook, Visio, and ERM software proficiency

John Ruben

1313 7th Ave SE Somewhere, IA 51123
Phone 555-001-0001 Email johnruben@jourrapide.com

S U M M A R Y

- 2+ years progressive management & administrative experience
- BS in Business Management
- Proficient with MS Office, Word, Excel, and the Internet

W O R K   H I S T O R Y

Grocery Store Inc.   **Assistant Manager**   Some Town, SD
2010–2015

- Full-time assistant manager w/in 6 months
- Supervise staff of 15–20 employees
- Maintain budget over $45,000
- Place product orders over $20,000
- Manage inventory control over $30,000
- Assist with payroll processing

World Dairy Inc.   **Summer Help Freezer**   Some Town, SD
2009–2010

- Worked in extreme conditions, 60+ hours a week
- Palletized products
- Loaded trucks for shipment

E D U C A T I O N

Associates Degree in Business Administration   **May 2013**
Western Tech   GPA 3.0   Another City, IA
3.6 on a 4.0 scale
Phi Theta Kappa member

Bachelor of Business Administration in Management   **May 2015**
Midwest University   GPA 3.0   A City, SD

- Accounting I & II
- Operations Management
- Advanced Excel
- Management Across Cultures
- Business Management Review
- Organizational Communications
- Organizational Behavior
- Human Resource Management

FRANK ROLLINS

2345 General Avenue
New Orleans, Louisiana 77777
555–001–0001
FrancisRollins@fleckens.hu

Objective: To obtain a position in **Business Management**, utilizing my education, training, and proven management skills.

Skills:

Software Systems:	Operating Systems:	Languages:
• Microsoft PowerPoint	• Windows Server 2012	• JAVA
• Microsoft Word	• Windows 8	• VB
• Microsoft Excel	• Windows 7	• ASP
• Microsoft Access	• Windows Vista	• HTML

Education:

Midwest University   Kansas City, Missouri
Bachelor's Degree Business Management
GPA: 3.9   May 2015

South College   Metairie, Louisiana
Associate of Science, Computer Information Systems
GPA: 3.78   May 2013

Military: **United States Marine Corps** (E-5 Retired)   May 1991 – August 2011

- Held Military Top Secret Clearance.
- Managed/Coordinated 50 accounts for the Express Travel Management Division.
- Developed, implemented, and directed government travel for musical groups throughout the United States.
- Maintained loss prevention program and supporting plans to protect $2 million in assets of unit materials and facilities.
- Created 150 presentations for military and civilian organizations for all musical commitments and government public relations performances.
- Graduated Non-Commissioned Officers School.

Experience: January 1997 – May 2001

Orleans Parish Prison
Sheriff Deputy

Louisiana Department of Labor   September 2003 – April 2009
Veterans Representative Assistant

Professional Membership/Certification:
American Legion   August 2009 – Present
Marine Corps League   January 2013 – Present

References Available Upon Request

Paul A. Smith

101 N. Main St #1, Maintown, SD 01020 ∗ 555-001-0001 ∗ PaulAlanSmith@dayrep.com

Education

Whitlock State University	**Western, SD**
*In Progress	
Master of Public Administration 3.83	
Professional project topic: *The Effects of Ethics Training on Law Enforcement Personnel*	

Whitlock State University	**Western, SD**
May 2011	
Bachelor of Science Human Services 3.3	
Law Enforcement & Probation concentration; Minor: Earth Science	

Presentations

- Presenter, Law Enforcement Intelligence Unit, *Digital Surveillance Techniques,* Bigtown, MO, 2011
- Presenter, Fraternal Order of Police, *Digital Surveillance Techniques,* Smalltown, SD 2010

Teaching/Volunteer Work

Smalley Library	**Southeast, SD**
2013 – present	
Volunteer archivist assistant working with the J. L. Smalley Collection	

Southwest Private School	**Northern, NM**
2013	
Substitute teacher for K-12 grades	

First United Methodist Church Outreach Committee	**Atown, SD**
2013	
Secretary for mission's appropriations	

Core Competencies

Interviewing, report writing, project coordination, instructing, research, data collection, team leadership, writing, editing, human relations, communication, criminal investigations, civil investigations, procedural compliance, crisis and disaster response and mitigation, interrogating, surveilling, search warrant writing and execution, court testimony and security, observing, administration, management

Professional Experience

Graduate Research Assistant	**Western, SD**
08/14 – present	

Political Science Department
Whitlock State University

- Provide assistance to faculty conducting research by collecting and arranging data, developing source materials, summarizing reports, searching the literature, compiling bibliographies, developing and operating research equipment, preparing and caring for research materials, assisting in the conduct of interviews
- Assist faculty in evaluating student work and examinations; preparing course materials and aids
- Assist in the instruction of students by conducting discussion groups within an online format

UPS Store	**Atown, SD**
04/13 – 08/14	

Sales Associate

- Provide customer service to a variety of consumers, editing documents, shipping and packaging goods, strong Internet and computer software skills

Special Agent	**Someplace, SD**
02/10–08/12	

Some State Commission

- Investigated violations of state gaming rules and laws
- Inspected licensee's operations, evaluated licensee's record keeping and internal control systems
- Presented findings from financial, criminal and civil investigations to the gaming commission and courts

Special Deputy Sheriff   **Sometown, SD**
10/07 – 02/10
   County Sheriff's Office
   • Patrolled the National Forest Service boundaries enforcing county/state/federal laws
   • Assisted National Forest Service officers with juvenile alcohol and drug violations

Patrolman S   **Sometown, SD**
06/05 – 10/07
   Sometown Police Department
   • Enforced city ordinances & state/federal laws
   • Investigated observations and/or reports of alcohol and narcotics violations

Chief Deputy Sheriff   **Some Place, SD**
6/03 – 06/05
   County Sheriff's Office
   • Instructed and supervised deputies
   • Coordinated day-to-day operations & investigations
   • Responded to calls for service, enforced county ordinances & state/federal laws

Financial Advisor   **Some City, SD**
11/02 – 08/03
   Waddell & Reed
   • Financial consultations: investment, retirement, and insurance analysis
   • Sales of financial and insurance products, licensed NASD series 6, 7, & 63

Patrolman   **Some Town, SD**
9/99 – 12/02
   Some Town Police Department
   • Answered calls for service, enforced city ordinances & state/federal laws
   • D.A.R.E officer trained

Client Manager Supervisor   **Some Town, SD**
1997 – 1999
   Community Alternatives of the Someplace Hills
   • Trained and supervised 10 client managers within a private correctional facility setting
   • Coordinated operations & investigations, case management, budget management
   • Testimony before probation and parole boards

Professional Training

   • Focus Group Interviewing, Dr. Jim Jones & Dr. Mary Greene, Univ. Minn., 2014
   • FEMA IS-700 & IS-100.LE, Atown, SD, 2012
   • Law Enforcement & Criminal Activity, UNLV Las Vegas, NV, 2009
   • Basic Narcotics Investigations (DEA), Some Town, SD, 2007
   • Rapid Deployment to High Risk Situations (SPD), WSD, 2003
   • Narcotics ID & Investigation (IPTM), WSD, 2001
   • Interview & Interrogations (IPTM), Atown, 2001
   • D.A.R.E., D.C.I., WSD, 2001
   • Certified Law Enforcement Officer, Law Enforcement Training & Standards, WSD, 2000

MANDIE MARIE BERGIN

1234 Juniper Dr. • Sterling Hts., MI 48313
mandiebergin@einrot.com • (555) 001–0001

QUALIFICATIONS PROFILE

Highly accomplished **Customer Relations Advisor** with over 14 years experience in sales, warranty administration, and customer service across a variety of automotive dealership environments.

➢ Proven leadership abilities in monitoring department operations, supervising staff productivity and performance, and collaborating with management to achieve corporate goals.

➢ Top performing service advisor with track record of driving up to $48k in monthly sales.

➢ Strong organizational and multi-tasking abilities in greeting walk-in customers, coordinating service and warranty, addressing phone inquiries and written correspondence, maintaining detailed documentation, and monitoring customer satisfaction levels.

➢ Excellent communication and interpersonal skills with customers, staff, and management.

PROFESSIONAL EXPERIENCE

KEY FORD   Present

VILLAGE FORD—Dearborn, MI   2014 to 2015

   NEW CAR SALES

   INTERNET SALES

KEY FORD—Troy, MI   2012 to 2014

Customer Relations/Service Advisor

Monitored service department operations and customer relations. Supervised 4 service advisors and 3 service porters in daily operations. Communicated with customers regarding service complaints and scheduled phone and in-person appointments. Coordinated remedial action and follow up by phone or correspondence. Maintained customer files. Interacted with customers, staff, and management.

Key Achievements:

◆ Instrumental in driving sales of automotive services from $29k to $48k a month within first year of employment.

◆ Provided leadership in identifying customer service issues, monitoring employee performance and reporting customer feedback to management.

◆ Demonstrated outstanding interpersonal skills in addressing and resolving customer concerns.

◆ Increased quality control scores by 11% within 3 months through continuous process improvements.

◆ Achieved Master Certification as Service Advisor.

VOYAGE FORD—Dearborn, MI   2005 to 2012

Service Advisor

Provided customer support regarding automotive service. Coordinated repairs including diagnosis, cost estimate, and scheduling. Maintained service documentation. Interacted with customers, service porters, customer relations, and management.

Key Achievements:

◆ Provided the highest quality service for phone, walk-in, and repeat customers to ensure 100% satisfaction and retention.

◆ Increased service sales and developed strong client base through effective listening skills, industry knowledge, cost estimating skills, and ability to gain client confidence.

◆ Earned reputation for positive attitude and motivation in a high volume, fast-paced auto service environment.

ROME FORD—Sterling Heights, MI
2001 to 2005

Warranty Administrator, Cashier

Oversaw processing of directly insured auto warranty contracts. Discussed warranty issues with customers; monitored auto diagnosis and cost estimates; reviewed repairs requiring prior approvals. Processed warranty documentation for reimbursement. Tracked accounts payable/receivable. Interacted with service advisors and parts personnel.

Key Achievements:

♦ Monitored all aspects of warranty administration for the repair of factory defects.

♦ Developed ability to price material parts and labor costs to ensure dealership and technicians were properly compensated for auto repairs.

♦ Earned promotion to Warranty Administrator within 4 months of employment.

EDUCATION

Major: Criminal Justice
(2013 to Present)

ONLINE UNIVERSITY—Virtual, IA

CERTIFICATIONS AND SEMINARS

FORD MOTOR COMPANY, Master Certification Service Advisor

Combination Resume Example 5

EMMA PATTERSON, PHR

123 Valley Circle ⊠ Hometown, AL 52345 ⊠ 555-001-0001
EmmaMaryPatterson@gustr.com

PROFESSIONAL EXPERIENCE

Arrowhead Country Club
Hometown, AL

July 2012 to present – *Human Resources Director*

• Counsel and guide 150+ employees and management on personnel issues.
• Propose, publish, and administer personnel policies and employee handbook.
• Monitor labor laws and provide direction and training to management staff.
• Prepare, recommend, and maintain records and procedures for controlling personnel transactions and reporting personnel data.
• Designed personnel forms and directed the maintenance of personnel records by all departments.
• Direct payroll processing, safety program, worker's compensation claims handling and tracking.
• Direct benefits administration, enrollment, and open enrollment meetings.
• Obtain bids upon renewal, inform management regarding benefits costs, make recommendations for employer/employee cost sharing.
• Manage open enrollment and benefits meetings.
• Developed database of 75+ organization job descriptions.
• Designed and implemented an effective recruitment program.
• Implemented procedures / provided training to hiring managers on proper way to conduct successful interviews.
• Review resumes and applications; interview and assist with the final decision process.
• Conduct needs assessment, develop training curriculum and conduct training sessions on various HR topics. Conduct orientation programs.
• Finalize year-end reconciliation audits and reports.
• Finalize all HR internal audits and approve necessary adjustments.

TRP Staffing, Inc.
Hometown, AL

September 2011 to July 2012 – *Operations Manager*

- Managed operations of branch office from general office operations to placement of temporary and direct hire labor.
- Expanded client base by 22% and extended services to new industries.
- Developed proposals and negotiated contracts with clients for continued business services.
- Effectively and efficiently managed office personnel and temporary staff assigned to clients.
- Provided leadership and training to Staffing Supervisors.
- Resolved disciplinary issues and provided counseling of temporary staff. Interpreted policies and procedures for client specific policies.
- Communicated, translated and provided interpreter services for clients' Spanish speaking staff.
- Directed the development of staffing strategies for building client base and led sourcing and recruiting initiatives and processes to leverage networking and employee referrals.

External Word Television Network
Another Town, AL

May 2010 to September 2011 – *Human Resources Generalist*
February 2007 to May 2010 – *Human Resources Specialist*

- Designed, managed, and performed daily recruitment operations.
- Established internship program to present and recruit at colleges and universities, technical schools, public employment offices, community groups, and minority organizations locally and throughout the United States.
- Benefits administrator—managed annual benefits open enrollment. Consulted, educated, assisted, and informed employees on benefits-related problems and issues.
- Developed, designed, and conducted appropriate training curricula and instructional methods for employee's individual training, group instruction, demonstration, and workshops.
- Assisted and advised senior management on Human Resources issues.
- Liaison between employee and attorney's for H1B document processing.

Vitner Painters Inc.
Some Town, AL

March 2006 to January 2007 – *Personnel Manager*

- Managed all human resource related issues for 200+ employees.
- Formulated and initiated Human Resources policies and objectives for the company, and ensured policies developed guarantee compliance.
- Trained and directed senior management on employee relations issues.
- Administered benefits programs.
- Prepared and processed payroll, month-end payroll taxes, union dues, and garnishments.
- Managed Workers' Compensation-related issues.
- Functioned as primary contact with external labor counsel including union, federal, state, and local governmental agencies.
- Recruited staff to fill positions at all levels for work on public, private, and governmental jobs.
- Developed and managed all safety training materials (in Spanish and English) in accordance with OSHA guidelines.

EDUCATION

A.S., Human Resource Management, *Virginia College*	June 2015
Certificate in Accounting, *Lawson State*	June 2009
Certificate in Human Resource Management, *University of North Alabama*	February 2008
Certified Needs Assessment, *University of Alabama*	February 2008

PROFESSIONAL AFFILIATIONS

March 2009 to present	Member of Society for Human Resources Management
March 2009 to present	Member of Birmingham Society of Human Resources Management
March 2009 to present	Certified Professional in Human Resources

COMMUNITY INVOLVEMENT

September 2011	Vice President Alabama Association of Colleges and Employers
January 2009 to December 2015	Advisory Board for Herzing College

REFERENCES

References available upon request

References For

Paul A. Smith

*101 N. Main St #1, Maintown, SD 01020 * 555-001-0001 * PaulAlanSmith@dayrep.com*

References

Dr. Hawkens	CJ Professor	Western University	555-001-0005
Sandy Smith	Attorney	Smith Law Firm	555-001-0003
Pat Wren	Sheriff	Specific County	555-001-0008

Education

Whitlock State University
Master of Public Administration   3.83
Professional project topic: *The Effects of Ethics Training on Law Enforcement Personnel*

Western, SD
*In Progress

Whitlock State University
Bachelor of Science Human Services   3.3
Law Enforcement & Probation concentration; Minor: Earth Science

Western, SD
May 2011

EMMA PATTERSON, PHR

123 Valley Circle ◇ Hometown, AL 52345 ◇ Cell: 555-001-0001
EmmaMaryPatterson@gustr.com

PROFESSIONAL REFERENCES

Dr. Michael Slone Director ~ Technical College / Workforce Development
123 River Drive
A Town, KY 40119
1-555-001-0001 Ext. 1234
michaelslone@wfd.gv

Trish Austin RN ~ Shift Supervisor Telecom @ A Town Medical Center
PO Box 123
A Town, KY 41234
1-555-001-0001
trish.austin@medcen.com

Karen Fries LPN ~ Staff Nurse
13 Upper Cal Road
A Town, KY 41234
1-555-001-0001
fries.k@rhs.du

Krista M. Olsen

530 Hackberry Circle, Cedar City, SD 57703   *   555-555-5555   *
KristaOlsen@email.com

Education

Paralegal Studies

Western Dakota Technical Institute   (WDT)   **Cedar City, SD**   2002
Associate Degree

Core Competencies

Outstanding attention to detail, organization, client relations, excellent oral and written communication skills, procedural knowledge, legal terminology, strong work ethic, efficient, effective, meticulous, ambitious, punctual, flexible, problem solver, team worker. Strong computer skills - Microsoft Office, Odyssey E-File & Serve.

Professional Experience

Paralegal

04/14-Present

Murphy, Johnson & Vanderbeek Prof. L.L.C.

Primary paralegal to Michal Murphy.

- Type, draft, summons, complaints, demand letters to insurance companies/defendants.
- Open new files, manage client database, calendar court dates, due dates and appointments.
- Prepare correspondence to counsel and clients.
- Organize and produce discovery to opposing counsel.
- Assist other attorneys and paralegals.
- Communicate w/counsel, clients, doctors' offices, to complete legal forms.
- Proficient with Odyssey E-File & Serve system.
- Detailed knowledge of legal terminology, procedures and processes.

Legal Secretary

12/03-01/14

Ember County Public Defender's Office   **Cedar City, SD**

10+ years Legal Secretary

- Primary legal secretary for 6 criminal defense attorneys.
- Typed, drafted, modified, corrected and prepared appeals for the South Dakota Supreme Court.
- Assisted heavy client load for 24/7 Sobriety Program.
- Ordered transcripts, corresponded with State Attorney's Office, typed motions, prepared notice of appeal.
- Managed 3000+ case files in 10 years.
- Proficient with Odyssey E-File & Serve system.
- Detailed knowledge of legal terminology, procedures and processes.

Deputy Court Clerk

06/02-11/03

Unified Judicial System Clerk of Courts for Ember County   **Cedar City, SD**

- Provided exemplary client services at counter and phone.
- Efficiently received and filed documents with the court system.
- Accurately prepared files for Judges.

Krista M. Olsen

Store Assistant/Baker   **Cedar City, SD**

06/95-05/02

Best Food and Drug Supermarket

- Superior customer service.
- Baked and packaged food; decorated cakes.

Performance

- Noted for excellence in interpersonal communications, legal documents, attention to detail, teamwork, flexibility and reliability.
- High performance with or without supervision.

References

References, transcripts, additional work history and any further information available upon request

chapter 6

Professional Cover Letters and Applications

> " *Until one is committed there is hesitancy, the chance to draw back,*
> *always ineffectiveness . . .*
> *[T]he moment one definitely commits oneself, then Providence moves too.*
> *All sorts of things occur to help one that would never otherwise have occurred.*
> *A whole stream of events issues from the decision, raising in one's favor all*
> *manner of unforeseen incidents and meetings and material assistance,*
> *which no man could have dreamt would have come his way. . . .*
> *Boldness has genius, power, and magic in it.*
>
> —W.H. Murray "

target competency > *Develop professional cover letters and complete error-free applications.*

learning outcomes

After studying this chapter, you should be able to:

LO 6-1 Understand the components of a professional cover letter.

LO 6-2 Write an effective cover letter to accompany your resume.

LO 6-3 Demonstrate how to complete an error-free application.

High Expectations

Twenty-year-old Alison DuBois expected to graduate next month from Green Valley School of Massage Therapy at the top of her class. She hoped to work in an upscale salon. In preparation, she had been checking listings on the Internet, and was elated to find the following ad:

Massage Center, Massage Bliss
Professional Massage Therapist needed for busy clinic. Principal duties include: Perform consecutive 50-minute quality massage therapy sessions; Design specific sessions based on client's individual needs; Promote the health and wellness benefits to clients receiving massage therapy on a regular basis; Create excellent experience for members/guests through friendly and helpful attitude; Generate new clientele through promoting member referral and guest pass programs; Help maintain professionalism and cleanliness of therapy rooms and common areas.

License Required: New York State Massage Therapist

Experience Required: No experience needed; submit online application together with resume and cover letter online.

The position sounded ideal! Though Alison knew that the job market was competitive, she didn't want to lose out on the opportunity. She had been working on her resume in her career exploration class and thought it was in pretty good shape. She immediately forwarded her resume to the e-mail address listed with the ad. After rereading the listing, though, Alison noted that she was also supposed to send a cover letter and the application. She had not learned how to create a cover letter in her career class yet, so without consulting her instructor or the Career Services Department at Green Valley, she wrote the following e-mail message to the Massage Bliss clinic:

To whom it may concern,

I saw your ad for a massage therapist on jobs.com. I would like to apply for the position. I'm a top student at Green Valley School of Massage Therapy. I've already sent you my resume. I hope to hear from you soon. I'll send in the application you want, too. Please consider me.

Thank you,
Alison DuBois

As she began to tackle the online application, she thought to herself *"Wow, this is long and complicated!"* She noticed that much of the information, such as references, employment history, and education were already on her resume, so she assumed she didn't need to fill out those sections. She also left several of the application questions blank, or wrote "see resume." In addition, she felt that several of the questions were somewhat nosey and intrusive. Why did they need to know if she had been convicted of a crime? She assumed the question was just fishing for information, and decided not to answer it. *"After all,"* she thought, *"the application is just a formality. No one really reads it."*

Finally, Alison reached the last section on the application. One of the questions asked "Do you hold a New York State massage therapist license?" Alison was planning to take the licensing exam right after graduation, so she answered "Yes." If she was hired for this position, she had no doubt she would pass the test by the time she began working there. She submitted her application, confident that she would receive a positive response from the salon right away.

One week later, Alison received a reply e-mail from the clinic. Instead of inviting her for an interview as she had expected, she was stunned at the response:

Thank you for your interest in the Massage Therapist position with Massage Bliss. We regret to inform you that we are considering other applicants at this time.

Alison had no idea what she had done wrong. She had submitted all of the materials the clinic had asked for, and would certainly be well qualified for the job after completing the Green Valley program and passing her licensing exam. She felt confused and didn't know how to move forward with her job search after reading the e-mail.

Discussion Questions

1. What mistakes did Alison make?
2. How do you think Alison should have handled the question about the required massage therapy license?
3. Was Alison correct in assuming she didn't need to answer certain questions on that application that were already covered in her resume?

» LO6-1 The Components of Professional Cover Letters

Your cover letter is more than an introduction to your resume. Some employers view a resume without a cover letter as an incomplete application. Students often write cover letters that contain just a few vague sentences, wrongly assuming that they just need something to send in with their resume. In this chapter, you'll learn how a cover letter can support your resume, and the key parts that make up an effective cover letter.

The cover letters shown in Figures 6.1 and 6.2 would cause an employer to be less enthusiastic about the accompanying resumes—and the candidates. Your cover letter is another marketing tool and should be used to frame your skills and experiences as much as your resume. If you do not put in the time and effort to create a valuable cover letter, it can be a turn-off that keeps employers from reading your resume. Also, your cover letter can come in the form of an e-mail. If you have been asked to send an electronic copy of your resume and are not sending a hard copy, then you will send your cover letter as an e-mail.

A resume without a cover letter is like an incomplete pass in a game—even if your resume is great, you might not score the interview.
—Dr. Karine Blackett

Your cover letter is the opportunity to show the employer how you can add value to the organization.

Cover Letter Workshop

Your cover letter and your application are often the first impressions you make with a potential employer. Your cover letter is the opportunity to show the employer how you can add value to the organization.

You must include several items such as the following in your cover letter:

- **Return address:** This is your address. Include your phone number and e-mail address.
- **Date:** The date you send the letter.
- **Inside address:** This is the company's address and the name of the person you are sending the application to.

World News Inc.
123 Nowhere Avenue
Auburn, FL 33214

To Whom it May Concern,

I am interested in the administration position you have listed on careerbuilder.com. I wanted to introduce myself as someone that can bring a great deal to your company.

Please see my attached resume and you will see that I am fully qualified for this position. I feel that I would be a great asset to your company.

You can reach me at 555-1234.

Thank you for your time,

Tammy Dunn

Tammy Dunn

Figure 6.1 **Ineffective Cover Letter #1**

August 5, 2015

To Whom It May Concern:

I am responding to the full-time position as a paralegal at Banks & Banks law firm. Please see my resume. I believe I would enjoy this position, and I look forward to your response.

Thank you for your consideration.

Missy Wilson

Missy Wilson

Figure 6.2 **Ineffective Cover Letter #2**

- **Greeting/Salutation:** Call and find out the name of the hiring person, so you can address the greeting to a specific person. Make sure you ask for the correct spelling. Use Mr., Mrs., Ms., or Dr. and a colon after the name. Do not begin your letter with "*To Whom It May Concern.*" That greeting is impersonal, and suggests you didn't do the necessary work to find out who will be reading the letter. This will put a negative spin on your letter and resume. "*Dear HR:*" is also not the best option. If you absolutely cannot find a person's name to send your cover letter and application to, use "*Dear Members of the Search Committee:*" or "*Dear Sir/Madam.*" Address the letter to the manager of the specific department you are applying to if you do not have a name.

Body of the Letter

Three paragraphs are customary for the body of your cover letter. The body is where you have the opportunity to further sell yourself to the hiring manager.

Opening sentence to paragraph one The first sentence in your letter should grab the hiring person's attention and set you apart from other candidates. Do not state the obvious in this first sentence. For example, this is a common and lackluster opening sentence in a cover letter: *I was very excited to see your advertisement for the XYZ position on May 16 on Monster.com.* If you have a contact name to mention for the position, the first sentence is the place to do it. Here are a few examples of strong opening sentences:

- Seven years as a certified Network Administrator with experience in LAN/WAN network design, implementation, and support is what I bring to the open Senior Network Administrator position.

- Kevin Beck suggested I contact you directly regarding the open [position you are applying for] position with [company name]. With over 10 years in the [industry] field, and proven experience with [specific skill], [specific skill], and [specific skill], I will add value to your organization.

- Please accept this letter and attached resume as my application for the open [position you are applying for] position.

Paragraph one This paragraph states the purpose of your letter, including which position you are applying for, if someone referred you, and where you saw the advertisement (if there was one). Capture the reader's interest by highlighting some of your qualifications.

Paragraph two This is where you market your skills and target them to the position. The second paragraph needs to clearly explain why you should be interviewed. Focus on your actual accomplishments, skills, and experiences, and target them to the position's requirements. Look at the description of the position. What is the employer looking for in terms of skills and experience?

As with your resume, why is it critical for you to target the skills on your cover letter to the specific position opening?

Be sure to quantify the skills you are highlighting. Numbers catch the eye and are great marketing tools. Do not make vague statements about your soft skills, such as how reliable you are, and that you are a great communicator. The following are soft skills you should limit in your cover letter and resume unless you back them up with examples:

Communication skills	Multitasker
Creative	Organized
Detail-oriented	Patient
Driven	Punctual
Empathetic	Quick learner
Flexible	Self-motivated
Honest	Strong work ethic
Listening skills	Team player
Multicultural	Tolerant

Soft skills should be used sparingly in your resume and cover letter because they rarely make an impact. Think about it—you say you are a great communicator, but there are thousands of other people looking for a job who may also be great communicators. Instead, use a specific example to demonstrate each soft skill you are trying to highlight. Prove that you have the skill you are stating. For example, you could show evidence of strong communication skills by providing specific examples of your writing or public speaking experience. Another pitfall to avoid is overusing the pronoun "I." Mix your sentence structure so you are not starting every sentence (or every other sentence) with "I."

A simple way to target your cover letter to a position is to use a two-column bulleted skills format in paragraph two. This type of format presents the skills that the employer seeks in the left-hand column and the applicable skills or experience you have that match each requirement in the right-hand column. Title the first column "You Require," or "Requirements for Position," followed by a brief bulleted list underneath. Title the second column "I Have," "I Offer," or "My Qualifications," and bullet your related skills underneath. It would look something like this:

Requirements for Position	My Qualifications:
• BS/BA in Computer Science, IT, or 7 years applicable professional experience and education.	• AA degree in Computer Technology plus 8 years as a Network Systems Administrator.
• Experience in network design, implementation, and troubleshooting of network devices.	• Responsible for the design, configuration, installation, and troubleshooting network devices (switches, router and firewalls).
• Cisco CCNA certification minimum required. Cisco CCIE preferred.	• Cisco CCNA certified in April 2014. Currently studying for CCIE certification.

Action paragraph The final paragraph in a cover letter that takes action by asking for the interview, and stating when you will call the employer to follow up on the application.

Paragraph three The third paragraph is your action paragraph. The **action paragraph** is the final paragraph in a cover letter that takes action by asking for the interview, and stating when you will call the employer to follow up on the application. Politely request the interview. Let them know when you will contact them, and then do it. You can also add that you look forward to the next step or discussing the position further with them.

Closing Acceptable closures include *Yours sincerely*, *Sincerely*, and *Respectfully*. The last, *Respectfully*, is recommended for letters to law firms. Leave room for your signature and remember to sign the letter and add contact information immediately under the closing, or in the heading. If sending the cover letter electronically, there are several options for your signature. Some people prefer to use a script-like font, which can be set in an ink color such as blue, to create a signature. Others prefer to insert a small image file with a picture of their actual signature, while some simply type their name. As long as the closing is professional, you can choose how to handle your digital signature. Finally, write "Enclosure" at the bottom to indicate that you are sending your resume as an attachment to the e-mail.

Additional tools for cover letters

- **Limit Abbreviations:** Keep abbreviations limited to words that are universally abbreviated, such as states. For example, write out Bachelor of Science rather than using the abbreviation B.S.
- **Follow the Resume Style:** Use the same header, font, formatting, and paper as your resume. Your cover letter should work together with your resume.
- **Don't Restate Resume:** Keep your cover letter fresh. Do not repeat the skills and verbiage that you used on your resume.

Why do you think it is important to include a handwritten or electronic signature at the end of your cover letter?

- **Focus on the Company:** Show the company and hiring agent what you can do for them, not focus on what they can do for you. State the special skills and personal attributes that you bring to the table. Focus on how you can add value to the company.

- **Business Format:** Do not handwrite your cover letter. Always use a business letter format (find a template in Word, or conduct an Internet search). Use one-inch margins and double space between paragraphs.

- **Accurate:** Have your cover letter checked by one or more trusted professionals for spelling and grammar, as well as content.

- **One Page:** Keep the cover letter length to one page.

- **Attitude:** Write in a positive style. Demonstrate your enthusiasm.

- **Contact Information:** Make sure you add your phone number, e-mail address, and mailing address in the letter. Your contact information can be located in the heading above the company information or below your name. Do not embed your contact information within the letter itself, as it is more difficult to locate.

- **Bullets:** Add impact and organization to a cover letter with bullets, but use them sparingly. Your cover letter is not your resume.

careercoach6.1

How to Handle the Salary Requirement

Some employment ads will ask you to list your salary requirements on your resume, cover letter, or application. It is crucial that you are diplomatic and careful in how you word this information. You don't want to be eliminated from the candidate pool for not answering this question, and you don't want to be eliminated for stating a salary that is out of the company's range. If the employer insists on knowing your salary requirement, then you are better off giving one. One way to handle this is to know what the job is worth and use a desired range, such as $45,000–$55,000. You can use an online salary calculator, such as www.salary.com or www.payscale.com/, to find salary ranges in specific geographic locations. However, if you can avoid a specific number, do so. State instead that salary is negotiable, or that you would like to know more about the specifics of the job to properly discuss the salary. Be aware that if you state a number, the employer may try to hold you to it. It will not leave much room, if any, for negotiation. Some students have reported posting their resumes on job boards online, and stating their desired salaries. Later they were held to that salary range when offered the position—much like a contract. For this reason, leave salary information off job boards as well. Use the terms *Negotiable* or *Open* instead when referring to your desired salary.

Putting It All Together

The cover letter template in Figure 6.3 demonstrates the popular and effective one-column bulleted list.

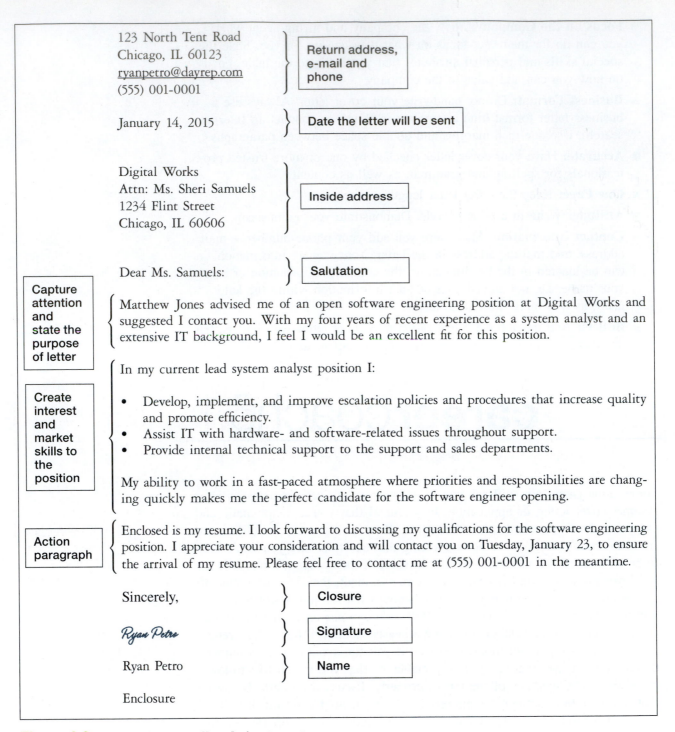

123 North Tent Road
Chicago, IL 60123
ryanpetro@dayrep.com
(555) 001-0001

Return address, e-mail and phone

January 14, 2015

Date the letter will be sent

Digital Works
Attn: Ms. Sheri Samuels
1234 Flint Street
Chicago, IL 60606

Inside address

Dear Ms. Samuels:

Salutation

Capture attention and state the purpose of letter

Matthew Jones advised me of an open software engineering position at Digital Works and suggested I contact you. With my four years of recent experience as a system analyst and an extensive IT background, I feel I would be an excellent fit for this position.

Create interest and market skills to the position

In my current lead system analyst position I:

- Develop, implement, and improve escalation policies and procedures that increase quality and promote efficiency.
- Assist IT with hardware- and software-related issues throughout support.
- Provide internal technical support to the support and sales departments.

My ability to work in a fast-paced atmosphere where priorities and responsibilities are changing quickly makes me the perfect candidate for the software engineer opening.

Action paragraph

Enclosed is my resume. I look forward to discussing my qualifications for the software engineering position. I appreciate your consideration and will contact you on Tuesday, January 23, to ensure the arrival of my resume. Please feel free to contact me at (555) 001-0001 in the meantime.

Sincerely,

Closure

Ryan Petro

Signature

Ryan Petro

Name

Enclosure

Figure 6.3   One-Column, Bulleted List Cover Letter

Student Sample Cover Letters

Even though there is a prescribed format for a cover letter, there are still many winning variations, as you can see in Figures 6.4–6.7.

PATRICIA SMITH
1234 Bakers Street • Dallas, Texas 77777 • (555) 555-1234
PatriciaRSmith@cuvox.de

December 17, 2014

Dr. Mary Windham
Director of Personnel
Dallas Independent School District
PO Box 1234
Dallas, TX 77777

Dear Dr. Windham:

Dallas ISD possesses a reputation for providing an exceptional education and achieving above-average scores on standardized tests, and I would like to assist Dallas ISD with continuing to offer a high level of education to the students within this district.

I have taken the following actions to meet the requirements to teach within Texas:

- Bachelors of Management with Education minor, from South University.
- Completed an alternative teaching certificate program with *A Career in Teaching* in Dallas, Texas, from September to October 2014.
- Passed TEXAS EC-4 Generalist Exam for teaching December 2014.

In addition to the above actions, I also obtained experience working with children through supervising YKID After School Programs from August 2004–May 2014, which were operated in cooperation with Dallas ISD.

Please accept my letter of interest and resume for the Kindergarten through 3rd grade teaching positions that are open within Dallas ISD for the 2015–2016 school year. I look forward to the opportunity to give back to a school district that provided me an exceptional education from elementary school through high school graduation. I will contact you next week to arrange a time that is good for both of us, or feel free to contact me before that time at (555) 001-0001.

Sincerely,

Patricia Smith

Patricia Smith
Enclosures

Figure 6.4 Sample Cover Letter #1

Valerie Herns
213 Johnson Drive
Anywhere, NC 23456
December 17, 2015

Robert Boyd
Down To Earth Computers
1100 Commerce Avenue
Jacksonville, NC 28546

Dear Mr. Boyd:

I am writing in response to your advertisement in the Jacksonville Daily News for a Computer Field Technician. After reading your job description, I am confident that my skills and my passion for technology are a perfect match for this position.

I would bring to your company a broad range of skills, including:

• Hardware installation and troubleshooting
• Software installation and troubleshooting
• Driving knowledge of Eastern NC
• Parts inventory record keeping
• Great customer service skills

I would welcome the opportunity to further discuss this position with you. If you have questions or would like to schedule an interview, please contact me by phone at (555) 001-0001 or by e-mail at valerieherns@rhyta.com. I have enclosed my resume for your review, and I look forward to hearing from you. I will be calling your office on Wednesday, December 20, to see if there is a good time we can meet.

Sincerely,

Valerie Herns

Valerie Herns
Enclosure

Figure 6.5 Sample Cover Letter #2

Tamara Schultz
2123 Oak St
Brooklyn, NY 11212
May 14, 2015

Mr. John Cunningham
Human Resource Manager
Valley Microsystems
123 Lead Pkwy.
Las Vegas, NV 25684

Dear Mr. John Cunningham:

I am writing in response to your advertisement on Vegashotdice.com for a network administrator. Your advertisement addresses my qualifications perfectly. I can offer you the precise skills for which you're searching.

You seek someone with the ability to:	Do I possess this ability?
• Train and support local and remote area network users.	✓ Yes
• Plan and support LAN based on Microsoft Windows 2012.	✓ Yes
• Manage security, capacity planning, and database support for Microsoft SQL Server™ database and maintain LAN/nationwide office links.	✓ Yes
• Deal effectively with Windows and provide SQL Server database support.	✓ Yes

I hope you'll agree that your needs and my capabilities are a perfect match, because it would be a thrill to join a firm with the technological talent yours employs.

Please contact me at (555) 001-0001 evenings or weekends, or by mail at the address above. I'd be pleased to set up a meeting whenever it's convenient for you.

Sincerely,

Tamara Schultz

Tamara Schultz

Enclosure

Figure 6.6   Sample Cover Letter #3

Dr. Tamara Khelly
Assistant Chair, Professional Studies
College of Arts and Sciences
Online University

Dear Dr. Khelly,

I am a firm believer that providing sound structure and support for faculty and students are two key factors for faculty and student success. Due to my strong background in higher education instruction, design and administration, I feel I demonstrate the qualifications and skills you seek for the Assistant Academic Department Chair.

You seek a Department Chair:

- Who is adept at metrics, surveys and curricular development

- Who can schedule classes, train, assign, supervise & monitor faculty
- Who can provide seminar coverage
- Who has positive working relationships with peers and external departments

- Who can teach online, contribute scholarship and service

I have:

- Curriculum development experience including designing & assessing online courses with rubrics, outcome standards, and course surveys
- Hired, trained, assessed, monitored & mentored online faculty from 3 universities
- Substituted for other faculty/able to cover seminars
- A proven 7 year history of positive work relationships internally and among other campuses and departments
- Over 6 years online teaching experience, published, Master's in Higher Education, and service experience professionally

In addition to my extensive teaching and instructional design experience, I have strong writing skills, education, and administrative experience. My broad background in online instruction at XYZ University and American University Online make me an excellent candidate for this position.

Thank you for your consideration. I look forward to the next step.

Sincerely,

Maria Ortiz

Maria Ortiz
555-001-0001
mortiz@jourrapide.com

Figure 6.7 Sample Cover Letter #4

Cyber Trip 6.1

Cover Letter Tutorial and Quiz Visit Quintessential Careers at http://www.quintcareers.com/cover_letter_tutorial.html to work through an online tutorial and quiz on cover letters. Practice makes perfect when it comes to your marketing tools!

Have someone critique your cover letter as well as your resume.

e x e r c i s e 6.1

Critique the Cover Letter

Use the grading rubric in Figure 6.8 to critique the cover letter below.

> *January 20, 2016*
> *1234 Jones Way W. North Platte, NJ 08666*
>
> Dear *Whom It May Concern,*
>
> I have just graduated from Country South University's Fraud Investigations Program and saw your ad regarding a Fraud Investigator in the Bucks County Courier Times.
>
> I look forward to further discuss this job opportunity and how I can contribute to the success of *unknown name. Please see my attached resume.*
>
> Hopefully, we will be able to sit down and talk more about me. I want to tell you about the things that that I posses that will benefit your company. If time permits, I will call you.
>
> Sincerely,
>
> *[sign your name] Tricia Moore*

Student Name:		Circle Score		
		Not Included	**Needs Improvement**	**Present**
1	Contains all structural elements: date, inside addresses, salutation, body, closing, enclosure	0	1–2–3	⟨4⟩–5
2	Signed or e-signed	0	1–2–3	4–⟨5⟩
3	Has short, action-oriented, concise paragraphs	0	1–2–3	⟨4⟩–5
4	Addressed to a specific person	0	⟨1⟩–2–3	4–5
5	Interesting, captures attention	0	1–2–3	⟨4⟩–5
6	Positive and assertive	0	1–2–⟨3⟩	4–5
7	Identifies and targets a specific position	0	1–⟨2⟩–3	4–5
8	Targets skills and experiences to position	0	1–2–3	4–5
9	Identifies method of follow-up	0	1–2–3	4–5
10	Correct grammar, spelling, and punctuation	0	1–2–3	4–5
11	Limits starting sentences with "I"	0	1–2–3	4–5
12	Limits abbreviations	0	1–2–3	4–5
13	Uses action words	0	1–2–3	4–5
14	Left-justified with no indents for paragraphs	0	1–2–3	4–5
15	Brief—no more than one page	0	1–2–3	4–5
16	Appropriate font and print size, matches resume	0	1–2–3	4–5
17	Professional	0	1–2–3	4–5
18	Neat and easy to read	0	1–2–3	4–5
19	Double spaced between paragraphs	0	1–2–3	4–5
20	Uses business letter format—single space	0	1–2–3	4–5
21	If template was used, all prompters from template are removed or hidden (such as *sign your name here* or *date here*)			
22	Includes verbiage "Enclosure" if the resume is attached under the signature			
	Comments:			

Figure 6.8   Cover Letter Grading Rubric

 **SELF-CHECK**

1. What is the purpose of a cover letter?

2. Who should you address in your greeting of a cover letter if you do not have the hiring person's name?

3. How many paragraphs are customary for a cover letter?

» LO6-2 Writing an Effective Cover Letter

Cover letters are more than an introduction to your resume. They are an essential marketing tool.

The cover letter demonstrates that you can write complete sentences, construct paragraphs, organize your thoughts, and make strong statements. To ensure your cover letter is a cut above other applicants, remember to:

> Cover letters are an essential marketing tool.

1. Personalize your cover letter.
2. Reference the title of the position.
3. Use the hiring agent's name, along with Mr., Ms., or Dr. to greet them.
4. Target your skills to the position.
5. Avoid using soft skills unless you provide specific examples.
6. Use an action paragraph to close.
7. Use varied sentences; avoid using "I" too much.
8. Write clearly and concisely.
9. Use the same fonts, paper, and headings that are on your resume.
10. Include your contact information.
11. Use the business letter format.
12. End your letter with *Sincerely, Yours sincerely,* or *Respectfully* (the last is most appropriate when applying to attorney offices/law firms).

Cyber Trip 6.2

Cover Letters   Listed below are a few websites where you can learn more about cover letters. You can also search online for additional sources using keywords such as "cover letter samples" or "writing a cover letter" in your favorite search engine. Share your findings with the class. Resume Resource: http://www.resume-resource.com/cover-letter-examples-professional-writers/Quintessential Careers: http://www.quintcareers.com/cover_letter_samples.html Purdue Online Writing Center:https://owl.english.purdue.edu/owl/resource/698/01/

exercise 6.2

Practice Writing a Cover Letter

Read the following job posting, and draft a cover letter for this position using what you have learned about professional cover letters. You can improvise your skills for this letter. Use correct professional business letter formatting.

A busy ophthalmic retinal practice is seeking an energetic individual with impeccable organizational skills to function as a full-time Clinical Study Assistant for multiple ongoing clinical trials. A detail-oriented person is desired. Duties to include scheduling of patient study visits, organization and maintenance of medical charts, completion of Case Report Forms, filing of study correspondence, answering phones and drug accountability. Prior clinical study or medical office experience is preferred, but not required. We offer an excellent compensation and benefit package. Please e-mail resume/application to MidwestEye@rhyta.com, or mail to Mid-West Eye Specialists Attention: Mark Wells, 629 17th Street, Somewhere, CO 80555.

Think about what you want to include in your cover letter. Do the skills that you want to include complement the skills and experience on your resume?

Now that you have the basics down for creating cover letters, you can begin to think about what skills you want to showcase in your own cover letter. To do this, refer to your transferable skills, adaptive skills, and job seeking skills that you identified in Chapter 2, and look at the skills you listed in your resume. Just as you targeted your resume, you will want to target the cover letter to the position you seek. At this point, you might not know the exact job title, so you might need to improvise for the following portfolio project.

my portfolio 6.1

Draft Your Cover Letter

Choose one of the two cover letter formats from Figure 6.9 or Figure 6.10 and fill in your information. Later, transfer this information to a business letter Word document. Use the Cover Letter Checklist in Exercise 6.3 to ensure you have all of the needed elements for a winning cover letter.

(Continued)

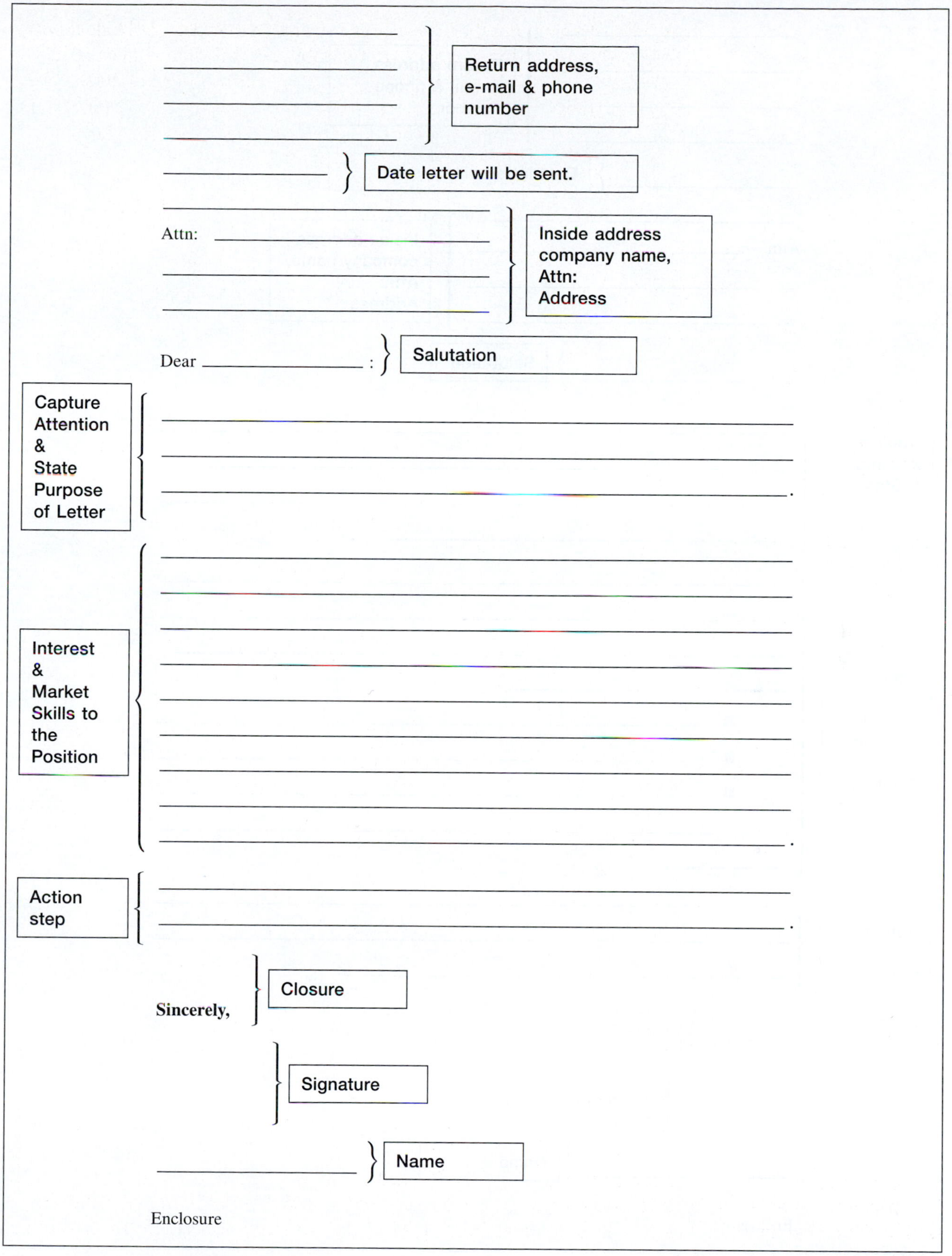

_____ } Return address,
_____ } e-mail & phone
_____ } number
_____

_____ } Date letter will be sent.

_____
Attn: _____ } Inside address
_____ } company name,
_____ } Attn:
                             Address

Dear _____ : } Salutation

Capture Attention & State Purpose of Letter

_____
_____
_____.

Interest & Market Skills to the Position

_____
_____
_____
_____
_____
_____
_____
_____
_____.

Action step

_____
_____.

Sincerely, } Closure

} Signature

_____ } Name

Enclosure

Figure 6.9   **Cover Letter Template #1**

(Continued)

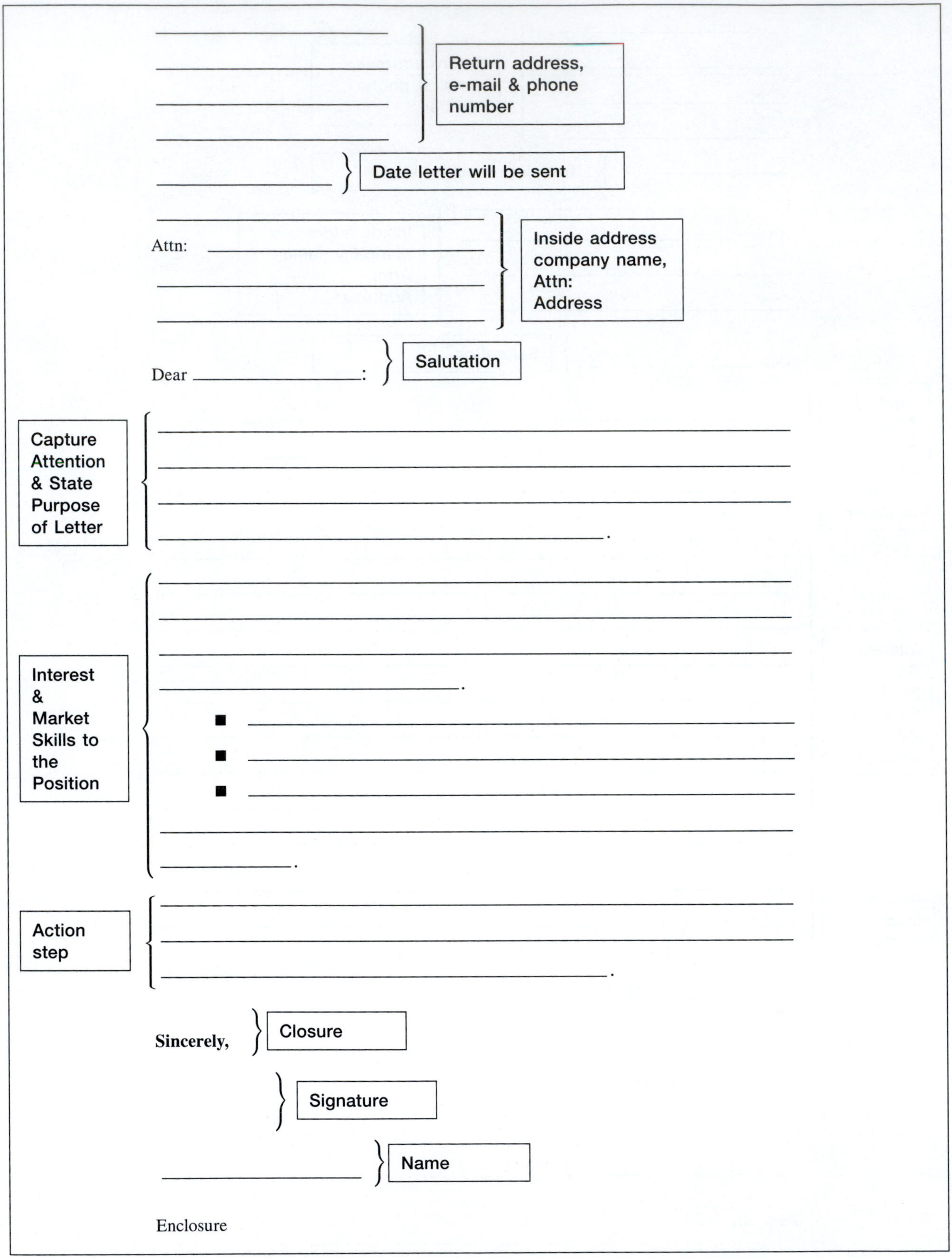

_____

_____   Return address,
                             e-mail & phone
_____   number

_____ } Date letter will be sent

_____

Attn: _____ } Inside address
                            company name,
_____   Attn:
                            Address
_____

Dear _____: } Salutation

Capture Attention & State Purpose of Letter
_____
_____
_____
_____.

Interest & Market Skills to the Position
_____
_____
_____
_____.
■ _____
■ _____
■ _____
_____
_____.

Action step
_____
_____
_____.

Sincerely, } Closure

} Signature

_____ } Name

Enclosure

Figure 6.10   **Cover Letter Template #2**

exercise 6.3

Cover Letter Checklist

Use the checklist in Figure 6.11 on the cover letter(s) you created in My Portfolio 6.1. The cover letter checklist can be used on each letter you create and will help ensure you have included all of the critical elements in each one.

Name:		Not Included	Present
1	All structural elements present: date, inside addresses, salutation, body, closing enclosure		
2	Signed		
3	Action-oriented, concise paragraphs		
4	Addressed to a specific person		
5	Interesting, captures attention		
6	Positive and assertive		
7	Targets a specific position		
8	Targets skills and experiences to position		
9	Identifies method of follow-up		
10	Correct grammar, spelling, punctuation		
11	Limits starting sentences with "I"		
12	Limits abbreviations		
13	Uses action words		
14	Left-justified		
15	Brief—no more than one page		
16	Appropriate font and print size, matches resume		
17	Professional format		
18	Neat and easy to read		
19	Double spaced between paragraphs		
20	Uses business letter format with single spacing and no indent for paragraphs		
21	If template was used, all prompters from template removed or hidden (such as *sign your name here* or *date here*)		
22	Includes verbiage "Enclosure" if the resume is attached under the signature		
	Comments:		

Figure 6.11 Cover Letter Checklist

» LO6-3 Completing an Error-Free Application

Job applications are designed to keep you out of the hiring pool—not in it.

Applications, like resumes, often receive only a few seconds of the hiring person's time before he or she makes a decision to continue reading or place in the "no" pile. While many companies still ask job candidates to fill out paper applications, some will ask you to complete an application online. However, many companies do not use formal applications or have a human resources department for screening applicants. If you do need to complete an application, keep in mind they are designed to eliminate as many candidates as possible. They ask very specific and limited questions, and the answers do matter.

Think of the application as the first "job" an employer gives you. This should reframe the task of completing it! Employers are screening for reasons to remove your application from the hiring pool. With that in mind, there are some things you can do so that your application takes you to the next step in the hiring process.

What can you do to ensure you shine above the other candidates when filling out your application?

Application Guidelines

Applications are more than a tool for employers to gather contact information and work history. By using the following guidelines, you will dramatically increase your chances of completing a winning application and making it to the next step in the hiring process.

- **Follow all directions**. Employers are trying to screen out candidates who cannot follow directions. Read the entire application before you begin.

- **Neatness counts.** If the application is paper, rather than electronic, use an erasable pen and print clearly and carefully. If the application is electronic, you can complete a "neat" application by being sure to use proper capitalization and punctuation.

  - **Take your own pen—or take two!** It is better to be prepared with your own pen. Take two pens, just in case one runs out of ink before you finish the application.

  - **Use black ink.** Avoid using bright ink colors such as green, orange, red, or purple. Stick to traditional black or dark blue ink.

  - **Do not use a pencil.** Pencil can be hard to read, and most employers will ask you to use a pen.

  - **Spell correctly.** If the application is paper, bring a small dictionary with you. If it is electronic or online, use spell check. Most Internet browsers have an automatic spell check for most dialog boxes, including applications. If your preferred browser does not automatically check your spelling, you can usually find a spell-check

Fill in every question.

add-on, extension, or plug-in. Just search "spell check" plus the name of your browser.

- **List your best references.** List professional references who will make you shine. This includes supervisors, instructors, co-workers, employees whom you've supervised, and supervisors of internships or volunteer work.

- **Be truthful.** You will sign this document, and it is binding that the information is correct. Do not make up information, exaggerate, or lie. Misrepresentation of application information can be grounds for dismissal from employment.

- **Fill in every question.** If the question does not apply to you, then use N/A (not applicable) or a dash. You can also state, *"will discuss,"* if that is applicable.

- **Less is more.** If they ask about criminal history and you do not have one, check the *no* box. Do not add more information about a petty incident such as a traffic violation, unless that is part of the question. If you do have a felony, then answer the question "yes," and briefly explain details only if asked to do so. Do not give unnecessary negative details.

- **Add value.** Do add extra details if there is room, and if it will add value to your application. For example, add a high GPA next to your high school or college information. You can also list words such as *supervisor* next to your job title if it applies.

- **Target your qualifications to the job.** Do not merely list skills. Write a concise statement that highlights your skills. For example: *Over $20K in direct hire revenue generated in one month.*

- **Apply for a specific job.** Employers are not going to take the time to see if they have a position for which you might qualify. You need to tell them exactly which job you are applying for on the application. Do not leave this blank. If you do not know the job title, state the department.

- **Word choice matters.** If you were downsized, say that. Do not say *"let go"* or *"fired."*

- **Avoid abbreviations.** Write out Road, Street, Avenue, etc. The only exception to this includes titles in the salutation, such as *Mr., Dr.,* or *Ms.*

- **Use action verbs and power words.** See the list in Chapter 5 regarding power words or action verbs to emphasize your skills.

- **Do not write *"See Resume."*** You should fill out all sections of the application completely, even if you attach your resume.

- **Take your resume and list of references.** If you have to fill out the application in person, versus online, you will need any required dates, names, and addresses on hand. If the application asks if you know someone who works at the company, only list people whom you know are good workers, as any names you list will reflect upon you.

- **Take other key items.** You may also need your Social Security number, license numbers, school addresses and dates, past and current employer addresses, dates of employment, and phone numbers.

- **Dress for a possible interview.** If you are required to fill out the application in person, you are making a first impression—even if you only sit in the lobby to fill it out. You might meet the hiring manager at that time, or even get an interview. Business casual is appropriate attire.
- **Sign the application.** Do not print your signature.

The Master Application

Master application An application you fill out and take with you to interviews or places of employment, so all of your information is in one place and easy to transfer to the application you will turn in.

Take a completed application with you! Do not turn it in, though. Use it for reference only. This application is referred to as your master application. A **master application** is an application you fill out and take with you to interviews or places of employment, so all of your information is in one place and easy to transfer to the application you will turn in.

To create yours, download or obtain a general application form. Even a fast-food restaurant application will work. Complete the application as if you were filling it out for a real job. Once you have completed it correctly and thoroughly, you will have nearly all of the information you need in one document. You can simply transfer the information on the master application to the application your potential employer wants you to fill out.

Employers pay close attention to information on applications that can help them narrow down the pool of applicants. How can you ensure employers will want to meet you, rather than be cautious of you?

Challenging Questions

The difficulty with applications is that you do not have the ability to talk to the hiring manager to explain any circumstances behind your answers as you fill out the application. Some of the information sought on applications is quite personal. In order to smooth over what may be seen as potential red flags in your application, the following suggestions are provided.

Criminal record: Again, be honest, but do not give more information than they ask for. If they ask whether you have been convicted of a crime, whether a misdemeanor or felony, state that fact, what it was, and how you have changed.

Fired or downsized: If you have been fired or downsized from a prior job, state it diplomatically on your application. Do not criticize your boss or past place of employment. Many times you can still get a letter of recommendation from a former employer, even if they let you go. Ask!

Gaps in work history: If you have frequent gaps in your work history, try using seasons in place of specific dates, such as "Spring 2004 to Winter 2005." There are legitimate reasons for gaps, including family obligations, children, health, traveling, school, or a home business.

Frequently changing jobs: If you were a job-hopper, be prepared to explain this. The following are several legitimate and acceptable reasons for leaving a job: temporary jobs, seasonal work, laid off, stay-at-home parent, relocated, growth opportunity, academic endeavors, military service, career change, or health.

Health questions: Some health questions may be illegal. For example, employers may not ask generally if you have a disability, but they may ask if you have a disability that would affect job performance. If asked about your health, mark *excellent,* unless you have a limiting condition. Again, do not give them a reason to remove your application from the pool. If you have health problems, but they will not interfere with your work, you can state: *I have no health problems or limitations that would affect my work performance.*

Salary questions: The best answer at this point (until you have a job offer) is to state "open" or "negotiable." If they ask what your current or past salary was, give accurate information. Do not screen yourself out of the pool by stating what your expectations are for the job unless they state the application will not be considered without this information. Whenever possible, wait for the job offer to discuss salary.

Cyber Trip 6.3

Online Applications   Find three different online applications, and review the differences and similarities. Then complete one for practice. There are many applications that you can find online by searching for "employment application form." The Internet has increasingly become the most common way to apply for job openings. Though applying online is now the norm, you must be careful. The following shows how important it is to be aware of whom you are sending information to:

I had an interesting experience online: I applied for an Administrative Assistant position and quickly received a reply e-mail. The employer told me that I was well-qualified and that out of the 200 resumes he received, mine was one of the best. He stated that the company wanted to interview me, and told me that the job would start at $20 an hour. He also stated that before I went to the interview, I was to bring a credit report with me because they didn't want to hire anyone who had poor credit. He provided a link to a credit report website, and told me I could use it, or use another one of my choice. He told me to e-mail him when I had completed and printed my credit report.

I clicked on the link in the e-mail, and it took me to a website that offered free credit reports. I filled out all the information and printed my report. I e-mailed the employer and didn't hear anything from him. I waited a week and then e-mailed him again. It has now been over three weeks and I have yet to hear from him. I am getting emails from the credit report company, but I am afraid the "employer" somehow might have obtained all of my information to use for identity theft purposes. I should have done some research on the company. I hope others can learn from my experience, and don't do what I did when they apply online.

© Used with permission of Wendy McKenzie, NAU student

Create Your Master Application

Use the information you have learned in this chapter to correctly complete the following application form in Figure 6.12.

APPLICATION FOR EMPLOYMENT

Master Employment Application

AN EQUAL OPPORTUNITY EMPLOYER

PLEASE READ BEFORE COMPLETING THIS APPLICATION AND PRINT ALL INFORMATION REQUESTED EXCEPT SIGNATURE

I. PERSONAL DATA   DATE _____

Name _____
       Last   First   Initial

Soc. Sec. Number: _____

Address _____
    Street   Apt.   City   State   Zip

Telephone (_____) _____ (daytime)   (_____) _____ (evenings)

(_____) _____ (Mobile)   E-Mail address _____

Have you previously been _____ Yes   When? _____
employed by this organization? _____ No   Where? _____

Will you travel if a job requires it? _____ Yes   _____ No

Driver's License No. _____ Issuing State _____

What is your means of transportation to work? _____

Have you had any accidents in the past three years? _____ How Many? _____

Have you had any moving violations in the past three years? _____ How Many? _____

Are you prevented from lawfully becoming employed
in this country because of Visa or Immigration status?   _____ Yes   _____ No
If hired, you will be required to show proof of employment authorization.

Have you ever been convicted of a crime that may
relate to the position for which you are applying?   _____ Yes   _____ No
(*Note: The existence of a criminal record does not create an automatic bar to employment.*)

Have you ever had any job-related training in the United States Military? _____ Yes   _____ No

If yes, please describe _____
_____

Are you able to perform the duties of the job for which
you are applying with or without accommodation?   _____ Yes   _____ No

Have you smoked or chewed tobacco at any time
within the last two years to the present?   _____ Yes   _____ No

---

Figure 6.12 Master Employment Application

II. EMPLOYMENT DESIRED

Position(s) applied for: _____

When available for work? _____ Salary desired:
_____

Are you available to work? _____ Full Time _____ Part Time
(Check all that apply.)

_____ Shift Work _____ Temporary

III. EDUCATION/SPECIAL TRAINING DATA

	Elementary School	High School	Undergraduate College/University	Graduate/ Professional
School Name/Location				
Years Completed	4 5 6 7 8	9 10 11 12	1 2 3 4	1 2 3 4
Diploma/Degree				
Major	Undergraduate:		Graduate:	
Describe any specialized training, apprenticeship, skills and extracurricular activities				
Describe any honors, commendations you have received				
State any additional information you feel may be helpful to use in considering your application				

IV. REFERENCES

(Please list three references other than relatives, or previous employers.)

Name, Address, Phone Number, E-mail	Known How Long	Occupation/Company

Figure 6.12 (Continued)

V. EMPLOYMENT HISTORY

Please list all previous employment. Start with most recent job. Include any job-related military service assignments and/or volunteer activities. You may exclude organizations that indicate race, color, religion, gender, national origin, disability, or other protected status. If you were self-employed, provide firm name.

1. Employer	Employment Dates		Work Performed
	Yrs.	Mos.	
Address	Hourly Rate/Salary		
	Starting		
E-mail Address	Ending		
Telephone Number ( )	Name of last supervisor		
Last Job Title			
Reason for Leaving			
2. Employer	Employment Dates		Work Performed
	Yrs.	Mos.	
Address	Hourly Rate/Salary		
	Starting		
E-mail Address	Ending		
Telephone Number ( )	Name of last supervisor		
Last Job Title			
Reason for Leaving			
3. Employer	Employment Dates		Work Performed
	Yrs.	Mos.	
Address	Hourly Rate/Salary		
	Starting		
E-mail Address	Ending		
Telephone Number ( )	Name of last supervisor		
Last Job Title			
Reason for Leaving			
4. Employer	Employment Dates		Work Performed
	Yrs.	Mos.	
Address	Hourly Rate/Salary		
	Starting		
E-mail Address	Ending		
Telephone Number ( )	Name of last supervisor		
Last Job Title			
Reason for Leaving			

May we contact your present employer? _____ Yes _____ No

Did you complete this application yourself? _____ Yes _____ No

If not, who did? _____

If you need additional space, please continue on a separate sheet of paper.

Summarize any special job-related skills and/or qualifications acquired that may not be listed above. Also provide any additional information necessary to describe your full qualifications for the specific position.

_____

_____

Figure 6.12 (Continued)

Now use the application form checklist in Figure 6.13 to ensure your application is accurate and complete. Once you have completed, verified, and finalized the information on the form, you can use it as your master application.

	Name:	Not Included	Present
1	Followed instructions		
2	Typed or printed information		
3	Used a black pen		
4	Neat and easy to read—printed		
5	All questions answered thoroughly		
6	Complete, accurate information		
7	Used N/A or a dash for questions that did not apply		
8	Correct information in correct spaces		
9	No scratch-outs or white-out		
10	Correct grammar, spelling, punctuation		
11	Information stated in positive terms		
12	Specific position/title listed		
13	Specific past or current salary stated (if requested)		
14	Addresses with zip codes		
15	Phone numbers with area codes		
16	E-mail addresses		
17	Application form is signed and dated		
18	Employed history listed chronologically, starting with most recent		
19	"Negotiable" or "Open" stated for salary desired, unless the employer states it will not accept an application without salary information		
20	No acronyms		
21	Included skills for position		
	Comments:		

Figure 6.13 Application Form Checklist

exercise 6.4

Analyze an Application

Use the application form grading rubric in Figure 6.15 to critique the application shown in Figure 6.14.

APPLICATION FOR EMPLOYMENT

PERSONAL INFORMATION   **DATE OF APPLICATION:** ___ May 23 ___

Name: lisa   felton   k.
_____
                    Last   First   Middle

Address: 1234 oak street   M-1   somecity, state   55515
_____
                    Street   (Apt)   City, State   Zip

Alternate Address:
_____
                    Street   City, State   Zip

Contact Information: (   )   555-4567 sassygirl123@superrito.com
_____
                Home Telephone   Mobile   Email

How did you learn about our company?   My mom

POSITION SOUGHT: _____ Anything/Open _____   **Available Start Date:** ____ ? _____

Desired Pay Range: _____ $12-17 an hour _____ **Are you currently employed?** _____ yes

I do child care with my monm _____

EDUCATION

Name and Location	Graduate?—Degree?	Major / Subjects of Study
High School	yes	randall high school Yes / Yes
College or University	i took a few classes in phycology	
Specialized Training, Trade School, etc.		
Other Education	nothing	

Please list your areas of highest proficiency, special skills or other items that may contribute to your abilities in performing the above-mentioned position:

i am really good with people, I can type 35 wpm, I have good computer skills like email, internet, txting. i also worked at the yougurt store and my boss would tell you i am super hard working, friendly and most of the time i am on time. i don/'t mind staying late either.

PREVIOUS EXPERIENCE
Please list beginning from most recent:

Date Employed	Company Name	Location	Role/Title
2011 to now	my mom's day care in her house	1234 oak St somewhere, state	child care

Job notes, tasks performed, and reason for leaving:
child care I still work there

Dates Employed	Company Name	Location	Role/Title
trudi's yougurt shop	2009-2211	at mini mall	counter server

Job notes, tasks performed, and reason for leaving:
this was as sjummer job, but i worked there a couple different summers then my mom opend her day care and needed me to help out.

Figure 6.14   Inadequate Application for Employment

Student Name:		Circle Score		
		Not Included	**Needs Improvement**	**Present**
1	Followed instructions	0	1–2–3	4–5
2	Typed or printed information	0	1–2–3	4–5
3	Used a black pen	0	1–2–3	4–5
4	Neat and easy to read—printed	0	1–2–3	4–5
5	All questions answered thoroughly	0	1–2–3	4–5
6	Complete, accurate information	0	1–2–3	4–5
7	Used N/A or dash for questions that did not apply	0	1–2–3	4–5
8	Correct information in correct spaces	0	1–2–3	4–5
9	No scratch-outs or white-out	0	1–2–3	4–5
10	Correct grammar, spelling, punctuation	0	1–2–3	4–5
11	Information stated in positive manner	0	1–2–3	4–5
12	Specific position/title listed	0	1–2–3	4–5
13	Specific past or current salary stated (if requested)	0	1–2–3	4–5
14	Addresses with zip codes	0	1–2–3	4-5
15	Phone numbers with area codes	0	1–2–3	4–5
16	E-mail addresses	0	1–2–3	4–5
17	Application form is signed	0	1–2–3	4–5
18	Employment history listed chronologically from most recent to least recent	0	1–2–3	4–5
19	"Negotiable" or "Open" stated for salary desired	0	1–2–3	4–5
20	No acronyms	0	1–2–3	4–5
21	Included skills for position	0	1–2–3	4–5
Comments:				

Figure 6.15   Application Form Grading Rubric

Cyber Trip 6.4

More Bad Applications   Gain additional practice using the application form grading rubric by critiquing an application filled with mistakes. Ask your instructor for a blank copy of the grading rubric, and visit http://www.kent.ac.uk/careers/cv/badaf.htm to view the erroneous application.

✓ SELF-CHECK

4. What is the real purpose of a job application?

5. What color pen should you use to complete the application form?

6. What should you write in response to application questions that do not apply to you?

High Expectations—Alison Learns that Details Matter

Although she was confused after receiving the denial letter from the Massage Bliss clinic, Alison was determined not to lose out on another opportunity to be seriously considered for a massage therapist position. On the advice of her career exploration instructor, Alison contacted the Career Services Department at Green Valley School of Massage Therapy and made an appointment to meet with her advisor, Justin Harvey.

Justin explained to Alison that applications are more than just a formality and employers not only read them, but also look for problems such as grammatical errors and incomplete applications.

"Alison," he said, "in order to be seriously considered you must present a complete package of a well-crafted resume, a complete and truthful application, and a cover letter that is going to set you apart from other candidates. It also goes without saying that your application documents must be mistake-free."

Justin further recommended that Alison develop a master application form to use as a reference and guide when completing applications online, as well as in person.

"What a great idea!" said Alison. "I'll have all my critical data in one place. This will definitely help to ensure that my applications are complete and perfect. Before, I was having trouble keeping track of all of my papers and information."

Something else has been troubling Alison though. "I notice that many of the ads are seeking someone with a state license—how should I handle that?" she asked. "I'll be taking the licensing exam in a few weeks."

Justin assured Alison that it was always best to answer the question honestly, and while she is awaiting notification of passing the exam, she should refer to herself as a *license candidate.* He noted that Alison should explain this on the application and in her cover letter.

"But what if I don't get the job because I answer 'no—I'm not licensed'?" said Alison.

"Employers seeking entry-level therapists are aware that the licensing process can take some time," replied Justin. "Very often they are willing to offer an intern or trainee position to someone they really want to hire, or they will be willing to reconsider your application once you have your license. Being dishonest will never help you get a job, though."

Finally, Justin and Alison worked on an attention-grabbing cover letter that conveyed important information about Alison's skills and training as a massage therapist. They used the proper format, key words, and framed information that helped set Alison apart from other possible applicants.

"Employers want to know what you will bring to their business and how you will fit in with their needs," explained Justin. "Let's look at that job ad you responded to last week, and compare you to the desired candidate they describe. A bullet format would work well, and it can be adapted to every situation. That way, you can easily tailor your cover letter to each specific job you apply for."

Two weeks later Alison stopped by Career Services.

"Great news, Justin!" she exclaimed. "I have an interview at Chez Spa downtown tomorrow. The work we did on my cover letter worked!"

Discussion Questions

1. Why was it important for Alison to fully complete and submit a cover letter, application, and resume to Massage Bliss?

2. Although the ad for Massage Bliss did not ask this, how would you advise Alison to answer questions about her desired salary?

3. Draft the cover letter that Alison should have sent to Massage Bliss.

[chapter summary]

Cover letters can make you or break you. Since the employer will give only about 30 seconds to your cover letter and resume, make sure the cover letter is powerful and worthy of the employer's attention. Pay attention to the details.

1. Personalize your cover letter.
2. Reference the title of the position.
3. Use the hiring agent's name along with Mr., Ms., or Dr. to greet the prospective employer.
4. Target your skills to the position.
5. Stay away from listing too many soft skills unless you present specific examples.
6. Use an action paragraph to close.
7. Use varied sentences and not too many beginning with "I."
8. Write clear and concise sentences.
9. Match font, paper, and heading to your resume.
10. Include your contact information.
11. Use business letter format for writing.
12. End letter with *Sincerely, Yours sincerely,* or *Respectfully* (consider using when applying to attorney offices/law firms).

Applications are often used for entry-level positions. Some companies require them for all potential employees. When completing an application, use your master application for an easy way to transfer information. In addition:

1. Read and follow directions.
2. Be neat and accurate.
3. Use a black ink erasable pen; not a pencil.
4. Answer truthfully but stay positive.
5. Find way to list skills.
6. Apply for the job you seek—use job title.

[skill/term check]

1. What is the purpose of an action paragraph in a cover letter? Where should the action paragraph be located? **(LO 6-1)**

2. In what ways does a cover letter function as a marketing tool? **(LO 6-1)**

3. Provide an example of an acceptable salutation and closure for cover letters. **(LO 6-2)**

4. What can you communicate in a cover letter that you cannot communicate in a resume or application? **(LO 6-2)**

5. What is a master application, and how would you use one? **(LO 6-3)**

6. What guidelines should be used to answer the salary question in the application? **(LO 6-3)**

7. What are three do's and three don'ts for completing applications successfully? **(LO 6-3)**

[KEY TERMS]

Action paragraph: The final paragraph in a cover letter taking action by asking for the interview and stating when you will call the employer to follow up on the application. **(LO 6-1)** [p. 168]

Master application: An application you fill out and take with you to interviews or places of employment, so all of your information is in one place and easy to transfer to the application you will turn in. **(LO 6-3)** [p. 184]

Moving Forward:

Interview, Follow-Up, and Managing Change

In Part 2, you carefully crafted your marketing tools and learned how they work together to promote your product—you! Part 3 shows you how to bring your hard work full circle by interviewing, following up, and negotiating successfully with potential employers. The work you have done in Parts 1 and 2 has prepared you well. Now it is time to put your skills and success tools to the test by learning how to present yourself and communicate your worth effectively.

Chapter 7 discusses the steps involved in the interview process, as well as the various types of interviews and interview questions. You will learn how to answer difficult questions and create a list of your own questions to ask the interviewer, so you are fully prepared for each interview you attend. Chapter 7 will also stress how important it is to create a professional image. Projecting yourself with confidence and a polished appearance is imperative when you are searching for your ideal career. Chapter 8 then guides you through successful follow-up and negotiations, ensuring that you take necessary steps after each interview and are fully prepared to negotiate effectively when you receive the job offer.

Learning successful interview and follow-up strategies in Part 3 provides you with the confidence to present a professional image of yourself. You will learn to effectively communicate your skills and value to each company you interview with, and master the challenging art of negotiation.

Chapter 9 looks forward and shows you how to manage your career, including how to make a great impression at work, prioritize your time, manage work-life balance, and successfully advance your career. As more people change jobs frequently throughout their lives, whether by choice or not, it is also imperative that you have an action plan to stay organized and lessen your stress level in these situations. Chapter 9 provides you with this action plan. You also will learn the importance of lifelong learning and continual goal setting.

Each part of this book works together with the other parts synergistically. As you read the final chapter, reflect on the work you have done, what your career plans and goals once were, and where they are now. Whatever your circumstance—whether you are looking for your first job or making a life-altering career change—the tools and skills you have gained throughout this book will ensure you are prepared to grow, reach, and exceed your personal career goals.

chapter 7

Successful Interviews

" Walk in like you own it, and walk out like you sold it. "

—Thomas Labrie

target competency > *Interview successfully*

learning outcomes

After studying this chapter, you should be able to:

LO 7-1 Understand the seven interview steps.

LO 7-2 Differentiate among the types of interviews and understand how to prepare for them.

LO 7-3 Understand the different types of interview questions and know how to answer them successfully.

LO 7-4 Recognize how to create your professional image through proper attire and presentation.

LO 7-5 Conduct a mock interview.

Be Prepared!

Hew had found an open position posted online for a marketing coordinator at Marketing Solutions, LLC, and felt he would be a good fit. Hew had a degree in business administration and had just completed a recent internship with Palmer & Anderson Marketing. He sent his cover letter and resume for the open position and was called for an interview a few days later. Hew was elated at landing the interview and went in the following Tuesday to meet with the panel of interviewers for the position.

The first question one of the interviewers asked Hew was, "Why do you want to work for Marketing Solutions?"

Hew had so many answers racing through his mind, but couldn't seem to organize his thoughts. He said something to the effect that the job sounded interesting and it was near where he lived.

The second interviewer then asked, "What do you know about our company?"

Hew could feel his face burn. He had meant to go online and do some additional research about Marketing Solutions, LLC, but had not done so. He had hoped they would not ask him many questions about the specifics of the company; in fact, he was upset they were not asking him about his work ethic and recent internship experience. Hew tossed out a few vague statements that could be true for any marketing firm. He knew the interview was off to a bad start.

The next gentleman (whose title and name Hew could not remember) asked Hew, "Based on the advertisement, what about it drew you to the position the most, and why do you feel you are qualified for it?"

Hew replied, "Well . . . I don't have the ad with me, but from what I remember, I thought I would like doing the responsibilities it listed and the title of the position fit me as a business person." Hew quickly glanced up at the interview panel after answering, but they did not look impressed.

The final person on the panel then asked Hew the interview question he hated the most: "What are some of your weaknesses in the workplace, and can you give me an example of how you turned a workplace problem into a solution?"

Hew's mind went blank. Each time he was asked this question in an interview Hew made a mental note to create an answer for it for the next interview, but he just hadn't gotten around to it. He replied, "Well, ahh . . . I . . . umm . . . gosh, that is a really hard question. I, ah . . . I can't think of any real weaknesses I have in the workplace. Umm . . . what kind of weaknesses do you have in mind? I mean . . . at a job I had in high school, I once got in trouble for chewing gum . . . so I quit chewing gum—is that what you mean?"

Hew felt his face still burning, and now his hands were getting clammy. *"Why are interviews so painful?"* he thought to himself.

The only thing worse than the fear of death is the fear of looking stupid.
—Marty Neumeier, author of *The Brand Gap*

Discussion Questions

1. Why is researching the company a valuable interview strategy?
2. What are some ways Hew could have found out more about Marketing Solutions, LLC, the position, and even the people who interviewed him?
3. What else could Hew have done to improve his interviewing results?

The Seven Interview Steps

You have a great product (you), excellent marketing tools (resume, cover letter, and networking business card), and all of your hard work got you in the door (either literally or virtually) of the company to audition for the job. That's right, you got the interview! Now what are you going to do in that short time to gain their confidence, wow them with your skills, and differentiate yourself from the competition? There is a marketing saying that goes like this: *Companies differentiate themselves in one of three things—product, price, or service.* The same goes for job candidates. The interview is your opportunity to demonstrate what you can do for the company that is different and better than the other candidates. This will be stressed over and over in this chapter as many candidates incorrectly view the interview process as "What can the company do for me?" That question is asked later when you actually receive a job offer. Until you get the job offer, you need to remember that the interview is all about *them*. What can you do for the company? Why should they hire you and not another candidate?

Seven Steps to a Stellar Interview

The interview actually begins long before you have a formal discussion about the position. There are seven steps in the interview process, and you can master each of them to achieve a winning interview.

Step 1	Prepare for the Interview
Step 2	First Impression
Step 3	Face-to-Face Interview
Step 4	Closing
Step 5	Follow-up
Step 6	Job Offer and Negotiation
Step 7	Making Your Decision

Step 1: Prepare for the Interview

Do your homework: Take time to research the company and the position. Interviewers may even ask you, "What do you know about our company?" Learn what the company needs. How can you add value? Make notes of how your skills, experiences, and education can meet those needs and include specific examples. Candidates who do their homework take the lead in receiving job offers. Let's briefly review how you can research a company:

- Visit the company website. Find the mission statement, core values, and "About us" sections. The way a company presents itself on its website is how it wants to be seen, so what you read on the site will help you understand the image the company wishes to present to the world. Think about how you can support those efforts.
- Check out the company's presence on social media. Reviewing the social media pages will help you get to know the company and its personality, and it may help you come up with ideas for questions you can ask in the interview. Peruse industry trade magazines. Even if you don't find anything about the company in these magazines, it is valuable to know what is happening in the industry.

- Do a news search on the company. Most search engines offer a news-specific search (try Google's at https://news.google.com/). This will bring up articles about the company that have appeared recently in the news. Ask others if they know anything about the company or anyone at the company.

- Call the company's human resources department and ask any questions you may have about the company.

Voice message and phone etiquette: As soon as you send out resumes and begin searching for a position, make sure the outgoing greeting for your voice mail is professional. For example, if an employer called you right now, would he or she be impressed with your outgoing message? If the employer has to listen to several minutes of some new hip-hop tune before your greeting, or has to wait through a long recording that says something more than simply, "I'm sorry I can't take your call, please leave a message," you may not win any points. If you have put a shared phone number on your resume (such as a home number you share with your family or with roommates), you need to know if others who might answer at that number know how to answer the phone politely, take a message, and remember to give you the message. You may need to prompt them. Some employers are hesitant to hire single parents or people with children (because they may expect that you will need to take more time off due to child concerns), so if your voice-mail greeting currently lists all the people in your family you, might change your message to say something like "You have reached the Smiths, please leave a message and we will return your call."

Contact the employer prior to the interview: You can send a professional e-mail or note to the hiring manager thanking him or her for the opportunity to interview. Also reconfirm the time and date, and ask where you should park, and if there are any parking restrictions you need to know about. See Figure 7.1 for an example.

Include one of your networking business cards if you send the confirmation note in regular mail. You can also electronically attach one of your NBCs to an e-mail confirmation.

Time the drive and plan for parking: This tip is often overlooked but could ruin the entire interview if ignored. If you are going to an in-person interview, and you are unfamiliar with the interview location, considering mapping and

---

Dear Ms. Leonard,

Thank you for the opportunity to interview with (company name) for the position of (position title) next Tuesday, July 17, 2016.

I look forward to learning more about the position and discussing with you how I can add value to your company.

Sincerely,

Your name
Phone number
E-mail address

Figure 7.1   Professional E-mail

If you need to drive to an interview, plan ahead for parking and potential driving obstacles.

driving the route prior to the interview and time it to see how long it takes. If this is not an option, use GPS, a mapping app on your phone, or an online mapping service to make sure you know how to get there and about how long should take. If you can test the route in advance, be sure to look for parking so you know what to expect. See if the roads are open, if there is construction, and how to navigate the alternate routes. Check if you need extra change for parking meters or cash for parking attendants. Attending to all of these little details can eventually add up to a big win for you.

Test the technology: Sometimes your first interview with a company will be by phone or videoconference, particularly if you are interviewing for a job in a different town. If this is the case, make sure all the technology you need for a successful call is ready to go. Find a quiet room where you will not be interrupted, and make sure your phone gets a strong signal or that you have a strong Internet connection there. If you are using videoconferencing technology, make sure you have downloaded the software (such as Skype, Google Hangout, or GoToMeeting) in advance, and test it to make sure it works and is ready to go. (See the next section for more on phone and video interviews.)

Arrival time: Plan to arrive 10 to 15 minutes early. Visit the restroom and do a once-over. Check your teeth, take out your gum, pop a breath mint. Turn off your cell phone. Get a drink of water.

Take essentials and leave the rest: Leave your large items such as big purses or bags in your vehicle. Take a padded portfolio for your legal pad, nice pen, resume, and networking business cards (NBCs). You can also tuck your resume and NBCs in the back of your legal pad if you do not have a padded portfolio. Consider leaving your cell phone at home or in the car; if you take it into the interview, turn it off beforehand.

Waiting: It is recommended that you stand until asked to sit. Remember to be friendly to all you meet in the company, but not overly chatty. Now is not the time to get the receptionist's phone number. A good human resource manager will be interested in how you conducted yourself while waiting. As stated earlier, the interview starts long before the face-to-face discussion.

Step 2: First Impression

Your image: Interviewers will size you up as a candidate in the first 15 to 30 seconds after you meet them. Make sure you are dressed the part (even if your interview is a videoconference and not face-to-face). This subject will be covered in detail later in this chapter.

Why is it important to make eye contact with the interviewer? Practice making eye contact with those you encounter in day-to-day life.

The handshake: As you learned in Chapter 4, the handshake says a great deal about you. Reach out your hand and give a solid handshake with two pumps while looking the person in the eye. While this gesture may seem trivial, it is not.

Eye contact and smile: Look the hiring manager and others in the interview in the eye. Don't stare, but use the two-second rule for eye contact. That is, look them in the eye and count to two. Use it periodically, to make sure you are not avoiding their eyes. It is noticed and does make a difference. Smile. You want to be friendly and professional.

Keep it comfortable: For many employers, interviewing can be the worst part of their job. Keep that in mind. Unless you are being interviewed by someone from human resources, the person interviewing you may be more uncomfortable than you are. If so, you can do one of several things to make him or her at ease. Make small talk by commenting on something nonthreatening. For example, you could comment on the weather or sports, especially if you notice, for instance, a team photo displayed in the person's office. You can comment on a picture in the person's office as well.

Remove doubt or negative thoughts from your mind: If you have negative thoughts, just notice them and remind yourself that such thoughts are part of your "mind chatter." Negative mind chatter is often a sign that you are out of your comfort zone. Replace the chatter with a psych-out message such as "I am the best person for this job," "They would be lucky to have me work here," or "I am in demand." Anything that counters the negative and builds you up will work. Think of Muhammad Ali. He used the statement "I am the greatest." And it worked. It does not need to be complicated, but you do need to replace doubting statements with confident statements, even if you do not feel confident.

> *Any face-to-face meeting with someone who could hire you is an "interview." This might be at a ball game or in the boardroom.*

Step 3: Face-to-Face Interview

Belong there: Put yourself in the hiring manager's shoes. He or she needs to hire the right person for the job. Give plenty of reasons you are that person. Use language that makes you a part of the company's team, not an outsider. When possible, answer and ask questions using language as if you had the job. For example, say, "Would we have the opportunity to . . . "

Prove your answers: Each time you give an answer make sure you provide an example. Don't just say you have such and such skill without backing it up. Think of the quantified skills listed in your cover letter and resume. Use quantifying statements when discussing your skills during the interview. For example, *I have a great deal of management experience* is not as strong as, *I currently supervise more than 23 employees and have been a manager for the past seven years.*

Sell yourself: During the interview, explain how you improved processes or solved problems in other positions. Then ask if that would be helpful for this company or position. You increase the likelihood of getting the job offer if the hiring manager agrees that you would add value.

Keep to the point: Answer the question by providing relevant examples. Then zip it. Stop talking. No answer should go more than one to two minutes.

Answer the problem questions: Problem questions will be covered in detail later in the chapter, as well as how to deal with illegal questions. Be prepared for the tough questions and practice your answers.

Focus on the employer: The *interview* is about how you can benefit the employer, not what the employer can do for you. Remember, you do not yet have a job offer, so you need to sell your strengths. The *job offer* is about what the employer can do for you. Ask questions about what the employer can do for you when you get the offer. For the interview, focus on the employer and how you can add value to the organization.

Step 4: Closing

Ask the right questions: There will be an opportunity for you to ask questions, usually toward the end of the interview. There are some great questions you can ask and some you definitely want to avoid. You do want to ask a few questions, as it demonstrates you have thought about the position and you are interested. Some good questions to ask include:

- What is a typical day like for this position?
- What areas are the highest priorities for this position that need immediate solutions or attention?
- What is the division's management style?
- What is the next step in this process?
- When do you plan on making a decision?
- Why is the position open?
- What are the avenues for advancement with this position?
- Do you offer assistance with professional development, training, or furthering an employee's education?
- Is an advanced degree required, or preferred, for promotions?
- Who would I report to?
- How is performance for this position measured?
- With your firm, is there an hourly quota that must be met each year?
- What other departments does this position interface (or cooperate) with and is there anything I should know about that role in connecting with these other parts of the organization?

Some questions to avoid include:

- What is the salary for this position?
- When will I get a promotion?
- How soon would I receive a raise?
- How much flex time is allowed?
- How much vacation time does the job offer?
- Do you do background checks/drug checks?

Do not ask about money or benefits until you get an offer: Yes, money and benefits are very important to you, but do not ask about them in the interview. This is not the time to discuss salary. You do not have a job offer. When you are interviewing, you do not want to be eliminated from the hiring pool. You want to get the job offer. If those interviewing you really like you, they may be able to meet your needs when you are negotiating. The interview is not a negotiation. The interview is when you sell yourself as the best person for the job. Remember, the interview is about the company and what you can do for them. The job offer is about you and whether the company can meet your needs. Discuss money, benefits, and other negotiation items when you get the offer. Another reason to avoid the money issue is that whoever mentions it first is at a disadvantage. You want them to make you an offer. Wait for the offer. Get the interview, then the offer, and then negotiate a winning job: one that is a win–win for both you and the employer. The hiring manager may bring up money in the interview, and how you answer this very important question is discussed later in the section on difficult interview questions.

The interview is not a negotiation.

The interview is about the company, and what you can do for it. The job offer is about you, and whether the company can meet your needs.

Ask for the job: Most candidates fail to ask for the job. This might seem out of your comfort zone, but with practice you will find it pays. Asking for the job is such a simple, yet often omitted step. Ask for the job while you are preparing to leave. Shake hands and say something to the effect of *"I want you to know that after our discussion today, I want to join your firm. I want the job."* You are more likely to get an offer when you are truly interested and committed to working for them. The interviewer will sense this interest, so close the deal. While bold, there is a time when it is more than appropriate to make a statement of intent such as, *"I want this job, I am ready to start."*

Thank you and handshake: Remember to say thank you and shake hands to close. Ask for business cards containing their contact information that you can use for follow-up.

Step 5: Follow-Up

- Review your interview.
- Send an e-mail thank-you the day of the interview.
- Send a regular postage mail (snail mail) thank-you card that they will receive in a couple of days.
- Send multiple thank-you notes if you had a panel interview. If this is not possible, send the thank-you note to the hiring manager and ask him or her to extend your thanks to the panel.
- Check the status of the job in a week or when the interviewer mentioned a decision would be made. Do not hound them, but by the same token, people like to hire people who are eager to work for them.

Step 6: Job Offer and Negotiation

This subject will be covered in detail in Chapter 8.

Step 7: Making Your Decision

This subject will be covered in detail in Chapter 8.

careercoach7.1

It's a numbers game, like anything else. When you have no personal stake in how many responses you get; when you take your ego out of it, you can do yourself a lot of good.

—Mimi Tanner,[1] relationship coach and author

The job search and interview process is a numbers game. Again, think of anyone who tried and succeeded at something great, from the thousands of attempts Thomas Edison made to invent the lightbulb, to J.K. Rowling, who was an impoverished, single mom with many manuscript rejections before the wild success of Harry Potter. The numbers game principle holds true whether you are looking for your ideal mate or a job.

If you lock onto one company and one interview for one job, you may find you don't get what you want. You limit yourself from finding or receiving what might be a better fit for you. The rule of thumb for this principle is to *rack them up*: interview for the sake of interviewing. See each interview as a great experience and one step closer to your ideal job. Each "no thank you" is a good sign. It means you are doing the work and you are in the game. If done right, the interview process includes many rejections. If you are not getting rejected (or are rejecting offers), then you are not applying the success principle: *it's a numbers game.*

» LO 7-2   Types of Interviews

It has been said that intelligence is the art of guessing correctly, and anything you can do to increase the chances of improving your guesswork adds to your intelligence. With this in mind, anything you can do to increase the likelihood of improving your chances of receiving the job offer is wise. Preparing for the different types of interviews you might receive will help you increase your chances of getting the offer. Review the following list of different types of interviews. Think about your particular field and what type of interview is most commonly used. If you don't know, then ask around. Knowing what type is part of the research you will do and is critical to your success.

Standard or Traditional Interviews

The **standard interview**, or traditional interview, is an interview during which the applicant is asked a variety of typical questions. Expect questions like, *"Why do you want to work here?" "What are some of your strengths and weaknesses?"* Proving your answers is the best way to successfully approach this type of interview. You prove them by providing specific examples.

Standard interview An interview during which the applicant is asked a variety of typical questions; also known as a traditional interview.

---

[1]Used with permission of Mimi Tanner.

Competency-Based/Behavioral Interview

The **competency-based interview**, or behavioral interview, is based on the premise that your past employment behavior will dictate your future behavior in the new position. This type of interview is becoming the new standard for interviewing. In a competency-based interview, you will be asked scenario questions where the interviewer wants to know how you handled past workplace situations. You will want to focus on specific examples to provide a successful outcome for this type of interview. The interviewer will ask you follow-up questions and may focus on specific details of the event and what you did. The hiring manager is looking for specific skill sets or characteristics. It is harder to fool the interviewer about whether or not you have the skill or qualification in this type of interview. A helpful tip is to answer the question using specific details and put a positive spin on your explanation, even when describing negative situations. Also, quantify (support with numbers) your answers whenever possible. Prepare for this interview by reviewing the behavior-based interview questions provided later in the chapter. Practice with someone in a mock interview session using the questions. The **mock interview** is a simulated interview used for practice. It will be explained more in depth later in this chapter.

> **Competency-based interview** An interview based on the premise that your past employment behavior will dictate your future behavior in the new position; also known as a behavioral interview.
>
> **Mock interview** A simulated interview used for practice.
>
> **Lunch or dinner interview** An interview that takes place during a meal and may be part of a daylong interview process, or it may be the interview itself.

Cyber Trip 7.1

The Interview Game   Practice your interviewing skills by visiting https://www.careerswales.com/en/tools-and-resources/games-and-activities/job-interview-game/ and playing an interactive interview game.

Lunch or Dinner Interview

A **lunch or dinner interview** takes place during a meal and may be part of a daylong interview process, or it may be the interview itself. Either way, it needs to be treated as an interview. People behave differently when they eat, and how you handle yourself in this social situation may be the deciding factor in whether you get hired. The hiring manager wants to hire the right person—someone who not only fits into the culture of the organization, but also someone who will not embarrass the company if sent out with clients. Do not order any alcohol at these interviews, even if everyone else does. Abstain. You can drink with them later when you are employed and are part of the "family."

Choose your menu selection carefully. Select something fairly easy to eat with less likelihood of spilling. Follow your host's lead (except in drinking alcohol). Order food in the price range the others are ordering in. Skip dessert if they do. This is the time to eat less, listen more, and come off as polished and professional. To prepare for this type of interview, have someone practice a mock interview with you in a restaurant. While this might seem uncomfortable or odd, it will take the edge off of having to interview with the hiring manager over dinner. For example, have whoever is participating with you in the mock interview ask you questions right when you start eating. This will

Be careful what you order at a lunch or dinner interview.

allow you to get a feel for how the dinner or lunch interview is much different than dining with friends. Other suggestions include things your parents might have told you growing up such as:

- Say "please" and "thank you."
- Be gracious to the server as well as those you dine with.
- Chew with your mouth closed.
- Put your napkin in your lap as soon as you sit down.
- When you leave the table, excuse yourself and place your napkin on the seat or over the arm of your chair.
- Wait for the interviewers to ask you to sit down. If they don't, then sit after they do.
- For utensils, the rule of thumb is to start at the outside and work your way toward your plate.
- Begin eating after everyone is served and the interviewer begins to eat.
- Keep elbows off the table.
- As far as removing your jacket, follow the lead of the interviewer.
- Don't talk with food in your mouth. If you are asked a question while you have food in your mouth, raise your finger as if you will speak in just a moment. Finish swallowing and answer the question.
- Stay away from messy food, such as those with sauces or those that need to be eaten with fingers.
- Spoon the soup away from you.
- Do not drink alcohol at the dinner interview. It is an interview, not a social engagement.
- Place your knife across the top of your plate while you are still eating.
- To let the server know you are finished eating, place both fork and knife, with handles toward you, on the side of the plate in the "three or four o'clock" position. Also, place your napkin off to the side of your plate.
- Women should visit the restroom to touch up makeup or lipstick. Do not reapply while seated at the table.
- Thank them for your meal and for the interview.

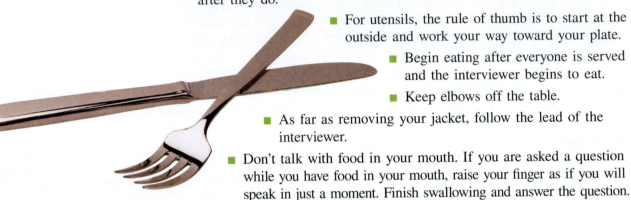

What are some ways you can use utensils properly during a lunch or dinner interview?

Nondirective or Work Sample Interview

A **nondirective interview**, or work sample interview, is often used in fields where the candidate needs to demonstrate his or her skills or wares. For example, a graphic artist may bring and share his or her portfolio, or a sales position may require a demonstration. The job candidate often leads these types of interviews. Again, practice by presenting your portfolio or demonstrating your sales pitch to someone in a mock interview.

Panel or Group Interview

The **panel interview**, or group interview, usually takes place around a conference table, where a group of individuals will collectively ask the candidate questions. This is a common type of interview in higher

Nondirective interview An interview often used in fields where the candidate needs to demonstrate his or her skills or wares; also known as a work sample interview.

Panel interview An interview that usually takes place around a conference table, where a group of individuals will collectively ask the candidate questions; also known as a group interview.

education institutions. Sometimes it is organized where the panel takes turns asking you questions, but other times it might seem like an interview firing range.

When you enter the room, take the time to shake each person's hand, look them in the eye and smile. Your first impression matters and you need to connect quickly with each individual on the panel. Take out your pen and paper for the interview. If possible, jot down the panel members' names (and titles) so you have this information when answering their question and later for follow-up. Don't focus on just one member of the panel. Make sure you look at all members when you are answering questions, even if one person seems more attentive or friendly. Panel interviews often use competency-based or behavioral interview questions. Take time to review this format before the interview.

Close the panel interview by shaking the hand of all members of the panel and thanking them while addressing them by name. Remain formal by using Mr., Dr., and Ms., unless they tell you otherwise. Smile and leave them with your NBC.

Phone Interview

A **phone interview** is conducted over the phone, usually before ever meeting the hiring manager in person. A phone interview is different from a prescreening interview (discussed in the next section) in that it might be the only interview you will receive. With the increase of online positions and telecommuting in the expanding global marketplace, companies are relying more and more on the phone interview. As mentioned earlier, in some cases you may be asked to interview by videoconference. The following are some tips to help you nail the phone interview. Unless noted, these tips also apply to video interviews:

> **Phone interview** An interview conducted over the phone, usually before meeting the hiring manager in person.

Prior to the Phone Interview

1. Confirm the phone interview just as you should confirm a face-to-face interview. You can do this by sending a professional e-mail message to the interviewer, such as the one in Figure 7.2.

Dear Ms. Hollis,

Thank you for the e-mail inviting me to interview with (company name) for the sales representative position. I would like to accept the phone interview. To answer your question, three times that work for me are:

Eastern Time: 12 pm June 2nd; 2 pm June 4th; or 3 pm June 4

I look forward to hearing from you and to visiting about the sales position.

Thank you for contacting me.

Sincerely,

Your name
Your phone number with area code that you want to use for the interview
Alternate phone number
Your e-mail address

Figure 7.2 Interview Confirmation

2. Confirm who is going to make the call (you or the interviewer) and confirm the time zone for the appointment. Confirm either the number you will call or your number that you want the interviewer to call. For a video call, confirm the technology you will use.

3. Find a quiet place where you will not be interrupted during the interview. If you are using your mobile phone, make sure you get good reception in this spot. If you are conducting a video interview, make sure you get a strong Internet signal.

4. Have the following with you for the phone interview:
   - Your resume and cover letter so that you can quickly refer to your employment history and skills during the interview.
   - Your transcripts.
   - Your questions for the interviewer.
   - A pen and pad to write down information and further questions.
   - Bottle of water to drink, if needed.

It helps to dress up for a phone interview, as it can help you feel more attentive.

5. Take a few minutes to get centered and use positive self-talk for a successful interview.

6. Dress up for the phone interview. If you are hanging out in your sweats you may feel casual and comfortable, but not necessarily professional. Your answers may reflect this. If that seems like too much effort, ask yourself, *"How much do I want the job?"* The habit of talking on the phone may cause you to be overly relaxed. Time on the phone is often for chit-chatting. Remember to focus and remind yourself this is an interview.

7. Conduct a mock phone interview with a friend to practice before the actual interview.

During the Phone Interview

1. The interviewer will introduce himself or herself.

2. If you do not have the correct spelling for the interviewer's name, ask for this for follow-up correspondence.

3. Listen to the questions and ask for clarification if needed.

4. Do not take a call that comes in on call-waiting. Disable this feature if you can for the interview. If you are on a video call, turn off the ringer on any phone in the room so you will not be interrupted.

5. Do not use a speaker phone even if the person interviewing you is using one.

6. Answer by providing specific examples and quantify when you can (use numbers to support).

7. Don't multitask; focus only on the conversation. If you are doing anything else, it comes across over the phone.

8. Keep all answers to less than two minutes in length.

9. If you accidentally interrupt, apologize and allow the interviewer to continue by being silent.

10. Speak slower than you normally speak and make sure there is no background noise.

11. Smile; it comes across on the phone to the listener.

12. Stand; your voice will have a better resonance.

13. Sound interested and enthusiastic.

14. Hold your questions until the end, or until asked for.

Ending the Phone Interview

1. Thank the interviewer.

2. Ask for the job! Say something to the effect of "After visiting with you today, I am even more interested in this position and I want to join your team."

3. Ask what the next step is in the selection process. Don't allow the phone call to turn into chitchat. This is still an interview.

After the Phone Interview

1. E-mail a thank-you note to the hiring manager the day of the interview and follow up with a conventional (snail mail) postage stamp thank-you note, if you have an actual address. You want to be fresh in the interviewer's mind when he or she is interviewing others or making the decision.

2. Follow up with a phone call either one week later, or when they said they would be making a hiring decision.

Spontaneous Phone Interviews

Occasionally, a hiring manager will call the candidate without warning and begin to interview on the spot. If it is a bad time for you to talk (you are walking out the door or the kids are screaming or playing nearby) you should say, *"I am so glad you called and want to give you my full attention, but unfortunately I cannot at the moment."* Then ask to schedule a time to visit about the position. This is a reasonable request that will allow you time to gather your notes as well as your thoughts.

Screening or Prescreening Interview

A **screening interview**, or prescreening interview, is used to evaluate and narrow a large applicant pool. This type of interview could be in person or on the phone. The goal for the hiring manager is to establish your qualifications and to determine if you are a good fit to proceed to the next step. This interview may be conducted by an outsourced hiring firm or by human resources. Helpful tips for this interview are to have your marketing tools organized and handy so you can literally reach for them if needed (resume, transcripts, etc.) and be prepared to interview on the spot. Fields that rely heavily on prescreening interviews include sales positions and pharmaceutical representatives. Other forms of screening include speed interviews and preemployment or computerized testing.

Speed Interview

This interviewing format is often used to quickly screen candidates down to a smaller pool or for a large recruitment drive. Candidates typically receive a very short (5- to 15-minute) rapid-fire interview. If

Screening interview An interview used to evaluate and narrow a large applicant pool; also known as a prescreening interview.

the speed interview is successful they will move to a longer, more traditional interview. Successful candidates are usually prepared. Remember your *30-Second Commercial* from Chapter 4. This tool would be ideal to use in a speed interview.

Preemployment Testing/Computerized Testing

These screening tests can take place at the company, or more often, online. Types of tests include the IQ or aptitude test, behavior-based test, technology-based test, knowledge-based test, honesty and integrity test, personality test, drug testing, background check, or a test with a variety of objectives. This form of screening is on the rise and it is wise to be prepared. Check the employer's website before the interview to see if it mentions preemployment testing. Some employers even post sample tests online for job candidates to prepare.

Second Interview

After the initial interview, there is often a **second interview**. The second interview includes candidates who made the first cut and have been screened down to a small pool of people in which the company is truly interested. The questions may be deeper and the candidate may be interviewed by a panel or supervisor at this point. This could also be a peer or group interview, to make certain you fit into the culture of the organization. The same advice for the first interview works for the second interview as well: making a good first impression, using specific examples when answering questions, staying at ease, and asking for the job.

Second interview An interview that occurs after the initial interview and involves candidates who made the first cut and have been screened down to a small pool of people in which the company is truly interested.

Stress interview An interview with the goal of seeing how you actually handle stress in the workplace, rather than just asking you questions about how you handle stress.

Structured interview An interview in which each job candidate receives the exact same questions.

Stress Interview

You may not know you have walked into a stress interview, but you certainly will know it by the time you leave. Your interviewer will do more than ask questions; he or she will make you feel less like a job candidate and more like an intruder or enemy. Your interviewer will grill you, interrupt you, and generally try to cause you stress. The goal of a **stress interview** is to see how you actually handle stress in the workplace, rather than just asking you questions about how you handle stress. If you feel the pressure of a stress interview, breathe, do not react to the stress you are feeling, and focus on answering the questions and keeping your cool.

Also, watch out for silence in a stress interview. An interviewer's best friend for increasing stress and increasing the likelihood of gaining illegal information is silence. The interviewee thinks he or she has answered the question and the interviewer remains silent. The recommendation is to regain eye contact, smile if appropriate, and remain silent and still. Wait for the interviewer to ask the next question. Silence is an interviewer's most powerful tool. Luckily, most don't use it.

Silence is an interviewer's most powerful tool.

To practice succeeding at the stress interview, videotape yourself in a simulated or mock stress interview. Play the video to friends or the interviewer to receive helpful feedback.

Structured Interview

In a **structured interview**, each job candidate receives the exact same questions. With the increase of lawsuits, many companies resort to this type of interview style to avoid criticisms of bias from applicants who did not get the offer.

Technical Interview

During a **technical interview**, technical questions are asked in order for you to demonstrate that you have the specific knowledge or skills the employer is seeking. Some questions might be specific to programming languages or programming tools. If you do not know the answer, do not pretend that you do or allude to the fact that you have the specific requirement. Rather, use your transferable knowledge and skills and emphasize that you are a quick study and willing to learn the language, software, or skill. If you have learned a specific technical skill quickly in the past, describe that experience.

> **Technical interview** An interview during which technical questions are asked in order to demonstrate that you have the specific knowledge or skills the employer is seeking.

careercoach7.2

Don't Settle

Dating coach Paige Parker has an excerpt in her book, *Dating Without Drama*, relating the dating process to job interviews. When you think about success principles, there is a definite parallel between the two subjects. Paige stated it this way:

Dating Is Like a Job Interview[2]

Let's say that you're a journalist, and it's your dream job to write for *In Style* magazine. You send your resume and, miraculously, you are called in the next day for an interview. You go into the *In Style* offices and meet with the executive editor. Immediately you click. You have so much in common—you share an alma mater, you both have a love for people and fashion, and until that day, you'd never met someone who has the same quirky sense of humor as you. It's a perfect match. She loves your portfolio of writing samples and is impressed by your work experience.

When she shakes your hand at the end of the interview and tells you she'll call you soon, you're feeling confident that the job is yours.

So when *Glamour, Cosmopolitan,* and *Elle* magazines call you the next day and ask you to come in for an interview, do you say, "Thanks, but no thanks. I've already found a job."? Of course not.

You haven't been offered the job yet. There's a chance you may never be offered the job. You should interview with those other great publications just in case. Also, if *In Style* calls you in for a second interview, you've had the opportunity to brush up on your skills in the meantime. (Not to mention that with another offer on the table you'll be in a better position to negotiate!) And—who knows—maybe by meeting with these other magazines you'll discover that there's another editor who you could learn even *more* from; there might be a better career match out there for you that you didn't even know existed (Parker, 2009).

Paige Parker is referring to dating, but this excerpt is a perfect illustration of valuing your worth in the interview process. Like dating, you are looking for a great match. By the same token, you need to stir the pot (get the word out) and you may end up interviewing with many companies before

---

[2]Used with permission of Paige Parker.

you land your ideal job. It has been said that it takes one month of a job search for each $10,000 in salary you are seeking. So if you are seeking a $60K job, plan on spending up to six months working the market until you land it. In the meantime, you might want to get a temporary job as you search.

✓ SELF-CHECK

1. Why do you think behavioral interviews are becoming so popular with employers?

2. Which types of interviews are you familiar with, and which ones do you need to practice?

3. What type of interview is used most commonly in your field?

» LO 7-3 Understanding and Answering Interview Questions

While scripting interview answers is not recommended (you may not come off as sincere), knowing the types of interview questions you might be asked, and being prepared to answer them successfully, is a great idea. The following lists of questions will give you an idea of the types of questions you are likely to run into and suggested ways to answer them.

We will review the following:

Standard or traditional questions
Competency-based/behavioral questions
Illegal questions
Top 10 difficult questions

Standard or Traditional Interview Questions

These questions run the gamut from scenario questions to those that help the interviewer determine if the candidate would be a good fit for the company and culture. The best way to answer them is using the Three-Step Formula.

The Three-Step Formula for Answering Traditional Questions

Step 1: Understand what interviewers are really asking. There is usually a question behind the question. Answer the real question, not just the question they asked you. For example, if they ask, "What do you do for fun?" interviewers are not trying to find out about your hobbies. They are trying to find out

There is usually a question behind the question.

if you fit into the culture, or if you might embarrass them by going "clubbing" Thursday through Sunday. You want to answer the underlying question. In this case, you would let them know you are a well-balanced person with acceptable hobbies. You might go a step further and match hobbies that the interviewer is interested in, such as golfing or boating—if they are truly your hobbies as well.

Step 2: Answer the question. In less than two minutes, answer the question, remembering to focus on the real reason the question is being asked. Relate the answer to your skills and how you can add value to the organization.

Step 3: Support your answer with specifics. Prove your answers with examples or facts to support what you are saying. To say you like to do social things with your friends is a vague answer; but to say you often go to movies or go camping on the weekends proves your answer.

Practice Interview Questions

The following are questions that are commonly asked during standard interviews. Become familiar with them, and expect to hear some of them if you find yourself in a standard or traditional interview.

1. Tell me about yourself.
2. Where do you see yourself in five years?
3. What are your short- and long-term goals?
4. Why should we hire you over other qualified candidates?
5. What job have you had that you enjoyed the most and why?
6. How do you prefer to be supervised?
7. How do you supervise others?
8. Describe a problem you had at work and how you dealt with it.
9. What motivates you?
10. Are you available for traveling or overtime?
11. Why do you want to work for us?
12. Are you a big-picture person or a detail-oriented person?
13. How do you handle stress or pressure?
14. Describe a pressurized job situation that you encountered in the last few years and explain how you handled it.
15. Name some of your accomplishments that you are most proud of.
16. What do you do in your leisure time?
17. Why did you leave your last job?
18. Are you a team player or do you prefer to work alone?
19. Can you explain these gaps in your work history?
20. What would your last boss say about your work performance?
21. What are some of your professional strengths and weaknesses?
22. How do you feel you can add value or contribute to our company?
23. Have you ever been fired?
24. How flexible are you?
25. How do you handle change?
26. What do you know about our company?
27. Are you comfortable working in a stressful situation?
28. Are you willing to relocate?
29. What are you thinking in terms of salary?
30. Give an example of how you showed initiative at work.

Competency-Based/Behavioral-Based Interview Questions

When answering competency-based or behavior-based questions, you can follow a three-step acronym technique known as **STAR**, or Situation/Task, Action, Result. Variations of the acronym include STAR: Situation or Task/Action taken/Results; SAR: Situation/Action/Result; or PAR: formulate Problem/Action/Result. Essentially each of these is asking you to do the same thing. The acronym is a way to remember what to do when you are under stress in the interview.

What are the three basic steps to follow when answering a behavioral-based interview question?

The Three-Step Formula for Answering Competency-Based/Behavioral-Based Interview Questions

Step 1: Present the *Situation* or describe the *Task*.
Step 2: Explain the *Action* you took with examples to support it.
Step 3: Describe what happened. What was the *Result* of the action you took?

STAR A three-step acronym technique used to answer competency- or behavior-based interview questions; also known as SAR or PAR.

The hiring manager is looking for a specific example that demonstrates your competency, not a general overview. To do this successfully, you want to focus on proving your answer by providing an example of the situation.

The competencies that are being assessed are typically:

- Your personal attributes such as your flexibility, how well you make decisions, and your integrity and ethics.
- Your managerial or leadership abilities, such as demonstrating how well you lead, plan, organize, and supervise.
- Your administrative skills in terms of budgeting, organizing your time and space, and scheduling others.
- Your interpersonal skills, including how well you communicate, your teamwork abilities, and your approachability.
- Your technical skills, including computer software and computer knowledge.
- Your analytical skills, including number solving and basic critical thinking.
- Your motivation style, ability to focus, and energy level.

The following are several examples to help you get a better understanding of using the STAR process.

Question 1: Describe a situation where you had to work with a difficult co-worker.

Answer strategy: You want to demonstrate that you can *build relationships* with someone under difficult circumstances. Sometimes this is not possible. If you did not have success with a difficult co-worker, describe the efforts you took to make it work. Stress what you feel is needed to maintain good working relationships in the workplace.

Question 2: Give an example where you had too many assignments and too little time and how you handled the situation.

Answer strategy: This question pertains to time management, organization, delegating, and prioritizing. Your answer should address one or several of these skills.

Question 3: Tell me about a time where you had to go along with the group or a decision even though you did not agree with it.

Answer strategy: This question is about compromises and flexibility. It is also about the balance between leadership and cooperation. Depending on your situation, you might reflect on a time when you were outnumbered by the group, and later the decision was reversed, moving the group in your direction. It is a time to stress being a team player, while not being stuck in group thinking.

Question 4: Tell me how you plan your day, including how you schedule and organize your time.

Answer strategy: This question is focusing on your effective work habits and your self-motivation. You would give specific examples on how you use Microsoft Office Outlook or another system to manage your day appointments, tasks, and assignments as well as your month (or year). You could also discuss how you make your daily (or weekly) to-do list and how that helps you.

Question 5: Describe the culture of your current or past organization and explain how you worked in this type of corporate culture to achieve your goals.

Answer strategy: This question is focusing on your organizational awareness, your understanding of corporate culture, and how you adapt to meet your goals. Corporate cultures are hidden and you need to be alert to clues, artifacts, and subtle nuances to understand your company's culture. Each company has a unique culture and you want to be able to give specific examples to support your ideas. You will learn more about corporate cultures later in this book.

By utilizing the STAR three-step formula, you will successfully navigate behavior-based interviews. Behavior-based questions reveal your ability to answer questions and your skill level completing particular tasks. Remember that framing your responses to behavior-based questions according to the STAR three-step formula requires that you determine the situation or task (ST), the action required to resolve the situation (A), and the response after implementing the action (R).

STAR in Action

The following is a behavior-based interview for the position of city ordinance enforcement manager.

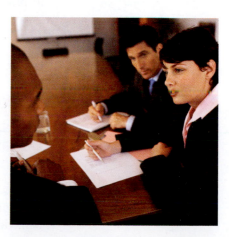

How does Victor use the STAR formula to answer Joy's question?

Prior to hosting interviews, the city council advised that they would like the person hired to have some skill or knowledge of how to handle falling parking revenue trends. Joy, the city human resource manager, outlines her interview questions to include one that asks an appropriate behavior-based question that should flush out the skills they are looking for in the person they eventually hire. The first job candidate is Victor, a parking enforcement supervisor for a neighboring city.

After the initial greetings, Joy got down to business by asking, "Victor, how would you attempt to correct a significant fall in parking revenue?" Banking on some collateral experience and direct knowledge, Victor quickly organized his thoughts utilizing the STAR formula. "I have experience with a similar situation (**ST**). Our contracted parking ramp revenue dropped off and I was asked to look into it. I found that business owners and patrons had little incentive to extend their contracts when other parking ramp contracts in the downtown vicinity were of equal price and value. I briefed the city council and received approval to offer a 15 percent discount to anyone willing to purchase annual parking ramp contracts (**A**). After implementing the new incentive, parking ramp revenue stabilized quickly and increased by years end (**R**)."

Victor expertly navigated the STAR technique when answering Joy's question. He left no doubt in Joy's mind regarding his ability to tackle and solve the parking revenue problem. What you don't want to do in any interview, and in this type in particular, is answer vaguely and in general terms. That is a sure-fire way to sink a behavioral-based interview.

exercise 7.1

Choose the STAR Technique Answer

Read the interview question and the three possible answers that the job candidate, LaTina, could provide. Choose the answer that best reflects using the STAR method of answering behavioral-based interview questions.

Interviewer

LaTina, please explain why you left your last job at ABC Furniture.

   a. LaTina: Well, I got too stressed with all the hours they kept piling on. With a young child at home and my husband working nights, it was just too much.

   b. LaTina: I enjoyed working for ABC Furniture, but now that I have my degree in management, I am ready for new challenges and there was nowhere for me to grow at the company. I did bring an excellent reference letter from my supervisor, the owner of ABC Furniture, in my portfolio for you to read.

   c. LaTina: I like new challenges and felt it was time to move on.

Which answer did you choose? Why?

From this exercise, it should be easy to see why it is important to prepare for behavior-based questions. The next exercise will give you an opportunity to practice your behavior-based interviewing skills.

exercise 7.2

Behavior-Based Questions and STAR Approach Answers

In this exercise you will practice recognizing behavior-based questions and appropriate responses using the STAR approach. First, write down three new behavior-based questions you foresee being asked by future employers. You can make them up or find them on the Internet. Remember, the interviewer wants you to prove that you have certain qualifications and skills that the company is seeking. Behavioral-based questions often start with phrases such as "Think of a time when . . . " or "Provide an example when . . . " or "Have you ever had the experience of _____? What did you do?"

Now you try:

1. _____

   _____

   _____

2. _____

   _____

   _____

3. _____

   _____

Once you have listed your behavior-based questions, formulate each answer according to the STAR outline. Write the letters (ST), (A), and (R) near the wording that illustrates the format correctly. If you are unsure, see the parking enforcement interview for an example.

1. _____

   _____

   _____

2. _____

   _____

   _____

3. _____

   _____

   _____

If you run into this situation, and feel your interview is going nowhere fast, use your control statement. A **control statement** is a statement that you make during the interview that changes the direction of the interview. See Career Coach 7.3 below for further information on the control statement and how to use it.

> **Control statement** A statement that you make during the interview that changes the direction of the interview.

career coach 7.3

The Control Statement

There is a coaching tool that you can keep in your back pocket and hopefully never need to use. It is called the *control statement* and is only used on rare occasions when the interview is going from bad to worse. If you have found yourself in this situation, you know the sinking feeling of not being able to turn the interview around as it goes down the drain. Fortunately, there is a tool to use to turn the situation around. Remember, it is only to be used in rare interview emergency situations. When called for, this tool works, and it could land you the job.

A control statement is a statement that you make in the interview that changes the direction of the interview. You take control of the interview. Here is what you do: Once you have determined that the interview has gone from bad to worse, and you know there is no hope for your having a remote chance at being selected, you stop answering questions. That is right. The hiring manager will ask you a question, and instead of answering it you say, "I know we don't have much time left to discuss this position and I really would like just two minutes to tell you why I applied with your company, why I want to work for you, and how I can add value to your organization. I want to quickly explain how I can meet and exceed your expectations in this position."

The floor is yours. Ninety-nine percent of the time you will get the two minutes. Use it well. Tell the interviewer exactly what you can do for the company. Give specific examples to prove that you have what it takes to make a difference. Demonstrate the research you've done on the company and how you align with its mission and values. Remember, keep this brief. Do not ramble on and on or you will once again lose them. Then, thank the hiring agent for the opportunity and ask for the job.

Do not use this tool in 99 percent of your interviews. It is an emergency tool. Perhaps you were so nervous that you fumbled the ball during the first part of the interview; the control statement is your "save." Use it sparingly, but know how to use it. Some students have reported that they actually got the job by using their control statement.

Illegal Questions

In an interview when you are asked an illegal question or one that is bordering on illegal, one thing to keep in mind is that most people doing the interviewing are not professional interviewers. Many have never been properly trained to interview. That does not excuse illegal questions, but the lapse may not have been intentional. With this in mind, you can decide if you will point out that the question is illegal, file a formal complaint, or let the situation go. What you do in this situation is up to you and there is not a right or wrong answer. The goal of this section is to educate you on illegal interview questions, increase your awareness, and provide you with options if you are ever faced with this issue. Illegal interview questions revolve around the categories that follow.

Affiliations

Prohibited question: *What groups or organizations do you belong to?*

Allowed question: *Are there any professional trade organizations you feel are relevant to your ability to perform this job?*

Age

Prohibited questions: *How old are you? What is your date of birth? What year did you graduate?*

Allowed questions: *Are you over the age of 18? Are you over the minimum age requirements established by the law?*

Arrest Record

Prohibited question: *Have you ever been arrested?*

Allowed question: *Have you ever been convicted of a felony or one of the following crimes?* (The crime needs to be related to the job.)

Citizenship

Prohibited question: *Are you a U.S. citizen?*

Allowed question: *Are you allowed to work in the United States?*

Disabilities/Health

Prohibited questions: *Do you have any disabilities? Have you had any major illnesses in the past five years? Have you been hospitalized? How many days of sick leave did you take last year? Have you been treated by a psychologist or a psychiatrist? Are you taking any prescribed medications? Have you been treated for drug addiction or alcoholism? Do you smoke?* It is also illegal to ask you to fill out a medical history form.

Allowed action: After the job is thoroughly described, the employer may ask the applicant if he or she can *perform the essential functions of the job.* A medical exam may be required after the job offer has been made. There are stipulations on confidentiality regarding such exams.

Gender

Prohibited questions: *How do you feel about supervising men (or women)? Have you ever been sexually harassed? What do you think about office romances?*

Allowed questions: *Tell me about your previous experience with supervising. Has there ever been a situation where you were disciplined for your behavior at work?*

Height/Weight

Height and weight are allowed only if there is a minimum standard for the safety of the job.

Prohibited questions: *How tall are you? What do you weigh?*

Allowed question: *As it is part of the job description, are you able to lift 50 pounds and carry it 100 yards?*

Marital/Family Status

Prohibited questions: *Who do you live with? Do you have children? What kind of child care arrangements have you made? Are you married, engaged, divorced, or single? What does your spouse think about your career? Do you have plans to start a family?*

Are you required to answer questions about your family status during an interview? What can you do if you don't feel comfortable answering the question?

Allowed questions if all candidates are asked: *Are you willing to relocate? Are you willing to travel as part of the job? Are you willing to work overtime as needed for the job?*

Military

Prohibited questions: *Were you honorably discharged from the military?*

Allowed questions: *What branch of the Armed Forces did you serve? What training or education did you receive in the military?*

National Origin/Race

Prohibited questions: *Where are you from? That is an unusual spelling or name; what is the origin?*

Allowed questions: *What is your name? Have you ever worked under a different name?*

Religion

Prohibited questions: *What holidays do you like to celebrate? What church do you attend?*

Allowed question: *Are you a member of any professional trade organizations you feel are relevant to your ability to perform this job?*

Answering Illegal Questions

Only you can decide whether to report an employer who violated regulations on interview questions. If you are asked a prohibited question in an interview, you have options. These include:

1. Answer the question truthfully, and risk losing the job offer.
2. Lie (not recommended).
3. Refuse to answer the question. You can state that the question makes you uncomfortable.
4. Answer the question without providing the information requested. For example, if you are asked about disabilities or medical history, you could answer that you are fully capable of meeting the job position requirements.

How you respond is a personal choice, and only you can make that decision. To recap, the questions that are prohibited by law in the United States generally fall into the following categories:

- Affiliations
- Age
- Arrest Record
- Citizenship
- Disability/Health
- Gender
- Height/Weight
- Marital/Family Status
- Military
- National Origin/Race
- Religion

This list is not all-inclusive and there are always exceptions, especially for positions that involve security. In addition, some types of positions require not only criminal history disclosure, but also credit history disclosures.

SELF-CHECK

4. Describe the three-step formula for answering traditional interview questions.

5. What does the acronym STAR stand for?

6. What are your options if you are asked an illegal interview question?

Cyber Trip 7.2

EEOC   Visit the website of the U.S. Equal Employment Opportunity Commission at www.eeoc.gov to learn more about what questions are prohibited during interviews, and how to report an employer.

Top 10 Difficult Questions

The following represent 10 of the toughest questions to answer during an interview. The questions themselves are not illegal, but if you are not prepared to answer them, you might easily get flustered by some of them, and share information you are not required to provide. Your response to these questions and to open-ended statements can tell the interviewer a great deal about your skills and experience, how you respond to pressure, and how you present yourself. Likewise, they are also questions through which many interviewees might find themselves offering unsolicited information that interviewers are not permitted to ask about. Become familiar with these questions, and know how to answer them so you are never caught off guard.

Question 1   Tell Me About Yourself

In response to this common question, many candidates provide information about themselves that would be illegal for interviewers to ask for, or they share irrelevant information that does not add value to the interview. The open-ended statement, *tell me about yourself*, is used because it potentially provides the interviewer with information that he or she would not be able to ask for, such as if the candidate is married, has children, a religious affiliation, or political affiliation. Sell yourself by describing why you chose your profession. Provide information about your education and work experience. Keep in mind, the interviewer may be fishing for information.

Question 2   What Is Your Personal Situation?

Again, this is a prime opportunity where a candidate might go overboard and share information that is illegal to ask. Make sure the information you provide enhances your candidacy for the job. Focus on your education, past employment, and career goals.

Question 3   What Are Your Strengths?

This is the time to shine. Describe your skills that match the qualifications of what the interviewer is looking for. Provide specific examples of how you excel at work by having this particular skill or quality.

Question 4   What Is Your Greatest Weakness?

This question is all about taking what might be perceived as a weakness and making it a strength. For example, let's say you are a huge procrastinator.

If you say that procrastination is your greatest weakness, you are most likely going to be taken out of the hiring pool. Remember, you are marketing yourself. Negative marketing does not sell. Your job is to shine. You can answer the question by framing it into your past. Here is how that is done. *"I used to be a huge procrastinator, but through help from my mentor I have found ways to not only turn in projects on time, but early, without sacrificing quality. For example, I use simple time management tools such as the 5-minute rule and use daily to-do lists to stay on track* (the 5-minute rule, simply stated, is that if you have 5 minutes, do something on your to-do list that does not take too much time, but needs to be done, like a phone call or quick e-mail). Here is another example: *I used to think that to get something done right, I needed to do it myself, and consequently, I was working 70+ hours a week on some things that really needed to be delegated. Now, I trust others more, explain what needs to be done, and delegate tasks, so I can focus on the heavy-hitter projects that need my full attention.*

Question 5   Why Do You Want to Leave Your Current Job?/Why Did You Leave Your Last Job?

Whether you chose to leave or were terminated, always speak in positive terms about your employer. If you were fired, explain how you and your supervisor (or the company) were not a good fit. Put a positive spin on any negative aspects of your employers, past or present. For example, *"My supervisor had a way of getting the employees motivated,"* instead of *"My boss was a drill sergeant."* Discuss how you learned from the experience to research the company and position more thoroughly. If you are still employed, discuss how you have advanced as far as you can in your current position and you are seeking new opportunities to grow that match your goals and education.

Always speak in positive terms about your current and past employers.

Question 6   What Are Your Plans for the Future?

While you may have no idea where you will be in 5 or 10 years, this question is asked to help hiring managers learn about your ambitions and long-term commitment. You want to send the message that you want to grow with their company. You might mention furthering your education.

Question 7   Why Do You Want to Work for Us?

You want to answer this question by referring to the research you did on the company. Frame your answer in terms of the things that the company is doing well or that you want to be involved with. You also want to say something about the job you are applying for—why you are interested in it and why it is a good fit for you.

Question 8   What Would Your Current Employer (Co-Worker or Boss) Say About You?

This question is related to your strengths, so pull from them. *They would say that I go the extra mile without being asked to make sure the job not only gets done, but is done well.*

Question 9 Why Should We Hire You for This Position over Other Qualified Candidates?

The question within the question is two-fold: the hiring agents want to see how you handle the question and how you sell yourself. Don't be defensive. You want to give specific examples of how you can meet and exceed the company's needs. You know more about their needs by listening to them during the interview and from doing your research. Explain how you, as a professional with your unique background, experience, and education, can add value to their company. You do this by demonstrating how you added value for others. This is how you close the sale.

Question 10 What Are You Looking for in Terms of Salary?

Please refer to Career Coach 7.4 to discover the secret to answering this question.

careercoach7.4

The Secret to Answering the Money Question

As noted earlier, *never bring up money in the interview*. If the interview panel or manager asks you questions regarding salary in the interview, there are a few ways you can handle this successfully. The interviewer might lead with: *What are you currently earning in your position? What did you earn in your last position? What are you hoping to earn for salary?* or *What will you need in terms of salary to join our company?* Answer these questions by focusing on your willingness to negotiate, and by being open or flexible. Don't give an exact number.

If pressed further, you should be prepared to know what the position is worth. You can find salary information on websites such as the Department of Labor's Occupational Handbook at http://www.bls.gov/oco/home.htm or www.salary.com. You can also conduct an Internet search using keywords "salary survey" or "salary calculator." Use this information to state a range. You might say something like "With my five years experience and education in the field, the salary range for positions such as this in this area is $ _____ to $ _____." Reiterate how you will add value to their organization.

You want to keep the focus off the money question until you get a firm job offer. In fact, you might follow their question about salary with "Are you making me an offer?" Be sincere when you ask this question.

As a recap on how to go about checking the salary for a specific position:

1. **Locate your job position.** You can use any of the online job boards including Monster.com or Careerbuilder.com.

2. **Research the salary range** for that job using one of the salary calculators, such as salary.com, http://www.rileyguide.com/salary.html, or the Bureau of Labor Statistics at http://www.bls.gov/bls/blswage.htm.

Create a List of Questions to Ask

Review the list of possible questions to ask in the interview and select three you like the best by circling the numbers from the following list.

1. What is a typical day like for this position?
2. What areas are the highest priorities for this position and need immediate solutions or attention?
3. What is the division's management style?
4. What is the next step in this process?
5. When do you plan on making a decision?
6. Why is the position open?
7. What are the avenues for advancement with this position?
8. Do you offer assistance with professional development, training, or furthering one's education?
9. Is an advanced degree required or preferred for promotions?
10. Who would I report to?
11. How is performance for this position measured?
12. What other departments does this position interface (or cooperate) with, and is there anything I should know about that role in connecting with these other parts of the organization?

Write down two additional questions to ask during the interview:

Question 1: _____

Question 2: _____

Type the list of questions you plan to ask during an interview into a Word document. You will want to save this list and modify it for each interview so you can print and take a copy with you.

» LO 7-4 Creating Your Professional Image

First impressions count! Projecting yourself through dress and attitude is extremely important when interviewing. Even if you have had a terrible day, or you are down to your last $20 and urgently need the job, leave your worry, desperation, or anger at the door as you walk into the interview. Likewise, while you want to demonstrate your uniqueness during the interview, what you wear is not the best way to do it. Going to an interview wearing a T-shirt, flip-flops, and nose ring will probably differentiate you from the other applicants, but not necessarily in a good way. The interviewer won't want to waste his or her time, regardless of your stellar portfolio. Get the job first, then decide if you are going to wear your nose ring to work (check the company handbook for the dress code). While there may be a time and place for all things, the interview is not the time or the place to challenge societal norms. If you want the job, then cater to the industry standard for interviewing.

Professional Attire Guide

Today, the dress code in many workplaces is business casual. **Business casual** is attire that falls between jeans and a formal suit; each company defines what fits into this category. The technology, automotive, factory, or trade industries tend to lean toward business casual. However, even if business casual is appropriate for a typical workday, you should dress more formally for an interview.

Following the guidelines below will ensure that you present yourself properly and professionally for interviews. You want to walk into the interview as the most successful version of yourself. This has to do with image. The last thing you want to do is put time and effort into your skills, interview preparations, and marketing tools, only to disappoint the hiring manager upon meeting him or her due to an unprofessional appearance.

Business casual may be worn to certain interviews, depending on the industry. Whether your industry is retail, business, technology, legal, culinary, corporate, small business, or any number of other options, why is it imperative for you to research the most appropriate attire for each interview you attend?

Women

- Clean and pressed clothing.
- Wear a pantsuit, or a jacket and coordinating knee- or calf-length skirt.
- Appropriate colors for interviews are black, gray, navy blue, tan, and brown. Pinstripes also work well, as long as they are small and conservative.
- Tailored blouse in a color that complements your suit. A small print also might work, but stay away from trends, and stick to traditional styles and colors.
- No dresses.
- Leave your purse in your vehicle, or use a small purse.
- Clear or neutral nail polish; stay away from red, pink, or any other bright colors.
- One set of conservative earrings.
- Conservative watch.
- One ring per hand or less.
- Conservative closed-toe shoes; pumps are acceptable, but avoid high heels and stilettos.
- Clean makeup that looks natural and fresh.
- Skin tones for hosiery; no bare legs.
- Cover tattoos if possible.
- Apply little to no perfume, hairspray, or other scents that might offend or cause allergic reaction to others.
- A good rule of thumb is that if you could wear it to a club or bar, don't wear it to the interview.
- Hair should be clean, neat, and out of your eyes.
- No book bags or bulky briefcases.
- No gum, candy, food, or cigarettes. Refrain from smoking prior to the interview in the clothes you plan to wear. The interviewer cannot legally ask you if you smoke, but may smell it.
- You can take a bottle of water.
- Bring a padded portfolio with a legal pad and nice pen.

Business casual Attire that falls between jeans and a formal suit; each company defines what falls into this category.

Men

- Clean and pressed clothing.
- Wear a suit and tie, unless business casual is accepted. It is not recommended that you wear jeans to an interview.
- Good colors for interviews are black, gray, navy blue, tan, and brown.
- Silk necktie with a conservative pattern.
- Nails should be short and clean.
- Only a wedding band or college class ring.
- Cover tattoos if possible.
- Little to no cologne.
- Hair should be clean, neat, and out of your eyes.
- No book bags or bulky briefcases.
- No gum, food, candy, or cigarettes. Refrain from smoking prior to the interview in the clothes you plan to wear. The interviewer cannot legally ask you if you smoke, but may smell it.
- You can take a bottle of water.
- Facial hair should be neat and trimmed.
- Bring a padded portfolio with a legal pad and nice pen.

Self-Worth in Interviewing

Sometimes we can be our own worst enemy, and inadvertently put more emphasis on our weaknesses than our strengths when interviewing. This can happen for a variety of reasons. Some people have been criticized their whole lives, so they take that feeling of low self-worth to the interview. Others are perfectionists who feel they need to make excuses for any potential weakness they might have. And still others are just plain nervous and don't do well in interviews. Regardless of why this might happen, there are things you can do to interview like a highly confident, successful candidate, even if you don't feel that way on the inside.

Self-esteem is partly a skill and partly an attitude.

—Ken Fraser, Australian representative on the International Council for Self-Esteem

Here are some pointers:

- Don't compare your insides to other's outsides. This means that even if you are nervous, don't assume other people have it "all together." You are worthy of the job.
- Focus on the work you did in Chapters 1 and 2 on your goals, skills, talents, and abilities.
- Know you are innately worthy of having what you want and of being treated with respect.
- Smile; practice kindness and courtesy before, during, and after the interview. If you are angry at the "bad" drivers on the way to the interview, you are setting up your emotions for distress rather than ease during the interview.
- Act as if the job is already yours. Bring your best, confident, friendly self to the interview.
- Remember that the past is the past. Your tomorrow starts at this moment.

- Use the positive self-talk we learned in Chapter 1.

- Remember: If you don't have the skills they seek in the interview you can acquire them. You can get the certification or sign up for a class or learn the skill on the job. You can sell the fact that you are a quick learner and willing to go the extra distance.

- If you don't get the job, remind yourself it is "not about you."

- Each interview is part of *hammering away at the rock*. We don't know which blow will shatter the rock or land the job, so hang in there.

- Remember to use your self-talk if you don't get the job offer. You can say, "It is their loss" or "Next time I interview I will do this or that better."

The more you interview, the better you will get at interviewing! And soon you will land a job that is perfect for you. It is a process. Don't put all of your self-worth into any interview.

Project Confidence

Despite possible difficult or stressful factors going on in your life, you must keep calm and project professionalism and confidence during each and every interview. The interviewer will watch you closely not only for your verbal answers, but also for your body language. Nervousness, anger, and anxiety can be difficult to manage, and you might not even realize you are projecting the wrong energy during an interview. Become aware of the factors in your life that might be affecting your confidence, and stay in tune to the image you put forth in front of the hiring manager.

> *The interviewer will watch you closely not only for your verbal answers, but also for your body language.*

Many students tell me they don't enjoy interviewing because they get too nervous and bomb the interviews. The solution to this problem is practice. Practice dressing the part and presenting yourself to peers, family, friends, acquaintances, and even strangers that you meet day to day. Interview more, not less. Apply for jobs you are not that interested in, but know you can get the interview. Use these interviews for experience and networking, and let go of having a personal stake in getting the job offer. This will free you up to enjoy the process more and not appear desperate or needy to the prospective employer. This is also one reason that it is best to look for your ideal job when you have a job. Employers can sense that you are not desperate for the position and this makes you more attractive as a candidate. That desperate, needy energy repels what you seek.

career coach 7.5

Desperation Does Not Win the Job

The biggest problem I have with trying to walk away from an unsuitable offer is the fact that we are so desperate for me to get a job right now. I just have to remember that I have a right to get what I deserve. I also know that I should not appear desperate.
—Stacy Major, paralegal studies, Virginia College Online student

You might be thinking that you are, in fact, desperate for the job. Perhaps you have recently been laid off or are soon to graduate and have not found your ideal job. When the stakes are high and the stress is higher, it is wise to remember there is an opposite principle to *like attracts like*, or the Law of Attraction. If you are hammering away at your positive career self-talk, career goals, and marketing tools, yet you are not getting the results you seek, consider this: feeling desperate, worried, and locking onto only one possible outcome is a deal breaker for getting what you are seeking. If you are focused on not having what you want, you end up getting more of what you don't want. This causes you to lose instead of win. If you find that happening, you can turn it around. Simply focus on all that you do have. Do some of the clearing work we discussed in an earlier chapter. Make another gratitude list. Spend time doing something you love to get back the feeling of joy and being alive. Get out of your rut. You can use any challenge you are facing to actually propel you further in your career goals. Taking all of these steps will enhance your self-image, which will in turn enhance the confident, professional image of yourself that you project onto others.

✔ SELF-CHECK

7. Why are open-ended interview questions sometimes difficult to answer?

8. Define business casual attire. For what type of interviews might this attire be appropriate?

9. List two ways you can build your self-confidence.

» LO 7-5   Conduct a Mock Interview

As you learned earlier in this chapter, a mock interview is a simulated interview used for practice. Unfortunately, the mock interview is often overlooked in the interview process. One of the best ways to improve your interview skills is practice. You can go to many interviews to get this practice and you can also set up your own mock interview. Mock interviews are beneficial for several reasons. They allow you to increase your confidence as well as requiring preparation, execution, and follow-up. Mock interviews provide you with the perfect setting to convey your skills in a controlled setting.

e x e r c i s e 7.3

Mock Interview with a Professional

Schedule a mock interview with someone who will ask you interview questions and provide you with helpful feedback. It is recommended to use someone in human resources, or someone who does this as part of his or her job.

By selecting someone in the hiring capacity to conduct the mock interview, the feedback you receive should be constructive and helpful.

Use the Interview Checklist in Figure 7.3 for the mock interview. Have the interviewer (not you) fill out the checklist. It is helpful if the interviewer gives you specific comments, not just checkmarks or points. Consider videotaping the mock interview so you can see exactly where and how you can improve.

Your Name (student) _____

Interviewer's Name _____

INTERVIEW PERFORMANCE RATINGS			
No = 0 POINTS	Needs Improvement = 1 POINT	Yes = 2 POINTS	Comments
INTRODUCTION			
On time			
Introduced self			
Firm handshake			
Used interviewer's name			
Stated purpose of visit			
PERSONAL APPEARANCE			
Wore neat, professional clothing			
Well-groomed			
COMMUNICATION			
Good eye contact			
Smiled			
Calm and professional			
Confident and enthusiastic			
Good answers to questions; supported with examples			
Marketed skills and experience			
PREPARED FOR INTERVIEW			
Had necessary materials: resume, paper, pen, etc.			
Asked questions			
CLOSE OF INTERVIEW			
Asked for the job			
Asked about follow-up			
Thanked interviewer			
OTHER COMMENTS:			

Figure 7.3 Interview Checklist

exercise 7.4

In-Class Mock Interview

For this activity, you will conduct mock interviews in class with your peers. You will have the opportunity to be both an interviewer and an interviewee.

As the Interviewer

Before you act as the *interviewer*, you must first decide what type of an interview you will be conducting (see the types of interviews presented earlier in this chapter such as behavioral interview or stress interview). Next, prepare a set of interview questions to ask the prospective employee (your peer). Make certain you ask questions that are aligned with the type of interview you are conducting. For example, traditional interview questions are different from behavioral interview questions, as we discussed earlier. Use the Interview Checklist from Exercise 7.3 above to take notes and critique the other student. This will provide him or her with feedback to use in the future.

As the Interviewee

As in a real interview situation, you will not know in advance which type of interview you will be having for your mock interview, so be prepared. Bring the list of questions you plan to ask the person who conducts the interview. While much of a mock interview is improvised, do your best to make it real. Consider videotaping the in-class mock interviews, so you can replay them and gain additional insights to ways you might improve your interview skills in the future.

exercise 7.5

In-Class Round-Robin Mock Interview

For this exercise, students sit in a circle. One at a time, each student asks the person to his or her left an interview question. Each student has up to two minutes to answer the question. Once the student answers, he or she then asks the student to the left a new interview question. Once this activity is complete, students provide feedback to each other.

Log of Contacts Expanded

In Chapter 3, you learned how to create and keep a log of your contacts. You can do this in a notebook or electronically. As a review, the following chart contains a sample of the information you will want to include in your log. Now you can expand your log of contacts by including postinterview notes.

LOG OF CONTACTS	
Company name:	
Address:	
City:	
State:	
Zip code:	
Website address:	
Contact person Name/and title:	
Phone #:	
Fax #:	
E-mail:	
Comments:	
Date applied:	
Follow-up:	
Title and name of interviewer:	
Date interviewed:	
Postinterview notes and follow-up taken	

Figure 7.4   Log of Contacts with Postinterview Notes

career coach 7.6

It's Ok to Be Nervous

Simply noticing your feelings about interviewing will enable you to interview better. When you don't fight the fear, but rather notice it like this—*"Yep, that is it. I am feeling butterflies in my stomach and I don't want to interview"*—you will do better than if you fight the fear. It is far better to just be nervous. Don't fix it; just be aware of it and be sure you are projecting yourself calmly and professionally. Athletes use nervous energy to propel them to the next level; so should you (Chopra, 2005; Kane & Kane, 2008; Kasl, 2005; Forleo, 2009; McColl, 2007; Price, 1998; Rutherford, 1998; Proctor, 1997; Shinn, 2008).

Cyber Trip 7.3

Practicing Interviews on the Web   Visit http://www.oet.ky.gov/des/vws/interview/interview_workshop.asp to walk through an interview workshop step-by-step.

Be Prepared!—Hew's Practice Makes Perfect

Hew left the interview with Marketing Solutions, LLC, feeling let down and worn out. He knew that interviewing was not one of his strengths. Later that night, Hew got a call from Renetta, one of the managers at Palmer & Anderson where he had interned. Renetta had become somewhat of a mentor for him, and she wanted to know how the interview had gone.

Hew said, "It wasn't good, Renetta. I just could not find the words."

Renetta felt bad for Hew, as she knew how badly he wanted a job at a marketing firm. "Hew, how did you prepare for the interview?" she asked.

"That is just it, Renetta; I didn't prepare. I don't know how to prepare—I hate interviews!"

Renetta replied, "It takes practice. Don't be down on yourself. More opportunities will come your way, and with each one you will get better at selling yourself. By the way, did you put together the portfolio we talked about?"

Hew thought about it and said, "I meant to, but I didn't take the time. I didn't know it mattered that much." Renetta reminded Hew that his work shined, and since interviewing was still difficult for him, his confidence might be stronger if he put together a solid portfolio demonstrating some of the projects he had completed in school and during his internship.

Based on his answers so far, Renetta could already guess his answer to the next question. Nevertheless, she asked, "Hew, did you take any letters of recommendation to the interview?"

"No," answered Hew. "I don't like asking for those. I don't want to bother anyone like you or one of my instructors to write a letter."

Renetta smiled on the other end of the phone, "I know you are not asking, but I would be happy to write one for you if you promise to put together your portfolio for your next interview." Hew was surprised at Renetta's generosity and willingness to write a letter of recommendation for him. His mood began to lift. He had applied to other positions, and he started to think about the next interview as a real job opportunity, not a dreaded event.

"Thank you, Renetta, I feel much better and I appreciate you calling me and offering me a letter of recommendation. I will put the portfolio together. Would you be willing to look at it when it is ready?"

"Absolutely!" Renetta replied. "I will also e-mail you a draft of that letter in the next few days. You are a wonderful worker and you are going to get the job you want. Hang in there, OK?"

The next day, Hew took action and contacted his friend Melissa, a human resources manager for a local company. He told her his difficulty with interviews. Melissa suggested they get together for a mock interview and videotape it. As he prepared, Hew was surprised at how the mock interview was nearly as nerve-racking as the real interview. A couple of days before they met, Melissa called Hew and gave him the name of a real company and suggested he conduct some research on the company on the Internet to be more prepared. Based on what had happened in his last interview, Hew took this advice to heart!

During their mock interview, Melissa used behavior-based interview questions and asked Hew how he handled different situations. Hew came to the mock interview prepared with a list of questions to ask. After the mock interview, Melissa and Hew reviewed the video, and she made comments regarding what Hew might change in the future.

With the additional practice from the mock interview, plus his new portfolio, Hew found himself more confident when interviewing. Hew also learned to make a log of his contacts and to save job postings that interested him in a file on his computer. He knew now that he needed to refresh himself on the job position before each interview and even take a printout of the job listing with him in his folder to the interview, in order to have information about the job at hand. While his next few interviews did not result in job offers, he kept practicing by mock interviewing and remained organized about his job search. A few weeks later, Hew's practice and preparation paid off and resulted in an offer for a great marketing position that he was not only excited about, but that also fit his career goals perfectly.

Discussion Questions

1. How does participating in mock interviews help in the real interview situation?
2. What can you do to prepare for different types of interviews?
3. Name three items you can add to your own portfolio in addition to your cover letter and resume.

[chapter summary]

Interviewing is the grand finale of the job search. For the interview to be successful, all of your hard work networking, preparing marketing tools, and conducting research must come together in this 30 minute or less face-to-face exchange of information. Using the STAR formula as an approach to answering many interview questions will help make the interview come out in your favor. In a nutshell:

- Research online the company and position, including average salary base.
- Practice interview questions and answers using the STAR approach.
- Dress appropriately and be well-groomed for the interview.
- Take your marketing tools with you and include a legal pad and pen.

- Determine the simplest route to get to the interview.
- Decide in advance on the best place to find a parking spot.
- Plan to get to the interview at least 15 minutes early.
- Use a professional handshake and smile.
- Listen attentively and answer using the STAR approach. Prove your answers with examples.
- Ask for the job!
- Ask for a business card for follow-up.
- Thank the interviewer and leave with a professional handshake and a smile. Present your networking business card.

[skill/term check]

1. Identify and describe two of the seven interview steps in detail. (LO 7-1)
2. What are the main differences between the traditional interview and the competency-based/behavioral-based interview? (LO 7-2)
3. How might you handle the stress interview? (LO 7-2)
4. What is the value of answering interview questions using the STAR technique? (LO 7-3)
5. What is a control statement, and when would you use it? (LO 7-3)
6. Provide an example of an illegal interview question. How might you answer it? (LO 7-3)
7. Name three professional image tips. (LO 7-4)
8. What is the purpose of a mock interview? (LO 7-5)
9. What specific things can you work on in mock interviews to help you perform better in real interviews? (LO 7-5)

[KEY TERMS]

Business casual: Attire that falls between jeans and a formal suit; each company defines what fits into this category. **(LO 7-4)** [p. 225]

Competency-based interview: An interview based on the premise that your past employment behavior will dictate your future behavior in the new position; also known as a behavioral-based interview. **(LO 7-2)** [p. 205]

Control statement: A statement you make during the interview that changes the direction of the interview. **(LO 7-3)** [p. 217]

Lunch or dinner interview: An interview that takes place during a meal, and may be part of a daylong interview process, or it may be the interview itself. **(LO 7-2)** [p. 205]

Mock interview: Simulated interview for practice. **(LO 7-2)** [p. 205]

Nondirective interview: An interview often used in fields where the candidate needs to demonstrate his or her skills or wares; also known as a work sample interview. **(LO 7-2)** [p. 206]

Panel interview: An interview that usually takes place around a conference table, where a group of individuals will collectively ask the candidate questions; also known as a group interview. **(LO 7-2)** [p. 206]

Phone interview: An interview conducted over the phone, usually before meeting the hiring manager in person. **(LO 7-2)** [p. 207]

Screening interview: An interview used to evaluate and narrow a large applicant pool; also known as a prescreening interview. **(LO 7-2)** [p. 209]

Second interview: An interview that occurs after the initial interview and involves candidates who made the first cut and have been screened down to a small pool of people in which the company is truly interested. **(LO 7-2)** [p. 210]

Standard interview: An interview during which the applicant is asked a variety of typical questions; also known as a traditional interview. **(LO 7-2)** [p. 204]

STAR: A three-step acronym technique used to answer competency- or behavior-based interview questions; also known as SAR or PAR. **(LO 7-3)** [p. 214]

Stress interview: An interview with the goal of seeing how you actually handle stress in the workplace, rather than just asking you questions about how you handle stress. **(LO 7-2)** [p. 210]

Structured interview: An interview in which each job candidate receives the exact same questions. **(LO 7-2)** [p. 210]

Technical interview: An interview during which technical questions are asked in order to demonstrate that you have the specific knowledge or skills the employer is seeking. **(LO 7-2)** [p. 211]

chapter 8

Follow-Up and Negotiation

Attempting to negotiate a better offer is almost always in your best interest.
—Richard Castellini, VP, CareerBuilder.com

 **target competency >** *Demonstrate successful follow-up and learn how to effectively negotiate.*

learning outcomes

After studying this chapter, you should be able to:

LO 8-1 Demonstrate the two-step follow-up procedure.

LO 8-2 Apply the art of successful negotiation.

LO 8-3 Understand the elements in making a sound career decision.

LO 8-4 Negotiate once you have a job.

LO 8-5 Manage obstacles and frustrations in the job search.

What Now?

Tracy had been through three rounds of interviews for a pharmacy technician position with CRV Pharmacy, one of the largest pharmacy chains in the country. Her last interview was with Mrs. James, the head pharmacist at the location she would be working at. This was Tracy's dream job as she had completed pharmacy technician training, passed the certification exam, and become a certified pharmacy technician. Tracy left the final interview feeling very good about getting the job. She went home immediately and sent a thank you e-mail to Mrs. James, the person who had interviewed her last. Tracy received a call the next day offering her the position. She was very excited until she heard the offer. The salary offer was much lower than she was expecting. If she took the position, it would mean less money than she was currently making. In addition, she would have a longer commute to the new job. Tracy composed herself and asked the following questions:

1. When would they need her to start?
2. How often were performance reviews given?
3. Are there opportunities for promotion?

After her questions were answered, Tracy asked Mrs. James if she could get back to her the next day, as she would need to think about the offer. Mrs. James said yes, but she asked Tracy to call her within 24 hours with her decision. She needed to fill the position quickly. Tracy said that she would and thanked Mrs. James.

Perplexed and not knowing what to do, Tracy called the career development director at her college to ask for advice. The director reminded Tracy of what she had learned in the career development course about negotiating a salary and suggested she review the relevant chapter in her textbook. The director was the person who had taught the course and was more than happy to help former students and to offer suggestions.

Tracy pulled out her book, read over the chapter on negotiation, and wrote down what she would say when she called back the next day, hoping that her strategy would work. She called Mrs. James bright and early the next morning and told her that she did appreciate the offer, but that she was unable to accept it at this time. Mrs. James asked her why and Tracy told her that the salary offered, coupled with the commute, would put her at a disadvantage. Tracy thought that by saying this, Mrs. James would make her a better offer. Mrs. James said that she understood, and that she appreciated Tracy's honesty. She reiterated that Tracy had excellent qualifications and wished her luck in her continued job search. She did not make Tracy another offer.

Discussion Questions

1. Did Tracy have the right reasons for not accepting the job with CRV?
2. Did Tracy try to negotiate or did she turn down the offer with her remarks?
3. What is a different way Tracy could have negotiated a better salary?

» LO8-1 The Two-Step Follow-Up Procedure

The Interview Is Not Over until the Thank You Note Is Sent

Very few job candidates take the thank you note seriously. We live in a time when thank you notes are considered too formal by many job seekers, a nuisance by others, and totally overlooked by some. The fact is that to separate yourself from the pack and show your sincere interest in the position, you want to send a thank you note. Since you made sure you had the hiring manager's business card when you left the interview, you are ready to send a thank you note.

> *Gratitude can shift everything.*
> —Joe Vitale

Two Thank You Notes Are Better than One

Your *thank you strategy* (and it is a strategy) goes like this:

Thank you strategy 1—the e-mail thank you: An **e-mail thank you** is simply an e-mail note sent the day of the interview to show your immediate interest in the position. After you interview, send an *e-mail thank you,* preferably that day. You want to do this to show your immediate interest in the position and gratitude for the interview.

E-mail thank you An e-mail thank you note sent the day of the interview to show your immediate interest in the position.

Thank you notes do not need to be elaborate, but they do need to be professional and they do need to be sent. You can refer to the notes you took in the interview so that you can mention something specific in your note and formal follow-up letter. If you do not have a physical address, then the *e-mail thank you* will be the only one you send. Figure 8.1 shows an example of an e-mail thank you note. The subject line of the e-mail for this example should read "Thank you Accounting Position Interview" so that the person receiving the message will not think it is spam.

Thank you strategy 2—handwritten follow-up: Follow the e-mail note with a *snail mail (postage stamp) note.* Buy professional thank you cards. Do not buy note cards with butterflies or other cute details; just the words

---

Dear Mr. Williams,

Thank you for the opportunity to interview with you for the accounting position with Server Pros. I hope I answered all of your questions. Should you have any more questions, please do not hesitate to contact me.

I am very interested in the position and look forward to the next step.

Sincerely,

Your name

Phone number

E-mail address

Figure 8.1 E-Mail Thank You Note

Dear Mr. Williams,

Once again, I want to express my appreciation in meeting you and discussing the networking administrator position with Nel-Tech.

I look forward to hearing from you in the near future.

Sincerely,

Your Signature

Phone number

E-mail address

Figure 8.2   Handwritten Thank You Note

"Thank You" should be on the outside of the card, and the card should be blank inside. Handwrite your thank you message in the note card. If your handwriting is not legible, then have someone else write the message for you. You will write only a couple of lines, much like the e-mail thank you. Change the verbiage from what you sent in your e-mail follow-up. See Figures 8.2–8.5 for examples.

I am a huge apostle for thanking.
—Marshall Goldsmith

The reason you want to follow up with a formal thank you note or letter is that you want to be fresh in their mind when interviewers are interviewing other candidates or making their final decision. This way, while interviewing other qualified candidates, they will be reminded and affirmed of your character in the form of a thank you letter. This not only separates you from the other candidates, but also positively influences their focus back onto your application. Include one of your networking business cards (NBCs) in the note. This is another opportunity to market yourself. If your contact information (phone, e-mail, and address) is not on your NBC, make sure to include it in the note.

Dear Ms. Mitchell,

Thank you for arranging the interview today. It helped me gain a better understanding of how the Technology Solutions Group functions.

I appreciated the discussion this morning, as it also helped me see how I could add value to the team. The Web Designer position is aligned with my skills, experience, and career goals.

Thank you again for answering my questions and for meeting with me.

Kathy Martin

Phone number

Figure 8.3   Thank You Note Sample 1

Dear Mr. Davis,

I want to take a minute to tell you how impressed I was with the atmosphere and what I learned about *(name the company)* today. Thank you for meeting with me and answering my questions about the marketing position.

From our discussion, I feel my skills, education, and experiences would be a good fit for the position and that I would work well with your team.

Thank you again,

Jeff Hoffman

Phone number

Figure 8.4 Thank You Note Sample 2

Dear Ms. Norman,

I appreciate you taking the time to discuss the *(job title)* position with me today. I learned more about what *(name of company)* is accomplishing and what is on the horizon.

I am interested in joining such a motivated, cohesive team. The purpose and duties of the *(position title)* position are aligned with my personal career mission and goals. I believe my skills, gifts, and experience could be well-served in this position.

Thank you again,

Josie Woods

Phone number

Figure 8.5 Thank You Note Sample 3

If you do not care for formal thank you note cards or if you prefer the note to be typed, you can send a thank you in the form of a business letter that matches the style of your cover letter and resume.

Another reason you want to send the formal thank you note is that it is the right thing to do. In fact, some hiring managers think less of candidates who do not send a thank you note. Again, if you do not have an e-mail address, then the formal thank you note is the only one you will be able to send. That is fine. One is better than none.

Why is it important to follow up each interview with a formal thank you letter?

Cyber Trip 8.1

Follow-Up Letters to the Interview   Visit one or more websites for ideas on what to write in a thank you letter. To do this, use your favorite search engine and type in the keywords *"interview follow-up letter"* or *"interview thank you."* Your search will yield many samples of the types of letters and thank you notes you can send.

Catherine B. Delaware

555 NE Florida Ave #100
Somewhere, IA 50000
(515) 001-0001
cdelaware@dayrep.com

January 4, 2016

Kent Lewis
Brice & Lewis Law Group PC
500 Buena Vista Building
505 5th Avenue
Somewhere, IA 50000

Dear Mr. Lewis,

Thank you for the opportunity to interview today. The information you shared with me about Brice & Lewis Law Group was most intriguing, and I am excited about the possibility of applying my education and experience in the position of Legal Administrative Assistant for your firm.

The possibility of working with Workers' Compensation and Product Liability is especially intriguing.

If I can provide you with any additional information, please let me know. I look forward to hearing from you soon.

Respectfully,

Catherine Delaware

Catherine B. Delaware

Figure 8.6   Formal Thank You Letter Sample 1

Two of the most powerful words in the English language for bringing about change are 'thank you'.
—The Universe[1]

P.S. 'Happy Hour' is not a word.

If you had a panel interview, tedious as this may sound, send a thank you to each member of the interview. Be sure to vary the message in the thank you in case they are shared. If you do not have their addresses or e-mail addresses, ask the hiring manager for their contact information so that you may follow up with them directly. You can also send a thank you to the chair or head of the interview committee, asking him or her to share your thank you with others on the panel. Try to avoid doing this, as the formal thank you note or letter leaves a positive and lasting impression and is worth the effort. Samples of the formal thank you letter are shown in Figures 8.6–8.8.

[1]www.tut.com

200 NW 7th Terrace #919
Somewhere, FL 33333
555.001.0001
rebeccabeal@gustr.com

January 9, 2016

Ms. Patricia Bowman
Hiring Manager
Solution Corporation
6000 Solution Avenue
Somewhere, FL 33333

Dear Ms. Bowman,

It was a pleasure to meet with you yesterday to discuss the Operations Manager position available at Solution Corporation. The information you shared with me about Solution's Operations Department was excellent, and I am very interested in applying my skills and experience to such a dynamic organization.

As we discussed, my qualifications seem to be an excellent match for the position. My previous work history, with over 10 years of operations management experience, has prepared me to meet the challenges of this position. In addition, my work ethic and solid management experience will allow me to adapt easily to your organization.

Enclosed is an official copy of my transcript, which you requested. If I can provide you with any additional information, please let me know. Thank you for the interview and for considering me for the Operations Manager position.

Sincerely,

Rebecca Beal

Rebecca Beal

Enclosure

Figure 8.7   Formal Thank You Letter Sample 2

careercoach8.1

Gratitude as a Success Tool

Gratitude is an interesting and powerful coaching principle. When you are thankful for something before you get it, in this case a job offer, you are affirming the outcome you desire. Sending a thank you message following an interview is a good marketing tool as well as a manifestation tool. You are appreciating the fact that the hiring manager chose you to interview out of all of the candidates who applied. You appreciate the networking opportunity the interview gave you, and you appreciate the opportunity to land a job with the company. While you might not get the job offer, letting them know that you

are grateful for the interview with them makes a difference. Sometimes the candidate that is selected for the job does not work out and the company needs to find a quick replacement. Your effort of gratitude may be the one thing that sticks out in their mind from others they interviewed. The few minutes it takes to write and send a professional thank you is worth it (Canfield & Hansen, 1996; Dooley, 2009; Fengler & Varnum, 1994; Gage, 2006; Gregory 2004; Klauser, 2001; Matthews, 1990; McColl 2007; Proctor, 1997; Ray, 1999; Rutherford, 1998; Shinn, 2008; Vitale, 2006, 2007, 2009; Heer, 2012; Zimmerman, 2011).

Thank You Notes When You Are Turned Down

Believe it or not, it is a good idea to send another thank you if you find out you were not selected for the position. As noted earlier, the person selected for the position may not work out, and you could still be offered the position. By sending this note, you show your spirit of fair play in the workplace and your professionalism. Companies that are growing are going to need more workers; people retire and people move. Therefore, anything you can do to network with the company is recommended.

---

333 Lodge Avenue
Second Floor
Somewhere, NJ 07777

July 8, 2015
Richard Scott
Technical Recruiter, ITT Systems
The Plaza, 2nd Fl.
Somewhere, NJ 07777

Dear Mr. Scott,

I want to take this opportunity to tell you how impressed I was with the atmosphere and customer service at ITT Systems. You and your staff were very informative regarding the available position of Network Manager, which has furthered my interest in working with your organization.

I also want to thank you for covering all the details involved with this position. After our conversation, I am convinced my prior skills and experience would be an ideal match for your department. I am also convinced my customer service skills and professionalism would be a fine addition to your team.

Enclosed for your convenience is my contact information. You may contact me at 555-001-0001 or e-mail me at weberthomas@rhyta.com. I look forward to hearing from you on Monday afternoon.

Thank you,

Thomas Weber

Thomas Weber

Figure 8.8 Formal Thank You Letter Sample 3

Write a Follow-Up Letter

Directions: Use the samples in this chapter to help you formulate a professional thank you letter. Create it in a Word document using the business letter format (the same format you used for your cover letter). The follow-up letter should consist of three short paragraphs, single spaced with no indents, and an extra space between the paragraphs. Make sure you include your contact information as you did for the cover letter.

The first paragraph begins by thanking them for the interview. You can also use verbiage such as *"I would like to express my appreciation for the opportunity to meet with you and discuss the XYZ position."* Mention something specific you learned from visiting with them about the job or company.

The second paragraph is where you communicate that you are ready to begin working for the company, and provide a *new example* of how you are a great fit for the job.

In the final paragraph, again thank them for the interview. Assure them of your continued interest in working for them in this position. You can mention that you *"look forward to hearing from them"* or *"look forward to the next step."*

Use a formal closing such as *Sincerely* or *Respectfully,* and sign your name with your typed signature beneath it.

✓ SELF-CHECK

1. Describe the two-step follow-up procedure.

2. Why are two thank you notes better than one?

3. Should you still send a thank you even if you are not hired? Why or why not?

» LO 8-2 Applying the Art of Successful Negotiation

Occasionally, toward the end of an interview, the hiring manager will say something that sounds like they want you. If you are fortunate, it will be obvious and sound something like this: *"We would like to make you an offer."* Or, it may be subtle like this: *"What would it take for us to get you to work for us?"* Be alert for these types of cues that the negotiation process has begun. If you get the less obvious cue posed in the second scenario, make sure you follow this with a question to clarify that they are actually making you an offer, not just seeing what you want for salary. If they are not actually offering you the job, you are not negotiating. You are still selling yourself to them, so answer that you are *open* or *negotiable.* If hiring

Are you making me an offer?

managers affirm that they are indeed offering you the job, then the negotiation process has begun. The following are examples of what you say next, after each negotiation cue:

Hiring manager: *We would like to make you an offer.*
Job candidate: *That is great, as I am ready to consider your very best offer.*

Or

Hiring manager: *What would it take for us to get you to work for us?*
Job candidate: *Are you offering me this position?*
Hiring manager: *That is correct; we want you to work for us.*
Job candidate: *Terrific! Thank you. I am ready to consider your very best offer.*

In the second dialog, do you see how the candidate deferred the discussion on salary back to the hiring manager? Do that. Allow this person to offer you a salary amount for the position. You want the hiring manager to state the price. Remember, whoever brings up an exact money amount first is at a disadvantage.

> *In negotiating, it's always far better to let the other person talk first. When you get to listen first, you ALWAYS have the advantage. You know exactly what the other person wants . . . and knowledge is influence and power.*
>
> —Christian Carter

The initial offer to you is just that, the beginning. Even if you are told it is a firm offer, very few times is it. The government and military are places where offers are often fixed; the corporate world has wiggle room in negotiating salary and/or benefits.

If you do not get an offer in the interview, you may get it in the follow-up phone call or even in a letter. Again, the above dialog works. Thank the hiring manager, and say that you are prepared to consider (not accept) the best offer.

careercoach8.2

Breathing Room: Ask for Time to Make Your Decision

Now that you have a solid job offer with a salary amount attached to it, you want to do two things. First, thank them sincerely for the offer and let them know you are enthusiastic about the position. You do this even if the offer is too low. Second, you ask for time. You ask for 24 hours or a short block of time to consider the offer. You want to do this even if the offer is perfect. During the 24 hours you will consider all aspects of your situation and the offer. You will then be in a solid frame of mind to either accept the offer as it was presented to you or to counter the offer.

Asking for time also lets the employer know you are serious and valuable. I know of one candidate who asked for 24 hours and, while waiting for the candidate to accept the position and proposed salary, the manager actually called her back with a better offer. They did not want to lose her and they thought the delay in response meant she was not going to accept.

Key Negotiation Questions to Ask

Once you have been offered the job, but before you accept, you are in the position to gather more information. Consider asking some of the following questions to help you evaluate the job offer:

- When would you like me to start?
- How and when will my performance be reviewed?
- What are the promotion opportunities with this position?
- What are the benefits added to the position in terms of vacation, insurance, and other perks?
- Is there mileage reimbursement for commuters or parking benefits?

The following student story exemplifies the importance of evaluating and negotiating in order to ensure that the position fully fits your goals, as well as your needs.

I have a nightmare story about an interview that I hope will help others. Sometimes we are so scared that we won't get a good job that we don't do our homework and end up accepting a job only to be miserable from day one.

I had an interview with a company to be the director of training. I "nailed" the interview and knew I got the job as soon as I walked out. The president of the company asked what I needed in order to get started and I told him: I need a computer, someone to answer the phone when I am out, and a copier. Later, I will need a computer lab.

When I showed up the first day of work, my "computer" was one I shared with another employee and it was also the Internet server for their ISP business. The "someone to answer the phones" was a $10 answering machine, and my copier was Kinkos. It went downhill from there.

I stuck it out for six months before resigning, but I learned from that point on to interview the company while they are interviewing me and to ask questions when offered the job. Just as I need to prove that I am a good fit for them, they need to show me that likewise they are a good fit for me. Make sure that it will be a good place for you to work.

Nothing is worse than getting a job and realizing that you soon need to go on another job hunt because you hate your job.

Remember to ask for time to consider any offer you receive. How much time is typically acceptable to take to consider?

© Used with permission of Saundra Johnson, National American University student

How could this student have made sure there would be an opportunity for evaluation and negotiation after starting her job? What questions could she have asked before accepting and after beginning her job?

Do you have any plans you can't put off?

Other Questions to Consider

Ask if there is anything you can do before you begin working to get a head start in your job, such as reading recommended material or participating in any meetings. If you have an upcoming event you need to attend, such as a wedding or scheduled vacation that cannot be postponed, you will want to broach this topic with them before you accept the offer. You can ask, *"Before this position became available, my husband and I planned and purchased a trip to Hawaii to celebrate our anniversary. I would like to take this vacation. Would there be a way for me to do this even though you do not offer annual leave for six months?"*

careercoach8.3

Negotiate for a "Win—Win" Agreement

When you negotiate your job, come from a place of having and getting what you want, not from a place of scarcity. Think *win–win,* not *me versus the company.* You want the company to prosper and you want to add value to the company. In return you want to be rewarded for your efforts. When your energy is added to the company's, all prosper. Win–win negotiation works. You are building relationships. After all, you will be working with, or for, the person with whom you are negotiating the terms of your employment. Bully tactics do not work in job negotiation, or in much of life for that matter. Both parties want to walk away feeling they have an edge. You may need to give a bit in order to get what you want. As you contemplate the position, think about your short-term and long-term goals and how well the job meets your vision. Research and preparation will help you determine if the position is a good fit for you (Jandt, 1985; Covey, 1990).

Nonnegotiables

Nonnegotiables The few items you must have in order to take the job.

Make sure you have your nonnegotiable items in mind. **Nonnegotiables** are the few items you must have in order to take the job. For example, if you need to be able to flex your lunch hour to pick up your child after school, then having that particular need met might outweigh the need to negotiate other benefits. These two or three nonnegotiable items become your line in the sand; you are saying that if the employer can't work with you on them, you are willing to walk away from the offer. If you have more than two or three, then you may be walking away from some decent offers. You can have many "wants" on your ideal job list, but you want to narrow your list down to a few things you absolutely must have.

Cyber Trip 8.2

Job Negotiation Advice on the Internet Use your favorite search engine and the keywords *"job negotiation advice," "win–win job negotiations,"* or *"successful job negotiation"* to find two or three tips on job negotiation that will be helpful for you. In addition, visit http://jobstar.org/tools/salary/negostrt.php to read more useful negotiation advice.

e x e r c i s e 8.1

Your Nonnegotiables

The work you did in the first few chapters had you prioritize your ideal job and what you value in the workplace. You also drafted your career mission statement. This is a good foundation for this exercise and for negotiating.

Directions

First, list as many things as you can think of in five minutes that you want in your ideal job. Do not censor yourself; however, do stop after five minutes.

Your Negotiable List		

Next, circle only *two or three* items that you must have. These are *nonnegotiable* for you in any position you would consider and the items may change over time. For example, if you have small children, flexible hours might top your list today, but as your children get older that need might change.

Listening is a key to winning in negotiation. Listen for cues of what the company representative really can offer you. Listen for phrases that might mean they can go higher. For example *"We are offering you just about the best terms we have for someone with your experience."*

You can also ask questions to find out if they support your goals. For example, if one of your goals is to be reimbursed for mileage but mileage reimbursement is not in their budget, you can ask, *"Would you support taking steps to budget for mileage reimbursement?"* If the answer is yes, you might be able to negotiate for the following year's mileage reimbursement assuming you agree to work for the remainder of the current fiscal year without this perk.

» LO 8-3 Making a Sound Career Decision

Nearly everything is negotiable in a job offer. It is much like buying a house. You can ask for anything. You may not get it, but you can ask. Once you accept a job offer, it is very difficult to renegotiate. A Society for Human Resource Management survey found that 8 of 10 bosses were willing to negotiate salary and benefits with job applicants. Yet only 33 percent of applicants surveyed said they felt comfortable negotiating (salary.com). Be sure you are part of that 33 percent.

> A survey of 875 hiring managers found that about 60 percent leave some wiggle room when they extend an initial pay offer, while just 30 percent say their first offer is final. For the other 10 percent, it depends on the candidate: For the right person, hiring managers will up the ante.
>
> About 1 in 10 hiring managers said they actually think less of a candidate who doesn't try to nudge the numbers up a little. When asked what was most likely to persuade them to sweeten their offer, the largest group (34%) said they want to hear you explain why you're worth more by highlighting specific accomplishments. (CareerBuilder.com)

As you make your decision, you want to know what you are really being offered so you can negotiate what is most important to you. Here are some of the items that you can negotiate:

- Base salary
- Responsibilities
- Vacation time
- Insurance paid
- Signing bonuses

- Yearly bonuses
- Promised reviews with salary increases
- Office assistant
- Stock options/profit sharing

- 401K matched contribution level
- Relocation expenses
- Mileage reimbursement
- Toll fees paid
- Tuition reimbursement
- Day care paid for or supplemented
- Parking space and parking fees
- Flexible schedule (especially if you have children you need to take to school or pick up)
- Option to telecommute on certain days or when needed
- Time off for travel days (if you are traveling for work over a weekend you would have two extra days off)
- Company car
- Title
- Office space
- Equipment you need to work on the road or at home, such as a laptop
- Equipment fees
- Uniform allowance
- How shift work is assigned
- Home Internet (especially if you are expected to put in overtime from home or telecommute)
- Employment for your spouse

Find out what your work environment could be as part of your negotiable list.

All of the items mentioned have a price to them and do add value to the total package. After looking at this list, you might want to add some more items to your negotiable list. For entry-level positions, stick to the basics. After you have more information regarding the position, you are ready to weigh the package and make a decision.

Cyber Trip 8.3

Additional Research on the Company   For statistics on pay and benefits, visit the website of the Bureau of Labor Statistics, a division of the U.S. Department of Labor, at http://www.bls.gov/bls/wages.htm. There you will be able to find the standard of pay for your field. While you may want to ask for the moon, you also want to keep your requests reasonable. This is another time when knowing what the position is worth will help you negotiate.

Negotiation Student Success Story

The following example shows how one student achieved her desired salary by following the proper steps and asking her prospective employer the right questions.

Student's Inquiry:

Hi Professor!

The interview on Monday went great and today they offered me the job! The only problem is that they're only offering $38,000/yr and I was making $45,200 at my previous job. That's quite a pay cut! It does cost a bit less to live in the Carolinas than it did in south Florida, but still it would be difficult to live on that salary. The job itself seems great though and would teach me a lot in my field. Is there a good way to let them know I'm interested in taking a job but need more money?

Thank you for any advice you can give me!!

—Sandy

Hi Sandy,

Did you go to www.salary.com, http://www.bls.gov/bls/blswage.htm, and other helpful websites to research what the average earnings are for this position? You can find the range.

When you call them back, ask if there is any wiggle room in their offer, as it is quite a bit lower than you are currently making. If they ask you what you were expecting, you can state you want to make a lateral move, or if you had to take a slight pay cut that the benefits and/or time off would at least offset the difference.

Since they will probably ask you to define lateral move, be prepared to give a number. Only you have the answer. Use the information you find on salary.com.

If you would accept the position at $40K, then indicate a range of $40K to $50K depending upon benefits and time off. Explain that those two factors play into that range. This tells the HR manager that $40K is what you are seeking for a base salary without benefits.

Do not talk about your need for the money. Rather, emphasize your education and experience, what the job is worth in the area, potential for growth, etc. They don't care about your need for cash, but they might pay more if you are worth more.

Keep me posted,

—Kari

Professor:

It worked!!! He offered me $43K plus a full benefit package which I accepted. First he emailed me a copy of the original offer. I had some small questions, such as what the shift hours were, how often employees get paid, etc., so I emailed him back with those questions and then I asked the following:

"And my final question is regarding the starting salary. Is there any wiggle room in that offer? I was making $45,200 at my previous job, and while I'm not necessarily looking for a lateral move, I was not expecting such a large pay cut.

I look forward to your answers so that I can make a decision."

He emailed me back saying he would call me in the morning to discuss. Then he called me around 11:30 today and answered all of my questions, one at a time. When we got to the salary question, he said that he had budgeted between $33,000 and $45,000 for the position (like it said in the ad), but that he couldn't offer me the full amount because my programming skills are not very strong at this point. I agreed with him on that point and he said he could come up to $43K and I said that would work for me. He also made sure I knew that he offers increases and bonuses on a regular basis, so I have a feeling that my salary will increase to a more comfortable level before too long.

I plan to start next Wednesday! Thanks again so much for the advice! It really helped!

—Sandy

Systematically Weigh the Alternatives

An easy method to evaluate the job offer is make a line down the middle of a sheet of paper. On one side list all of the advantages or reasons you would take the job and on the other list all of the disadvantages.

The student in the example above could have also used the 70/30 rule to evaluate whether or not the offer fit her needs. The **70/30 rule** states that if the job offer has 70 percent of what you desire (advantages) and less than 30 percent of what you don't want (disadvantages), then you may be in the ballpark for accepting. Please see Career Coach 8.5 for further information on the 70/30 rule.

> **70/30 rule** If the job offer has 70 percent of what you desire (advantages) and less than 30 percent of what you don't want (disadvantages), then you may be in the ballpark for accepting.

careercoach8.5

The 70/30 Rule

The 70/30 rule states that if the job offer has 70 percent of what you desire (advantages) and less than 30 percent of what you don't want (disadvantages), then you may be in the ballpark for accepting. This also assumes that the most crucial factors, or *nonnegotiables*, are in the offer, such as salary and commute time. This success tool can be helpful when making career decisions. You can also use the 70/30 rule to see if you need to ask for something specific to make the offer work.

Another 70/30 rule in job negotiation is to listen 70 percent of the time and speak 30 percent of the time. Ask open-ended questions when you are negotiating and let the hiring manager speak.

How to Diplomatically Ask for What You Want

Words are very powerful, and the ones you choose in negotiating make a difference. Consider these sentences: *"I want the job, but I would need more money"* and *"I am very interested in this position and working for you, and I am wondering, is there is any wiggle room in your offer for the salary amount?"* or *"I am very interested in the position and I am wondering, is there is any room for negotiation in the salary?"* The first sentence is demanding, while the next two are more flexible and open for negotiation. The rule of thumb is to ask for more than what you are willing to settle for and negotiate for what you want. You do this from the employer's perspective. Explain how your skills and experiences are worth more. You also use the information from the research you have done regarding what the job is worth in that region.

If they cannot meet your negotiation goals, then you have options. You can look for another job, perhaps a better job. Another option is to ask for a performance review in three to six months with an option to increase the salary and/or bonuses pending a positive review.

How can minor differences in wording make or break a negotiation situation? Practice phrasing negotiations correctly with your peers, family, or friends.

Get the Offer in Writing

Once you accept the offer and its terms, it is reasonable to ask for a contract or to have the offer in writing.

One way to do this is to send a follow-up e-mail as a thank you and to state what you understood to be the agreeable terms of the job offer. The hiring manager would respond to your e-mail confirming your understanding or with changes. A handshake agreement is nice; however, in negotiation, it is important to have the terms of the job offer in writing. This is more about memory than honesty. You may have negotiated a three-month review with a salary bump, but if the hiring manager does not recall that part of the conversation, you will be sorely sorry. It is recommended that you state, *"As we have discussed many facets of this position today, could you please send me the terms in writing so I can review them?"* Any business-minded person will appreciate your desire for details.

> *Once you accept the offer and its terms, it is reasonable to ask for a contract or to have the offer in writing.*

Job Offer Acceptance Letter

Most offers will be negotiated and verbally agreed upon over the phone. Once that occurs, send a formal *job offer acceptance letter* (see Figure 8.9). Use the business letter format for this letter restating the particulars of the offer. Use the letter to confirm the salary and your start date. If you have further questions, call the hiring manager or supervisor and ask them directly. Do not ask questions in your acceptance letter.

Cyber Trip 8.4

Job Offer Acceptance Letter Samples Visit http://www.quintcareers.com/sample_accepting_letter.html, or http://www.career.vt.edu/jobsearchguide/acceptingoffer.html to find additional examples of how to write a professional acceptance letter.

"Don't Sell the Farm" Yet

When you take a position, you are often under a review period for the first three to six months. While you might be relocating for this position, keep in mind your employer could decide your performance is not meeting the company's standards, thus ending your employment. While this is rare, one suggestion is to postpone selling your home during this review period. This is especially important if you would not have relocated had it not been for the new job. Rent an apartment until you have successfully met the probationary period.

Juggling Offers

Juggling offers is one of the good problems in life. However, it can be a problem. You want to make certain you are making the best possible decision

Nina P. Hanson
1234 Blue Spruce Court
Fort Worth, TX 7555
June 13, 2015

Mr. Pete Jones
Operations Manager
Jones Construction Company
1234 Main Street
Dallas, TX 77777

Dear Mr. Jones:

I am pleased to accept your offer of employment as the office manager for the Fort Worth branch with Jones Construction Company, starting on July 6, 2015. The position sounds both exciting and challenging, two of the most important aspects of work to me.

I have thoroughly reviewed the details of your offer as outlined in the offer letter. I have signed and enclosed a copy of the offer letter as you requested. If I need to complete other paperwork before my first day of work, please mail it to me at my home address above. Thank you for your confidence and the opportunity to work with Jones Construction.

I am looking forward to working with you.

Sincerely,

Nina P. Hanszon

Nina P. Hanson

Enclosure

Figure 8.9 Job Offer Acceptance Letter

for you and perhaps your family. So, what is the best way to successfully juggle offers? What are you supposed to do if you receive an offer from one company while waiting for an offer from another? You can ask for more time to think over the offer. Do not explain why; simply ask for an extension. In the meantime, call the hiring manager of the other position to see if they will give you a timeline for their decision. Once you have this information, you need to decide if you are willing to tell the first company that you are waiting to hear from another firm. This decision comes with risks, as most companies would like to think you want them as much as they want you. Telling them might also elevate your desirability to the first company, but you won't know this.

How to Turn Down an Offer Successfully

Some fields such as nursing, information technology, and health care experience the glory of being in demand. It is easy to feel confident turning down offers when you are in a seller's market. Keep in mind that networking is part of your career, and how you turn down the offer matters more than the fact that you decline. When turning down an offer your goal is to leave the impression that you are a person of integrity and to keep the hiring manager as one of your professional networking contacts. The following are more tips on declining a job offers:

- **Stay friendly and positive to all.** View the interview as a networking opportunity with colleagues in your field.

- **Be honest.** Let the interviewer know in the interview that *you have other offers you are considering, but are very impressed with their company and would like to work for them.* You do want an offer.

- **Gather more information.** Follow the preceding statement by finding out *when the company will be making its hiring decision.*

- **Buy time.** You can ask for more than 24 hours, but two weeks is not a good idea. You can tell the hiring manager you would like a few days to review the offer and in that time gather as much information as you can about the hiring time frame of other companies.

- **Can you afford to turn them down?** If you are offered a position, and put them off, you may lose that offer and the job you were hoping for may not come through. Make sure you are prepared for that to happen.

- **Decline professionally.** Thank the company representative for the time he or she spent interviewing you (and money if they flew you in, etc.). Let the hiring manager know it was a difficult decision. You can state a direct reason for your decision such as salary, location, or benefits. Ideally, you want to keep the door open, at least as a professional contact.

exercise 8.2

Mock Negotiation

Write your answers to the following scenarios or use the scenarios to conduct practice mock negotiation in class.

Scenario 1: You were the top candidate in the interview for the marketing manager position with the ABC Marketing Firm. The hiring manager calls and offers you the position with a base salary of $58,000, plus benefits. With your extensive experience and now your degree, you were hoping for an offer of around $75,000, plus benefits, since you currently earn $63,000 as a marketing manager at your current firm without your new degree. How would you handle this situation? What research could you do to back up your asking for more base salary? Write out a script for what you would say on the phone to the hiring manager at that moment:

_____

_____

_____

_____

_____

Scenario 2: Congratulations! The Department of Corrections just called to offer you the position of parole officer with a starting salary of $38,000, plus benefits. While you are happy for the offer, you believe that $38,000 is quite a bit lower than the starting salary for parole officers in your area. What do you say at this moment? What can you do to negotiate a better offer? Then what will you say if you call them back in the near future to renegotiate?

_____

_____

_____

_____

It is always important to follow your instincts when evaluating an offer, but why do you think it is also critical to weigh the pros and cons on paper?

Cyber Trip 8.5

Salary and Negotiation Quiz   Visit the website links that follow to quiz yourself on how much you now know about job and salary negotiation: http://www.quintcareers.com/salary_job_offer_quiz.html; http://www.quintcareers.com/job-offer-tutorial; and http://www.academictutorials.com/quiz.asp?id=64.

Make a Decision—Then Make It a Right Decision

Sometimes the hardest part is making a decision. If you find that *all things seem equal* and you are at an impasse in making a decision, then it is time to make a decision. This is done after you have weighed all of your options and evaluated the job offer(s). When you are making a decision, write out the pros and cons of the offer on paper and weigh them, consult with those who help advise you, and listen to your intuition (gut). If you follow these steps and still do not get a clear "Yes, take it" or "No, don't take it," then at this point you need to believe in your ability to make a good decision. Make a decision and then go about making it a right decision.

> One little known secret to making precisely the right move, at precisely the right time in your life, is knowing that in all cases, there is more than one right move and more than one right time.
> —The Universe[2]

_____

[2] © www.tut.com

4. Describe the acceptable way to ask for additional time to consider an offer.

5. What are two of your nonnegotiables?

6. What are the appropriate steps for turning down an offer?

» LO 8-4 Negotiate Once You Have the Job

Negotiation does not stop the moment you are hired. There are many opportunities to negotiate and renegotiate after you are employed. Just as you took well-planned negotiating steps before you were hired, how and when you negotiate after being hired are just as important.

Asking for a Raise

Most employees find it hard to ask for a raise. Usually this is because the employees aren't sure when would be the best time to ask. Sometimes, they're afraid to ask at all, for fear their manager will turn them down even if the time is right for a raise. If you're wondering if the time is right, here are a few questions to ask yourself:

- Has it been more than 12 months since my last raise?
- Have I been given additional job responsibilities, or worked longer hours?
- Am I supervising more people?
- Have I increased company profitability in a significant way?
- Has my job description changed?

If the answer to any of these questions is "Yes!" then you have a good opportunity to speak with your manager about a raise.

When you feel you are in a position to negotiate for more salary or benefits, you want to be prepared. For starters, document your successes. You might think that your supervisor is doing this for you. Most likely, that is not the case. Gather documents on how you add value to the organization. This could include any of the following:

1. Times when you worked excess hours to finish projects or solve problems.

2. Situations where you helped outside of your job duties.

3. E-mails or documents that support and praise your work from your supervisor or other stakeholders such as clients, customers, vendors, or others in the company.

4. Professional development you undertook to improve your performance.

5. Education and training that adds to your value in the organization.

6. Ideas you brought to the company that were adopted.

7. Projects you initiated successfully.

8. Committees for which you volunteered.

When you are ready to ask for a raise or negotiate more benefits, turn the above items into a list. Quantify the items on the list, as you did for writing your skills in your resume. Detail how much you saved the company in terms of time and/or money. Provide specific examples on how you contributed to the organization.

Just as if you were applying for a new job, you need to do some research on what your position is actually worth. You need to find the standards in your industry. Do not ask others in the company what they earn, as that is not professional nor is it allowed at some firms.

Timing Matters

Don't ambush your supervisor by asking for a raise in an unscheduled meeting. Request a time to visit with your boss. Do not schedule this meeting at these times:

- Right when the workday starts.
- Right before lunch.
- Near the end of the day.
- During or before an audit.
- During or before a very important merger or event.
- If your company is not doing well financially or is in a scandal.

Good times to ask for a raise include:

- Mid morning.
- After lunch or midafternoon.
- When your job responsibilities have expanded.

Don't ambush your supervisor to ask for a raise; schedule a meeting in advance.

Turn the Performance Evaluation into a Negotiation Opportunity

Your performance evaluation is an opportunity to discuss many elements of your position. Assuming your performance has been productive to the organization, you can negotiate for more benefits and salary. For example, you might ask for an office, or a better office, better technology, or more vacation time. Essentially, everything that can be negotiated in starting a new position can be negotiated in the position you have. The key is how to ask for what you want.

Be prepared and spend a good amount of time listening in the performance review. Now is not a good time to get defensive or emotional. If you were verbally promised something during the year contingent upon performance, and you met the stipulation, now is the time to bring that to the forefront. Other suggestions include:

- Do not discuss why you need a raise.
- Do not compare yourself or your salary to others in the company.
- Bring your list of accomplishments.
- Stay confident and professional.

Industry standards The compensation levels for different fields.

- Ask for more than what you want within the ballpark of the **industry standards** for your position. Industry standards are the compensation levels for different fields.
- Listen.
- Be willing to take on more responsibility for extra compensation.
- Don't put your job on the line unless you are prepared to leave.

» LO 8-5 Managing Obstacles and Frustrations

The interview process is often a blow to the ego. While it would be ideal to receive a job offer for every position you seek, more often than not, you will be met with ample amounts of rejection. Keeping perspective, having a good support system, and keeping your sense of humor are all important during this time. If you are not offered the position, you can ask the hiring manager what you could improve for your future interviews and why you did not get the job. More often than not, they will talk about others having more experience or skills than you did. Take the information they provide you as data, but not the absolute truth.

You also want to send a thank you letter or note when you are not selected. Figure 8.10 is an example of a rejection thank you note.

What you want to do is improve your interviewing skills, work on acquiring more skills, and keeping your attitude positive. When you are desperate for a job, it is hard to stay positive. Unfortunately, employers can sense your desperation and despair, which does not add to your desirability. Make sure you are feeding your ego and engaging in activities you enjoy. For example, if you are a youth leader and receive praise for your efforts and personal rewards for the work you do, make sure you devote time to that activity. Even if you are feeling you should spend more time hunting for jobs, the value this adds to your spirit is equally important. You need to feed your self-esteem

Dear Mr. Davis

Thank you for letting me know the outcome of the search.

I appreciate having had the opportunity to learn more about *(name the company)*, and discuss the position with your group.

While I am disappointed that I am not joining your team at this time, I look forward to future possibilities with *(name the company)*.

Thank you again,

Jeff Hoffman

Phone number

Figure 8.10 Rejection Thank You Note

with your hobbies and passions. Your self-confidence and well-being will show in the interviews to come.

Job Search Rejection Tips

The following are ways to keep your perspective in the job search:

- Remind yourself of the number of applications most companies receive for one open position.
- Remember it is a numbers game. You need to keep at it.
- Tell yourself "It is their loss."
- Have an expert in human services or other professional review your marketing tools to see what you can improve.
- See if there are other ways you can improve for the interview: Conduct a mock interview, get advice on style from experts at clothing stores that sell clothes for professional workers.
- Consider contacting a recruiter to help you search and prepare for interviews.

careercoach 8.6

Overcome "There are no good jobs out there"

When you experience rejection, it is easy to develop a belief that there are no good jobs out there. It is important not to buy into this feeling. Remember the definition of frictional unemployment from earlier chapters? Frictional unemployment is when jobs are created due to people retiring, being promoted, passing away, moving, and other real circumstances that create a position in the job market. Those are not only *real* jobs, but they also are often very good jobs. The only problem is that due to networking, over 70 percent of those jobs are not advertised. This is not a problem for you, however, as you now know how to network to find and land one of these good jobs.

Get Support

When you are feeling rejected and down, that is not the time to isolate yourself. Isolation can cause you to mentally replay all of your negative tapes and self-talk. It is also not the time to hang around people who do not believe in you, or who want you to settle for less in life. These individuals might love you, but they are not helping you; don't seek their advice. They should not get a vote in your career decisions. In fact, limit your contact with them during this time. Instead, seek out and spend time with positive people who make you feel better about yourself when you are around them. Call them, ask them if they would like to grab a cup of coffee. Let them cheer you on when you feel hopeless. They are out there.

If you cannot think of someone in your life to lift your spirit when you are feeling dejected, then find them. You can also be your own cheerleader. Find biographies and autobiographies of people who made it in spite of the odds. Read their stories. These are individuals who succeeded in business, sports, politics, or overcame health problems against the odds. Any librarian or bookstore worker can lead you to these books. Read their success stories every day, especially before you go to bed. They will inspire you to persevere against the odds and challenges you have been experiencing.

Who are the people in your life who will lend support through the rough times? If you can't think of anyone, what are some alternative ways you can surround yourself with positivity?

Do not abandon your goals. Keep the goals; change the plan.

Roadblocks, Side Trips, and Detours

The job search is often full of roadblocks, side trips, pit stops, and detours. When these are expected, it makes the trip less stressful. Do not personalize these experiences; they are just a part of the journey and can lead to something better than you originally had in mind if you are open to the serendipity of how life works. Getting stuck in linear thinking can shut out opportunities that come from unlikely sources. To open yourself up to new ideas, new plans, and new solutions, get out of your rut. Simple as this sounds, do something new. Meet new people. Uncomfortable as it is, get out of your comfort zone and be open to detours and side trips.

Plan B and C

Does it mean you have abandoned your goals if you have a plan B? Not at all. Having a plan B or plan C gives you breathing room to know that you have a solution. You can continue to interview for your ideal job while you take a position that will pay your bills for now.

Armed with a plan B or C, always remember the **11th hour principle** as well. The 11th hour principle is the idea that when things seem the bleakest in the job search, it is a good sign, as the tide generally turns at that point. Please see Career Coach 8.7 for further information regarding the 11th hour principle.

11th hour principle When things seem the bleakest in the job search, it is a good sign, as the tide generally turns at that point.

careercoach 8.7

The 11th Hour Principle

There is a coaching principle that addresses how things work out in the last few minutes. It may seem the universe is testing your patience and ability to hold out for the job you seek. This is called the *11th hour principle*. The principle says this: In the 11th hour, the tide turns. The events change and what seemed would never happen comes to pass in your favor. This principle reminds us not to settle and to persevere. In other words, you may need to go to one more interview, and write one more thank you letter, and shake one more hand . . . even when you feel like quitting—*especially* when you feel like quitting. Many people do not know about the 11th hour principle and perceive the bleak circumstances of not getting interviews or the job they want as signs they should settle or give up. While you might need to take a job you don't really want while you strategically search for your career, you can rest assured with this principle that what you seek is out there waiting for you. You will know you are in the 11th hour when you feel at your wits' end and not sure you can take one more rejection. You can start seeing that as a good sign. When you have done the job search work, systematically and consistently, you are much closer than you think to landing that job. The rule of thumb at this time is to press on. It is happening.

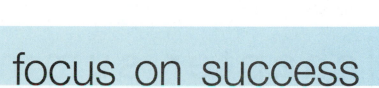

What Now? Tracy Negotiates

Tracy did not really think she was turning down the offer. She thought if she said she could not take the job due to the salary, the hiring manager would counteroffer. When that did not happen, she was surprised and confused. After she realized that she had indeed declined CRV Pharmacy's initial offer, she decided to further research the art of salary negotiation. Through the career development director, career counselors, and websites, Tracy learned the correct steps involved in negotiating. She reviewed her textbook in more depth, and refreshed her memory by completing all of the exercises and activities the text suggested. She also practiced mock negotiations with the career counselors, which allowed her to experience what a successful negotiation felt like. While asking for more money was extremely uncomfortable, Tracy would have the opportunity to use her new skills and ideas on Mrs. James of CRV Pharmacy, whom she had interviewed with earlier that month. She had initially turned down a job with CRV, and never thought she would have another opportunity to work for them. She had sent them a follow-up letter thanking them for the offer. Fortunately for Tracy, circumstances had changed.

Tracy was at home when the phone rang. It was Mrs. James from CRV Pharmacy. She remembered Tracy from an earlier interview and liked her honesty. She still felt that Tracy would be a good fit for the pharmacy.

"Hello?" Tracy said when she answered the phone.

"Hello, Tracy, this is Mrs. James with CRV Pharmacy. You interviewed with me earlier this month, but you could not take the position at that time. Are you still interested in coming to work for CRV? We have another position that has just become available."

Though a bit stunned to hear from Mrs. James again, Tracy was very excited. Remembering what she had learned from the career director, career counselors, and her research, she composed herself and told Mrs. James that she was still interested. Tracy asked if she was being called for the same position or if CRV was interested in her for a different position.

"It is the same position," said Mrs. James, then she paused. Tracy remained silent, waiting for Mrs. James' response. Finally Mrs. James continued. "What type of salary are you looking for?" she asked.

"Are you making me a formal offer?" asked Tracy sincerely. Mrs. James assured Tracy that she was. Tracy continued, stating the salary range she desired, and noting it was based on the industry standard and her experience level.

Mrs. James thought for a moment. "I can see you have thought about this range, and while I was very much impressed with your skills, I was even more impressed with your honesty, and hiring an honest person is a benefit to the company. I think the value you would bring to the company reflects this range you are asking for." Mrs. James then offered Tracy an attractive number within the range, and after talking through several details regarding the benefits CRV offered, Tracy verbally accepted the offer.

Tracey was excited that she was finally going to accomplish her dream and that she would be doing it while making her target salary. She thanked Mrs. James for offering the position to her, and asked when she should come in to finalize everything. Mrs. James told her to be at the pharmacy at 8 a.m. the next morning.

Discussion Questions

1. What types of negotiation skills do you think Tracy learned from her research?
2. What role did honesty play in Tracy getting the position with CRV?
3. What additional advice would you give Tracy about future negotiations?

[chapter summary]

Follow-up and negotiation are often neglected. Very few applicants take the time to show appreciation. By taking the time and effort to send a follow-up note, you will be setting yourself apart from the vast majority of applicants. Follow up after the interview with the *e-mail thank you* and snail mail thank you card or note. If you are unable to secure a position, know that you put your best foot forward; you may find you are selected to join the company at a latter date due to your professional follow-up skills and by sending a note of appreciation even after you were not selected. The other major skill to use in this process is negotiation. While it is exciting to land the job, if you don't know how to negotiate the terms successfully, you may be short changing yourself and be frustrated working at the company in the long run. To avoid this, negotiate an acceptable package utilizing the win–win approach covered in this chapter.

[skill/term check]

1. What are the two thank you strategies suggested for follow-up? **(LO 8-1)**

2. What marketing tool should you include in a job acceptance letter? **(LO 8-1)**

3. What are two negotiation questions you might ask? **(LO 8-2)**

4. Why is it important to ask questions about the position before accepting an offer? **(LO 8-2)**

5. Explain the 70/30 rule in your own words. **(LO 8-3)**

6. Name one bad time of the day and one good time of the day to ask for a raise. **(LO 8-4)**

7. How can one avoid frustration from job search rejections? **(LO 8-5)**

8. How can you turn a rejection into something positive? **(LO 8-5)**

[KEY TERMS]

11th hour principle: When things seem the bleakest in the job search, it is a good sign, as the tide generally turns at that point. **(LO 8-5)** [p. 260]

E-mail thank you: An e-mail thank you note sent the day of the interview to show your immediate interest in the position. **(LO 8-1)** [p. 237]

Industry standards: The compensation levels for different fields **(LO 8-4)** [p. 258]

Nonnegotiables: The few items you must have in order to take the job. **(LO 8-2)** [p. 246]

70/30 rule: If the job offer has 70 percent of what you desire (advantages) and less than 30 percent of what you don't want (disadvantages), then you may be in the ballpark for accepting. **(LO 8-3)** [p. 251]

chapter 9

Step Up Your Career

> " *Bring your best self to the workplace everyday.* "

target competency > *Develop a career management plan for short- and long-term career goals.*

learning outcomes

After studying this chapter, you should be able to:

LO 9-1 Make a stellar impression.

LO 9-2 Know how to advance in the workplace.

LO 9-3 Manage job changes, stress, and life balance.

LO 9-4 Understand the importance of lifelong learning and goal setting in reaching the next level.

Fitting In

Tim was excited about his new job at Graphic Solutions. He had stayed up all night thinking of ways to make a great first impression and fit in. With his new degree in Graphic Design and Visual Communication, Tim was positive this opportunity was going to be the launch of his career. On the first day, Tim was his exuberant, charismatic self. He laughed, cracked jokes, and visited others' offices and cubicles to network. Tim even brought doughnuts to the office as a gesture of gratitude. He was so caught up in the excitement, he failed to study his environment. Had he done this, Tim would have realized the company atmosphere was quiet and formal. People e-mailed each other rather than picking up the phone, and no one touched his doughnuts.

Undaunted by his first day, Tim kept up his extremely social ways, and his hearty laugh carried throughout the office. What he did not realize was that he was not fitting in to the company culture. Others were annoyed by his boisterous ways. He was soon excluded from meetings and e-mails, which was the organization's way of sharing communication and bonding. After just a few weeks, Tim was starting to feel depressed and his work was suffering. He had noticed that he was often not included in meetings, and his co-workers were no longer friendly when he dropped by their desks. Tim was confused and saddened that his promising career seemed to be going nowhere fast. The harder he tried, the worse things seemed to get.

Jennifer, one of the more tenured employees in the office, could see that Tim was struggling to fit in. She decided that she would speak with him and give him a few pointers about navigating the office environment. One day while they were both at the copier, Jennifer asked Tim if she could speak with him. "Of course!" said Tim.

"Tim," Jennifer began, "I can see that you are having difficulty fitting in here, but I don't want you to think nobody wants you here. You were hired for a reason. Perhaps try to let people come to you, instead of trying to make them like you. Give them a chance to see what you can do. You know, Tim," she said laughingly, "this was a pretty quiet office before you got here. It's a traditional environment, so just give everyone some time; they know you are a talented employee, and soon enough they will accept and like you for who you are as a person as well."

Tim shrugged and replied, "I know you are right, but this is my first job since graduating, and I know that if I do well here, it will be the perfect start for the career I have always dreamed of. I just want to fit in and feel like I am a part of a team."

"Sure! I completely understand," Jennifer said, "but if you don't make it a priority to understand the culture of this office—you know, its environment, what makes it tick—you will never be able to connect with your co-workers. It might become an environment you don't want to stay in, and you may decide to leave and never see your dream come true."

Tim knew that Jennifer was trying to help, and he appreciated her concern and the fact that she had reached out to him. He did understand what she was saying, but it also sounded like Jennifer was telling him that in order to fit into his workplace, he would have to change his personality. He wasn't sure if that was something that he could do or wanted to do. He thanked Jennifer for taking the time to talk to him. He had some thinking to do.

Discussion Questions

1. Is Tim a good fit for this office environment and its culture?

2. What changes will Tim have to make to be successful in this environment?

3. Do you think Tim would be better off sticking it out or finding another job with an environment that better fits his personality? Explain your choice.

» LO 9-1 Making a Professional Impression

Your first few days on the job will be the time when others will size you up quickly, and the impression you make will be lasting. How can you make your stellar, professional reputation?

Fit into the Company Culture

Company culture The norms, customs, attitudes, values, and ways of operating in an organization.

One of the best ways to thrive in the workplace is to learn the **company culture.** Company culture includes the norms, customs, attitudes, values, and ways of operating. Culture is something that is not stated overtly in the employee handbook, but something you can figure out by paying attention. People like to surround themselves with like-minded individuals. To blend in, you can listen for cues and follow suit, *without changing who you are.* Use good interpersonal communication skills. Even following another person's body language contributes to bonding and fitting in. They may not know why they like you, but you will be forming that good first impression, which is hard to change.

How you perform in the first few months of your job will create your workplace reputation.

Observing what people wear and who holds the power will help you fit into the culture. You can usually get a feel for a company's culture as you interview. Learning and understanding a company culture is not about judging the culture or you; it is about fitting the mold, not breaking it. If you find yourself in a situation like Tim in the opening vignette, you will need to decide if you want to work at changing or look for a better fit. Fortunately, the basic relational tools discussed in this section can assist you in being a good fit, without losing your personal identity.

Considering you got the offer and landed the job, your employer must feel you would fit well on the team. When you start a new position, be alert for the group norms. Many times this varies by department. Things to watch for include:

1. What types of jokes are told?
2. What are the company stories being shared?
3. What are people wearing? Is it a conservative office or more casual?
4. When do most employees arrive and leave?
5. Do employees take scheduled breaks? If so, what do they do or where do they go?
6. What do employees do for lunch?
7. What about gossip; what or who is being talked about and why?
8. What is the noise level? Is the department noisy or quiet?
9. Who holds the formal power (position power) in the department? Who holds the personal power?
10. How are decisions made?
11. How is communication delivered?

Often people leave jobs because they, or their supervisor, felt they did not "fit in" to the corporate culture. You can often make many mistakes on the job, but if you fit in, the mistakes will be forgiven. Learn to fit in, or start looking for a different job. Do not take it personally if you don't fit in. Instead, remind yourself that you are not a good fit for that particular culture, period. You might find that you fit into a different department in the same company. Figure out if you are bonding and relating to employees in other divisions, which may be a sign for you to network into that department.

Have a Positive Attitude

This is probably the number one determining factor for job success. Having a positive attitude means you are willing to learn, you are enthusiastic and motivated. You do more than asked; you go above and beyond. You are helpful, and you leave your personal problems outside the workplace.

Project Professionalism

From being organized in your work space to wearing appropriate attire, make sure you project confidence and professionalism.

Smile and Shake Hands

When you meet someone new at work, smile and offer a handshake. You can go out of your way to make the first move by saying, "*Hi, my name is Mandy. I just started working here in marketing.*"

Take Initiative

Once you start to feel comfortable with your job, ask for more work. When you see something that needs to be done, offer to do it, rather than waiting for someone else to do it. Show your team spirit and volunteer to help others. Do this from the standpoint that you want to learn as much as possible. Ask questions when you don't know something. People like to help, and offering to help will open communication with others.

Show Confidence

While you are new on the job, you may feel overwhelmed, but remember that you were hired for your great skills and that you have much to contribute. Be confident. Make eye contact when speaking with others. While you should listen more than you speak when you are new on the job, if you have an idea or see a problem, don't be shy—speak up. Introverted personalities need to double up on the effort to express confidence to establish their presence.

Be an Active Listener

When you are fully present and listen, you will make a connection. People love talking, but very few actively listen. Instead, they jump in with ideas, interrupt, and cut others off in an attempt to voice their great ideas. While you do want to contribute, your active listening skills will serve you well.

Use Names

People love hearing their name. Use them. Add titles if appropriate. If you forget a name, just say, "*I'm sorry, I forgot your name.*"

Remember Your Netiquette

While etiquette is defined as using social convention and good manners, netiquette connects Inter*net* with et*iquette*. **Netiquette** means using manners, civility, and general rules of respectable communication online.

Netiquette Using manners, civility, and general rules of respectable communication online.

Think about how you typically write e-mails. Can your netiquette be improved? Name three specific ways you can improve it.

Workplace e-mail is different from your personal e-mail account. There are certain expectations written and assumed regarding company e-mail. First and foremost, your work e-mail account should be used for work-related e-mails. While some companies allow employees to use their work account for personal e-mails, it's a good idea to keep a separate personal account and use that for e-mailing friends and family. Check your employee handbook on this topic to find the specific rules for your workplace. Follow them, even if others do not. To make sure you know when an important e-mail comes in, consider turning on the e-mail notifier. When you turn on your notifier you will receive notification of new messages on your desktop. If you are out of the office, turn on the automatic reply letting senders know that you are out of the office until a certain date.

Follow these suggestions for professional e-mail correspondence:

- Check your e-mail several times a day.
- Answer mail promptly, within 24 hours or less.
- Acknowledge e-mail you received. For example, if someone sends you a report, reply that you received it and thank them.
- Make a clear subject line: Let the reader know what the message contains.
- Remember work e-mail is property of your workplace and can be retrieved or read by others. Never write anything in an e-mail that you would not mind being published.
- Use professional verbiage; leave texting codes to your personal e-mails and cell phone.
- Keep e-mail messages brief and clear.
- Spell and grammar check each e-mail you send. You can usually turn on the automatic spell check option for outgoing messages.
- DO NOT YELL. Do not use all capital letters in writing. It is considered yelling and somewhat rude.
- Use punctuation properly. Leave smiley faces for your friends ☺
- Use names. Start the e-mail with the person's name and in some companies you will want to address e-mails with proper titles, such Mr., Ms., Dr., etc.
- Save your e-mail. Organize e-mail into folders and keep past messages that may help you in the future. E-mail is the modern version of a paper trail. It can save your reputation and help your career.
- Find out the company policy for popping or automatically forwarding your work e-mail to your personal account. Some companies allow this and encourage it so that you keep on top of work when you are not at the office. Check the employee handbook or with HR to find out if that is acceptable or recommended.

» LO9-2 How to Advance in the Workplace

Professionalism is key to your career success. This section covers a few other ways you can advance in the workplace.

Meet and Exceed Expectations

How you perform in the first few months of your job will create your workplace reputation.

What are four actions you can take to impress your employer during your first months at a new job?

Make sure that you *wow* them from the beginning. There are many things you can do to add value to your organizational and professional image. One way to do this is to give more than you get. When you enter your profession and focus on delivering high-quality service, whatever that may be, you will prosper. This is true even if you are in a bad work situation. You will develop a reputation that will take on a life of its own. People change jobs all the time and you may be recruited at some point due to your great reputation.

The following are tips to meet and exceed expectations and to add to your first impression and work reputation:

- Show up early and stay a bit late.
- Dress the part. A good rule is to "dress for the job you want, not for the job you have." Pay attention to what your boss and those above you wear, and take your style cues from them. Remember, if you would wear it out to the club, it does not go to the office.
- Decorate your office or cubicle to match the culture of the office of those above you, not below you. If the intern has a fun, hip office, with a radio and 15 photos of her boyfriend on the wall, while your boss displays diplomas, one family picture, a small globe, and plant—it is time to frame your diplomas and buy a small plant.
- Learn the culture from clothes to habits to decor and learn to "fit in." Adapt. For example, if your boss walks at lunch and invites you to join her, bring your sneakers to work the next day!
- Remember that you now represent the company, when you are at work and when you are at play. Keep your activity on Instagram, Facebook, Twitter, and other online social networking sites respectable and professional. Make sure that what comes up on the Internet when someone Googles your name is the image you want to project to your new boss and colleagues. Connect with your new co-workers on LinkedIn or another professional networking site, rather than on a personal social networking site.
- Contribute ideas, energy, and in other ways to prosper your workplace.
- Take care of your co-workers. Compliment them.
- Share the credit when credit is due.
- Solve problems.
- Solve your boss's problems, big or small.
- Keep your boss informed of your activities.
- Let your boss take the credit for your good work (at least for now).
- Invest in your professional life, from dress to learning new skills.
- Consider joining Toastmasters (http://www.toastmasters.org/) to improve your presentation and verbal skills.
- Speak highly of your workplace, boss, and co-workers.
- Do not participate in workplace gossip.
- Do not let others' opinions sway you. Instead, get your own data.

- Don't run people over trying to leave the building at 5 p.m. Don't shut down your computer every day at 4:55 p.m. unless you have an appointment. Stay 10, 15, even 30 minutes or more to get caught up, plan for tomorrow, and so on. Once you establish a reputation for working late, you can leave earlier.
- Use lunch time—not work hours—to run errands and make medical appointments, if needed. Remember, you are setting a tone; your reputation is at stake.
- Keep personal business to a minimum. Use your break time for personal business.
- Be willing to take work home or work extra hours to get the job done.
- Volunteer to help others.
- Answer all e-mail, not just the e-mail from those who are higher on the organizational chart.
- Drop everything to help a customer or client. When a client of the company (a worker delivering a package, someone wanting to fill out an application, or a client) needs help, drop everything and help them.
- Treat all people with dignity and respect, from the cleaning staff to the CEO. Do not change how you treat people based on a title.
- Show appreciation.
- Find a mentor.
- Keep networking.
- If your schedule permits, join your co-workers for after-hours activities.
- Keep track of your accomplishments for when it's time to negotiate.

Power over Your Schedule

When you are starting a new position, it is difficult to take total control over your time when it does not belong to you. It belongs to your boss and the company. This section is about finding ways to get more power over your schedule. The following practices will help you grow your career.

The top 3 percent of achievers leverage their abilities through effective planning.
—Brian Tracy, personal and professional development expert

Daily To-Do List

There are many ways to make a to-do list. How you make the list is far less important than making it a part of your routine. One tried and true suggestion is to take a legal pad and draw a line down the center (Abraham-Hicks, 2009). At the top, draw a line across. On the left, write "What I Intend to Do Today" and on the right, "For the Universe to Handle" or something to that effect. (You can use your higher power for example—whatever works for you in terms of verbiage and belief.) In other words, list on the right whatever you really have no power over, but is weighing you down with worry. Then release it. Let it go. We consciously let go of the problems on the right by symbolically writing them down as "For the Universe to Handle." The result is peace of mind, an increase in productivity, and more focus.

Complete both lists and don't be surprised if this process takes on a life of its own. If you have never tried this, you may be amazed by the energy this process unleashes. You can make a place for personal things to remember at the bottom of the left side. A very short version of what this to-do list might look like is below:

What I Intend to Do Today	For the Universe to Handle
_____ Check e-mail	_____ Dale in hospital
_____ Finish executive summary	_____ Promotion ???
_____ Lunch with division heads	_____ Sedona trip?
_____ Meeting: 1–3 Expansion topic	
_____ Get Susan by 6	
_____ Pick up dry cleaning	
_____ Meet Mark for dinner	
_____ Pay sitter for next month	

Prioritize

Number or circle the items on your list that are essential. When all items are equally essential, choose the ones with the biggest payoff or nearest deadline. Which matter most to your boss? Which matter more to your boss's boss?

The 5-Minute Rule

The **5-minute rule** is that when you have that few extra minutes between scheduled events, you have "time." This small amount of time is an opportunity to get work done on your to-do list that does not require a large time commitment. Look at your to-do list and find one of the tasks that you can work on for a few minutes. For example, make a short phone call or send an e-mail.

Avoid Time Wasters

Examples of time wasters include surfing the Internet, instant messaging, chatting, participating in office gossip, redoing work a second time because you were too tired to do it right the first time, and some meetings.

> *The highest paid, most successful executives use time differently than the average person. They think about it in advance. They allocate it in very small amounts. They think in 5-, 10-, 15-minute chunks of time.*
>
> —Brian Tracy, motivational speaker and business consultant

Cyber Trip 9.1

Internet Success Tips for the First Month on the Job Using your favorite search engine and appropriate key search terms, find two websites that offer additional information about making a great impression when you start in a new workplace. See if you can find three new tips to add to those in this chapter.

Energy Management

Energy management is consciously choosing how you use your energy, allowing you to be efficient and effective. Energy management is probably more important than time management, because if you have the energy, you can be efficient and effective. In focusing only on time management, you might have the time, but you might not be very effective. To use this tool well, you need to know yourself well. Pay attention to your energy levels for different tasks. For example, you decide to use the first 30 minutes of the workday to take care of top priority e-mail, and plan your to-do list. Next, you allocate 90 minutes for a project that needs your focus and concentration. At this time, you shut your door or put on headphones if you can (even if there

5-minute rule Use the extra minutes between scheduled events to get work done on your to-do list that does not require a large time commitment.

Energy management Consciously choosing how you use your energy, allowing you to be efficient and effective.

is no sound, people will assume you are listening and leave you alone) and you work. Next, you take a 15-minute break and walk outside. You then attend two back-to-back meetings and go to lunch. You spend the afternoon putting out fires that do not take a great deal of concentrated effort, but take their toll on your energy. If you had put out fires all morning, you could be emotionally wiped out for the rest of the day.

Do Something Daily that Takes You Toward Your Goals

You might not be able to pull off a perfect priority system, but what sometimes happens is that we get so pulled into daily emergencies and busywork, we never do one thing toward achieving our overall career goals. Revisit your career goals daily and make a concerted effort to do one thing that takes you closer to them. Add this to your to-do list. For instance you could research seminars you want to attend, call your mentor to have lunch in order to discuss your next promotion, or contact the university to register for classes that you have been meaning to take.

Navigate Office Politics

Just as who you know is important in landing a job, it is equally important on the job. Those who think they will avoid office politics may find themselves without a job. Navigating office politics successfully will allow you to advance in your career, while maintaining your integrity. Learn to connect with others, listen, and make time for networking in your office. You do this by learning the culture and the personality of the office and letting your best self shine.

careercoach9.1

Be Good for Your Word

> When you speak with impeccability, your words have power not only with yourself but also with others.
>
> —Jack Canfield

If you say you will do something, do it. If you say you will complete a project by a certain time or date, stay on course to meet the deadline. Your word is more powerful than you may know. The more you are good for your word, the more your value increases. If you cannot keep your word, you dilute your ability to be trusted. Keep your word in all matters. The truth is it all matters.

Moving Forward through Performance Appraisals

Every company has its own type of appraisal system. Depending on the organization, the reviews occur at different time increments. Common time frames include the three-month review, the six-month, the nine-month review, and the annual review. Sometimes companies will conduct several reviews the first year, and then only a six-month review and an annual review for subsequent years. The goal of performance evaluations is to identify the employees' strengths, weaknesses, and opportunities for growth in the company as well as establishing goals for the next year or next time frame. They are also used to determine raises and promotions.

Often appraisals use weighted averages to score the employee in terms of categories such as poor, fair, quality, outstanding, and excellent.

Some companies outsource appraisals, where they have their managers use a contracted firm that focuses on performance reviews. The managers/supervisors complete performance evaluations using the contracted firm's software. Examples of this are the web-based companies such as Performance Pro or Halogen eAppraisal, which provide talent management software. Other companies develop their own in-house systems of performance evaluation. Regardless of how the review is conducted, it is essential that you know how to use this process to grow in the company.

What is the purpose of a performance appraisal? How can you prepare yourself for each evaluation and be sure you are meeting your employer's expectations?

New employees often fail to ask to see the performance rating fairly soon after they start working. In the first day or two after you begin your new job, ask what criteria you are being evaluated on for your performance, and how often you will be evaluated. You can also ask for a copy of the performance review form, so you know exactly how your performance will be measured. You might think you are doing all of the *right things right,* but may overlook something important because you did not know it was a part of your employee performance review. An example of this might be professional development. If you did not know this was part of the evaluation, you might fail to "accomplish growing professionally" due to being focused on your day-to-day work commitments in a new job.

Some tips to move ahead through appraisals include:

- Take the performance reviews seriously.
- Prepare for the performance appraisal.
- Review and reflect.
- Request clarification if any goal or comment in your review is not clear to you.
- Acknowledge areas you can improve.
- Don't assume your supervisor is documenting your success.
- Highlight and document your accomplishments.
- Keep a file updated with your successes. For example, save e-mails that praise you and your work, make notes of projects you successfully complete or initiate, and list committees you work on as well as outside professional growth opportunities and clubs and organizations you belong to.
- Find ways to document your job knowledge, staff relations, client relations, dependability, and job production, including any way you contribute to the organization.
- Keep track of the criteria that your company uses so you know that you are meeting and exceeding expectations.

Your appraisal is a record that is typically housed with human resources. Make sure the information in your file is accurate. Also, remember that often budgets are set prior to performance reviews, so you may want to ask for a bonus or raise in another meeting before the actual review.

If Your Employer Doesn't Use Performance Reviews

While most companies conduct regular employee performance reviews, not all do. However, just because your supervisor isn't evaluating you through a formal performance review, don't assume that you are doing a great job. If you want to know how well you're doing, you need to ask.

If you ask about performance reviews in your first few days and learn that there isn't a formal review process, ask your supervisor if you can meet to discuss how you will be evaluated. Be sure you understand what success looks like, as well as things your boss wants you to avoid. Then ask if you can meet on a regular basis to get informal, verbal feedback on your performance. When you are new to a position, it's a good idea to have these check-ins more often, such as once a month. As you get more established in the company and more comfortable in your role, you will get a better sense of how you are performing and will need these feedback sessions less frequently. Remember, whether your company has a formal performance review process or not, you are responsible for your performance.

Managing and Advancing a Small Business: The Basics

Perhaps you are going to work for yourself. Some additional tips and tools for managing and advancing your private business include:

1. Visit http://www.irs.gov, and apply for your Employer ID number (EIN).

2. Find a system for organizing your finances. You might consider QuickBooks accounting software, hiring out to an accounting firm, or developing your own system. Consider asking your mentor or others in your field how they manage the business side of their personal business.

3. Get informed. The U.S. Small Business Administration has a website for professionals such as you. Visit it at http://www.sba.gov.

4. Another great website for the small business owner is Entrepreneur. com (http://www.entrepreneur.com/).

5. Learn how to market yourself and to attract clients. Consider joining your local Chamber of Commerce or other business-networking organization.

✓ SELF-CHECK

1. List three things to do to help you exceed expectations in your workplace.

2. How can you improve your netiquette?

3. What are two ways you can manage your energy during the workday?

» LO 9-3 Managing Job Changes, Stress, and Life Balance

No one expects to lose a job or to be downsized, but it happens. With advances in technology and globalization, change is the one constant you can count on. Unexpected change can wreak havoc on your well-being. This section will provide you with coping skills, options, and support if you lose your job, as well as balancing skills to avoid job burnout.

Job Loss Triage

Triage is a process where ranking occurs in a crisis. Everything is handled in terms of importance or priority. For example, it is used in emergency medical situations where emergency workers assess and prioritize injuries. A job loss is also a crisis, and a priority plan is provided in this section in case you or someone you know needs it. **Job loss triage** involves using triage or prioritizing skills when downsizing or job loss occurs to ensure the situation becomes a temporary setback rather than a tragedy. This way, your recovery time should be reduced and you will restore balance back into your life more quickly.

Job loss triage Using triage or prioritizing skills when downsizing or job loss occurs to ensure the situation is a temporary setback rather than a tragedy.

Priority Plan of Action

If the unexpected occurs and you find yourself out of a job, following this priority plan of action can help you organize your next steps and reduce your stress.

Before You Leave

You have the right to negotiate with your employer (or at least ask) for a couple of very important items. First, you can negotiate what they will say to future employees about your work. Ask for a letter of recommendation. While that might seem odd, management might see some very good skills and strengths in your work that they would be willing to describe in a letter. You can ask that your termination be documented as a position that was eliminated or that you mutually agreed that you were not a good fit and left. Those reasons are very different from being fired. They may agree to that. You have a right to view your file and should do so while employed and before you leave. You can also ask for a copy of your personnel file.

Remember to negotiate the terms of your departure. It may be painful, but it can be very important for your new job search.

Negotiate a Severance Package

Check your company policy manual regarding severance pay. The rule of thumb is that it is case-by-case at the discretion of the employer. Often the offer is one to two weeks of pay for every year you have been employed with the company. Federal law states that if you are over 40 you have the right to review a severance package and to not sign it for up to 21 days and you have up to seven days to change your mind if you do sign. This regulation is under the Older Workers' Benefit Protection Act of the Age Discrimination in Employment Act[1] and can give you time to contact your attorney and negotiate a better severance package.

Register for Unemployment

Many times people are so overwhelmed by losing a job, they postpone this step. Unfortunately, in many cases unemployment insurance is not retroactive. In other words, it starts only when you file a claim. There is no need to put this off as most states now allow unemployment insurance claims to be filed online. The Department of Labor website, CareerOneStop, can guide you to the information on unemployment services state by state. Visit the following map, and click on the state in which you reside or work: http://www.service-locator.org/OWSLinks.asp.

---

[1]http://www.eeoc.gov/types/age.html

Figure 9.1 Target Your Opportunities

Circle labels: 10% Jobs to float while you search • 40% Second-choice jobs • 50% Ideal positions

Contact Your Creditors Immediately

Many times you can negotiate temporary lower monthly payments with your creditors. Contact your service providers such as phone, gas, electric, and water to see if you can defer payments or even negotiate a lower payment for a few months. Many will work with you if you work with them. That means contacting them immediately, being honest, and asking for lower payments until you get a new job. You might be able to consolidate your bills. Do this with caution and watch your interest rates. Contact your bank for options. Your goal is to keep your credit in good standing through this trying time. Be wary of high interest loans from commercial loan stores.

Update Your Resume and References

Polish your resume and update your references. Call your references and let them know you are actively job searching. Confirm with them that they will continue to be a professional reference for you. Explain your circumstances so they are not caught off guard if they are called to provide a reference to your skills. Stay positive when you speak to them and allow them to offer you any tips, support, and suggestions.

Target Employment Opportunities

Revisit earlier chapters in this book, and target your job search. Have a three-tiered plan (see Figure 9.1). The first tier centers roughly 50 percent of your time targeting ideal jobs. The second tier focuses about 30–40 percent of your time seeking "second-choice" jobs, those that bridge the gap between being unemployed and employed. The final tier captures whatever time is left. It might include applying for temporary jobs, menial work, and even day labor. These are jobs that pay bills, and keep you afloat. Continue seeking your first-choice jobs as you work your second-choice, or your temporary job. For all you know, the second-choice or temporary job you land will turn into your ideal job.

Firm Up Your Network

Over 70 percent of jobs are found through networking. Revisit Chapter 4 and hone your networking skills. Create your networking business card, if you have not already done so. Get connected. Network in person and online. Use LinkedIn, Facebook, and other online resources such as industry e-mail lists so that you are connected.

Temporarily Cut Expenses and Assess Assets

No one enjoys cutting expenses. Remind yourself and your family that this is temporary. Take an inventory of your assets. Could you take out a second mortgage if needed? How much savings do you have? Can you cash out your 401(k) fund or other retirement plan if needed? Find out. Do you have any family members who could assist you? Look at your bills. Consider giving up cable television for a while. While it might not be fun, local stations tend to be free.

The same goes with cell phones. If you are on an expensive cell phone plan, consider spending the fee to quit, and then use a *prepaid* cell phone until you land your job. If you do this, and have to get a new number, remember to change your cell number on all of your applications and marketing tools.

You may need to remind yourself and your family that this is not forever! Yes, it might not be fun, but going bankrupt and losing your house is less fun. Tighten the belt, and press on. Then reward you and your family when things bounce back and you are financially solvent again. If you have large monthly payments on your vehicles, consider refinancing them, selling them, or trading down to vehicles of lesser value. Depending on your situation, you might find an equally nice vehicle for half the payment. Another suggestion is looking into food co-ops. This is where you pay a small monthly fee or donation, and in return you receive fresh fruit, vegetables, meat, and other food products to prepare several meals. You can even use food pantries found at many local churches and synagogues. Check out movies and other free resources from the library rather than a store. The library is free. Again, none of these measures are designed to be your future. They are all part of your triage plan so you can bounce back quickly and reduce your stress level.

Increase Your Income

You will have the opportunity after this section to brainstorm how you can bring in more income while you look for new employment. This is a time to get very creative when it comes to making money. Some ideas include child care, lawn care, house painting—inside and out, house-sitting, personal assistant or shopper, typing for others, house cleaning, garage sales, pet sitting, selling baked goods, repairing things, paper routes, snow removal, rent out part of your house or a room, and the list goes on. Brainstorm what you or your family members can do to bring in more income. Again, this is a triage situation, not the rest of your life. Treat it as such and get creative.

Temporary Setback

You need to frame your situation as a "temporary setback." In fact, those are the words you can use daily with yourself and your family. You hit a snag. It happens to the best of us. It won't last forever, and the faster you work these tools, the faster you will have this behind you. Stop self-blame, or even blaming others. It does not put you in the frame of mind you need to move forward. If you get stuck in the "blame game" you will be giving your power away to people who probably don't even think of you anymore. While that might hurt, it is largely true. Work any forgiveness tools you have for yourself and others, and move forward.

Use Forward Thinking

Think about the vision of having this stress behind you. See yourself driving to work and enjoying your new job. Plan fun things to do that are inexpensive or free, until you can afford more. When needed, you can get very creative and still enjoy every day. Enjoy thinking of the future and allow yourself to dream. This is especially important for children, rather than saying, "*No, we can't do that now or buy that now*," keep a list on the refrigerator and when they ask for something that

"K. Anders Ericsson found in 'The Role of Deliberate Practice in the Acquisition of Expert Performance' that a significant difference between good performers and excellent performers was the number of hours they spent practicing. The finding was popularized by Malcolm Gladwell as the '10,000 hour rule.' What few people realize is that the second most highly correlated factor distinguishing the good from the great is how much they sleep. As Ericsson pointed out, top performing violinists slept more than less accomplished violinists: averaging 8.6 hours of sleep every 24 hours."
—lifehacker.com

you cannot afford during this time, explain that you will keep it on the list. Add things to the list with the intention to get them later. You will be shocked, when you look at that list in a few years and indeed see how many of those items were attained! This will also help you with forward thinking.

Actively Seek Support

A person's career or job is often one of the largest contributors to their self-esteem. Losing a job can make individuals want to isolate themselves and not tell anyone what happened. If this happens to you, remember you are not alone. *You are not your job.* You are much more than that, and there is more for you out there. It might take some time and creative thinking, but it will get better. If you have been spending more time working than at social and professional functions, get back into them.

Self-Care

Drowning your sorrows is the worst thing you can do during this time. While you may need to feel bad for a time, you also need all of the strength you can muster to move forward. Celebrate once you land your next job. Get plenty of sleep and eat healthy. Conversely, if you find you are sleeping all the time, and still tired, you may have moved into a downward spiral and need to seek medical or professional care. Don't let this happen: take good care of yourself now. Bet on yourself. It will pay off.

Treat Your Day as a "Workday"

Get up and get dressed. Complete your typical morning activities, such as taking the kids to school or the dog for a walk. Then go to the local library, or take your laptop (you will want to invest in one if you don't have one) to a local coffee shop that has free Wi-Fi connection. Turn your job search into your 40-hours-a-week job. If you do that, you won't be unemployed for long. Do not stay home and watch TV, use social media, or play video games while you feel sorry for yourself. You will find many people who are self-employed go to Internet coffee shops to do business. Once you are sitting among them, you will not only gain new connections, but you will also feel as if you are an independent businessperson. That sense of worth will help you. For the price of a cup of coffee, you essentially buy yourself an office for several hours.

Plan your day around the three-tier plan—scheduling interviews, contacting temp agencies, networking with friends and associates who may have leads for you, visiting job board sites, and tracking leads. Remember, only 25 percent of the jobs out there are advertised. The rest are found through networking. Timing has much to do with landing a job. Show up to companies with your resume; you may find your timing to talk to the hiring manager was perfect. Remember, you only need to land one job. Even if it is temporary or not perfect, it can keep you afloat while you seek a job that is a better match. People like to hire people who are employed, so the sooner you can start working the better. Then you can keep your options open for better jobs.

Headhunters and Temporary Positions

Recruiters are wonderful connections. They can help you find a job, plus they can help you improve your resume and expand your network. Even if they don't have something for you at the moment, they may have ideas or other leads you have not considered. Contact them, set up an appointment, and treat it like an interview. Again, while you don't need to go into great detail, be honest about why you left your last job. You can find temporary positions and recruiters online by searching for "Employment Agencies." When you speak with an employment agency, bring your marketing tools, including your resume, networking business card, and sample cover letter. Let the agency know about your skills and experience, and be honest about how you left your previous job. Explain the kind of position you are interested in, but also be open to suggestions. Employment agents often have a big-picture view of the job market that no single job seeker can have. Because of this broad perspective, they may be able to suggest jobs or companies that would be a good fit for your skills and experience that you had not considered. Even if some days it might not seem like it, there are jobs out there. If you spend too much time on job boards, however, you may get discouraged because most jobs are not there, as covered in previous chapters. Use your connections, including recruiters, to find a job.

Cyber Trip 9.2

Surviving Downsizing   For more information regarding how to cope and recover from company downsizing, please visit http://www.yoursoulatwork.com/Surviving_downsizing.htm.

Learn More So You Can Earn More

Go back to school. Take a night course. Seek out your local career learning centers. If the thought of racking up more student loans is counterintuitive to finding a job when income is scarce, think again. You may be able to use financial aid to help pay your living expenses while you complete your schooling. Every degree adds value to your worth, so even though you may take out more student loans, you should be worth more in the marketplace. Paying back financial aid is easier when are earning substantially more. If you are able to take some classes online, you can work and go to school. Anther option to finance school and work is to find graduate programs that have assistantships. Assistantships allow you to receive help with tuition and often a salary. Often, career learning centers offer free or low-cost training. Many colleges and universities now offer free courses online through their websites. These Massive Open Online Courses, also known as MOOCs, cover a wide range of subjects, including computer programming, personal finance, business management, and entrepreneurship. Even if you do not earn college credit for taking these courses, you can develop your skills and include coursework you've taken and skills you have developed on your resume. To find online courses that might interest you, search the keywords "free online courses" using your favorite search engine.

exercise 9.1
Temporary Setback

Aside from those already listed in the above section, brainstorm 20 things that you can do to increase your income or reduce your expenses during setbacks. Ideas might include reducing or temporarily cancelling cable service, reducing or cancelling cellular phone service, or walking/biking whenever possible to save on fuel costs.

1._____

2._____

3._____

4._____

5._____

6._____

7._____

8._____

9._____

10._____

11._____

12._____

13._____

14._____

15._____

16._____

17._____

18._____

19._____

20._____

Know Your Rights

As an employee, you are protected by federal laws against employment discrimination based on your race, color, religion, sex (including pregnancy), national origin, age (if you are 40 or older), disability, or genetic information, and you are protected against harassment by managers, co-workers, or others you work with based on those same things. The law also protects you against retaliation if you complain about job discrimination or assist with a job discrimination investigation or lawsuit. These rights are enforced by the U.S. Equal Employment Opportunity Commission (EEOC). If you feel you have been fired or harassed for a reason that is protected by the EEOC, contact the agency immediately to see if you qualify for assistance. You can learn more at the EEOC website, http://www.eeoc.gov/. Another employment law you should be familiar with is "at-will" employment. According to the National Conference of State Legislatures, at-will employment means "an employer can terminate an employee at any time for any reason, except an illegal one, or for no reason without incurring legal liability. Likewise, an employee is free to leave a job at any time for any or no reason with no adverse legal consequences." This law provides you with some protection; unless you have signed a contract that states otherwise, you are free to leave a bad work situation whenever you like. However, it also gives your employer the freedom to fire you without cause (meaning without a performance-related reason), as long as it is not for a reason protected by the EEOC discrimination laws. Learn more about at-will employment at http://www.ncsl.org/research/labor-and-employment/at-will-employment-overview.aspx.

Employees Don't Quit Jobs; They Quit Bosses

Your relationship with your boss can make you or break you. If you are working for a difficult boss, do what you can to improve the situation. Learn what others have done to have a better relationship with this person. On the other hand, if you work for a bully boss, the chances of your making that situation better are slim. Just as there are bullies on the playground, there are bullies at work.

Bully Bosses

"Workplace mobbing," "work victimization," "workplace bullying," "internal terrorists," "toxic leaders," as well as "nondiscriminatory workplace harassment," "general workplace harassment," or "status-blind harassment," are some of the terms used to describe a phenomenon where supervisors use covert or overt aggression to harm subordinates in the workplace. Skeptics dispute the existence of general workplace harassment, or bullying, and argue that such practices are actually tough management styles, necessary discipline, and effective organizational tactics. They also argue that the purported victims of nondiscriminatory workplace harassment are lazy, problematic, or low-performance workers.

Unlike protected victims such as those subject to harassment based on race, sex, or disability, victims of non-bias workplace harassment are not protected. Most companies take a zero tolerance approach to protected harassment covered under the EEOC, but much less legal protection is provided to victims of non-class-protected forms of harassment. This is especially true within private businesses and organizations in "employment at will /right to hire/ right to fire" states.

Status-blind harassment is described as persistent, unfair, and irrational managing (Wornham, 2003). This is not a not a trivial problem. In the United States, approximately one in six employees, or 16.8 percent of workers, are targets of status-blind harassment. The majority of such harassment, 75 to 81 percent, is inflicted by a manager or supervisor upon a subordinate (Vandekerckhove & Commers, 2003; Wornham, 2003). It usually includes isolating the victim employee, singling him or her out, and treating this person differently than other employees using both covert and overt tactics. While shouting or verbal abuse may occur, such behavior is often discouraged and too easily recognized. More often, the harassing supervisor employs tactics such as distorted or fabricated allegations, writing up the worker for poor performance, and giving low scores on performance evaluations over a long period of time (Ballard, 2004). They also use subtle forms of harassment such as depriving the worker of responsibilities, burdening the worker with an unreasonable amount of work, excessive monitoring of the employee's work product, and leaving the employee out of group e-mails or other forms of communication (Salin, 2003).

> The difference between the ways a person treats the powerless and the powerful is as good a measure of human character as I know
> —Robert Sutton, More Trouble than They're Worth

> The Workplace Bullying Institute is the sole United States organization dedicated to the eradication of workplace bullying through public education, help for individuals, employer solutions, and legislative advocacy.
> Source: http://www.workplacebullying.org/

Status-blind harassment Persistent, unfair, and irrational managing.

Bullying can take on many forms and can inflict a hard toll on its targets.

The targets of bullies are just as likely to be strong individuals as weak, male or female (Carey, 2004). There are also "serial" bully bosses, who systematically prey on many different individuals (Wornham, 2003). These managers harass subordinates for the "sheer pleasure of exercising power." They are known for "mobbing down" and "managing up." In other words, these harassers enjoy abusing power and are also very good at showing reverence to those with more power (Carey, 2004). The detrimental effect upon the harassed worker includes emotional, physical, and economic costs. These include severe anxiety, inability to concentrate, insomnia, depression, loss of income from using sick leave, and finally, being fired or "voluntarily" quitting as a result of the harassment (Vandekerckhove & Commers, 2003; Wornham, 2003). Status-blind harassment is rarely punished and often not reported or formally documented.

Cyber Trip 9.3

Workplace Bullies Visit http://www.extension.iastate.edu/mt/civility/bullying/ to find links to additional information on workplace bullies and how to handle them. You can also conduct an Internet search using the keywords "bully boss," "workplace bullies," "non-bias workplace harassment," or any of the terms provided in the Bully Bosses section.

The trend is that employees finally quit or are fired after receiving unwarranted performance evaluations. In North America, most harassed or bullied workers quit. This ends up costing businesses and society approximately $24 billion each year (Hood, 2004).

Constructive discharge When an employee's work environment is intentionally made so difficult that the employee feels forced to resign.

Some states allow employees who were victims of non-biased workplace harassment to sue on the grounds of the legal term, **constructive discharge**. Constructive discharge is when an employee's work environment is intentionally made so difficult that the employee feels forced to resign. Constructive discharge is an exception to employment at will.

If you find yourself in this type of situation, a few suggestions include:

- Document harassment situations in a calendar or journal. Include the date, time, what happened, and witnesses.
- Summarize the details of verbal conversations in e-mails, so it is documented in a paper trail. For example, *"Rick, as I understood our conversation earlier today, you would like me to migrate the data from our current database to the new one by 5 p.m. today. Is that correct?"* You are not saying that doing that task is impossible; you are forming a paper trail documenting an insurmountable task with an unreasonable deadline.
- Save all e-mails. Print them or forward to your outside e-mail address.
- Avoid contact as much as possible.
- Document your work. You want to demonstrate you are working hard and contributing when performance evaluations occur.
- Document your breaks so you have proof of how long they were if this is an issue.
- Ask someone to mediate or monitor private discussions between you and the bully boss.

- Consider a formal complaint to human resources.
- Stay calm and professional at all times.
- Check out emotionally.
- Seek other employment immediately; rarely do these situations improve.

Workplace Burnout

Americans are working longer hours and taking less vacation. In the past 20 years, Americans have added an additional work week to every year and work longer hours than any of the other industrialized nations (International Labour Organization, 2009). Many Americans are burning the candle at both ends and merely showing up to punch the clock. They show up to work, but their enthusiasm is down. Common signs of burnout include changes in sleep habits; impatience with family and co-workers; cynicism; loss of sense of humor; less effective work habits; inefficiency when compared to hours worked; self-medicating with food; loss of enthusiasm; boredom; alcohol or other drug usage; being unmotivated; chronic headaches, backaches, or stomach trouble; weight gain or loss; feeling emotionally drained; and general fatigue. To learn more about how to avoid workplace burnout, see Career Coach 9.2.

careercoach9.2

Avoiding Burnout

Once the signs of burnout are identified, take action quickly. This might be harder than you think if you are now depressed and unmotivated. But being aware that your situation can change for the better is the key. If your burnout is due to poor working conditions, a bullying boss, or excessive pressure, you may need to quit. That may sound unrealistic, but a nervous breakdown, heart attack, or being fired for lack of performance are worse scenarios. Most bad work environments are not likely to change; the change comes from you. If you choose to stay, you must be aware of anti-burnout tools and use tough self-care strategies.

While you want to be a star player when you start a new job, if you find yourself burning out then self-care strategies are vital to regain your edge. For example, force yourself to go home when the workday ends, regardless of what others are doing. Take your breaks. Check your employee handbook, most likely you are guaranteed two 15-minute breaks in an eight-hour day, so take them. Go outside for a walk, call a friend, read a non-work-related book, or meditate in your vehicle. The important thing is that you stop working and give yourself a break. Take your vacations. If you are truly sick, stay home. Burnout victims often keep working regardless of how sick they are. Eat healthy foods and get sleep. Going on prescription medicine to combat work-related stress, or insomnia, is an option, but one not to be taken lightly. If your work is causing you to need prescription medicine, look at the big picture and consider getting a different job. You might need to change your life and earn less for a while, but *your life,* the only one you have, is at stake.

Cyber Trip 9.4

The Dragon Test: How Do You Handle Workplace Stress? For this Cyber Trip, you will need your Kingdomality® type you determined in Chapter 2. If you do not remember it, you can find it again by repeating Cyber Trip 2.2.

Once you know your Kingdomality® type, find your *Resiliency Quotient* by going to http://www. careerdevelopment.com/rqtest/ and completing the Dragon Test. The score and explanation of how well you handle workplace stress will be sent to your e-mail. Be sure to check your junk mail in case the results went there as an unknown sender.

What activities do you enjoy that can help you create a positive career-life balance?

Career-Life Balance

While you are growing your career, you also need to take good care of yourself so that you avoid burnout. Remember this is a journey much like a marathon, not a sprint. You need to know your body's rhythm for work and play and how to fill your energy reserves when they are low. If you are a night owl, for example, waking early to meditate or work out might be counterproductive to your natural rhythm of what works for you. Let the following tips assist you:

- Make time to play. This includes spending time with family, friends, pets, and your hobbies.
- Use your annual leave/vacation time and use it well. Rest, play, take a vacation.
- Exercise. See if your workplace has a reduced membership at the local gym or YMCA. If not, consider joining anyway and use this time to network, socialize, and just plain exercise. Whether you walk or lift weights does not matter, just make time to move your body. Walk at work during breaks or lunch.
- Go to the doctor for annual checkups. Just as we take our vehicles in for tune-ups, take care of your health and teeth.
- Keep your spiritual life and social life as priorities. They will renew you.
- Volunteer. See if your workplace allows you to use work time for any civic groups or volunteer organizations. Some workplaces partner with schools. If your workplace has a formal partnership with a volunteer organization, get involved. If your employer has not established working relations with local nonprofits, you may find some renewed energy proposing such a program. Start a campaign to raise money or collect food for a local shelter. This type of work should actually help fill your reserves.
- Sleep and rest. Sleep allows you to focus. Clear vision and focus allow you to do more accurate work in less time. Studies have demonstrated that after about 55 hours of work each week, employee productivity actually drops. While you want to be an asset to your company, you don't need to turn into an ineffective employee who stays at work all the time. In fact, while workaholics are super busy, they are often the most inefficient workers (Tyler, 1999; lifehacker.com).
- Eat well and drink lots of water. Minimize or eliminate alcohol.
- Delegate. Consider hiring out for housekeeping, laundry, lawn work, etc. This is personal, but keep in mind that time is money. Your time is valuable. If you are spending a great deal of time on laundry and

house cleaning, consider hiring out. If you cannot afford to do this all the time, consider hiring help during high stress times.

- Give your brain a break. Rather than TV, consider going to a museum, watching a gorgeous sunset, or listening to music. Resting your brain is an important step toward staying creative, alert, and focused at work.

- See if you can use your annual leave in smaller chunks so you can go to your children's games and musicals, as well as other important parts of your family life. You might be able to flex your time by working late another night or on the weekend to have time for important parenting activities.

Rather than watching TV, consider going to a museum, going on a walk, or listening to music to rest your brain.

As it has been said, this is your life, not a dress rehearsal; make time to live it fully.

✓ SELF-CHECK

4. As part of your priority plan of action, name and describe four actions you should take in the event of an expected or unforeseen job change.

5. What are two reasons it is important to continue gaining education throughout your career?

6. What are some things you can do to avoid burnout?

» LO9-4 Lifelong Learning and Goal Setting

As you may recall from Chapter 1, the time to set a new goal is when you get close to achieving one of your current goals. The reason for this is that the drive and motivation you get from your subconscious by setting a goal in the first place goes away once you achieve the goal. If you set a goal to land your dream job, and don't set a goal to grow professionally or advance, you might find that you are dragging yourself to work each day and have no idea why. In order to avoid this, set goals for professional opportunities and advancement.

Career Management Plan: Taking Goal Setting to the Next Level

Use the same goal-setting techniques found in Chapter 1 to move up the career ladder and provide awesome performance on the job. Your career plan is based on the combination of short-term and long-term career goals, and your career mission.

Some workplace or professional goals you might make include:

- Performance indicators.
- Promotion or advancement.
- Professional development.

If we are not in harmony with our goals, no amount of efforting, struggling, or striving will draw them to us.
— Elyse Hope Killoran, prosperity coach[2]

Set goals for professional opportunities and advancement.

---

[2] http://www.choosingprosperity.com/

- Salary, bonuses, or benefits.
- Avocation opportunities.
- Networking opportunities.
- Work environment goals such as a new or better office.
- Relationship goals with bosses or co-workers.

Your subconscious will go to work on your behalf once you name the goals you seek. Remember to write them down. You can also create affirmations out of the goals you make.

Expand Your Toolbox

Just as a hammer is great for doing some jobs but not others, you need a variety of success tools to get you where you want to go. Goal-setting tools are designed to "take a day and a half off the race." Two tools that can help you do this are your reticular activating system (RAS) and self-talk. As you learned in Chapter 1, self-talk is the mental chatter that you say to yourself on a daily basis. The **reticular activating system (RAS)** is the mind's filter system for information. Please see Career Coach 9.3 for further explanation on how these two tools can help you.

Reticular activating system (RAS)
The mind's filter system for information.

careercoach9.3

Tools That Work!

Your mind has a filter system for information called the reticular activating System (RAS). This mental filter can be used to help you reach your goals by screening for important information. Most people do not use this mind tool consciously, but rather by default. Up until now, you have screened a great deal of information in and out of your mind. The process is similar to screening phone calls. The phone rings, you check the number on the caller ID, and then you choose whether to answer or not. Have you ever had the experience of buying a car and then seeing that make or model of car everywhere? That is the power of your mental filter (Klauser, 2001; Rutherford, 1998; and Tice & Quick, 2004).

Think of a group of teenagers at the mall. They can be surrounded by a thousand people, with the noise of the hustle and bustle pouring out in every direction, and they still can spot a good looking guy or girl 500 feet away barely within their radar. How is this possible? Not only will the RAS screen *out* information, but like a global positioning system, the RAS will *locate* information that you value, need, or consider important.

If you want to change what is happening in your career life, use this mental filter to locate new career opportunities. You can literally retrain your brain to consciously see opportunities that have been around you all along, but were not getting through. Goal setting is one way to break through your mental filter. Studies on high achievers have found that people who have goals achieve more than people without goals. And, those who write their goals down achieve them most of all! Your job is to start utilizing the power of your RAS in order to jump-start your career.

The Power of Visualization Tool

Visualization involves using your mind to form pictures of your goals. In a nutshell, it can be considered forward thinking.

> **Visualization** Using your mind to form pictures of your goals; forward thinking.

Visualization is not magic, it is a tried and true success tool used by nearly all high-performance people from leaders in business to athletes (Choquette, 1997; Gawain, 2009; Tice & Quick, 2004; Vitale, 2006; Canfield, 2004; Gage, 2006; Katz, 2004; McColl, 2007; Hansen & Allen, 2002; Fengler & Varnum, 1994; Ray, 1999; Gregory, 2004; Proctor, 1997; Dooley, 2014; Tracy, 2009). It is important to stress the mechanics behind visualization so it does not seem magical. Visualization has very

> *The most powerful command you can send to your mind is a mental picture.*
>
> —Brian Tracy, chairman of Brian Tracy International

scientific roots. Cognitive psychology is filled with studies on the value of visualization. See Cyber Trip 9.6 for a visualization activity. See Exercise 9.2 for a visualization activity.

exercise 9.2

Visualization activity

Career Vision Board

This is a very powerful tool with several variations, and you can modify this exercise to suit your needs. Essentially, you will make a visual of your career goals.

1. Cut out words, pictures, sayings, and ideas from magazines or fliers that have meaning to you and your goals. Place these in a folder or envelope and keep collecting until you feel you have a good supply of pictures and words that represent your career goals. You can include life goals such as owning your dream car or house—goals that represent the lifestyle your career will bring you.

2. Near the top of a piece of poster board, write your career goal. Find the words or letters in magazines and cut them out individually, rather than simply writing the words. This better stimulates your reticular activating system. Write your goal in the first person present tense as if it is happening or will happen in the very near future.

3. Add the date by which you want to achieve this goal.

For example, you might spell out: I am enjoying the view from my corner office as I work as a (insert job title) for (insert the type of company; not the name of a specific company) by September 30, 20XX.

This statement is very powerful as it tells your brain, "This is it! This is what I want." Make it clear and specific. Now add pictures and words that you have collected that help you feel or picture your goal.

In addition, you can:

- Include a picture of yourself.
- If you put a vehicle on your board, add a picture of yourself in the driver's seat.
- Attach words that express your feelings about having your goal, such as joy, gratitude, etc.
- Make one big poster of all your goals for the next year.

The Extra Bit of Effort Tool

This is a coaching tool for success that is about doing *a little more*. All great wins seem to happen not because of some monumental advantage, but because someone did just a little bit more. Your job is to keep focused on your goals and put in that added effort to land the job of your dreams and eventually live the life of your dreams. There is a short inspirational movie regarding this principle called *212° The Extra Degree*® (Simpletruths.com, 2009). It sums up the coaching tool of a little more effort perfectly (http://play.simpletruths.com/movie/212-the-extra-degree).

Professional Growth and Lifelong Learning

Staying current in your profession is vital in the technological, global, fast-paced marketplace we live in. To assist your career security, take the initiative

Lifelong learning is key to your professional growth. Consider reading trade journals, joining professional organizations, and continuing your education while you work.

to learn more about your field and also look into developing new skills. This adds value to the organization and will help you as you grow professionally. Subscribe to industry publications (trade journals) in your field and join professional organizations. Attend and present at conferences. Continue your formal education. See if your employer provides tuition assistance. Many degree programs are all online, so you can do this in your off-hours. While this might sound like a large commitment, you are worth it.

Companies are seeking workers who can grow with the company and do not become obsolete as technology and processes change. Employees with cross-functional skills and knowledge are in demand. The key is to be able to work at your present job, while increasing your knowledge and skills, so you are prepared for the future. That is why reading trade journals is recommended. You will learn the industry forecasts and trends. You can get a jump-start on training or education which will keep you in demand. While it would be nice to think your boss or employer has your best interests in mind and will assist you with professional growth, this may not be the case. Use your mentor to help you with professional growth.

Mentors

In Chapter 4 we discussed the importance of having a professional mentor. Find a mentor in your field who is doing what you want to do in your career—one who can help you make excellent decisions to foster your career. Your mentor should be able to help you navigate office politics, help you advance, and direct your attention to opportunities that will grow your career. A sign that your mentor is doing a great job is that you outgrow him or her and move to another mentor as you advance in your career. A good mentor would not be offended by your progress as he or she would have good intentions for you.

my portfolio 9.1

Map Your Future Career Goals

The final portfolio assignment is to map three professional and lifelong learning goals. These could include a variety of possible new skills, individual courses, certificates, or degrees. It could also include professional associations you might join, subscriptions to industry journals, or conferences and training. You might also include a goal to find and use a mentor. In the space below, list three future goals that will add value to your career.

1. _____

   _____

2. _____

   _____

3. _____

   _____

Fitting In—Tim Finds His Place

Tim had been working at his job nearly a month now and was trying very hard to navigate the office culture but continued to find it difficult. He was very outgoing and felt that since he had to spend most of his day at the office, he wanted it to be fun. He did not want to change his entire personality to make the job work. Although Tim's work was excellent, he was discouraged about not fitting in and was ready to put in his notice. As a last ditch effort, he called his mentor, Joyce, who had recommended he apply with Graphic Solutions. She knew Tim and his ability, and she also knew that he was a good worker and could go far in the business. She really felt that if he could navigate the office culture, he would be successful.

They met for coffee and Tim detailed his work problems. Joyce could see clearly there was a personality conflict between Tim and the majority of the office. Joyce asked a few more questions about the job and discovered that Tim liked what he was doing, but he felt isolated and this depressed him. Joyce asked Tim how much he really wanted to succeed at this particular place of employment. He answered, "I really want this." Joyce recommended Tim try a few more changes in toning down his need for contact at work, and suggested he consider joining a social club, a young professionals' club, a fitness club, or do volunteering. There he could be as social as he wanted. She also persuaded Tim to give himself another month to try and fit into the culture or to determine that he was not a fit and start looking for another job. Tim trusted Joyce and knew that it might be difficult, but he was going to really try to succeed.

What Tim found after another month was that he fit into his work environment more than he thought he did. He joined a young professionals' club, which convened twice a month, as well as a gym, where he made several friends. He also tried toning down his socializing at the office and learned that he didn't have to change his personality at all. It was simply a matter of being more professional. He was learning to balance how much he socialized at work, and rather than cracking jokes all day, he chose times when it was appropriate, such as employee lunch outings. He found that when he communicated through e-mails and remained at his cubicle, rather than going desk to desk, others sought him out because they missed his laugh and positive spirit. They had grown fond of Tim over the weeks because he broke up the monotony of the quiet office. He was complimented on his work and was even getting positive attention from upper management. Tim felt good and was finally feeling like part of the team. He was sought out by co-workers for his opinion on projects, and as his professional communication with the rest of the office improved, he was being included on more meetings. He now knew that this *was* the right place for him because he was not only feeling more accepted but was also growing professionally. Although this was what Tim had wanted and he felt he was back on the right track to achieving his dream, he was now careful always to understand his surroundings and navigate accordingly.

Discussion Questions

1. Why do you think Tim had a difficult time adjusting to his environment?
2. Why is it important to have a mentor?
3. How important is it to learn to navigate your surroundings? Why?

[chapter summary]

The purpose of this chapter is three-fold. First, it is designed to provide you with the principles and practices of highly successful people, so that you can accelerate your career. The second goal of this chapter is to empower you when things get off course. No one wants to lose a job, get laid off, or have a bullying supervisor. If you are lucky, you will avoid all three. If it happens to you, however, you now have strategies to turn the setback into a success. The principle *success is always failure turned inside out* provides the foundation for looking at job problems more like opportunities. The final purpose of this chapter is to move you in the direction you want to go in your career, and provide you with tools to get you there faster.

When you set new goals in your career, and use constructive self-talk, forward thinking, and energy management strategies, you give yourself an edge in the marketplace. Often winners win by only small margins. This has been demonstrated in batting averages, runner's speeds, and in nearly all competitive arenas; those who win do so by a very short margin. This book is full of the principles, practices, and tools to take you to the next level in your career. You are well on your way to great success!

[skill/term check]

1. List three things you can do to advance your career. **(LO 9-1)**
2. Define netiquette, and explain why this is important in the workplace. **(LO 9-1)**
3. What are three ways you can take control over your schedule? **(LO 9-2)**
4. Why are performance evaluations important? **(LO 9-2)**
5. What are three ideas you can use to avoid burnout? **(LO 9-3)**
6. How can your RAS help you reach your career goals? **(LO 9-4)**
7. Why is it a good idea to make new professional goals once you land your job? **(LO 9-4)**

[KEY TERMS]

Company culture: The norms, customs, attitudes, values, and ways of operating in an organization. **(LO 9-1)** [p. 266]

Constructive discharge: When an employee's work environment is intentionally made so difficult that the employee feels forced to resign. **(LO 9-3)** [p. 282]

Energy management: Consciously choosing how you use your energy, allowing you to be efficient and effective. **(LO 9-2)** [p. 271]

5 minute rule: Use the extra minutes between scheduled events, where you have opportunity to get work done on your to-do list that does not require a large time commitment. **(LO 9-2)** [p. 271]

Job loss triage: Using triage or prioritizing skills when downsizing or job loss occurs to ensure the situation becomes a temporary setback rather than a tragedy. **(LO 9-3)** [p. 275]

Netiquette: Using manners, civility, and general rules of respectable communication online. **(LO 9-1)** [p. 267]

Reticular activating system (RAS): The mind's filter system for information. **(LO 9-4)** [p. 286]

Status-blind harassment: Persistent, unfair, and irrational managing. **(LO 9-3)** [p. 281]

Visualization: Using your mind to form pictures of your goals; forward thinking. **(LO 9-4)** [p. 287]

appendix A

Career Affirmations

A way to change your self-talk is to use affirmations.[1] As discussed in Chapter 1, an affirmation is a conscious, positive statement you say to yourself even if it is not true at the moment. The explanation behind an affirmation is that whatever you say after the words, "I am. . . ," you become. Even in your self-talk, when you say to yourself, "I am. . . ," you have just given yourself an affirmation. Affirmations are tools. They are very powerful when used, but it is up to you to use them. To use affirmations to your advantage, make constructive statements and say (and feel) them frequently. For example, "I always say and do the right thing," or "I am always in the right place at the right time." You feed your brain constructive statements that are stated as if they are true in order to offset the defeating messages you have fed yourself or received in the past. Affirmations are most powerful when using positive, first-person, present tense language.

How to Use Career Affirmations

Type or write the affirmations that you want to use on 3 × 5-inch note cards and say them in the morning right when you wake up and right before you go to bed. That is when your mind can soak them up the best. Say them other times as well. Some experts recommend saying affirmations in front of a mirror. Say them with feeling. The more you say them, the greater impact they have. Affirmations help retrain your brain for success.

Chapter 1: Jump-Start Your Career

I am now living my career mission to its fullest.

Focusing on my career is easy for me.

I see opportunities to advance my career everywhere.

I always use positive self-talk.

Change is easy for me.

Today, I take the first steps toward my goals.

---

[1] The coaching tool, **Affirmations**, is recommended by success experts, including Jack Canfield and Mark Victor Hansen, *Dare to Win*; Randy Gage, success coach, *Why You're Dumb, Sick, & Broke*; Eva Gregory, *The Feel Good Guide to Prosperity*; Charlotte Kasl, *If the Buddha Got Stuck*; Henriette Anne Klauser, author and speaker; Andrew Matthews, cartoon artist, *Being Happy*; James Arthur Ray, success and psychology coach, *The Science of Success*, Sanaya Roman and Duane Packer, *Creating Money*; Darel Rutherford, author and life coach; Florence Scove Shinn, *The Writings of Florence Scovel Shinn: The Game of Life, Your Word Is Your Wand, The Power of the Spoken Word, The Secret Door to Success*; Lou Tice, *Smart Talk for Achieving Your Potential: 5 Steps to Get You from Here to There*.

I look forward to my career.

I am now attracting my ideal job.

I have a strong inclination of my career purpose.

Setting and achieving my goals is easy for me.

I now attract the career that best expresses my life's work.

Today, I am committed to my career goals and my success is assured.

I flourish in the career that best supports my life's mission.

All of my setbacks are temporary as I move toward my goals.

Today, I am eager to work and make my contribution.

Chapter 2: Skills and Interests—Your Career Assets

I find it easy to speak positively about my skills, abilities, and achievements.

I market myself in a positive manner with my skills vocabulary.

Promoting my skills and strengths in interviews is easy for me.

I am always the expert on me.

I enjoy learning new skills.

I know what I need to do to advance my career.

I use the power of my self-awareness to launch my career.

Wonderful new opportunities are opening up for me to use my gifts, talents, and skills.

I am prosperous as I work in the career field I enjoy.

There is a huge demand for my skills and abilities.

I choose my career with full awareness.

I am honest in my appraisal of myself and my abilities.

I acquire all I need to excel in my profession.

Career Coach: Turn Affirmations into Why Questions

Author and SuccessClinic.com founder Noah St. John realized that when you ask the question "*Why?*" your mind automatically begins to search for an answer. St. John discovered how to use this unique capacity of the mind to his own advantage by changing "affirmations" into what he calls *Afformations®*. In his 2006 book, *The Great Little Book of Afformations*,[2] he explains how *Why* questions have the ability to work directly on the subconscious mind. The subconscious accepts the *Why* question as a truth and immediately begins looking for reasons, results, or answers to back up this *truth*. If you have been asking yourself, "*Why am I always late?*" your subconscious will work on your behalf to make sure you are always late! Remember, it is more important to your

> To get the right answer, it helps to ask the right question.
>
> —Thomas Watson, IBM founder

---

[2] Noah St. John, with author permission, **http://www.afformations.com.**

subconscious that you are sane, not right. To use the power of afformations, you would instead ask, *"Why am I always punctual or on time?"* Your subconscious will scurry to find an answer, and in doing so will also force the human body to perform.

St. John tells the story of an insurance salesman who began asking positive afformations, and within one month, his sales tripled. By the end of the year, his sales increased 560 percent over the previous year. Afformations may be a way to get better results with less effort. The following are some empowering *afformations* you can use or modify for your career success.

Chapter 3: Where Are the Jobs? Maximize Your Career Options

Why do I have the energy and persistence to investigate the career I have chosen?

Why do I find all pertinent information on the companies I want to work for?

Why am I so magnetically attractive to powerful and growing employers?

Why am I always in the right place at the right time doing exactly the right thing?

Why am I so abundantly paid for doing what I love?

Why am I so good at seeing and seizing opportunities?

Why am I so confident about my career journey?

Why do employers value and appreciate me?

Why do I receive abundant pay for my service?

Why am I so successful in my job search?

Why do I have clear goals that provide me a road map to my enduring success?

Why am I on target with my purpose in life?

Why are my talents and gifts appreciated and recognized in my workplace?

Chapter 4: Networking—It's Always Who You Know

Affirmations:

I enjoy meeting new people and networking connections.

I am always in the right place at the right time.

I always say and do the right thing.

I expect the best to happen when I meet new people.

I value my time and energy and so do others.

I allow others to help me in my job search.

I am alert to new opportunities: I see and seize them.

I attract people who can assist me.

People value and honor my contributions.

The career I seek is also seeking me.

I have a wonderful mentor to help me in my job search.

I feel confident in asking for advice.

Like a radio frequency, I am tuned to those who can assist me.

Afformations:

Why does my life work?

Why am I highly regarded?

Why do my obstacles turn into stepping-stones?

Why am I one step closer to my ideal job?

Why do I see signs daily that I am attracting the right people and opportunities for my new job?

Why am I connected to enough people to find my dream job?

Reminder: To incorporate and absorb your *affirmations and afformations* into the neuron of your brain, repeat them often (read them, see a picture of them in your mind, and feel the positive emotion the affirmation brings). The assimilation of affirmations is most effective right before you go to sleep and upon waking. Of course you can repeat them anytime, especially if you catch yourself using negative self-talk. You can turn your negative thoughts around by using a positive affirmation.

Chapter 5: Professional Resumes the Easy Way

Because of my special skills, employers are attracted to my resume and call me for an interview.

I create the perfect resume and portfolio to market myself to employers.

It is easy for me to create a winning resume.

My resume is a success magnet for interviews.

I constantly update and improve my resume as I improve myself.

My resume promotes me.

Chapter 6: Professional Cover Letters and Applications

I believe in my ability to land my ideal job.

Every part of the job search is important as I reach my career goals.

I am rewarded for the effort I put in my marketing tools.

Writing a winning cover letter is easy for me.

I always know how to market myself effectively.

I pay attention to details.

I am confident as I pursue my career goals.

Chapter 7: Successful Interviews

I network when I interview.

I enjoy meeting new people when I interview.

It is easy for me to sell myself, my skills, and my education.

Because of my professionalism, I always get the job offer when I interview.

I stay calm in the interview and my words flow freely.

I always say and do the right thing in the interview.

I always remember to shake hands and ask for the job at the end of the interview.

I look forward to the interview.

Chapter 8: Successful Follow-Up and Negotiation

I am a confident negotiator.

I am a valuable employee.

I add value to any company I am with.

People can see my worth, and I am compensated for the excellent work I do.

Job opportunities are everywhere.

I am confident in asking for what I want in a job.

Chapter 9: Step Up Your Career

The job I am seeking is waiting for me.

I control my destiny.

I work effortlessly and efficiently.

I do a great job and I am rewarded for it.

I am totally focused at work.

I am always a peak performer.

I achieve great results at work.

I love my work.

I have financial abundance this year.

I always act with integrity.

I am successful in all I do.

Others look up to me.

I easily achieve my dreams.

Affirmations for Career Changes

Affirmations work surprisingly well in career changes. Choose some of the following affirmations, and post them where you will see them often.

I gain strength through temporary setbacks, and bounce back quickly, better than before.

I enjoy getting up every day as I move toward my new career.

Because I am a hardworking and awesome employee, finding a new job is easy for me.

I use this time wisely as I seek my new career.

I am immune to stress.

I am moving forward with my life.

Every day in every way, I am getting better and better.

Draft Your Career Mission Statement

You are the expert on you! With this in mind, you will construct a career mission statement that works for you and your life's purpose. Now that you have learned about the career mission statement, and viewed several websites to learn more about developing one, you are ready to draft your own. Remember that you can modify your career mission statement over time. At this point, draft your best guess. Write something on paper as a starting point about what you want to do with your life. This may be similar to an objective on a resume. Do not be afraid to revise it several times until you have determined your best career mission statement. When you are satisfied, either rewrite your career mission statement on a clean sheet of paper and keep it in a binder specifically for your portfolio documents, or type it into an electronic word processing document and save it to your computer or a portable storage device, such as a USB drive.

Career Assets Inventory

In the chart below, list each skill you already identified under Transferable, Adaptive, or Job-Specific. Then mark whether you are proficient or are an expert, depending on your skill level.

Type of Skill	List Skill	Proficient	Expert
Transferable Skills			
Adaptive Skills			
Job-Specific Skills			

Quantify Your Skills

This portfolio exercise sets the foundation for resume building, cover letter writing, and interviewing. First, identify several skills you wish to include in your marketing documents. Next, consider how you might be able to quantify each skill. This means that you will need to add numbers to the skill so it is measurable. Figure 2.2 shows examples of how to quantify your skills.

Skill	Quantified Skill
Typing/keyboarding	Type or keyboard 50 wpm (words per minute).
Selling	Top salesperson for two quarters last year, with over $150,000 in total sales per quarter.
Supervising	Supervised 12 employees on a daily basis.

Figure 2.2 **How to Quantify Your Skills**

Now you try it:

List Skill	Quantify the Skill

You will expand on the process of quantifying skills in upcoming chapters to help you create superior marketing documents.

Company Research

Research three companies that interest you or that you might like to work for. Use the Internet, library, trade journals, Chamber of Commerce, or other sources to locate this information. Most companies have websites, which are great places to start.

After you have researched your chosen companies, complete the following information:

Company 1

Company or organization name: _____

Briefly describe what the company does: _____

Location(s): _____

Website address: _____

Phone number: _____

Type of position you are interested in within the company: _____

How to apply: _____

Positive aspects of the company: _____

Negative aspects of the company: _____

Three things you learned about the company or organization. These might include size, mission statement, growth projection, etc.: _____

_____

_____

Company 2

Company or organization name: _____

Briefly describe what the company does: _____

Location(s): _____

Website address: _____

Phone number: _____

Type of position you are interested in within the company: _____

How to apply: _____

Positive aspects of the company: _____

Negative aspects of the company: _____

Three things you learned about the company or organization. These might include size, mission statement, growth projection, etc.: _____

(Continued)

Company 3

Company or organization name: _____

Briefly describe what the company does: _____

Location(s): _____

Website address: _____

Phone number: _____

Type of position you are interested in within the company: _____

How to apply: _____

Positive aspects of the company: _____

Negative aspects of the company: _____

Three things you learned about the company or organization. These might include size, mission statement, growth projection, etc.: _____

_____

_____

my portfolio 3.2

Log of Contacts

Transfer the information from one of the companies you researched to the contact log below. This is how you can keep track of the companies you target, their contact information, and what action you took or plan to take. Consider also creating a digital version of this log of contacts that you can keep on your computer or phone.

Log of Contacts	
Company name:	
Address:	
City:	
State:	
Zip code:	
Website address:	
Contact person name and title:	
Phone number:	
Fax number:	
E-mail:	
Date applied:	
Follow-up date:	
Additional comments:	

my portfolio 4.1

Create Your NBC

Again, your networking business card is your mini resume. It should contain the following information: your skills, contact information, and perhaps an image or icon associated with your career intent. You may find that you continue to use your NBC even after you land a job. The NBC is one of the most powerful, yet underused, tools in leveraging your networking efforts.

To start, see Cyber Trip 4.4 for links to several websites that allow you to experiment with designing your NBC. The suggested sites also provide additional samples for you to view.

Keep in mind there are various approaches to the construction of your NBC outside of the referred links, including Word/clip art, Power Point, and so on. Use the format that works best for you.

It costs nothing to create a design at many of the online business card stores. Explore the different logos. If you are going into an IT field, consider adding a computer icon on your card. These services are very inexpensive, and purchasing the minimum number of cards should last you a sufficient amount of time, depending on how often you hand out your card. It will only cost a few cappuccinos to make and deliver the cards to your home address. As an alternative, you can use heavy paper, also known as card stock, with your own computer software to make your cards. Many students add a photo of themselves to their NBC. Consider adding a picture of yourself as well!

Check to make sure your NBC is professional and easy to read and that it includes the following:

- Your name.
- Your degree (use the words "in progress" if you are still working on your degree).
- Your skills—a few that are essential to your field.
- Professional e-mail address and phone number.
- A visual related to your field.
- Professional and easy to read layout and type.

Lastly, turn in your actual NBC or the information you would include on one, depending on your instructor's requirements.

my portfolio 5.1

Create a Resume

Directions: First choose the format—chronological, functional, or combination—that best fits your experience and desired position. Practice with these formats using both the exercises in this book and online using various tools. You can find appropriate worksheets using your favorite Internet search engine, by entering the keywords "resume worksheet," "chronological resume worksheet," or "functional or skills resume worksheet." Revisit My Portfolio 2.1, and use your *Career Assets Inventory*. You already listed many of your skills in that exercise. Now you can organize, bullet, and quantify them for your portfolio. Keep in mind you do not need to use all of the skills you listed in your *Career Assets Inventory* for your resume. You are targeting a job, so use the skills that best support your qualifications for the position you seek. These should agree with your objective if you decide to use one.

(Continued)

Resume Header or Identification

_____

_____

_____

Objective (optional):

To _____

Summary of Skills (optional)

■ _____   ■ _____

■ _____   ■ _____

■ _____   ■ _____

Education
College name, address (city/state):
Degree:
Graduation date (month/year):
Majors/ minors:
GPA if above 3.0:
College name, address (city/state):
Degree:
Graduation date (month/year):
Majors/ minors:
GPA if above 3.0:

Work Experience or List of Positions (most recent first)
Company names, cities, states:

1. _____
2. _____
3. _____
4. _____
5. _____

Dates of employment at each company:

1. _____
2. _____
3. _____
4. _____
5. _____

Title held at each company:

1. _____
2. _____
3. _____
4. _____
5. _____

List skills gained from each company—follow the *Skills Formula*. Once you have a list, put them into bulleted format:

1. _____
2. _____
3. _____
4. _____
5. _____

Honors and Awards (optional)

_____

Activities or Community/Civic Involvement/Professional Affiliations (optional)

_____

Publications (optional)

_____

Figure 5.5 Chronological Resume Worksheet

(Continued)

Resume Header or Identification

_____

_____

_____

Objective (optional):

To _____

LIST SKILLS IN BULLETED FORM (follow the *Skills Formula*; skills and experience in functional groups such as management, computer skills, training, etc.)

Skill Heading I _____

Example _____

Example _____

Example _____

Skill Heading II _____

Example _____

Example _____

Example _____

Skill Heading III _____

Example _____

Example _____

Example _____

WORK EXPERIENCE OR LIST OF POSITIONS (most recent first)

Company name _____

City, state (abbreviate) _____

Dates of employment _____

Title _____

Company name _____

City, state (abbreviate) _____

Dates of employment _____

Title _____

Company name _____

City, state (abbreviate) _____

Dates of employment _____

Title _____

EDUCATION

Name of college or university _____

College address (city/state) _____

Degree: _____

Majors/minors: _____

Graduation date (month/year) _____

GPA if above 3.0: _____

Honors and Awards (optional):

_____

_____

Activities or Community/Civic Involvement/Professional Affiliations (optional):

_____

_____

Publications (optional):

_____

Figure 5.6 Functional/Skills Resume Worksheet

(Continued)

Resume Checklist			
	Not Included	Needs Improvement	Well Done
Categories arranged in order of importance			
Organization logical, clear, and consistent			
Information is targeted to position: keywords			
One or two pages only			
No sentences; concise statements			
Information accurate and positive			
Uses *Skills Formula*			
Power words used			
Verbs in correct tense (past or present)			
No slang			
Abbreviations avoided			
Correct spelling, grammar, and punctuation			
Unnecessary repetition avoided			
No use of *I, me, my,* etc.			
Appropriate headings			
White space, indentation, underlining, italic, capitals, and spacing effectively used			
Skills are bulleted			
Space between categories			
Layout: headings, spacing, type face, print size, etc., consistent			
Correct information in the heading			
Overall appearance pleasing, appealing, and easy on the eye			
High-quality paper used (if applicable)			

Reference Checklist			
Separate from resume			
Appropriate format			
Lists 3–5 references			
Heading matches resume heading			
Information is complete			
Phone numbers with area codes			
Addresses include zip codes			
Paper matches resume (if applicable)			

Figure 5.7   Resume Checklist

Resume Checklist and Grading Rubric

Use the Resume Checklist and Grading Rubric to either peer review another student's resume or double check your own. These tools will help ensure all of the elements are included in your winning resume.

(Continued)

	Resume Grading Rubric (100 points)	Circle Points		
		Not Included	Needs Improvement	Well Done
1	Categories are arranged in order of importance	0	1–2–3	4–5
2	Organization is logical, clear, and consistent	0	1–2–3	4–5
3	Information is targeted to position: keywords	0	1–2–3	4–5
4	One or two pages only	0	1–2–3	4–5
5	No sentences; only concise statements	0	1–2–3	4–5
6	Information is accurate and positive	0	1–2–3	4–5
7	Uses *Skills Formula*	0	1–2–3	4–5
8	Uses power words	0	1–2–3	4–5
9	Verbs are in correct tense (past or present)	0	1–2–3	4–5
10	No slang	0	1–2–3	4–5
11	Abbreviations are avoided	0	1–2–3	4–5
12	Correct spelling, grammar, and punctuation	0	1–2–3	4–5
13	Unnecessary repetition is avoided	0	1–2–3	4–5
14	Appealing and easy on the eye; high-quality paper if applicable	0	1–2–3	4–5
15	No use of *I, me, my,* etc.	0	1–2–3	4–5
16	Use of white space, indentation, underlining, italic, capitals, and spacing is effective	0	1–2–3	4–5
17	Skills are bulleted	0	1–2–3	4–5
18	Space between categories	0	1–2–3	4–5
19	Formatting and layout: headings, spacing, type face, print size, etc., are consistent and accurate.	0	1–2–3	4–5
20	Heading information is accurate	0	1–2–3	4–5
	Additional comments:			
	Total Points for Resume (100 points possible)			
	REFERENCES GRADING RUBRIC (25 points)			
1	Reference page is separate from resume; if hard copy, the paper matches the resume	0	1–2–3	4–5
2	Appropriate format	0	1–2–3	4–5
3	Lists 3–5 references	0	1–2–3	4–5
4	References heading matches resume heading	0	1–2–3	4–5
5	Information is complete: phone numbers have area codes; addresses include zip codes	0	1–2–3	4–5
	Total Points for References (25 points possible)			
	Total Points for References and Resume (125 points possible)			

Figure 5.8   Resume Grading Rubric

my portfolio 6.1

Draft Your Cover Letter

Choose one of the two cover letter formats from Figure 6.9 or Figure 6.10 and fill in your information. Later, transfer this information to a business letter Word document. Use the Cover Letter Checklist in Exercise 6.3 to ensure you have all of the needed elements for a winning cover letter.

(Continued)

```
   _____  ⎫  ┌─────────────────────┐
   _____  ⎬  │ Return address,     │
   _____  ⎭  │ e-mail & phone      │
   _____     │ number              │
                                └─────────────────────┘

   _____  ⎫  ┌─────────────────────┐
                            ⎬  │ Date letter will be sent. │
                               └─────────────────────┘

   _____     ┌─────────────────────┐
   Attn: _____  ⎫  │ Inside address      │
   _____  ⎬  │ company name,       │
   _____  ⎭  │ Attn:               │
                               │ Address             │
                               └─────────────────────┘

   Dear _____ :  ⎫  ┌───────────────┐
                         ⎭  │ Salutation    │
                            └───────────────┘
```

┌──────────────┐ ⎧
│ Capture   │ │ _____
│ Attention   │ │
│ &   │ ⎨ _____
│ State   │ │
│ Purpose   │ │ _____.
│ of Letter   │ ⎩
└──────────────┘

┌──────────────┐ ⎧ _____
│   │ │ _____
│ Interest   │ │ _____
│ &   │ │ _____
│ Market   │ ⎨ _____
│ Skills to   │ │ _____
│ the   │ │ _____
│ Position   │ │ _____
│   │ │ _____.
└──────────────┘ ⎩

┌──────────────┐ ⎧ _____
│ Action   │ ⎨
│ step   │ ⎩ _____.
└──────────────┘

       Sincerely, ⎫ ┌───────────────┐
                   ⎭ │ Closure   │
                      └───────────────┘

                   ⎫ ┌───────────────┐
                   ⎬ │ Signature   │
                   ⎭ └───────────────┘

   _____ ⎫ ┌───────────────┐
                    ⎭ │ Name   │
                       └───────────────┘

       Enclosure

Figure 6.9   **Cover Letter Template #1**

(Continued)

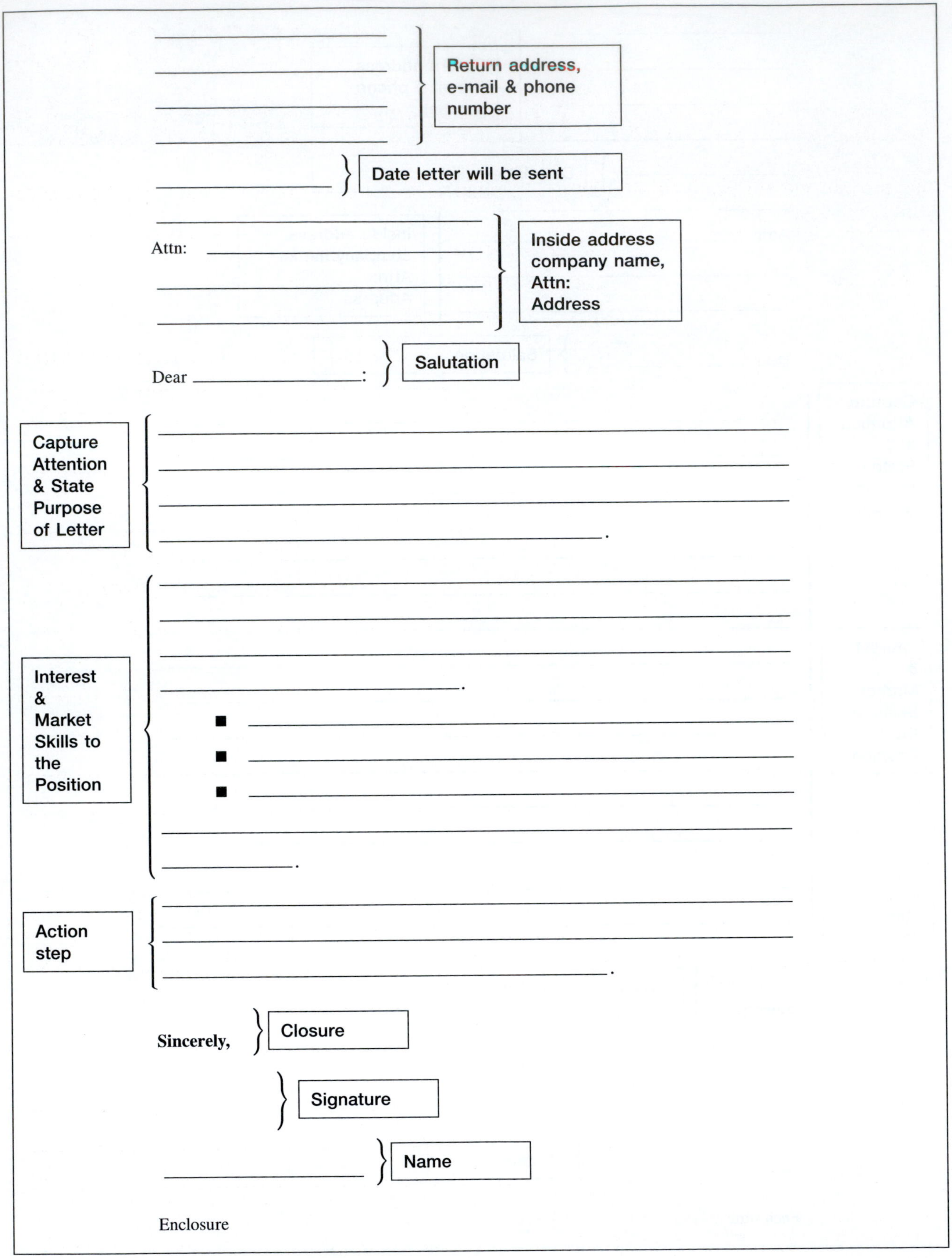

_____
_____ } **Return address,**
_____   e-mail & phone
_____   number

_____ } Date letter will be sent

_____
Attn: _____ } Inside address
_____   company name,
_____   **Attn:**
                                 Address

Dear _____ : } Salutation

Capture
Attention { _____
& State   _____
Purpose   _____
of Letter   _____ .

Interest   { _____
&   _____
Market   _____
Skills to   _____ .
the   ■ _____
Position   ■ _____
                   ■ _____
                 _____
                 _____ .

Action   { _____
step   _____
                _____ .

Sincerely, } Closure

              } Signature

_____ } Name

Enclosure

Figure 6.10   **Cover Letter Template #2**

Create Your Master Application

Use the information you have learned in this chapter to correctly complete the following application form in Figure 6.12.

APPLICATION FOR EMPLOYMENT

Master Employment Application

AN EQUAL OPPORTUNITY EMPLOYER

PLEASE READ BEFORE COMPLETING THIS APPLICATION AND PRINT ALL INFORMATION REQUESTED EXCEPT SIGNATURE

I. PERSONAL DATA   DATE _____

Name _____ Soc. Sec. Number: _____
     Last   First   Initial

Address _____
     Street   Apt.   City   State   Zip

Telephone (_____) _____ (daytime)   (_____) _____ (evenings)

(_____) _____ (Mobile)   E-mail address _____

Have you previously been employed by this organization? _____ Yes   When? _____
_____ No   Where? _____

Will you travel if a job requires it? _____ Yes _____ No

Driver's License No. _____ Issuing State _____

What is your means of transportation to work? _____

Have you had any accidents in the past three years? _____ How Many? _____

Have you had any moving violations in the past three years? _____ How Many? _____

Are you prevented from lawfully becoming employed in this country because of Visa or Immigration status? _____ Yes _____ No
If hired, you will be required to show proof of employment authorization.

Have you ever been convicted of a crime that may relate to the position for which you are applying? _____ Yes _____ No
(*Note: The existence of a criminal record does not create an automatic bar to employment.*)

Have you ever had any job-related training in the United States Military? _____ Yes _____ No

If yes, please describe _____

Are you able to perform the duties of the job for which you are applying with or without accommodation? _____ Yes _____ No

Have you smoked or chewed tobacco at any time within the last two years to the present? _____ Yes _____ No

---

Figure 6.12   Master Employment Application

(Continued)

II. EMPLOYMENT DESIRED

Position(s) applied for: _____

When available for work? _____   Salary desired:
_____

Are you available to work?   _____ Full Time   _____ Part Time
(Check all that apply.)
                                  _____ Shift Work   _____ Temporary

III. EDUCATION/SPECIAL TRAINING DATA

	Elementary School	High School	Undergraduate College/University	Graduate/ Professional
School Name/Location				
Years Completed	4 5 6 7 8	9 10 11 12	1 2 3 4	1 2 3 4
Diploma/Degree				
Major	Undergraduate:		Graduate:	
Describe any specialized training, apprenticeship, skills and extracurricular activities				
Describe any honors, commendations you have received				
State any additional information you feel may be helpful to use in considering your application				

IV. REFERENCES   (Please list three references other than relatives, or previous employers.)

Name, Address, Phone Number, E-mail	Known How Long	Occupation/Company

Figure 6.12   (Continued)

(Continued)

V. EMPLOYMENT HISTORY

Please list all previous employment. Start with most recent job. Include any job-related military service assignments and/or volunteer activities. You may exclude organizations that indicate race, color, religion, gender, national origin, disability, or other protected status. If you were self-employed, provide firm name.

1. Employer	Employment Dates		Work Performed
	Yrs.	Mos.	
Address	Hourly Rate/Salary		
	Starting		
E-mail Address	Ending		
Telephone Number ( )	Name of last supervisor		
Last Job Title			
Reason for Leaving			
2. Employer	Employment Dates		Work Performed
	Yrs.	Mos.	
Address	Hourly Rate/Salary		
	Starting		
E-mail Address	Ending		
Telephone Number ( )	Name of last supervisor		
Last Job Title			
Reason for Leaving			
3. Employer	Employment Dates		Work Performed
	Yrs.	Mos.	
Address	Hourly Rate/Salary		
	Starting		
E-mail Address	Ending		
Telephone Number ( )	Name of last supervisor		
Last Job Title			
Reason for Leaving			
4. Employer	Employment Dates		Work Performed
	Yrs.	Mos.	
Address	Hourly Rate/Salary		
	Starting		
E-mail Address	Ending		
Telephone Number ( )	Name of last supervisor		
Last Job Title			
Reason for Leaving			

May we contact your present employer? _____ Yes _____ No

Did you complete this application yourself? _____ Yes _____ No

If not, who did? _____

If you need additional space, please continue on a separate sheet of paper.

Summarize any special job-related skills and/or qualifications acquired that may not be listed above. Also provide any additional information necessary to describe your full qualifications for the specific position.

_____

_____

_____

Figure 6.12   (Continued)

(Continued)

Now use the application form checklist in Figure 6.13 to ensure your application is accurate and complete. Once you have completed, verified, and finalized the information on the form, you can use it as your master application.

	Name:	Not Included	Present
1	Followed instructions		
2	Typed or printed information		
3	Used a black pen		
4	Neat and easy to read—printed		
5	All questions answered thoroughly		
6	Complete, accurate information		
7	Used N/A or a dash for questions that did not apply		
8	Correct information in correct spaces		
9	No scratch-outs or white-out		
10	Correct grammar, spelling, punctuation		
11	Information stated in positive terms		
12	Specific position/title listed		
13	Specific past or current salary stated (if requested)		
14	Addresses with zip codes		
15	Phone numbers with area codes		
16	E-mail addresses		
17	Application form is signed and dated		
18	Employed history listed chronologically, starting with most recent		
19	"Negotiable" or "Open" stated for salary desired, unless the employer states it will not accept an application without salary information		
20	No acronyms		
21	Included skills for position		
	Comments:		

Figure 6.13 Application Form Checklist

Create a List of Questions to Ask

Review the list of possible questions to ask in the interview and select three you like the best by circling the numbers from the following list.

1. What is a typical day like for this position?
2. What areas are the highest priorities for this position and need immediate solutions or attention?
3. What is the division's management style?
4. What is the next step in this process?
5. When do you plan on making a decision?
6. Why is the position open?
7. What are the avenues for advancement with this position?
8. Do you offer assistance with professional development, training, or furthering one's education?
9. Is an advanced degree required or preferred for promotions?
10. Who would I report to?
11. How is performance for this position measured?
12. What other departments does this position interface (or cooperate) with, and is there anything I should know about that role in connecting with these other parts of the organization?

Write down two additional questions to ask during the interview:

Question 1: _____

Question 2: _____

Type the list of questions you plan to ask during an interview into a Word document. You will want to save this list and modify it for each interview so you can print and take a copy with you.

my portfolio 8.1

Write a Follow-Up Letter

Directions: Use the samples in this chapter to help you formulate a professional thank you letter. Create it in a Word document using the business letter format (the same format you used for your cover letter). The follow-up letter should consist of three short paragraphs, single spaced with no indents, and an extra space between the paragraphs. Make sure you include your contact information as you did for the cover letter.

The first paragraph begins by thanking them for the interview. You can also use verbiage such as *"I would like to express my appreciation for the opportunity to meet with you and discuss the XYZ position."* Mention something specific you learned from visiting with them about the job or company.

The second paragraph is where you communicate that you are ready to begin working for the company, and provide a *new example* of how you are a great fit for the job.

In the final paragraph, again thank them for the interview. Assure them of your continued interest in working for them in this position. You can mention that you *"look forward to hearing from them"* or *"look forward to the next step."*

Use a formal closing such as *Sincerely* or *Respectfully,* and sign your name with your typed signature beneath it.

my portfolio 9.1

Map Your Future Career Goals

The final portfolio assignment is to map three professional and lifelong learning goals. These could include a variety of possible new skills, individual courses, certificates, or degrees. It could also include professional associations you might join, subscriptions to industry journals, or conferences and training. You might also include a goal to find and use a mentor. In the space below, list three future goals that will add value to your career.

1. _____

_____

2. _____

_____

3. _____

_____

glossary

Achievement An accomplishment or success that you attain.

Action paragraph The final paragraph in a cover letter taking action by asking for the interview, and stating when you will call the employer to follow up on the application.

Adaptive skills Soft skills related to your work style that help you function as a good employee on a day-to-day basis.

Affirmation A conscious, positive statement you say to yourself even if it is not true at the moment.

Afformation Turning affirmations into "why" questions.

Avocation An activity or hobby that is done for enjoyment in addition to one's regular work.

Baby boomer Someone born between 1946 and 1964.

Brand identity Your personal marketing image that highlights your worth and value to employers.

Business casual Attire that falls between jeans and a formal suit; each company defines what falls into this category.

Career A profession built on one's skills, passions, experiences, education, and preferences.

Career mission statement A brief description of your overall career purpose.

Career plan A series of steps taken over a period of time to achieve a desired career.

Chronological resume A resume that lists specific skills under each position held.

Cold contact A person with whom you have no connection but you are going to call or connect with regardless.

Combination resume A resume that combines both the chronological and functional resume types; also known as a custom resume or hybrid resume.

Comfort zone The environment, situations, or people that make you feel the most safe and normal.

Company culture The norms, customs, attitudes, values, and ways of operating in an organization.

Competency-based interview An interview based on the premise that your past employment behavior will dictate your future behavior in the new position; also known as a behavioral interview.

Constructive discharge A termination of employment brought about by making the employee's working conditions so intolerable that the employee feels compelled to leave.

Contact log A way to record current and potential contacts during the job search and interview process.

Control statement A statement you make during the interview that changes the direction of the interview.

E-commerce company Business that is conducted electronically on the Internet.

11th hour principle Principle for perseverance: when things seem the bleakest in the job search, it can be a good sign, as the tide generally turns at the 11th hour.

Energy management Consciously choosing how you use your energy, allowing you to be efficient and effective.

E-mail thank you An e-mail thank you note sent the day of the interview to show your immediate interest in the position.

First cut When employers sort through a pool of applicants, and accept or reject them based on their applications or resume materials.

5-minute rule Use the extra minutes between scheduled events, where you have opportunity to get work done on your to-do list that does not require a large time commitment.

Frictional unemployment Unemployment that results because people move between jobs, careers, and locations.

Functional resume A resume that organizes skills and accomplishments into groupings that support the position objective; also known as a skills resume.

Globalization The growing economic interdependence of countries worldwide.

Hard skills The technical expertise you need to have to do a job well.

Hidden job market A network that consists of people you will associate with in your career search and while climbing the career ladder; also known as a hidden network.

Industry standards The compensation levels for different fields.

Informational interview An interview that allows you to gather information about a particular occupation or company.

Job A work situation in which you earn money.

Job loss triage Using triage or prioritizing skills when downsizing or job loss occurs to ensure the situation becomes a temporary setback rather than a tragedy.

Job-specific skills Skills that require special training, experience, education, or certification.

Keywords Terms related to specific skills or qualifications that employers search for in electronic resumes.

Leverage The power to do more with less.

Lunch or dinner interview An interview that takes place during a meal, and may be part of a daylong interview process, or it may be the interview itself.

Master application An application you fill out and take with you to interviews or places of employment, so all of your information is in one place and easy to transfer to the application you will turn in.

McDonaldization Term coined by George Ritzer to explain how society takes on the characteristics of a fast-food restaurant.

McJob A low-paying job requiring few skills and offering little chance of advancement.

Mentor An experienced person who helps and guides another.

Mock interview Simulated interview for practice.

Netiquette Using manners, civility, and general rules of respectable communication online.

Networking Using contacts for purposes beyond the reason for the initial contact, especially in business and career searches.

Networking business card (NBC) A personal business card that includes your name, contact information, desired field of employment, and a brief description of your skills or qualifications.

Nondirective interview An interview often used in fields where the candidate needs to demonstrate his or her skills or wares; also known as a work sample interview.

Nonnegotiables The few items you must have in order to take the job.

Outsourcing Hiring and paying an outside firm or third party to handle internal company functions.

Panel interview An interview that usually takes place around a conference table, where a group of individuals will collectively ask the candidate questions; also known as a group interview.

Personality assessment Categorizes your personality traits to determine if your personal attributes are a good fit in a particular work environment.

Personal reference Someone other than an employer who can make statements about your ethics, trustworthiness, and personality.

Phone interview An interview conducted over the phone, usually before meeting the hiring manager in person.

Plain text resume A resume with simplified formatting, in order to prevent errors when sending it electronically. Also known as electronic resume, e-resume, scannable resume, text resume, text-based resume, or online resume.

Portfolio A grouping of hard copy or electronic documents that represent your work and can be used during the job search.

Position power The power that a title brings to an individual.

Power words Verbs in your resume that best describe and emphasize what actions you did in the position.

Professional recruiter Professional agency or individual, also known as a headhunter, who works on your behalf to help you land a job.

Professional reference Someone who knows your work, such as an employer or co-worker.

Quantified skills Skills that include specific, measurable amount(s) in numerical form.

Reticular activating system (RAS) The mind's filter system for information.

Screening interview An interview used to evaluate and narrow a large applicant pool; also known as a prescreening interview.

Second interview An interview that occurs after the initial interview and involves candidates who made the first cut and have been screened down to a small pool of people in which the company is truly interested.

Self-talk The mental chatter that you say to yourself on a constant basis.

Service workers Those who perform services for the public.

70/30 rule If the job offer has 70 percent of what you desire (advantages) and less than 30 percent of what you don't want (disadvantages), then you may be in the ballpark for accepting.

Skills Formula™ Uses bullets, power words, and keyword skills to create quantified outcomes for your professional resume.

Skills gap The skills you must acquire to obtain your ideal job.

Skills vocabulary Identifying your skills in order to market and sell yourself to potential employers or to your current employer if you want to be considered for advancement.

Small to medium employer (SME) Generally defined in the United States as a firm employing between 1 and 500 full-time employees.

SMART goals An acronym technique that produces specific, measurable, attainable, realistic, and tangible goals.

Soft skills The skills aside from technical expertise that you need to do a job.

Standard interview An interview during which the applicant is asked a variety of typical questions; also known as a traditional interview.

STAR A three-step acronym technique used to answer competency- or behavior-based interview questions; also known as SAR or PAR.

Status-blind harassment Persistent, unfair, and irrational managing.

Stress interview An interview with the goal of seeing how you actually handle stress in the workplace, rather than just asking you questions about how you handle stress.

Stretch goals A goal that is large enough to create the energy and motivation needed to achieve it, but not so lofty that it is unattainable.

Structured interview An interview in which each job candidate receives the exact same questions.

Synergy The enhanced results when two or more people combine efforts or energy.

Targeted job search When you take the lead to research and select industries, companies, and even positions or people you want to work for.

Technical interview An interview during which technical or information technology questions are asked in order to demonstrate that you have the specific knowledge or skills the employer is seeking.

Temporary agencies Staffing companies that find jobs for people searching for employment, and find qualified people for companies that are seeking to fill specific positions.

Transferable skills The skills you gain from your experiences.

Virtual company Online companies that may or may not have physical locations.

Visualization Using your mind to form pictures of your goals; forward thinking.

Warm contact Someone you are comfortable contacting.

Working poor Individuals whose income falls below the official poverty threshold.

Workplace values Values that are upheld and honored in the workplace.

references

Abraham-Hicks. (2009). Retrieved from http://www.abraham-hicks.com/

Ballard, S. (2004, July). How to handle a workplace bully. *Jet 106* (4), 16–20.

Bowen, W. (2007). *A Complaint Free World*. NY: Doubleday.

Braden, G. (2009). GreggBraden.com. Retrieved from http://www.greggbraden.com/

Bristol, C. (1991). *The magic of believing*. NY: Pocket Books.

Canfield, J. & Hansen, M. V. (1996). *Dare to win*. NY: Berkeley.

Canfield, J. (2004). *The success principles: How to get from where you are to where you want to be*. NY: Collins Living.

Canfield, J. (2009). Jack Canfield Coaching. Retrieved July 8, 2009, from http://www.canfieldcoaching.com

CareerBuilder. (2009). CareerBuilder.com. Retrieved from http://www.careerbuilder.com/

Carey, B. (2004, June). Fear in the workplace: The bullying boss. *New York Times*, F1.

Center for American Progress, "Fact Sheet: The Women's Leadership Gap," http://www.americanprogress.org/issues/women/report/2014/03/07/85457/fact-sheet-the-womens-leadership-gap/ (visited August 02, 2014).

Chao, E. (2006, August 30). Minority Business Development Agency Luncheon Address: Acceptance of the Ronald H. Brown Leadership Award. Retrieved August 28, 2009, from http://www.dol.gov/_sec/media/speeches/archive/20060830_MinorityBusiness.htm

Chopra, D. (2004). *The spontaneous fulfillment of desire: Harnessing the infinite power of coincidence*. NY: Three Rivers Press.

Chopra, D. (2005). *The book of secrets: Unlocking the hidden dimensions of your life*. NY: Three Rivers Press.

Chopra, D. (2009). The Chopra Center. Retrieved July 14, 2009, from http://www.chopra.com/

Choquette, S. (1997). *Your heart's desire: Instructions for creating the life you really want*. New York: Three Rivers Press.

Covey, S. (2014). The 7 habits of highly effective people–Habit 4: Think win-win. NY: Simon & Schuster.

Demartini, J. (2005). *You can have an amazing life in just 60 days*. Carlsbad, CA: Hay House.

Dooley, M. (2009). Notes from the universe. Retrieved July 14, 2009, from http://www.tut.com

Dooley, M. (2014). *Notes from the universe: New perspectives from an old friend*. OR: Atria Books/Beyond Words.

Fengler, F. & Varnum, T. (1994). *Manifesting your heart's desire*. TN: Heartlight.

Ferguson, B. (2004). *Heal the hurt that sabotages your life* (2nd ed.). Houston, TX: Return to the Heart.

Forleo, M. (2009). MarieForleo.com. Retrieved from http://marieforleo.com

Gage, R. (2006). *Why you're dumb, sick, & broke . . . and how to get smart, healthy, & rich!* Hoboken, NJ: Wiley.

Gage, R. (2009). RandyGage.com. Retrieved from http://www.randygage.com/

Gawain, S. (2009). Shakti Gawain. Retrieved from http://www.shaktigawain.com/

Goldsmith, M. and Reiter, M. (2007). *What got you here won't get you there*. NY: Hyperion.

Granovetter, M. (1995). *Getting a job: A study of contacts and careers*. Cambridge, MA: University of Chicago Press.

Grant, B. (2005). The Woman Men Adore . . . And Never Want to Leave. Retrieved from http://www.relationshipheadquarters.com/

Grant, B. (2007). How to Get Him Back. Retrieved from http://www.relationshipheadquarters.com/

Gregory, E. (2004). *The feel good guide to prosperity*. CA: Leading Edge Publishers.

Hansen, M. V. & Allen, R. (2002). *One minute millionaire: The enlightened way to wealth*. NY: Harmony Books.

Hansen, M. V. & Allen, R. (2009). OneMinuteMillionaire.com. Retrieved from http://www.oneminutemillionaire.com/challenge/

Hayden, R. (1992). *How to turn your money life around*. Deerfield Beach, FL: HCI.

Heer, Dain. (2011). Being You, Changing the World. Big Country Publishing, LLC.

Heer, D. (2012). drdainheer.com Retrieved from http://drdainheer.com/

Hesselbein, F. & Goldsmith, M. (2009). *The organization of the future 2: Visions, strategies, and insights on managing in a new era*. San Francisco, CA: Jossey-Bass.

Hill, N. (1997). *Keys to success: The 17 principles of personal achievement*. NY: Penguin Group.

Holland, J. L. (1973). *Making vocational choices: A theory of careers*. Englewood Cliffs, NJ: Prentice Hall.

Holmes, E. (2009). *Creative mind and success*. NY: Classic House Books.

Hood, S. B. (2004, September). Workplace bully. *Business Source Premier, 77*(18).

Hyatt, M. (2014). 5 Reasons Why You Should Commit Your Goals to Writing. Retrieved from http://michaelhyatt.com/5-reasons-why-you-should-commit-your-goals-to-writing.html

International Labour Organization. (2009). Retrieved July 26, 2009, from http://www.ilo.org/global/lang–en/index.htm

Jandt, F. (1985). *Win-win negotiating: Turning conflict into agreement*. Hoboken, NJ: John Wiley & Son, Inc.

Kane, A. & Kane, S. (2008). *Working on yourself doesn't work*. NY: McGraw-Hill.

Kane, A. & Kane, S. (2009). Catalysts for instantaneous transformation. Retrieved July 14, 2009, from http://www.transformationmadeeasy.com/

Kasl, C. (2005). *If the Buddha got stuck*. NY: Penguin.

Katz, M. (2004). *The easiest way*. Woodland Hills, CA: Your Business Press.

Katz, M. (2009). Mabel Katz: The easiest way. Retrieved August 2009, from http://www.mabelkatz.com/

Katz, M. & Len, I. H. (2009). Discover love, wealth, and happiness with Ho'oponopono. Retrieved July 14, 2009, from http://businessbyyou.com

Keirsey, D. (1998). *Please understand me II*. Del Mar, CA: Prometheus Nemesis Book Company.

Killoran, E. H. (2009). Choosing prosperity. Retrieved July 26, 2009, from http://www.choosingprosperity.com/

Klauser, H. A. (2001). *Write it down, make it happen: Knowing what you want and getting it*. NY: Touchstone.

Kulish, D. General Manager, M.G. Oil Company, Inc. Used with permission. Copyright © 2014.

Latham, G. P. (2012). *Work motivation: History, theory, research, and practice*. Thousand Oaks, CA: Sage.

Lazzaro, J. (2009). Thought experiments: More than halfway to anywhere. Retrieved August 28, 2009, from http://www.asimovs .com/_issue_0603/Thougthexperiments.shtml

Len, I. H. (2009). IZI LLC. Retrieved July 14, 2009, from http://www .hooponopono.org/

Lin, S. (2002). *Optimum strategies for creativity and longevity*. National Council of Engineers. Retrieved July 5, 2009, from http://www.ruebusch.net/docs/Retirement_Longevity_Study.pdf

Matthews, A. (1990). *Being happy* (2nd ed.). NY: Price Stern Sloan.

Matthews, G. (2014). Goals Research Summary. Retrieved from http://www.dominican.edu/academics/ahss/undergraduate-programs-1/psych/faculty/fulltime/gailmatthews/researchsummary2.pdf

McColl, P. (2007). *Your destiny switch*. Carlsbad, CA: Hay House.

MindTools. (2014). Essential tools for your excellent career. Retrieved July 6, 2009, from http://www.mindtools.com

NACEWeb (2009a). Employers Cite Communication Skills, Honesty/Integrity as Key for Job Candidates. Retrieved October 1, 2009, from http://www.naceweb.org/press/display.asp?year=&prid=254.

NACEWeb (2009b). Hiring Flat for College Class of 2009. Retrieved October 1, 2009, from http://www.naceweb.org/press/display.asp?year=2008&prid=291.

NACEWeb (2009c). Tob jobs for the Class of 2009. Retrieved October 1, 2009, from http://www.naceweb.org/press/display.asp?year=&prid=307.

Nemeth, M. (2000). *The Energy of Money: A Spiritual Guide to Financial and Personal Fulfillment*. NY: Ballantine.

Nemeth, M. (2009). Academy for Coaching Excellence. Retrieved August 30, 2009, from http://www.academyforcoachingexcellence.com/?mvcTask = maria

Neumeier, M. (2005). *The brand gap: Expanded edition*. Berkeley, CA: Peachpit.

Newman, F., et al. (2004). *The future of higher education: Rhetoric, reality, and the risks of the market*. San Francisco, CA: Jossey-Bass.

Niven, D. (2006). *The 100 simple secrets of successful people*. NY: HarperCollins.

Osteen, J. (2007). *Your best life now*. NY: FaithWords.

Parker, P. (2009). Dating without drama. Retrieved July 22, 2009, from http://www.datingwithoutdrama.com.

Peale, N. V. (2003). *The power of positive thinking*. NY: Fireside.

Price, J. R. (1998). *The success book*. Carlsbad, CA: Hay House.

Proctor, B. (1997). *You were born rich*. Scottsdale, AZ: LifeSuccess Productions.

Proctor, B. (2009). Bob Proctor. Retrieved August 30, 2009, from http://www.bobproctor.com/splash.asp

Rann, M. & Arrott, E. R. (2005). *Shortcut to a miracle*. CA: Jeffers Press.

Rath, T. & Clifton, D. O. (2009). *How full is your bucket?* NY: Gallup Press.

Ray, J. A. (1999). *The science of success: How to attract prosperity and create harmonic wealth through proven principles* (3rd ed.). CA: SunArk Press.

Remen, R. N. (2006). *Kitchen table wisdom*, 10th anniversary edition. NY: Berkeley.

Roman, S. & Packer, D. (2007). *Creating money: Attracting abundance* (2nd ed.). CA: HJ Kramer/New World Library.

Rutherford, D. (1998). *So, why aren't you rich?* (2nd ed.). Albuquerque, NM: Dar Publishing.

Salin, D. (2003, October). Ways of explaining workplace bullying: A review of enabling, motivating and precipitating structures and processes in the work environment. *Human Relations, 56*(10), 1213.

Schein, E. H. (Aug, 1963). Review: March to Calumny: The story of American POWs in the Korean War. *American Sociological Review, 28*(4), 649–650.

Scheinfeld, R. (2003). *The 11th element*. Hoboken, NJ: Wiley.

Sher, B. & Gottlieb, A. (2003) *Wishcraft: How to get what you really want* (2nd ed.). NY: Ballantine Books.

Sher, B. (1997). *Live the life you love*. NY: Dell.

Shinn, F. S. (2008). *The collected writings of Florence Scovel Shinn*. VA: Wilder Publications.

Simpletruths.com. (2009). 212° The extra degree. Retrieved July 26, 2009, from http://www.212movie.com/

Stegemann, J. (2013). The six best ways to find your next job. Retrieved from http://www.forbes.com/sites/deborahljacobs/2013/03/22/the-six-best-ways-to-find-your-next-job/

Sutton, R. (2004). Breakthrough ideas for 2004: More trouble than they're worth. *Harvard Business Review, 83*(2): 19–20.

Sylver, M. (1997). *Passion, profit, & power*. NY: Simon and Schuster.

Tanner, M. (2009). Calling men e-book. Retrieved July 22, 2009, from http://callingmen.com/

Tice, L. (2005). *Smart Talk*. Pacific Institute Publishing www .thepacificinstitute.com

Tice, L. & Quick, J. (2004). *Personal coaching for results*. Nashville, TN: Thomas Nelson Publishers.

Tracy, B. (2009). http://www.briantracy.com/

Truman, K. (2001). *Feelings buried alive never die* (4th ed.). Brigham City, UT: Brigham Distributing.

Tyler, K. (1999). Spinning wheels. Retrieved July 26, 2009, from http://findarticles.com/p/articles/mi_m3495/is_9_44/ai_56973703/pg_2.

U.S. Department of Labor. (n.d.). Why America needs an educated and prepared workforce. Employment and Training Administration. Retrieved October 17, 2007, from http://www.doleta.gov/wired/files/Why_America_Needs_an_Educated_Workforce.pdf.

U.S. Census Bureau. (2005). Educational attainment in the United States: 2005. Retrieved July 7, 2009, from http://www.census.gov/population/www/socdemo/education/cps2005.html

U.S. Department of Labor, Bureau of Labor Statistics, "Civilian labor force by age, sex, race, and ethnicity," December 2013, http://www.bls.gov/emp/ep_table_304.htm (visited August 02, 2014).

U.S. Department of Labor, Bureau of Labor Statistics, "Employment Projections: Employment by major occupational group," http://www.bls.gov/emp/ep_table_101.htm (visited August 02, 2014).

U.S. Department of Labor, Bureau of Labor Statistics, "National Business Employment Dynamics Data by Firm Size Class," http://www.bls.gov/bdm/bdmfirmsize.htm (visited August 02, 2014).

U.S. Department of Labor, Bureau of Labor Statistics, "Number of Jobs, Labor Market Experience, and Earnings Growth. Results from a National Longitudinal Survey News Release," July 25, 2012, http://www.bls.gov/news.release/nlsoy.htm (visited August 02, 2014).

U.S. Department of Labor, Bureau of Labor Statistics, "Occupational Outlook Handbook: Fastest Growing Occupations," http://www .bls.gov/ooh/fastest-growing.htm (visited August 02, 2014).

U.S. Department of Labor, Bureau of Labor Statistics, "Occupational Outlook Handbook: Most New Jobs," http://www.bls.gov/ooh/most-new-jobs.htm (visited August 02, 2014).

U.S. Department of Labor, Bureau of Labor Statistics, The Editor's Desk, Share of labor force projected to rise for people age 55 and over and fall for younger age groups on the Internet at http://www .bls.gov/opub/ted/2014/ted_20140124.htm (visited August 02, 2014).

Vandekerckhove, W. & Commers, M. S. R. (2003, June). Downward workplace mobbing: A sign of the times? *Journal of Business Ethics,* 45(1), 41–50.

Vitale, J. & Len, I. H. (2007). *Zero limits: The secret Hawaiian system for wealth, health, peace, and more.* Hoboken, NJ: Wiley.

Vitale, J. (2006). *Life's missing instruction manual: The guidebook you should have been given at birth.* Hoboken, NJ: Wiley.

Vitale, J. (2007). *The key: The missing secret for attracting anything you want.* Hoboken, NJ: Wiley.

Vitale, J. (2008). *The attractor factor: 5 easy steps for creating wealth (or anything else) from the inside out.* Hoboken, NJ: Wiley,

Vitale, J. (2009a). Dr. Joe Vitale is . . . Mr. Fire. Retrieved July 14, 2009, from http://www.mrfire.com

Vitale, J. (2009b). The attractor factor: 5 easy steps for creating wealth (or anything else) from the inside out. Retrieved July 14, 2009, from http://www.mrfire.com

White House, "Did You Know That Women Are Still Paid Less Than Men?", http://www.whitehouse.gov/equal-pay/career (visited August 02, 2014).

Wilson, T. (2006). The prison of hopelessness. 302nd Airlift Wing. Retrieved from http://www.302aw.afrc.af.mil.

Workingpoorfamilies.org. (n.d.). Working hard still falling short. Retrieved July 7, 2009, from http://www.workingpoorfamilies.org/pdfs/NatReport08.pdf

Wornham, D. (2003, June). A descriptive investigation of morality and victimization at work. Journal of Business Ethics, 45(1), 29.

Zimmerman, R. (2011). 21 Secrets of the Universe. Rikka Zimmerman Publisher.

photo credits

index

Reiter, M., 15
Rejection
  getting support following,
    259–260
  method to overcome, 259
  thank-you notes following,
    242, 258
Religion, illegal questions
    on, 220
Remen, R. N., 140
Research, job search and,
    64–68
Resiliency Quotient, 284
Resume components
  education, 116
  header or identification, 115–116
  optional sections, 117
  references, 117–118, 160–162
  skills summary, 116
  work experience or list of positions,
    116–117
Resumes. *See also* Cover letters
  challenges when creating,
    129–130
  checklist and grading rubric for,
    136–137, 307–308
  delivery of, 132–133
  "don't do" list for, 112–113
  elements of professional,
    128–132
  first cut for, 114
  fonts for, 120–121
  identifying skills for, 43
  integrity of, 128
  keywords for, 121–122
  measurement of successful,
    138–139
  objectives in, 116
  overview of, 112–113
  paper for, 132
  peer review of, 138
  power words for, 122–125
  presentation on, 115–118
  roadblocks on, 141–142
  Skills Formula for writing, 125–127
  steps to create, 133–137, 304–306
  targeting jobs with, 128
  updating following job loss, 276
  visual impact of, 128
Resume types
  chronological, 114–115, 129,
    145–151
  combination, hybrid, or custom,
    118, 129, 153–159
  electronic, 118–120
  functional or skills, 118, 129
  scannable, online or plain-text,
    118–119
Reticular activating system (RAS),
    286, 287
Retirement, life goals and, 20, 21
Ritzer, George, 60

Roman, S., 6, 18, 23, 294n
Rowling, J. K., 204
Rutherford, D., 13, 15, 17, 18, 46,
    61, 231, 242, 286

Salary
  discussion of, 244
  educational attainment and,
    58–59
  on job applications, 185
  job interview questions related to,
    202–203, 223
  negotiating, 248
  requirements for, 169
  research on, 19, 68, 223
Salin, D., 281
Scannable resumes, 118–119
Scheinfeld, Robert, 82, 140
Screening interviews, 209–210. *See
    also* Job interviews
Second interviews, 210. *See also* Job
    interviews
30-second marketing commercial, 104
Self-care, 278
Self-employment, 274
Self-talk
  developing positive, 16–17
  explanation of, 15
  use of affirmations to change, 18,
    294–298
Self-worth, 226–227
Service workers, 57
70/30 rule, 251
Severance package, 275
Sher, Barbara, 7, 82–83
Shinn, F. S., 6, 18, 36, 46, 231,
    242, 294n
"Should have to" self-talk, 17
Simic, Charles, 74
Skills
  adaptive, 37
  hard, 39
  job-specific, 40–41
  listed in cover letters, 167
  quantifying your, 43, 301
  soft, 38–39, 167
  transferable, 39, 40
Skills formula, 125–127
Skills gap, 45–46
Skills resumes
  example of, 152
  explanation of, 118, 129
Skills vocabulary, 37
Sleep, 284
Small to medium employers
    (SMEs), 56
Smart-Band™, 16, 17
SMART goals, 18–19
Smiling, 201, 267
Social media
  background on, 90–91
  company information on, 198

job search and, 92
  leveraging through, 86
  networking and, 91
Soft skills
  in cover letters, 167
  explanation of, 38
  identifying your, 38–39
St. John . Noah, 295–296
Standard interviews. *See* Job
    interviews; Traditional
    interviews
STAR technique
  examples using, 214–216
  practice using, 216–217
  steps in, 214
Status-blind harassment, 281
Stegemann, Jorg, 77
Stress, workplace, 284
Stretch goals, 20–21
Structured interviews, 210. *See also*
    Job interviews
Success
  awareness and, 46
  money and, 6–7
  tools for, 21
Success principle, 6–7
Swindoll, Chuck, 33
Sylver, M., 15
Synergy, 76, 89

Tanner, M., 204
Targeted job search
  function of, 64–65
  research and, 65–68
Technical interviews, 211. *See also*
    Job interviews
Technological advances
  employment trends and, 60–61
  for job interviews, 200
Telephone interviews. *See* Phone
    interviews
Temporary agencies, 61
Thank-you notes
  e-mail, 237
  examples of, 237–241
  as expression of gratitude,
    241–242
  following panel interviews,
    203, 240
  formal, 240–242
  guidelines for, 243
  handwritten, 237–238
  when you are turned down, 242, 258
Tice, L., 15, 18, 20, 23, 36, 61,
    63, 81, 286, 287, 294n
Time management, 270–271
To-do lists, 270, 271
Tracy, Brian, 270, 287
Traditional interviews. *See also* Job
    interviews
  explanation of, 204
  job interview questions for, 212–213